Transported Styles in Shakespeare and Milton

Transported Styles in Shakespeare and Milton

Harold Toliver

METAPHORA, or the figure of transporte: A kinde of wrestling of a single word from his owne right signification, to another not so naturall, but yet of some affinitie or convenience.

—Puttenham, *The Arte of English Poesie*

The Pennsylvania State University Press
University Park and London

Library of Congress Cataloging-in-Publication Data

Toliver, Harold E.
    Transported styles in Shakespeare and Milton / Harold Toliver.

      p. cm.
    Includes index.
    ISBN 0-271-00646-3
    1. Shakespeare, William, 1564–1616—Criticism and interpretation.
2. Milton, John, 1608–1674—Criticism and interpretation.
3. Influence (Literary, artistic, etc.)   I. Title.
PR2976.T64 1989
821'.4—dc19   88-12614
                                                                                                            CIP

Copyright © 1989 The Pennsylvania State University
All rights reserved
Printed in the United States of America

Contents

Preface	vii
Introduction	1

Part One: Rhetoric and Poetry in the Theater

1	Playhouse Eloquence	19
2	Unnatural Language: Songs and Soliloquies	37

Part Two: Four Plays

3	Cleopatra's Phantom Marriage	65
4	The Polysyllabic Moor and Venetian Parlor Talk	87
5	Words of Command, Words of Suffering in *King Lear*	123
6	Going Between in *The Winter's Tale*	153

Part Three: Going Beyond

7	*The Tempest*'s Capable Spirits Vanishing, Milton's Ascending	183
8	Holy Signs and Songs	219
9	Kinds and Moments of Plot	239

Notes	259
Index	273

Preface

This study is more problem-oriented than historical in its concern with the nexus of drama, rhetoric and lyric. But in its joining of Shakespeare and Milton it maintains a more than incidental interest in literary succession as well and in the cross fire of perspectives we gain from antithetical periods. The passage of literary elements from one major figure to another is a complex matter that carries into the secrets of creation, re-creation, and literature-society relations. The Milton I propose here is a transformer of things Elizabethan and Jacobean, in other words of the legacy he inherited from within a counterculture. Hence although it is probably possible to read the Shakespeare and the Milton sections separately, the better way is to read them in succession. For Miltonists whose time does not permit all that—and I know this distant course to him asks a lot—I suggest the introduction and for the main course the seventh chapter ("*The Tempest*'s Capable Spirits Vanishing, Milton's Ascending"), which binds the two parts together, and then the rest.

I am grateful for James Calderwood's efforts with "Cleopatra's Phantom Marriage" and Robert Montgomery's with "The Polysyllabic Moor." Comments from both were helpful. I don't know who to thank for the three very able readings for The Pennsylvania State University Press, but for their going beyond the call of duty I am grateful, as I am also for a sabbatical from the University of California that came at a timely moment.

Introduction

> The eye's plain version is a thing apart,
> The vulgate of experience. Of this,
> A few words, an and yet, and yet, and yet—
> —Wallace Stevens,
> "An Ordinary Evening in New Haven"

Antony on Behalf of the Play

John Crowe Ransom offers wise counsel in advising against our putting plot and poetry into rivalry in Shakespeare and bothering "as to which had the honor to come first in his intention. Both are there, and both engage with our emotions, though apparently not quite the same ones." Yet he himself cannot resist going against that advice, not in finding "complete little poems" seated like polished diamonds within the plays but in discovering an excess of eloquence in characters who in soliloquy "burst the bonds of drama in favor of a freer poetry." That fretting of form is similar to the one he often finds within poetry itself when texture chafes at structure. Such concessions to metaphor suggest that we should not be too surprised at a texturizing Hamlet who keeps up an affair with words while revenge awaits a sparer mood. The resolve to act in Shakespeare sometimes has to wage a rearguard action against the rich contingency of the world's body rushing in behind its word-hoard, metaphors twisting away from the straight course. For Ransom that is all to the good if it weakens "the tyranny of science over the senses."[1]

If such a critic on his guard succumbs to temptation, it is perhaps because the internal struggle between poetry and drama gathers momentum in key passages where motives and passions are too complex and fables too brutally simple to brake the onrush. Antony does not necessarily speak in character, or at least not exclusively to dramatic purposes, when he asks Eros if he wishes to be

> window'd in great Rome, and see
> Thy master thus with pleach'd arms, bending down
> His corrigible neck, his face subdued
> To penetrative shame; whilst the wheel'd seat
> Of fortunate Caesar, drawn before him, branded
> His baseness that ensued?
>
> (4.14.72–77)

Although this appeal unquestionably owes much of its force to Antony's predicament, what we do not get—and come not to expect from Shakespeare's great Romans and English—is transparent language exclusively in the service of usable motive, motive convertible into action-moving persuasion.

The question is how the poetic elements influence our reception not merely of the impersonated Antony but of the play as performance, so notable here in the marching of clauses to the cadence of shame's procession. That Antony must be vivid to overcome Eros's revulsion in a general way justifies the bending of the once incorrigible neck and the penetration of a once inviolable integrity. Antony's sharply etched tableau assumes a hierarchy of moral qualities having to do with a chivalric system that equates inner worth with public image. It assigns its qualities to the parallel adjectives (pleached, corrigible, penetrative, fortunate, and wheeled), which it fastens to featured nouns (arms, neck, shame, Caesar, seat), three of them situated in parallel places in successive lines. Stature goes with equipage and is read in postures. Antony's once weapon-bearing, now useless arms he imagines bound while Caesar rides free and upright in a triumphal chariot. By such cinema-ready, medium-range shots and close-ups, the vignette recapitulates recent battles and prepares an entry in the historical chronicle for subsequent generations to read.

All the while Antony is trying to do something about a desperate situation, Shakespeare is stealing the demonstration, reminding us of the ways and means of eloquence, representing the Antony we see before us not exclusively as a paraded captive or the chief lover of the afterworld but also as an actor costarring in the production of a legend. It is Shakespeare who is gifted in syntactical variants and sound systems such as "subdued" and "ensued," who uses distant rhymes to stitch together highly patterned thought. Like the visual figures, the aural ones lift the procession of shame out of history's raw materials. That Antony only imagines the scene makes the moment all the more performative. His motives for self-slaughter pass through imagination until it is impossible to separate Antony inventing a minidrama for Eros's benefit from Shakespeare inventing Antony for ours. A good many questions that have interested both formalist criticism and new historicism hang on the decisions we make at such crossroads of rhetoric, poetry, and drama.

Up to a point, we have no difficulty seeing what any of this has to do with plot. Yet we cannot award everything to Antony or his situation. More than one rhetoric runs at a time, and more than one palpable design. As Ransom recognizes, the trick for the spectator or reader "consists, apparently, in guiding the imagination to the right places and then letting it go" (p. 289). That seems to be what Shakespeare too has done. Certain issues or *quaestiones* that have been held up to scrutiny in lecturelike thrust-ins Antony now brings to a new pointedness, many of them harnessed by the structural parallels and interwoven metaphors. These include a fifth-act equivalent from Cleopatra as well as the future that Antony himself soon projects in Hades. This particular vignette concerns the ultimate degradation of a shame culture. The lovers' promenade in Hades and the reunion that Cleopatra imagines would be showpieces of chivalric splendor freed of the struggle for autonomy.

The play at such pausal moments demands a well-spoken Antony to go with his very theatrical Cleopatra, each capable of maintaining personal authority, shored up by lyricism, against the wreckage the plot is inflicting upon them as they lose ground. By killing himself rather than Antony, Eros spreads the magnificence, which on several occasions proves capable of lifting subordinates into the legend and into the poetry that sustains its pretense to transcendence. None of these parallels depends on soliloquy or completely bursts the dramatic bonds; but together they point up a highly articulated structure of allusions and analogies as poetic as they are rhetorical and dramatic. Word and deed are reciprocal and mutually entangled but not indistinguishable. Nor could they be where eloquence departs so strikingly from ordinary talk. The graphic imagery of windowed mobs and folded arms belongs to the stuff of professional writers.

Speeches for their own sake fascinate minor as well as major characters in this and other plays and just as clearly fascinate Shakespeare. Interpreting departures from the common idiom goes better at times, however, if we reverse Ransom's assignment of texture to metaphor and of idea to dramatic action or structure. Politics, the bodily world, and psychological realism provide most of the stuff that moves plots, while poetry exits into fantasy or idealized second worlds. Both the Octavius scenario and Antony's Hades are imaginary, but one is politically realistic and would likely be the outgrowth of Antony's continued life; the other exceeds realizable limits and puts out-of-bounds a corner of the hypothetical self. The degradations of Rome do indeed agitate for self-slaughter; but beyond that they form a network of comparisons. They recollect the play's ancestry in North's Plutarch, Virgil, Ovid, and Daniel, and such common topics as the justification of suicide and the value of honor. The family resemblances among a tradition of writers suggest that bracketed moments like this are set up not only for pausal emphasis within a sequence of acts but for our consideration of the place of a given performance within literary history. In this case, it brings together a blend of tragedy and romance that puts *Antony and Cleopatra* somewhere between the plays immediately preceding and the romance comedies soon to follow. The more Antony extends himself as a dramatic character winding up toward his honorable Roman ending, the more Shakespeare establishes a subgenre and screens public obligation and private desire through standard topoi.

I have been assuming that one complication in the bard-playwright rivalry, both in Shakespeare and other Renaissance figures, is rhetoric and that rhetoric brings a substantial concern with logic and ethics in tow. That third factor, somewhere between the dramatic and the poetic, is virtually all-encompassing, although the poetry-drama-rhetoric amalgam looks somewhat different now than it did to Shakespeare's contemporaries (or even than it did to critics only a few years ago, as demonstrated by Joel Altman on drama and William Kennedy on rhetorical manuals and lyric). To oversimplify, the instruments of rhetoric and logic, to most users, once appeared neutral in themselves. They were rentable for whatever cause anyone wanted to pursue, since as Aristotle suggests, they constitute the entire available means of persuasion. For that matter, to an older historicism, the stock of Elizabethan ideas too was largely there, simply to be drawn upon. The Tudor "play of mind," as Altman calls it, is often neutral on such political, social, personal, and religious issues as the power of sovereigns, the obligations of courtiers, the relation of reason to passion or to faith, the nature of courtesy, the effects of humors, love, the rights and obligations of children and parents—and one can include, for Antony, suicide and honor, military and erotic chivalry.[2] Such topics can be taken up wittily (as in *Love's Labour's Lost*), or in deadly earnest (as in *Lear*); they speak to a range of people in several styles, some of them more suited to the Inns of Court than to the crowd at the Globe.

The revised view of the past few years expects to find dominant ideologies planted in both the pageantry and the rhetoric of these stock values, ideologies that are not necessarily recognized by the writer. It is left to criticism to demystify them. This newer view may follow its forerunners in searching for an elusive "Elizabethan mind," but it is decidedly more suspicious and it is apt to find rhetoric more likely than poetry to uphold the values of dominant ideas. Poetry tends to erode common assumptions, subtly, by virtue of the complex feelings and marginal associations that come with metaphor, especially in such figures as catachresis. For instance, Franco Moretti's account of the Shakespearean soliloquy and its poetry, unlike Ransom's, finds a counterpoliticizing creeping into the text without passing through a conscious definition of issues or into pointed rhetoric. Rather than forwarding an action, a typical soliloquy retards it and makes its implications ungraspable. Thus in place of a lucid Cornelian continuity between word and act, it finds a "radical discrepancy." Whereas Ransom reads figural twists as "astonishing lapses of rationality," Moretti finds in them an early manifestation of an indecipherable modern "poetry" that undermines suasion. Thus a soliloquizer in collaboration with the poet pulls speech out of its social setting and prevents it from being absorbed into cultural patterns or settled values. What such a poetry renders is not what the imagination discovers when it is turned loose in a given place but the "stupefied perception" of cultural forms that have defaulted.[3]

I will return to the notion of a subversive modernist poetry later in considering Macbeth's soliloquies and at the same time to added reasons for the bombardment of surplus feeling from the margin. Read in this way, the poetry of plays plunges into a maelstrom and never surfaces again; we do not so much understand its issues as reexperience them while being whirled about by them. Through Antony, then—to return to the implications for a status culture of his richly associative speech to Eros—Shakespeare encodes the Elizabethan neochivalric revival without totally thematizing it. He places the chivalric division of love and military honors under a magnifying glass and has Cleopatra drive them apart and Antony suffer their division. It is relevant to the emotions of Antony's dilemma that much Elizabethan literature deals with similar conflicts between erotic courtship and power, and all of it is *our* context for the speech. Similar emotions turn up in sonnet sequences, for instance, in the parallels and differences between courtship and courtiership (recently a factor in readings of *Astrophel and Stella* as well as *The Faerie Queene* and *Arcadia*).

To the literary historian, then, *Antony and Cleopatra* becomes one shot in an Elizabethan barrage. We hear echoes not only from Daniel and North's Plutarch but from progresses, masques, and courtly lyrics going back to Wyatt. If we want to violate chronology, we hear them again from the Jacobean disintegration of chivalry and from Puritan versions of love-duty themes, especially Milton's radically different love and heroic martyrdom. To be subdued just in the manner Antony imagines in the Roman parade is to be disgraced in essence. We understand that, but somewhat distantly, and see the culture itself less as an inevitability than a historical curiosity.

We thereby transform some of Shakespeare's poetry back into rhetoric—not into the kind Antony exercises against a reluctant Eros, but into Shakespeare's measurements of a stature too valuable to make its loss other than a pity. In sorting out who knows what, we proceed by stages from what Antony says to what Shakespeare means to what an informed critic understands or thinks he does. That Octavius and Antony agree in principle suggests that for him they are fighting over personal authority and chivalric honor. They are not two examples of imperialism as Milton might interpret them or displays of heroic drama as Dryden might. They are blinded advocates, neither of whom offers an alternative. They feel the tug of inner tensions, Octavius in the violations of their agreement, Antony in the two lives he lives. From any great distance outside, it appears that, whichever prevails, the empire will continue to levy its taxes and the play will honor its commitment to grandeur through chivalry and imperialism. The play as an action centering in Antony's ruin does not explicitly address these issues, although Cleopatra challenges the Roman version of the heroic ideal. The point with respect to side effects, however, is that, placed under duress, Antony is forced far enough outside the chivalric standard to get tangled in competing values. Some of the poetry is squeezed out of him, and we must grant a portion of the eloquence to legitimate heightening. If poetry in its formal, imagistic, and thematic dimensions still goes beyond anything he sees, we are prompted to ask what lies between lines, especially in his wistful and poetically amplified desire for a better place.

So far I have been constructing a more or less hypothetical view of the interplay of dramatic, rhetorical, and poetic elements that finds rhetoric and poetry changing places according to the reader's perspective. It is not precisely the one I want to propose myself, which has been implicit in the observation that Shakespeare capitalizes on the *showmanship* of Antony and Octavius. Representational approaches—and both kinds of historicism are heavily indebted to them—concede too little to the playhouse manner of making demonstrations. They also tend to lose useful distinctions among kinds and reduce all writing to a single discourse. The interplay of social realities and fictions seems mutually transformative, and rhetoric must surrender some of its traditional holdings. The theater resembles acroasis or esoteric fable in its veiling of intent behind plots recognized from the outset as parabolic. If behind Antony's desire not to be led through the streets of Rome are attitudes that Shakespeare silently assumes, those attitudes are smuggled in not by disguised rhetoric exclusively but by the right of fictions to say one thing and mean another. When we agree to the conditions of a play, we also agree to try to receive all the messages such acroasis is capable of sending.

Although rhetoric, drama, and poetry overlap considerably, then, they will sustain discrimination. Much of what the playwright delivers over the heads of characters he is granted by the license issued to fiction-makers. A speech before parliament may use drama and poetry but is dominated by its persuasive purposes. A poem may use dialogue and set speeches but is more open to the musicality and figural density of lyric. Unfortunately, just how to go about such discriminations in a reasonably realistic theater is less than self-evident. In some of Antony's iambic pentameter lines we can identify what makes them poetic, as we can attribute some features of his speech unequivocally to plot and character and still others (but more tentatively) to a rhetoric of chivalry. The question is whether or not we can profitably distinguish moments that follow one mode from those that follow another, and whether, even if we can, we absolutely need to. Does it matter whether Antony is speaking rhetoric or poetry to Eros or, to think of Milton again, whether Eve is using rhetoric on Adam in her seduction of him or is carrying forward some phase of Milton's edenic love lyrics? Even if we detect an authorial commitment to a recurrent idea, does it matter that its current speaker is a dramatic fiction and not the writer himself?

In some borderline instances, "no" is surely the appropriate answer. Distinctions are not always vital to either interpretation or theatrical experience. We do not particularly need them to raise such historical matters as the broad disagreement between Elizabethans and Miltonic Puritans. Rhetoric's infiltration of poetry and drama stems from impulses deeply embedded in humanist training in ethical and pragmatic language. The techniques of public speech or elocution have a direct application in the theater, since both orators and actors practice oral delivery and strive for quality of voice, the timely use of gestures, the open display of feelings, the weighting of argument by inflection and pace, the arrangement of timing and climax. And the bank of figures and devices, founded on classical rhetoric, loans to all users without discrimination, about equally for logic and for aural emphasis and embellishment.

This much of the neutral view of rhetoric, as simply an instrument, is surely valid. It reinforces the current tendency to make all literary forms one and the same discourse. Within drama, rhetoric is often aimed at the audience and raises questions to an explicit level while it sets them to work internally as motives. Meanwhile, poetry is ordinarily the most sustained and pronounced artfulness of the performance, especially in lineation, meter, and figures. It does not necessarily forward reciprocal commentary or champion ideas and issues. On technical grounds, poets do not employ persuasive speech or *inventio* in just the ways orators and logicians do. They may display ethical models, but usually not of a rigorously logical or issue-oriented kind; they may advocate, but again only as a subordinate part of a fictive strategy. The very act of composing so intricate a form as metrical language, so governed by conventions, makes the fictional occasion palpably just that. Whenever we actually hear the versification of a play, it reminds us of the play's right not to be occasional or directly representational. Shakespeare sets Antony up as a paradigm case to speak for all times and thus potentially as a universal emblem, marching highly articulate and arranged clauses in ranks. In filling out the impetus of poetry's golden world with a contrasting Hades scene, Antony ends up (with Cleopatra's help) positing a world more in keeping with a higher showmanship. He carries to a culmination what has been trying to have its day all along but could not in the fields of history, where drama gathers the materials of its plots. It is as though the potentials for self-projection, getting practice in improvisations under pressure, finally leap all the way into fiction's artful world of display. The drama that occasions the poetry is reinspired and transported not to an altogether different world but to one in which the lovers achieve the boundlessness to which they have been directing small lyrics since the first act.

That is a quite different balance of argument and poetic supplement than anything Shakespeare could have found in earlier drama, although he transcribes and reuses less sophisticated forms available through later sixteenth-century amalgamations that by his time had already blurred their medieval origins. In John Heywood's *Gentleness and Nobility,* to take a representative case, lower, middle, and upper classes are set squarely against each other in personifications that use a relatively spare style but also extended set speeches. The playwright's aim is not to award victory to Plowman, Merchant, or Knight but to set up their conflict for educational purposes and if possible move to higher ground, which Heywood does in having Philosopher apply a comprehensive concept of humankind that rises above partisanship. Plays with sharper acrimony (and no philosopher to step in) follow similar conflicts to tragic outcomes or disarm them with farce. Whatever their means of handling social and ethical materials, however, influences for ill or good can be labeled and seldom have much metaphoric spillover. In the balance of playhouse and rhetorical elements, rhetoric claims an extremely large share.

A polemical residue can still be seen in *Antony and Cleopatra,* as it can in plays like *Macbeth, Lear,* and *1 Henry IV* (after Shakespeare's more open experiments with it in the Henry VI plays and *Love's Labour's Lost*). Prince Hal, for instance, capitalizes on morality definitions in staging his coming forth as a secular salvation. Pieces of sophistic debate show in arguments for and against honor and in the behavior of the prince among roisterers. Such issues as what to do with the prisoners a feudal lord has taken and what the balance of power should be between sovereigns and lords guide the audience's assessment of character in action. In the tragedies, Shakespeare complicates that morality inheritance with the meditative intelligence of the protagonists. In a morality play, we would see just where Macbeth or Lear belongs and how to judge him; in the Macbeth and Lear Shakespeare gives us, to carry through with such judgment in the face of "Tomorrow, and tomorrow" or "Poor naked wretches, whereso'er you are" requires us to work against a sympathetic eloquence and poetic supplements.

Our implication in the metaphoric network is given new life with each line that comes forth as though from a consciousness like the normal reader's except more tormented and far more articulate. Through implanted lyrics, the forum clarification of issues yields a good deal to both that centralizing of sympathy and the implicit authorial presence. The perceptions that attend Macbeth, Othello, Lear, and Antony obviously cannot be completely answered by opposing dialogue.

Plots and Words

In the Aristotelian dramatic hierarchy, the strongest principle of coherence is action, and what makes an action seem probable is motive. Characters are thus conceived in such a way as to move the ensemble toward an end that uses up motives as motions. What enables interaction is thought given voice or gesture. In the context of that arrangement of secondary elements, not much language and character can be allowed to escape their assigned duties. Intelligibility is defined from the outset as a workable interaction of parts in sequence. One goal of the *Poetics* is thus to impose narrative order on mimesis and its recognitions. Coherence is not *above* events, in some stable and unlinear realm of thematized ideas—the territory of discursive prose and issue-oriented philosophy—but *in* them.

Although Shakespearean drama is sufficiently plot-oriented to make an Aristotelian vocabulary useful, it also imagines other relations among parts besides the linear structure of anticipations and recollections. It generates more wit and character than most actions can be said to require, either to make the events unfold or to comment on them. At certain moments it raises music and spectacle to prominence, and these too are likely to hold act in abeyance. Where the bard most often works loose from the plot-maker is neither in music nor in spectacle, however, but in copiousness, which leads us back to the figures and devices of rhetoric. Attention to epicycles of meaning in a mischievous language is not unique with Shakespeare of course. As Jane Donawerth points out, Thomas Wilson, Montaigne, Bacon, and others were well aware of the disruptive potential of double meanings and the unintended conflict they introduce.[4] That distrust of duplicity and the counterenergies of language is well justified. To the puns that spring loose, Shakespeare adds riddles and accidents of sound. Any of these may cause a speaker to say one thing when the playwright means another.[5]

Not all countermotions are plot-defeating, however. When Macbeth is told that he may laugh to scorn "The power of man, for none of woman born / Shall harm Macbeth" and that he will never be vanquished until "Great Birnam wood to high Dunsinane hill / Shall come against him" (4.1.80, 93), he naturally leaps to the wrong conclusions. But we easily perceive the deceit to be intentional on the witches' part and functional on Shakespeare's. It introduces variables that the play uses to set Macbeth and the audience on different courses. The misleading prophecy amounts to a linguistic subplot working in collaboration with the unborn and the Birnam wood that soon march on Macbeth's stronghold. That we discover the correct reading before Macbeth is a source of disequilibrium in a play whose point of view is often Macbeth's and whose concern is the trauma of uncertain anticipation. When the discrepancy is at last rectified and Macbeth too understands the message, the correction follows the rest of the play's righting of the ship. It cancels one direction the words have seemingly allowed. Meanwhile Shakespeare has built into the plot a shadow action and a further commentary on Macbeth's grasping at straws. The riddles are responsible to the play's passage through choices to the almost-certain end of the reign of terror. What is unpleasantly surprising to Macbeth (when the caesarian-born enemy comes from behind his branchy camouflage) makes good sense to us. The play is after all not going back on its premonitions or its moral commitments. Nor is it going back on its obligations, as a fiction, to limit the range of doubts and ambiguities.

Such uses of duplicity are widely conceded and do not require belaboring here, but another gesture toward a Miltonic difference is in order. One of the directions Milton moves the genres he adapts is toward Protestant rationalism and faith in an ultimate clarification. For instance, the ambiguous phrase "son of God" (in *Paradise Regained*) spurs Satan into devising elaborate traps for Christ—Satan serving as a false oracle who plays on the kind of future uncertainty and ambition that snags Macbeth. The ambiguity is a crucial one, since as Satan realizes any human or angel could be called "son"; and yet the future of the race depends on just what that means. With the advantage of the Synoptic Gospels, the poem obviously goes much further in defining it than Satan can. From Satan's perspective, is there a difference between Christ the son and salvageable people? To persuade Christ to seize his own kingdom is one way of finding out. The question about the name includes the larger questions of God's intent toward fallen humankind and angeldom and how it will be manifest. Will the solution to the Satan problem be a social or a spiritual one? Will the act be finished in a kingdom of this world, or will the world itself be sacrificed? The announcements that accompany the sign indicate a new manifestation of purpose, and if such a purpose truly does materialize in the desert, it will be dramatic and not merely prophetic.

But if the phrase "son of God" leads to eschatological transport *only,* what can actually be revealed now? The entire relation of dramatic demonstration to prophetic poetry hinges on Milton's answers. Will the plot convert things half seen into manifest act? Or will words continue to hint at the undemonstrable and be swallowed up in the Word? Either way, ambiguous language serves character and act both in goading Satan to investigate and in conducting the reader toward a detailed paradigm of rejections. Presumably somewhere, sometime, even if not in this brief epic, Milton assumes a truth receivable by all eligible parties. In the interim, what has to be lived through as either chronicle or drama must be brought bit by bit into the highest imaginative faculty of the prophets.

These are obviously not identical instances of misleading assumptions, but the alternatives in both cases could be said to fall under the pattern of an Aristotelian ironic plot. A delayed and complex coherence is no less a coherence, even if in *Paradise Regained* the ending of the great single plot can only be anticipated. The difference is the level of the working, which is mostly social (with hints of a providential Nemesis) in *Macbeth* and eschatological (with a renewed social level in the next phase of Christ's continued biography) in Milton. Puns and riddles require butts of jokes who do not understand all meanings instantaneously, who assume one meaning and are derailed when a second or third comes into view. They do not require an equal range of possibilities in the reader or an endless chain of meaning-detonation.

I make that point to concede the possible reincorporating of some unavoidable complexities into even action-dominated drama. It is not primarily what I intend to pursue, however, which is the discrepancy between act and copiousness, with its abundance of feeling and thought. In view of the imported life and body of words and all the literary, political, and cultural accompaniments they bring with them, it is not safe to assume that a play limits its improvements on randomness to causal sequencing. The contingency introduced by double meanings may not be harmonious; the possibilities of metaphor may conflict with as well as supplement one another. Whereas a commitment to dramatic action wants all elements to put their shoulders to the wheel, the repertory of devices that the Elizabethan stage and Miltonic masque or epic employ includes the singing of an Amiens, the truant high spirits and skulduggery of an Autolycus, the rhymed overeloquence of a Richard II, the full internal life of a soliloquizing Hamlet, the bardic insertions of an Attendant Spirit and epic narrator. Hearing the language of love sonnets in *Romeo and Juliet* and the formality of *Richard II*, a literate audience helps Shakespeare orchestrate a more fully developed set of relations than the motives suggest; hearing a synoptic angel choir recapitulate the story of mankind, the Miltonic audience interprets visible act as an emblematic likeness to something nowhere fully realizable from types or definable arguments.

On- and Offstage Hearing

I have been making use of a further assumption that had better be brought forward for scrutiny. It is that apparent people—images of people—craft their lines unaware of what they are. Such unawareness is something different from the dramatic irony of our realizing what the witches are up to before Macbeth does. We do not even necessarily use it to judge the ignorance of the unknower. When Lear winds up to an apocalyptic note in "we'll wear out, / In a wall'd prison, pacts and sects of great ones" and Edmund crosses him with "take them away," we hear much more in the contrast than either character does. Part of what we hear is poetry. Edmund's not hearing is almost as meaningful as the contrast itself, not for our understanding of his character but for our perception of the relation of Lear's second world to this one. Likewise, when we are prompted into remembering the squeaking boy who plays Cleopatra and take special note of Charmian straightening the crown, it is because Shakespeare for the moment is being a theatrical version of Escher.[6] A contrived and entertaining Bottom who acts different roles in the Titania farce and *Pyramus and Thisby* may not cease being the mechanic who imposes his doggerel on romance and tragedy, but we are encouraged to see behind him a mirrored view of the play in progress. His pounding away at metered alliteration and rhyme does nothing to make us forget it.

Speakers and onstage listeners themselves notice some aspects of special play talk. They often respond to hyperbole and quibbles, for instance. Fool's riddles in *Lear* seem enigmas to his listeners as well as to us; the wits of *Love's Labour's Lost* progress from point to point by well-noticed and answered turns of phrase. Songs too are heard as such, not as speech incidentally accompanied by music, although they are not answered in full.[7] But rhyme, more subdued double meanings, and meter (unless Orlando gallops it furiously and Rosalind and Touchstone take notice) are strictly for the audience. The actors who deliver them talk simultaneously to those they play with and to those they play before. While their messages carry forward the part of the design that is socialized and plotted, their artifice shows the something more that Escher's simultaneously ascending and descending stairs reveal about painterly perspectives.

This is one of several reasons that we must situate both the playwright and the poet in a society of writers, not exclusively among playwrights but among Homer, Virgil, and Ovid as well. In topical allusions, what contemporaries recognize as recent events comes into view. In allusions to Atlas or Venus and Adonis, a community of predecessors shapes not just the play but the expectation of what it is to be a poet on a certain scale. Such citations may or may not be available to a particular auditor, but they are assuredly not available to a Hamlet who is forbidden to know even revenge tragedies. The consciousness that permeates symbolic acts must have unusual prominence *as* consciousness, since it is called into being solely to read the text. Only through the text does it read anything else. A consciousness that applies what it gathers to live issues must return from absorption in the network of allusions and by an abstraction of principles reformulate images and ideas. That voyage into the fiction and back suggests that Milton, for instance, in reversing the rhetoric of chivalry enters the fictive landscape on its terms, entertains its allure, and responds in kind.

Almost as noteworthy as onstage ignorance and this meeting of minds behind or above what is acknowledged onstage is the fact that we can usually decide without much difficulty which failures to hear are significant. When Lear proves deaf to the oiliness of the rhetoric of his two elder daughters, as Cordelia is not, we know that tone deafness is a fault for which he can be held accountable; it is dramatic. His will to be deceived is based in the same flaws that cause him to stage the love contest to begin with. That we have heard worse things without kingdoms falling suggests that the play is taking advantage of its right to set up its own rules and attend to rhetoric as a special problem.

In contrast, no one onstage is commissioned to notice the rhyme of that same highly formalized first act. Only we hear it, and so it is not significant except indirectly, as another mark of playhouse talk and the establishing of a contract with the audience. Only a modern character who breaks the dramatic illusion would accost France upon hearing this melodramatic doggerel:

> God, gods! 'tis strange that from their cold'st neglect
> My love should kindle to inflam'd respect.

> Thy dowerless daughter, King, thrown to my chance,
> Is Queen of us, of ours, and our fair France:
> Not all the dukes of wat'rish Burgundy
> Can buy this unpriz'd precious maid of me.
> Bid them farewell, Cordelia, though unkind:
> Thou losest here, a better where to find.
>   (1.1.254–61)

This flowery outburst is far worse than anything Goneril and Regan say, but France's future wife, so sensitive to rhetorical nuance in her sisters, raises nary a protest over it. Shakespeare is working with stereotypes, and this one apparently accords with the play's undebated assumptions about dowries and inherited honors. We are to accept France as praiseworthy and Burgundy as something else and go on from there. Knowing that we have just witnessed what only fictions have the license to show, we begin to sort out sensibilities on- and offstage and to identify an authorial presence working through all the costumed and worded resources of the proceedings. But we will evidently not have an easy task with the rhetorical subtext and will in fact find ourselves still putting the pieces together in Edgar's (or is it Albany's?) final instructions on how to speak.

The ratio of heard to unheard signals changes from moment to moment. Even within a passage our awareness of it may have to adjust. (If the copier theory of the folio *Lear* has any validity, for instance, a theatrical hearing of pentameter blank verse catches more lines at the beginning and ending of a speech than in the middle.) Assuming that it is not always obtuseness that blocks the perceptions of those waiting to respond, we look for what does. That one of the possibilities is listed under dramatic irony again puts to work our alertness to the fictiveness of the occasion. When we see what Lear does not, we withdraw from him in a way comparable to the pulling back of a zoom lens to show someone lost in a labyrinth whose exit is just around the corner. It is more characteristic of dramatic than of lyric art or rhetoric to work seriously on blindness and give us both the recognitions and the comparative safety of playhouse perception. Yet even as we benefit from that manipulation of distances, we are likely to be only momentarily secure and about to undergo hazards peculiar to linear maze negotiations. Thus in watching Hamlet watching Claudius watching the play within the play, we are not totally outside the riddles he ponders. We can see what is at stake in Hamlet's deciphering; we may be less sure what kind of risk we are taking. All listeners on- and offstage inhabit a live ecology of interpretation, and any altered relation of two parts affects all others—but under the conventions of dramatic listening and at different rates to different parties.

Playwrights cannot control all the factors that go into responses to texts any more than Shakespeare could anticipate a reader like Milton, or Milton a modern liberal. I will have to ignore the majority of those factors in order to concentrate on those that bear upon differences between plotted or dramatic discovery and poetic implications, with their farfetched leaps to another range of speculations. They are too awkward to be acknowledged, like the similarity of a character to one's aunt or how differently a detail registers in a first as opposed to a tenth reading or in playgoing as opposed to a critical reconstruction. Such anomalies vary in significance from negligible to decisive. The best we can do is train ourselves not to ignore the more emphatic ones and to identify the conventions that bring them about.

That is basically why the temptation to forget the palpable interventions of theatricality and extraordinary language should be resisted. Stephen Booth speaks of a membrane between our consciousness of the playhouse (of actors, costumes, fat heroines, and forgotten lines) and our consciousness of what it represents. "We simply amend performances in passage in much the way we automatically correct or delete linotypers' errors while we read a newspaper," by entertaining two fused but distinct "realities" at once.[8] No doubt willed deafness and blindness *are* part of our general suspension of disbelief, at least while we are absorbed in the progress of an Antony toward his monument. Yet Booth also speculates inventively and interestingly on the strategic uses of role-doubling in which our recognition of the actor who plays Antony, reappearing as Dolabella, puts before us the actor as actor. That is obviously a more emphatic intrusion than the spotting of a misspelling, and we surely need to be more than subliminally aware of it.

A second instinct, to tear gaps in the membrane, seems to me apt for moments when a play makes a point of role-playing and formalized speech, especially if we add the leisure of criticism and all the devices of a richly textured Shakespearean poetry for it to work upon. As Bert O. States remarks, in the make-believe atmosphere of the play our awareness of actors, scenes, and stage impedimenta is acute in the congregation of reminders in opening and closing scenes: entering the theater with a preconceived notion of Hamlet, in States's compelling account, we have a moment's impression of a stranger speaking the lines until we gradually become used to this form of Hamlet among the others. Again at the end, the business of the theater thickens with parting lines, exits, bows, curtain calls, and applause.[9] The marked ends of scenes and an ostentatious formalism like France's add a layer of consciousness within the action as well. The marginal notation here is that the total of verse drama's nonmimetic resources is impressive, and many of them are at the disposal of specially coded communiques to the audience. Some of the most prominent of such communiques are set up as poetry and set against the represented world. My concern is mainly with those differences of idiom that suggest an authorial signature and some periodicity that we can use as clues to the successions of literary history. They serve as beacons to successors navigating the same fictional waters but to different destinations. Milton's quite different destination tells us a good deal about the poetry that breaks loose from an Antony and a Lear and the second world it is forced to build elsewhere for lack of a receptive kingdom in the dramatic present.

Part One

Rhetoric and Poetry in the Theater

1

Playhouse Eloquence

> For surely divine poetry has the heaven-given power to lift the soul with its crust of earthly filth aloft and enshrine it in the skies, to breathe the perfume of nectar upon it, to bathe it with ambrosia, to fill it with heavenly bliss and whisper to it of immortal joy. Rhetoric so ensnares men's minds and so sweetly lures them with her chains that at one moment she can move them to pity, at another she can drive them to hatred, at another she can fire them with warlike passion, and at another lift them up to contempt of death itself.
> —Milton, Third Prolusion

Vehemence Beyond Usable Motive

It is a very young and impressionable Milton who passes in a general defense of letters almost without transition from poetry's immortal joy to rhetoric's ensnaring.[1] Apt words in whatever mode catch a cosmos in their net, connect its parts, and seize the soul with timely deliveries of knowledge. In that confidence in language and running together of modes, he reflects the late medieval and Renaissance identification of rhetoric and poetry and perhaps some of its enthusiasm for classical eloquence made into English (although on this occasion he is writing in Latin). With a similar confidence, the Elizabethan theater did its share of moving pity and raising passions. As G. R. Hibbard indicates, Shakespeare's mature plays, even as they parody an earlier theater and Shakespeare's own loquacious works, use extravagant language liberally.[2] The question to be posed here is how much of that language should be assigned to legitimate characters in charge of making things happen and how much is left over for other uses. The larger question of what rhetoric and poetry are is involved in it. A good many Renaissance texts allow Milton's overlap and make exclusive definition impossible. Mimetic fictions, as Scaliger says, shape a "disposition" of mind; disposition in turn shapes the actions of those who return to the first world altered. Hence poetry too is rhetoric, only more embellished.

Plays not only exploit both poetry and rhetoric, but turn them back into a network of social exchanges and show them operative in the responses of one person to another. In doing so they ask dramatic propriety to compromise with the extraordinary language of poetry, as it must if a Richard II is to be allowed his hysteron proterons and Autolycus his balladry. Yet too great a premium on entertainment and novelties of phrase is likely to inhibit our identification with characters as believable people. The theatrical contrivance shows in such marks of the trade as gesture, vehemence, and conventions. Shakespeare's later romance comedies add to those a use of the marvellous that moves close to the *mirabile* that Patrizi allows the poet and thus still further from verisimilitude. The earlier plays observe plausibility more scrupulously but make their own concessions to the unusual. As Harriet Hawkins observes concerning Bottom, after getting a stage made into a green forest "Shakespeare brings into this 'green plot' a set of louts who declare they will use the place as a stage. They point in the direction of a tiring-room, which we might otherwise have taken for a 'hawthorn-brake,' and decide that it will adequately serve them as a tiring-house."[3] When people in the back of a playhouse hear distinctly what someone standing next to the speaker misses, the play assumes our ready allowance for stage practice. When Gloucester labors a few feet across the stage, jumps, and thinks he has fallen from Dover Cliffs, we are meant to see not a singular credulity but a stage trick that to some extent allegorizes falls and recuperations as a running authorial commentary not conveyed through any onstage intelligence. Such conventions can never be rendered totally invisible, and Shakespeare makes no attempt even to lower their profile.

The Triple Pillar Transformed

The impact of devices from pratfalls to soliloquies and fog machines is a matter less for general comment than for practical testing. The sheer variety from play to play, even from scene to scene, makes it difficult to typify. However, I want to establish an extended and complex example before going into the critical options that Shakespeare's conflation of poetry and dramatic speech seems to give us. *Antony and Cleopatra* proposes itself because of its highly figural language and a strung-out action that allows a good many playlets and performances to dominate.

Those who speak a primarily Roman vocabulary, with its stoic virtues and rhetoric of power, prod us from the outset toward a harsh judgment of love's truancy and the games it plays with public obligation. But the Roman judgment of the lovers is less than definitive, and to some extent Shakespeare is examining the power of charisma even as he delivers the play over to it. Eloquent role-playing, whether of a reasonably consistent self or put on for the occasion, puts theatricality to manipulative use in acknowledgment that charisma builds more ships than evidence and logic do. If Helen's beauty (as we are told) stirred up the Greeks, cannot Cleopatra aim to be not far behind when history records its electrified responses to her? When Philo directs Demetrius's attention to her entry, even he looks through a highly metaphoric window at her and Antony, in a rhetoric based on the assumption of Roman dominance but also tinged with Egyptian extravagance. Shakespeare is already setting up the fifth-act exchange between Dolabella and Cleopatra, which comes to a similar collision between things Roman and Egyptian. But by then Cleopatra can enshrine the memory of an idealized Antony without the embarrassment of his reappearing and challenging her portrait of him.

Philo is both expositional in getting the play underway and functional in erecting a barrier for other romantics to get past:

> Take but good note, and you shall see in him
> The triple pillar of the world transform'd
> Into a strumpet's fool: behold and see.
> (1.1.11–13)

As the audience settles in, the billing tacked up outside the theater is confirmed by this transition to an arena of the spectacular. Antony and Cleopatra are to begin at a high level, which depending on how we take it will be either puffery or magnificence. Consistent with the judgments that follow, Philo's juxtaposing of the pillar and the fool underscores the magnitude that goes with things Roman and the tawdriness of things Egyptian. In getting a start on the play's heroic style and the buildup that Cleopatra consummates, however, he says more than he intends. Ricocheting an explosive "strumpet" against great "pillars," he taps in the poster nails with a flourish that gives him a share of the play's generous allotment of grandeur. He initiates a sequence of displays and calls attention to the relation between performers and the fugitive selves behind them. The latter we have to piece together not only from what comes out in interviews in this very public play but from what the poetry consolidates in images and between-the-lines implications that cannot be said really to "come out" at all.

Getting a place in the story is a project for several characters, Enobarbus most critically and in some scenes even Antony, as though keeping an eye on the audience and on history books were as important as plotting a pragmatic course of action. If Antony and Cleopatra are to be celebrated eventually, their opponents and subordinates cannot be paltry now and must therefore practice *their* flourishes as well. The sounder the Roman critique and the more eloquent the Roman encomium when the dust clears, the more powerful the challenge of love's hyperbole to ordinary imperialism. Thus Octavius will eventually answer Philo's opening coronets with the observation that "No grave upon the earth shall clip in it / A pair so famous" (5.2.357–58). He doesn't say virtuous or justified, we notice, but sizeable enough in passion and disastrous enough in choices to make the news. That impressive sobriety settles the story into chronicle and sends us out past the same posters, now partly the memorials of a striking performance. Love's rhetoric may not have saved a place for the lovers in the empire, but it has salvaged a prominent collective memory by a quite different application of its power to move.

As the lovers enter and make the claims for magnitude that Philo's fanfare leads us to expect, Shakespeare sets going one of the patterns of Antony's own last performances. Antony's high style now as well as then is more dubious than Cleopatra's, the most formidable challenge to love's poetry being not Roman moralizing but love's own inflation:

> *Cleo.* If it be love indeed, tell me how much.
> *Ant.* There's beggary in the love that can be reckon'd.
> *Cleo.* I'll set a bourn how far to be belov'd.
> *Ant.* Then must thou needs find out new heaven, new earth.
> (1.1.14–17)

Fine answers to the prompts in both cases, concise, almost proverbial, flattering to both Cleopatra and himself, and more important, dramatic in the sense that he meets her challenge for pretty speeches by denying them, yet makes them anyway. The brevity of the lines suggests that poets reciting eclogues to nymphs have grown tiresome and thus offers an indirect critique of flowery speech. Unfortunately, Antony himself immediately undermines love's potentially better style by reckoning passions, each of which "fully strives / To make itself, in thee, fair and admired!" (1.1.50–51). They cannot stand forth among history's preeminent lovers if he allows them to blend into the chorus of sonnet voices.

That falling back on conventional hyperbole calls passionate transport into question as seriously as Philo does and reminds us that ministries of propaganda work best when their spokesmen convince themselves first. This has the sound of practiced rhetoric, cut to a minimum and adopted to a dialogue that suggests among other things the potential boredom of soldiers with too much leave time and too many feasts. But in the logic of courtly love, the costs of love cannot be exorbitant if they make such a purchase as Antony claims, and we know that without some passion there will be no conflict to run the plot. To set sail for love's boundaries, lovers must venture beyond the reach of both Rome and Alexandria, whether or not previous cartographers of love have charted a course. Thus in Antony's (pretended or believed?) view, their voyaging will be as ambitious as any military career.

As in Antony's projection of the scene of shame to Eros, what such phrases have to do with character is not completely self-evident, but they must do service for the play as a literary performance whose opening sets up a cross fire of genres and styles. Philo's generic clues, for instance, allow for both love story and tragedy. Cleopatra as strumpet and Antony as fool keep satire and dark comedy open as well and remind us of the way in which both tragedy and romance are undercut in *Troilus and Cressida*. When the two lovers come on speaking grandly, it is possible to hear their vigor and poise as emotional fraudulence, as courtly wit, or simply as the sound of two people quoting a better class of heroic romances. That Antony lets speechmaking sweep him along as though he projected a role, liked the sound of it, and felt obliged to continue in it leaves the satiric possibility open. It is never quite closed even in his dying speeches. Cleopatra wants an openly declared contract or at least some statement, preferably elegant, that will shower endearments on her in full view of admirers. It probably does not matter to her exactly what Antony answers so long as he agrees to perform, and for all we know he may be turning her down at first because he dislikes her attempts to issue his lines to him. (This is after all not the star-crossed love of innocents or the unsophisticated love of Othello and Desdemona.) Their contest sorts through available styles for appropriate ones and for a balance between potential lyricism, straining toward authenticity, and mere rhetoric. One subtext of the play is thus a dialogue between Shakespeare and a reading public capable of juggling character-relevant self-projections and a choral author-inscribing critique of reproduced legends. (But I'll reserve that largely for later.)

Despite his tempting slogan for harness-loosening, "Let Rome in Tiber melt," Antony is vulnerable to the charges that Romans bring against him, if not strictly from a moral standpoint, at least from a pragmatic one. As an aging campaigner getting phased out in a grubbier new age of politics, he would be vulnerable even without the distractions of Cleopatra. This phase of the empire is less for new conquests than for consolidating and ruling; it requires administrative skills and a certain amount of espionage. Neither of the lovers seems to understand the Octavian stretching of chivalric codes or the relationship between ethics and power. That much we can assume about their vulnerability simply by knowing that because of her Antony will in fact ruin his standing among the triumvirs. It prevents us from overruling Philo even while regret over that ruin prevents us also from dismissing so respected a warrior as nothing more than a strumpet's fool. As we discover eventually, Antony is still testing voices while competing with Cleopatra over the most throat-catching way to say "I am dying, Egypt, dying."

Antony talks in this grand way now and will again then because the play needs him to do so if he is to build upon the Rome-Egypt contrast and be prepared to step into Cleopatra's legend, which requires magnitude. It is the posthumous Antony, the one who no longer speaks for himself but is reconstructed, who must finally live up to the billing, when the game of charisma is turned over to the better poet and strategist of the two. Up to that juncture, the play collapses great into small and transforms small into great with maximum discredit to both sides. Nothing stays fixed in practical wisdom where axiom and ordinary speech might have stationed it in a morality play, but those who have come to hear loftiness are at least being given some, and in several varieties, in stoic Romans who back up poses with a generous and brave manhood, in political Romans who capitalize on a magnanimous chivalry, in loyal and perceptive friends like Enobarbus, and in the ornamentally splendid Egyptians.

If love is to escape the suspicion that all this conceals the defects Philo names without opening an avenue toward transcendence, either Antony or Cleopatra must "tell how much" somewhat more convincingly than the initial samples suggest that they can. The playacting of the great cannot be all posturing or the command language of empire all rhetoric. A Cleopatra who was the Cressida Philo assumes her to be could make no convincing demonstration. As it is, suicide is one tangible proof of something—sincerity perhaps—at least for Antony, in what he thinks is the pursuit of Cleopatra already dead, and perhaps even for her in pursuit of him assuredly gone. The question is whether it is really love or the momentum of earlier self-projections that carries them. Certainly the final deeds themselves are accompanied by the kind of proclamations we would expect from the opening style. Cleopatra's interest in Dolabella's reaction in "Think you there was, or might be such a man / As this I dreamt of?" may or may not be genuine, but what she *does* in the wake of voicing it suggests her conviction that such a man once existed and now summons her.

The question of response divides into what skeptics onstage think and, using them as foils or guides, just how we put poetic supplements together with acts—whether to the exposure of concealed rhetoric or as a revealing of new dimensions of spirit. It is reasonably clear that not to play by Octavius's rules is to lose in the world of kings and battles and that Antony and chivalry, whether amatory or military chivalry, are squeezed by those rules. The later arias swarm with secondary implications by comparison to what answerable speech in the command exchanges of empire or the gossip of relaxed soldierly moments would normally allow. When the ends of plays sound like résumés, as Cleopatra's last speeches do, we owe it to motif repetition and a kind of musicality or ritual technique, reprise being a formal device by which an ending goes to a final boundary while recapitulating the charismatic moments. Here the summing up is especially wrapped up in performances as such. When Cleopatra recalls Enobarbus's glorious vision of her in "I am again for Cydnus, / To meet Mark Antony" (5.2.227–28) or recalls Antony in her vignette of "realms and islands" dropping as plates "from his pocket" (5.2.91–92), or when she accidentally cites Philo's version of eye-socket plates (from "those his goodly eyes / That o'er the files and musters of the war / Have glow'd like plated Mars" [1.1.2–4]), the audience hears simultaneously the closing of a dramatic circuit and the further sounding of the poetic-visionary note that has been struggling to be heard throughout. This is surely all classifiable as poetry, since no orator trained under the principles of Cicero or Quintilian would venture so far into Puttenham's metaphoric far-fet; but again it has dramatic functions based on the principle of decorum and an implicit politics that grants an empress style.

What comes forward more boldly in that resounding is what we now see has had little chance to mature in either Alexandria or Rome and requires a legendary place. Whatever historical chronicles record is eligible for legendary nostalgia, but particularly the histories of great classical and English realms.[4] As death finishes this particular narrative among the bibliographical entries under Cleopatra's name, the performance not only echoes others but raises the type of the lover to its highest pedestal. It has the effect of disarming and converting into eulogy the moralizing with which Philo begins. In donning the robe and the crown of the empress as the chief impresario of power through charm, Cleopatra dresses for an act quite opposite to the indignities a continued life would inflict, as represented by "mechanic slaves / With greasy aprons, rules, and hammers" uplifting "us to the view" (5.2.208–10). As she once floated down to Antony and sent the Egyptian encounter of Rome into a new phase, so she now prepares to rejoin Antony in the realm of ghosts. As befits a structural frame that opens and closes the chronological story with like recurrences, the death voyage heads toward a union beyond drama and well beyond the normal boundary of rhetoric. It straddles the margin between imaginative invention and historical fact. Not all the advantage lies with the dream of an elsewhere, however. Unlike the full-blooded lovers who approach each other on Cydnus, ghosts are not capable of much variety; they are usually reduced to what drove them or gratified them most. That Antony and Cleopatra in Hades will be less various is both a diminution and a fulfillment of their amatory exhibitionism. Although they both think only of the escape and the fulfillment, the play does not totally abandon its skepticism and its acknowledgment of the usefulness of a more calculating power in the real world.

Among the echoes that Cleopatra sends ricocheting in "I am again for Cydnus" are several others from previous stagings of herself, none quite so exotic as the barge tableau. We are cast back to the ambiguities of the first scene that Philo trumpets as an *in medias res* example of her control over Antony, already practiced to the point of habit. What has bothered us about the beginning can now be put in better perspective, since death has a way of shrinking troubling questions. Enobarbus too is recalled as someone now shut out of the glorious part he helped to build. Foremost among the loyal ones who depart, he has come near to claiming a significant role but has just missed. To accept the unvarnished truth is to drop out of the competition for a place among the great ones. An audience can exit feeling that the play is as valedictory as it is tragic, as poetic as it is dramatic, and still not know whether it is better to participate in a private quest for greatness or to go over to Octavius and the consensus fictions of the less spectacularly deluded.

Mimesis and Command Performance

Antony and Cleopatra alerts us to theatrical practices and a range of poetic resources beyond rhetoric's normal ones, including a high incidence of metaphor, references to Hercules and Egyptian goddesses, elaborate sound systems, altered syntax, meter, and inventive fable. Its interior self-references and habit of circling back are not typical either of historical narrative or of discursive argument. Its disregard of the unities of time and place moves it toward episodic romance and shifts the structural burden to analogy and echo. It thus commits its argument to word-realized thought as opposed to the more integral workings of motives in compact actions. To be a more Aristotelian play it would require people whose hold on reality is stronger and more successful in winning and organizing allies. Its use of hyperbole (the "loud-lier"), the far-fetcher, the trespasser, the distributer, the transporter, and other such figures (in Puttenham's colorful English) sets even its prosier dialogues over against ordinary language for the sake not so much of embellishment or advocacy as supplementation of chronicle by imagination.

As to the critical options such a play allows us, one of them is the option to focus on personality. But the inflation of the performances cautions us against going too far in that direction. Gauging the boundaries of character criticism is notoriously difficult, but the extraordinary language of the more inventive speeches forces us to work at the task. Critics who derive stage language almost exclusively from individualized motives—whose sense of style is based primarily in propriety and mimetic idiom—are particularly abundant in studies of Shakespeare. A subset represented by G. R. Hibbard, Albert Cook, Michael Black, F. W. Brownlow, and Terrence Hawkes will be representative enough for our purposes—representative of those who, while sometimes resisting Bradley by name, tend to describe Shakespearean drama in terms of strong personalities.[5]

To Hawkes, for instance, when a Macbeth or an Othello turns to private recitation, the play does not grow more palpably stagey or eloquent among its echoes; it exposes the moral defects and psychological derangements of a character who draws progressively away from the common idiom and its social bonds. Othello's uncommunicative nature from the fourth act onward is a monstrosity, as indeed a variety of critics have no difficulty showing, especially in Othello's mad scurrility:

> Lie with her, lie on her?—We say lie on her, when they belie her,—lie with her, zounds, that's fulsome! Handkerchief—confessions, and be hanged for his labour. First, to be hanged, and then to confess; I tremble at it. Nature would not invest herself in such shadowing passion without some instruction. It is not words that shake me thus. Pish! Noses, ears and lips. Is't possible? Confess?—Handkerchief?—O devil! (4.1.35–43)

Since such a speech does not build upon sources or tragic conventions, it is eminently available for psychological description—particularized in idiom and useful in our tracing of Othello's disintegration. Macbeth's deviation from the open language of Duncan is damning for similar reasons. By granting the desirability of a sociable style, one concedes the rightness of a Duncan and the vileness of the excited, egoistic imagination. What better evidence of the offices society allots to kings, husbands, and wives than the brutal shattering of social forms that Macbeth, Lady Macbeth, and Othello work, and what stronger argument for the adjustment of ego to social constraints than the nightmare of their fantasies? We need to add, however, that the language of monstrosity is only marginally related to moral judgment.

It returns us to the speaker at another level of engagement, articulate beyond character in any way we perceive it outside of fictions. Duncan is neither as poetically nor as dramatically impressive as the one who murders him. Macbeth, not the voices of normality, is the play's most superb instrument for articulating its deepest consciousness. (More of that in a moment.)

Brownlow, Cook, Black, and Hibbard take parallel routes to the absorption of the poetry into the image of people in action. In Hibbard, a recapitulated theatrical history shows up in each successive Shakespeare outing, but the author is increasingly veiled behind the dramatis persona. Thus from *1 Henry IV* onward, Shakespeare learns to bring "his exuberant delight in words and figures of speech into harmony with the dependence of drama on action and character" (p. 35), which shows the playwright briefly but then whisks him out of sight again behind the characters. Thus when Richard II breaks into highly figured speech, in a verse that "would normally be felt as undramatic," we feel it as drama because Richard's self-indulgence is relevant to his crisis and to the contrast with Bolingbroke (p. 36).

That distinction between the flowery and the efficient speaker is in keeping with Jonas Barish's valuable distinction between Richard II and Richard III and suggests the most common means of assimilating style to character—the attributing of extraordinary speech to aberrations of character. The language of Richard II is the kind that "summons because it likes the feel of a summons," in Kenneth Burke's words; Richard III summons because something needs doing. Where the one "exhibits himself for the sheer pleasure or whim of it," for the other, however much he enjoys his roles, "they remain instrumental to his primary aim." Both are useful to an exhibitionist drama, but Richard II is the better example of speech issued for its own sake, because as he "basks in the gaze of his court, what he is really signalling to us is a defect of function."[6] He must not be allowed to signal anything a real king could not. This comes close to saying that in Richard II we see an imitation of a king acting and an actor playing king, but without ever quite confessing to the interposing consciousness of the play, let alone the play as a variant of the texts it draws upon and echoes. The play remains a window upon a reality that happens to be itself highly theatrical. In Cook's version of decorum, Shakespeare's language includes both a pointed, daily idiom and a golden refinement beyond "meantness," which is almost to say beyond psychologically plausible action, but not quite. Even where Shakespeare tends "toward the magnificence of the golden style" in a play like *Antony and Cleopatra*, he returns to a plainer style to offer breathing space and tangible characterization. To similar ends, he gives Macbeth's most striking language a trenchant folk wisdom (p. 160).

Michael Black's equally functional speech works within a developing sense of selves in a play's larger society. Unusual speech for him too reflects a tension between self and society. Poetry represents "the movement of a consciousness," a singular consciousness that even in so striking an idiom as Macbeth's is "not Shakespeare's, not ours" (p. 73). Hence in Black's account, young people love to speak such a part because they can grow "intoxicated by [a] sense of 'being' Macbeth." Granted that even the least promising talent can scarcely resist "Is this a dagger, which I see before me, / The handle toward my hand," would-be actors also like to recite in croaking voices "When shall we three meet again? / In thunder, lightning, or in rain?" and "Double, double toil and trouble: / Fire, burn; and, cauldron, bubble." The reason playhouse fictions march down school halls as well as across stages is undoubtedly the showing off and saturation in high emotion that they permit, voiced but not possessed, full of color and sound but emptied of serious identification with motive or character. A flair for parody and purposeful misreading may also show in it, as it does in Shakespeare's turning Bottom loose on the melodramatic world of the Romeos and Juliets. When we voice these metrically hypnotic lines, do we not put ourselves among reiterated cultural echoes that reach beyond Shakespeare to Mother Goose, to typical and archtypical diabolism, and to Sophoclean and Senecan tragic forms?

Is it Macbeth who attracts us, then, or Shakespeare masked one moment as Macbeth, the next as the Weird Sisters, giving enthralled actors and audiences a vicarious, complex literary life? Or is it perhaps neither of these exclusively but the sound and meaning of the words engaged in fictive mind-creations? Surely the beginnings of an answer lie in the stretching of sense by metaphoric association and the stylistic difference between what we hear on stage and what we hear daily. The attractions of the figures that Puttenham collects for the vernacular lie in their antithetical relation to uncostumed role-playing. The latter too balances indoctrinated patterns and altered, self-styled variants and allows some latitude in the improvisation of selves in different social contexts. But we are obliged to stake some enduring reputation on our usual speech; theatrical expression has fewer constraints. Nor do we necessarily sacrifice the particularized idiom of a Macbeth to gain the greater resonance of Shakespeare's play world—not if we acknowledge the fictiveness of characters to begin with and go beyond representation to the fictive states of mind and the indirect power of theatrical charm.

Certainly before we get acquainted with Macbeth as an apparent man, we enter the special atmosphere to which (along with the nightmarish intuitions of his wife and the riddles of prophetic devils) he contributes his share. The language that stirs up so much clatter at the outset of the play never really subsides. Once we catch its tonal register and begin gathering the perceptions and feelings it stirs up, we do not hear the common idiom (when it puts in occasional appearances) as we hear it elsewhere. That witchy energy is dampened but still detectable in the sound and fury of "Tomorrow, and tomorrow," for instance. The play is dominated by fearful anticipations cast in a melodramatic mode and converted to autumnal reassessment when most of the butchery is done. To say as Black does that "an interest in 'character,' then is an interest in drama" (p. 74) and to stop there is to lose the atmospheric envelope in which the poetry wraps character, and lose as well the play's return loops and symbolic networks. Interest in drama *as art*, then, is also interest in verbal texture, lighting, costuming, directing, scenic construction, song and dance, rhyme, ritual, and intertextuality. Even where no fury is in transcendent forms (to paraphrase Stevens building up "a quite normal life"), the Shakespearean actual candle blazes with artifice.[7]

But we need to continue at least one step further if we are to keep open as many of the critical options as can be put to good account in honoring the verbal range of a Macbeth or a Cleopatra. Black's analysis of "Tomorrow, and tomorrow" is useful in situating metaphoric speech within unfolding consciousness. The question is not only whose consciousness but also how it passes among speakers and resonates in different ears:

> What we have . . . here is not a philosophy, not even Macbeth's own "point of view", but a dramatic process in which a consciousness undergoing a traumatic evolution is revealed through the words character uses. We see and hear a crucial transition from false confidence to despair. . . . The language takes us down below the level of logical transitions. The image-shifts, the verbal associations, the central rhythmic ictus and its transformations and suspensions seem the immediate activity of another mind, understood and felt as we do not ordinarily feel other minds. (p. 58)

I would take "as we do not ordinarily feel other minds" in a slightly different way. It is not just another mind that we enter, but a pattern of withholdings and revelations that includes other plays and literary transumptions, as many as we actually detect. Authorial presence too, as I suggested, is unmistakable. It is as unlike Marlowe's or Webster's as Macbeth is unlike Hamlet or Lear and cannot be totally lost in the reverberations of demon voices and Greek furies from Aeschylus. We are also probably wrong to deny that something is being said about the intellectual foundations of other minds, if James I, the political context of overthrown kingships, and the implanting of generic features from one playwright to another enter our calculations. If no such community of reference reaches us, we have no basis for common ideas and experience. We leave the play world politically apathetic and remote. But the main point is that the concept of a romantic self from which an action stems would be questionable even if the character here were not a literary impersonation; it is doubly so with a representation entirely made up of signs and gestures and special voice imprints unlike those of the pulpit, the radio, and the tea table. In short, we need to take vicarious play life in at least two ways, recognizing both the performance as such and a transmittable, moving trauma.

The actor figures prominently in this double-talking. We associate actors with the several parts they play and yet dissociate the person from any particular part. Although the history of theater records no shortage of those who hold chameleon skill against actors and want them, for the sake of their souls, to have their own characters, convention grants them the license to do as instructed. At the same time, in some way related to craft and practice, actors assert themselves as common factors among roles. If a division of our attention between them and the play means our not taking in an episode as an eyewitness would take in a real incident, it is surely a gain: none of us (as has been frequently and wisely pointed out) would return to a theater that put us through the trauma of a real Macbeth or Lear. Such actor filtering is not precisely equivalent to aesthetic distance, nor is it the exclusive property of fictions; it is the complex product of experienced hearing, which teaches us to sort out degrees of evasion and sincerity and to attribute less of the latter to actors speaking their lines than to most others. Eloquence and meter, the chief instruments of stylistic distancing, are strong signals of the actor's performance. As vehement language mounts toward its higher passions, we join so-called character there for company (to borrow another line from Stevens), "But at a distance, in another tree." It is an interesting if often wobbly perch.

Grace to Use Time So

For Milton the relation between narrative or dramatic events and visionary poetry is often a foreground matter. The difference between his fully thematized otherworldly interest and an Othello speaking a language of Christian references is both typical and crucial to Milton's rhetoric-drama-poetry triangulation. It is also involved and difficult to summarize, and I will have to postpone the major consideration of it until we can devote extended and exclusive attention to it. But Milton's habit of conflating and crossing kinds is the source of a difficulty that can be inserted here as a perspective on Shakespeare and a further caution against some of the more common critical options. For instance, the symbols of monarchy that establish legitimate greatness in Shakespeare turn up as evidence of self-inflation in Satan, whose speeches to the fallen host are exposed as merely the parodic back side of celestial gatherings. Like Marlowe's and Shakespeare's figures of power, he too has charisma, but it is a front for something else. If we apply pressure to virtually any Miltonic dialogue in fact, whether among the fallen or the about to fall, it shows a mixture of rhetoric and poetry that forces us to rethink the matter of decorum. The explicit argument coaches us to distinguish among things demonic, human, and divine. Milton uses both polemic and dramatic dialogue not only in *Paradise Lost* but elsewhere to set the stage for what he takes to be well-established truths.[8] From the Prolusions onward, he makes set pieces serve thematized causes. Again in Abdiel's arguments in *Paradise Lost,* Christ's in *Paradise Regained,* and the expostulations of "Comus" and *Samson Agonistes,* he brushes aside error but requires it as a negative version of what the disciplined mind must overcome. These extended arguments are a vital part of an architectural stress system and a hierarchical arrangement of genres that culminate in the narrative farsightedness that frames the action. Among other things they are a rebuke to the Elizabethan yoking of the heroic to the chivalric.

Where dialogue sharpens into debate like this (as it surely does more often in Milton than in any other major writer in English), the reasons undoubtedly have to do not only with the pressure of absolutes on dramatic moments but with a rationalized universe. Milton's confidence in an open forum is shared by Lady and proved by the refutations that Abdiel and Christ make of glaring theological errors. In such contests, debate disarms any expedient advocacy that may be fogging the air with illusions and any manipulative use of deceit. The main difference between Milton's contemporaries and Shakespeare's in this respect is that debates for the former are always theological before they are civil, and of course they assemble both their truths and their admonitions chiefly from biblical sources.

Two brief examples will suffice to illustrate that difference—the negative example of Satan's seduction of Eve and "How Soon Hath Time," both of which worry the problem of decision-making under the far-off eye of the great taskmaster. In the former, both tempter and tempted pass back and forth between argument and poetic address under a rhetoric-poetry relation quite different from that of the third prolusion. The balance of immediacy and bardic scope that Eve *should* maintain Milton displays in the creation hymns and the morning orison. The temptation follows a different procedure, full of hyperbolic enthusiasm for sudden rises in intelligence granted by the fruit. As Cicero and Quintilian argue concerning displays of feeling, the orator cannot expect to move an audience if he is not himself moved, and so Satan drums up a display of "Zeal and Love" over the wrong that limited status imposes on one's growth. What drives a noble being is love of change and evolutionary self-improvement:

> now more bold
> The Tempter, but with show of Zeal and Love
> To Man, and indignation at his wrong,
> New parts puts on, and as to passion mov'd,
> Fluctuates disturb'd, yet comely, and in act
> Rais'd, as of some great matter to begin.
> As when of old some Orator renown'd
> In *Athens* or free *Rome*, where Eloquence
> Flourish'd, since mute, to some great cause addrest,
> Stood in himself collected, while each part,
> Motion, each act won audience ere the tongue.
> (9.665–74)

Milton's reference to oratorical theatrics is well-taken, since orators are virtual playwrights in inventing a character to reinforce an argument. Even beyond those who have a senate to move, Satan with this audience is accomplishing the redirection of human history. The rhetoric hangs in part on the Platonist contest between sophistic illusion and philosophic definition. In the reactions that then follow, what looks like the greatest lyric intensity that either Eve or Adam has mounted to this point masks what is really a further stage of rhetoric caught from Satan's sophistry: "O glorious trial of exceeding Love, / Illustrious evidence, example high!" (9.961–62). Eve's *exclamatio* is sufficiently convincing that critics sometimes find it forgivable. "Ingaging me to emulate" suggests a causal connection of eloquence to good example. But the relation of logic to rhetoric is now in such a tangle that it will not be straightened out until the second Adam remixes dialogue and rhetoric.

The ignorance that creates openings for dramatic conflict also generates self-debate and monologue, the latter an inward turn that grows out of moments when no one else is there to provoke responses. "How Soon Hath Time" is Milton's earliest illustration of that uncertainty and the patience it exacts. Denying drama and turning away from any specific course of action, it comes to what will be a typical Miltonic formula for successful protagonists—the decision to go against the evidence of the moment and accept an already determined future:

> Yet be it less or more, or soon or slow,
> It shall be still in strictest measure ev'n

> To that same lot, however mean or high,
> Toward which Time leads me, and the will of Heav'n;
> All is, if I have grace to use it so,
> As ever in my great task-Master's eye.

The lower registers of the word "grace" carry a suggestion of manners and metaphoric good breeding, to be practiced while one waits; but all told, the direction of the narrative is conceded to be beyond dramatic suspense. Milton typically gives such rounding off formal authority over the encounters that lead to it. Summaries rise from incident to precept and seek the edge between history and providence. Their place is outside the simultaneity of eternity but above the perilous situations that stir the investigative process.

They are usually qualified by an anticipated next phase as yet unspecifiable. The swain's fresh woods in "Lycidas" and the endings of *Paradise Lost* and *Paradise Regained,* for instance, turn to the near future with some confidence. In each case the glance forward renews the resolve for productive labor as though the historical effort will produce the second world. It is thus easy to err in either of two directions in accounting for that narrative framing—by delivering the speaker or a protagonist too completely from historical bondage or by leaving him too entangled in it. When poetry has performed its educational tasks, revealed wisdom is sustained and disseminated; when argument has done its work, it removes specious reasoning and obstructions. Each is incomplete without the other, and both work to overcome the obscurity of the moment. It is in that overcoming that Milton generally proceeds from argument to act to a visionary poetic that retrieves and consolidates biblical readings. The wholeness of the Bible's story liberates its readers from the fractional parts that otherwise keep us trapped in incident. The object is to open windows upon what is to come eventually by a framed reading of what lies within the materials at hand.

Speech-Act Ratios

The nexus of poetry, rhetoric, and drama in Shakespeare and Milton does not lend itself to easy schematizing or to charts. But a spectrum of possibilities might be useful both to survey the ground we have covered and to look ahead.

- Poetry may serve demonstrable character and still be in excess of anything required for specific dramatic tasks, as in *Hamlet* the soliloquies do much more than retard the action meaningfully.
- Poetry may be not only proleptic or recollective in its networks but far-

fetched, introducing a vision beyond any conceivable end of the action, as in Antony's projected afterlife. Such language inserts a "what if" amidst dramatic sequences otherwise limited to the probable. It is especially important to the rupture between drama and poetry that Milton tries to fix by reconnecting dramatic moments to end things.

• Poetry may go unused by anyone to promote an action, as in songs, interludes, and soliloquies. These insets (in Francis Berry's apt word)[9] are likely to stretch our concept of the unity of action to the breaking point.

• Poetry may be so complex and unsettling that it remains difficult to assimilate, yet situated in dialogue not used as choral commentary. This troubling category may be squeezed down by fuller interpretations, but I doubt that it can ever be totally eliminated in Shakespeare. Milton is determined to demonstrate the final relevance of every detail, but several poems leave a gap between what faith expects and what is actually knowable.

2

Unnatural Language: Songs and Soliloquies

Right and naturall language seeme[s] to have least of wit in it; that which is writh'd and tortur'd, is counted the more exquisite. Cloath of Bodkin, or Tissue, must be imbrodered; as if no face were faire, that were not pouldred, or painted? No beauty to be had, but in wresting, and writhing our owne tongue? Nothing is fashionable, till it bee deform'd; and this is to write like a *Gentleman.* All must bee as affected, and preposterous as our Gallants cloathes, sweet bags and night-dressings: in which you would thinke our men lay in, like *Ladies:* it is so curious.
—Ben Jonson, *Discoveries*

Drama organizes its means of presentation—dialogue, mime, dance, and song—with the help of transferable pieces of satire, pastoral, and romance that it twists into exchangeable talk and declamation. But it took its language initially from poetry. Besides the Homeric and Sophoclean sources that Aristotle names and issue-oriented disputational and morality forms, Elizabethan drama includes such verse sources as Ovid and Virgil. It draws also upon historical chronicles for materials and upon old and new comedy for form and manner—to name but a few of the staples in its diet. In acquiring that expanded literary ambience, it learned to tolerate a rhetorical copiousness guided by classical and English commentaries and to make some use of dialectic and formal logic, the latter primarily for entertainment in comic displays of choplogic. Its mainstay in comic prose is middle- to low-style conversation, but in verse, without straying totally from reactive speech, it allows inset sonnets, songs, and ritualized dialogue to go with its dumb shows, allegories, pantomimes, and soliloquies—such is the loose baggy monster that Jonson and Sidney survey in the making and Dryden tidies up in retrospect. In all this, the Elizabethan theater juxtaposes the vernacular and Latinate diction with a growing sense of national muscle-flexing.

I rehearse these well-known resources primarily to keep before us the sheer textuality of plays and the consequent critical need to balance representation and unity of action with a good deal that strains against them. To put it in the favorable terms often used for it, Elizabethan drama is "capacious"—generically diverse, energetic, unparaphrasable, unclassical. What Jonson objects to in its extremes, especially in Marlowe and other highly embroidered writers, is the bombast of its greater deviations from common idiom—the diction and the iconic and metrical heightening, the ostentatious sound systems and rounded periods. It is doubtful that he would have included the unjointed hopping or curt styles associated with Lipsius and Seneca, but both loose and abrupt periods could look affected in stage characters. Joseph Hall apparently has no single kind of embroidery in mind in the third satire of *Virgidemarium* when he sniffs the playwright's "pot-fury" leavings:

> weeneth he his base drink-drowned spright,
> Rapt to the threefold loft of heavens hight,
> When he conceives upon his fained stage
> The stalking steps of his great personage,
> Graced with huf-cap termes and thundring threats
> That his poore hearers hayre quite upright sets.

Senecan tragedy no doubt contributed as much as Cicero's orator to those decibels. Departures from prosiness become visual dislocations when raised voices are punctuated "With high-set steps and princely carriage."

The question of what is right and natural in language is notoriously difficult, but without putting too fine a point on it we can agree with Jonson about highly ornamental passages that glory in wit and artfulness. Perhaps equally assumable is Shakespeare's obtrusive speechmaking in the earlier plays and tendency in his maturity to parody similar speakers running to excess, even as he assigns eloquence to those who need it for specific purposes. Richard II's combination of meter, rhyme, and rhetoric, to take a relatively late earlier case, results in a pomp-epic style that he makes the first entry in a series of contrasts, to be juxtaposed with the efficient Bolingbroke and followed later by the prince learning a tavern idiom. As an impresario of emotions, Richard is both sympathetic and pathetic. Shakespeare associates his theatrical flair with chivalric ritual and spiritual obtuseness. Because speeches that look "pouldred, or painted" usually contribute something to performance, what seems to be at issue in such curious language is not so much realism or decorum as control of the audience's distance from and engagement in "artificial persons" (in J. Leeds Barroll's term). The distinguishing of classes and types, in part a matter of historical taste, also warrants some attention before we try to say what seems conventional and what natural in a given context, which I want to do here in a few specific cases drawn from *As You Like It, The Tempest,* and *Macbeth.*

Rhetoric and Aristotle's Imitation of an Action

English manuals in the tradition of *Ad Herrennium* and Quintilian—by Cox, Wilson, Day, Fenner, Sterry, and Peacham, for instance—have very little to say about the craft of verse beyond a common agreement that poetry is more embellished than prose.[1] It does not fall within their province to note that, whether or not poets exceed orators in abruptness (one sign of passion for Longinus),[2] fictionality gives them more freedom to make sudden climbs and plunges. Unfortunately for both poetry and rhetoric, tradition links them initially not as Puttenham's or Sidney's effective teachers and persuaders but as the objects of the Socratic attack on unprincipled persuasion. Any language fogged with sensory imagery and fleshed out with devices is suspect. It is not meter or eloquence that bothers Socrates but unprincipled appeals to the senses. Orators and poets are vivid stylists whose relation to dialectic and to unvarnished truth needs to be watched closely. That philosophic dialogues define their abstractions through interrogation makes them safer because it allows what the stranger in *The Sophist* calls the purging of error. By dividing issues into their logical components, contention makes for clearer vision and finer distinctions and allows fruitful pauses for the questioning mind. That poets are like forum orators in avoiding countervoicing thus tells heavily against them.

One aim of Tudor-Elizabethan rhetoric and poetry from the earlier manuals through Puttenham and Sidney is to combine what Plato pulls asunder—reason-governed example, dialectic, and poetic fictions—and thus build into poetry itself more offices of philosophical teaching. Jonson again reflects a common opinion in observing that "wheresoever, manners, and fashions are corrupted, Language is. It imitates the publicke riot. The excesse of Feasts, and apparell, are the notes of a sick State; and the wantonnesse of language, of a sick mind."[3] A play that deals with such an ailing state might offer up a feast of languages in illustration, as *Love's Labour's Lost* does, but otherwise "the true Artificer" should not "run away from nature, as hee were afraid of her; or depart from life, and the likenesse of Truth; but speake to the capacity of his hearers. And though his language differ from the vulgar somewhat; it shall not fly from all humanity," as he finds it doing in "the *Tamerlanes,* and *Tamer-Chams* of the late Age" with their "scenicall strutting, and furious vociferation, to warrant them to the ignorant gapers" (*Discoveries,* p. 587).

However, just how poets under such strictures are to enliven fables with the extraordinary is as arguable as what "natural" means in a London that mixes cockney, Scottish dialect, aristocratic poise and wit, French imports, and high talk over supper about Livy and Tacitus. Implicit in the Renaissance interest in the marvellous is a recognition of differences between symbolic fictions as delivered through dramatis personae and speeches by orators offered more or less in their own characters. That Castelvetro sanctions rare events and Sidney the golden age are signs of the dissatisfaction with plain truth.[4] Extraordinary invention, as Geoffrey Shepherd remarks in Sidney's case, is not necessarily a product of fantasy; it can be rather a "recognition of newly *discovered* patterns" in nature itself.[5] As Sidney is aware in straining against verisimilitude, poetic vividness can take many forms, the highest of them as eloquent as the best of biblical writers, undertaking to represent the "inconceivable" God who stands behind much seventeenth-century loftiness.

Pursuit of that line here, however, would lead us too far afield. I want instead to explore the borderline between the natural and the extravagant, if in fact one exists and not merely a large buffer territory. If the "material point" of metaphor enforces the registration of truth on our minds as Sidney says, one defense of transport is its vivid impact. Even Bacon is willing to acknowledge that. The other main defense is the imitation of disorderly thought processes. It is not by rational dialectic but by figures that one connects far-flung provinces. Even so, Sidney retains enough conservative Plato and Aristotle to condemn "material pointing" when it becomes far-fetched comparison. Sophists are forerunners to what the more sober and fact-minded later seventeenth century called enthusiasts:

> So is that honey-flowing matron eloquence apparelled, or rather disguised, in a courtesan-like painted affectation: one time with so far-fetched words, they may seem monsters, but must seem strangers, to any poor Englishman; another time with coursing of a letter, as if they were bound to follow the method of a dictionary; another time with figures and flowers extremely winter-starved.[6]

Like Indians not content with earrings who must "thrust jewels through their nose and lips, because they will be sure to be fine," the inflated stylist cannot get enough similitude and is "more careful to speak curiously than to speak truly" (pp. 138, 139). To flee nature in such a manner is to abuse art.

George Puttenham's admonitions are milder. He is at pains to keep courtly rhetoric and distinct class status safely above common speech. He is also convinced that poets from the beginning have been our best persuaders "and their eloquence the first Rhetoricke of the world." That may be little more than a concealing of ideology in origins, but we do not have to track down his motives to see that the practical matter is the repertory of figures rendered in English. Without writing an explicit defense of linguistic exuberance, he manages to encourage it. In the process, he makes civilization itself nearly equivalent to artifice. Because both poetry and rhetoric use the same figures, although in different amounts—poetry primarily auricular figures; rhetoric, figures of thought or conceit—no clear distinction can be made between them. No neophyte poet or dramatist is likely to come away from *The Arte of English Poesie* without feeling encouraged to practice anything from ablaser and ablatio to zeugma. The identification of art with eloquence is a gain for ingenuity. Puttenham's courtly aestheticism (which Heinrich Plett rightly opposes to humanist didacticism)[7] emphasizes figures of dissimulation such as enigma, ironia, and periphrasis. Its exhibitionist role-playing is as adaptable to the stage as it is to the podium.

Even in sacred matters, Puttenham claims, no style has served as well as the lofty one. The genealogical argument is that when once upon a time it came to be that "the high mysteries of the gods should be revealed and taught, by a maner of utterance and language of extraordinarie phrase, and briefe and compendious, and above al others sweet and civil as the Metricall is," the task fell to poets.[8] But the usefulness of poetic devices is not limited to divine mysteries. Something akin to poetic wit (without the meter) enables politicians, lawyers, engineers, and philosophers to pursue their occupations. Poetry in any of its services can be a mirror in which "are represented unto the soule all maner of bewtifull visions, whereby the inventive parte of the mynde is so much holpen as without it no man could devise any new or rare thing" (p. 14)—devise even bridges and bureaucracies. Figures may slow down or speed up a discourse, tune it or introduce a timely disorder, bring extension or abridgment, look backward or predict, understate or overstate, eclipse or display, offer the preposterous or the sententious and the clipped: their legitimacy lies not in naturalness or decorum but in the accord of meaning with a combination of beauty, service, expressive fullness, and impact.

Renaissance treatises like to recall Quintilian's definition of figuration (in

Institutio Oratoria) as a form of speech "artfully varied from common usage," or in Puttenham's variant, as "a certaine noveltie of language evidently (and yet not absurdly) estranged from the ordinarie habite and manner of our dayly talke and writing." The words to stress here are "evidently" and "not absurdly." Only the first shock of perception suggests the heterogeneity of tenor and vehicle and the short-circuiting of logic; second thoughts link this or that likeness to some phase usually of the Elizabethan correspondences. Those are not easy correspondences to keep within reason, as Browne's conflict between reason and faith and his love of enigmas and paradoxes suggest. The progressive strain of key Puttenham sentences betrays a need to spring loose from natural likeness—hence the vertical leap of metaleptic transport. Figurative speech he describes as "a certain lively or good grace set upon wordes, speaches and sentences to some purpose and not in vaine, giving them ornament or efficacie by many maner of alterations in shape, in sounde, and also in sence, sometime by way of surplusage, sometime by defect, sometime by disorder, or mutation, and also by putting into our speaches more pithe and substance, subtiltie, quicknesse, efficacie or moderation, in this or that sort tuning and tempering them by amplification, abridgement, opening, closing, enforcing, meekening or otherwise disposing them to the best purpose" (pp. 123–33). Such extravagant sentences are good examples of displacement by accumulation and a sidetracking syntax neither quite Ciceronian in balance and order nor Senecan in abruptness. This particular sentence has a good deal of parallelism and symmetry, but "disorder," "mutation," "superplusage," and "defect" toss and turn and disturb the repose of "purpose," "tuning," "tempering," and "closing." Do figures after all close down, by nailing thoughts to their syntactic and lexical places and to meaning, or do they open up, by crossing logical boundaries and allowing a vehemence and sublimity that might prove to be as subversive as Plato feared?

Puttenham deserves the special attention he has received in recent years because he culminates the sixteenth-century treaty between rhetoric and poetry more on poetry's terms and because a potential poet under his tutelage is not required to become merely nature's midwife or imitator. Like a utopian, he may surmount nature and reconstruct what is less perfect in it. Saying that leaves the apologist still a long way from a concept of imagination that would grant meter and figuration the authority actually to generate ideas and perceptions, but it does suggest that style is the man, placed on exhibit before others. A maker of elegant images helps us, as Sidney's poet does, "by a cleare and bright phantasie and imagination" and does not thereby like the painter "counterfaite the naturall by the like effects . . . nor as the gardiner aiding nature to worke both the same and the like, nor as the Carpenter to worke effectes utterly unlike, but even as nature her selfe working by her owne peculiar vertue and proper instinct and not by example or meditation or exercise as all other artificers do" (pp. 253–54). Figures render the metal of mind; manner of utterance renders "the very warp & woofe" of conceits (p. 124). Provided that the poet's purposes are laudable to begin with and keep him on the side of the humanist pedagogue and provided that he avoids the mingle-mangle of pompous speech, he has at his disposal ample justifications for both copiousness and a radical dislocation of speech from the natural.

Were there more apologists like Puttenham we would be justified in extracting from Renaissance theory a defense of unusual language as the best if not the only form an idea or an experience can take, suspended in rearranged syntax, in symmetry or effective asymmetry of clauses, and in similitudes of various closeness and distance. But Jonson's conservatism and Sidney's didacticism are more representative, and Jonson's view carries with it a suspicion that Shakespeare, like Marlowe, could have profited from curbing hasty writing. Macbeth in calling his "seeling Night" to "Scarf up the tender eye of pitiful Day" (3.2.46–47) and Edgar with his "crows and choughs that wing the midway air" (*King Lear,* 4.6.12) speak a language more "estranged from the ordinarie habite and maner" than rhetoric usually is and less answerable to any known order, social or intellectual.

The Poetic Sublime

Even Milton, scarcely noted for idiomatic speech or devotion to the common object world, is wary of certain kinds of grandeur that he associates with egoism. The legitimate soaring of inspired bards in that regard must be balanced against the windblown travel of the Limbo of Fools. The poet would also do well to remember Satan's launching forth to master the "universal hubbub wild / Of stunning sounds and voices all confus'd" (2.952–53), the ultimate image of extravagance (*extra vagari*—to wander outside, beyond the pale):

>   At last his Sail-broad Vans
> He spreads for flight, and in the surging smoke
> Uplifted spurns the ground, thence many a League
> As in a cloudy Chair ascending rides
> Audacious, but that seat soon failing, meets
> A vast vacuity: all unawares
> Flutt'ring his pennons vain plumb down he drops.
>   (2.927–33)

Satan's swimming, sinking, and creeping emblematized the sublime gone bathetic. No one can transport himself where the Word has not previously assigned ranks and hierarchies and thus laid out an implicit stylistic chart by exact propriety and the relation of unequal ranks. Like Sidney, Milton locates justifications for the sublime among biblical precedents, justifications he would not apply very often to a Marlowe or Shakespeare or to the far sailing of an Othello.

The latter is instructive for his incidental citation of the cosmos that for most Elizabethans justifies instant expansion from the local to the universal:

> Like to the Pontic sea,
> Whose icy current, and compulsive course,
> Ne'er feels retiring ebb, but keeps due on
> To the Propontic, and the Hellespont:
> Even so my bloody thoughts, with violent pace
> Shall ne'er look back, ne'er ebb to humble love,
> Till that a capable and wide revenge
> Swallow them up. Now by yond marble heaven,
> In the due reverence of a sacred vow,
> I here engage my words.
> (3.3.460–69)

Like other Othello speeches, this one uses an extended simile to persuade not another party but the self to a loathsome act. The replacement of normal afflatus is here deep water: vengeance, coming like Borealis from a hollow cave, is not a tempestuous sea played upon by gusts of feeling but a tidal flow. Alliterative explosions work a metrical buildup before easing into a marble heaven called upon to bless the current and give justice the stellar fixity to which Othello returns in "It is the cause." The illegitimacy of that stellification betrays not so much Iago's diabolism as Othello's egomania. The hellish and the heavenly are hyperbolic attendants on the wide circumferences of thought. "For it is not to persuasion but to ecstasy that passages of extraordinary genius carry the hearer," Longinus reminds us: "the marvellous, with its power to amaze, is always and necessarily stronger than that which seeks to persuade and to please."[9] Not that jealousy itself is marvellous, but Othello's near madness approaches an equivalent derangement in which illusions and errors overpower perception. In blowing fond love away just previously, he has exhaled divine breath to draw in "tyrannous hate." He claims here an already willing emotion inspired to vengeance. The self-gratulation suggests more an invocation than a ratification.

The faults of Othello's style are more obvious in isolated quotations than in the theater, where Shakespeare capitalizes on an impressive momentum to intensify dramatic interest and expose the monstrosity it feeds upon. He does not always offer to bring the audience safely back to chastened modesty from such moments. An Emilia, an Octavius, or a Kent is not a sufficient curb. Nor does he really use their counterstyles to allow a humanist morality to prevail over perversity. They are merely other alternatives in the juxtaposition of styles, and not always preferable ones. A Philo or an Edgar sets a meager measure for an Antony or a Lear. Linguistic strain is perceptual stretching and criticism of the ordinary.

The Games of Arden

Shakespeare's early histories cannot be said to need the hurly-burly of a Talbot for plot purposes or to use it very tellingly. It comes free of charge and proclaims an entertainment value in pomp and bluster that we have more difficulty appreciating than Elizabethans apparently did. By *1* and *2 Henry IV*, however, one style counters another in alternate scenes and comments on place and station. The babble of tongues from Mistress Quickly's to Henry IV's is set up for the education of a prince as an instrumental part of Shakespeare's probing of power-eloquence relations. Otherwise, very few generalizations about departures from ordinary language apply broadly. *As You Like It* and *The Tempest* are similar, for instance, in confirming rightful dukes and reforming wrong ones, but beyond that their inserted songs, image networks, and set speeches have little in common. Partly for that reason these two plays are useful to an exploration of extraordinary language. They use both songs and set speeches to persuade, but the advocacy we extract from Ariel's small productions and from the songs and sonnets of Amiens and Orlando obviously does not function as a propriety-based speech or argument does. The songs, for instance, make quite different deviations from ordinary language than historical pomp and tragic rant. Presumably neither Hall nor Jonson would object to them. It is the nature of singing that sets them apart from the context and engages audiences on and off the stage. Our distance from the singer as a person is not necessarily a barrier to sympathy with the mood of the song, which prevails through tone and voicing. Whereas a rhetorical performance calls attention to character-owned skills and whereas ordinary dialogue sends point of view back and forth, the audience of song lingers with the performative moment.

Very little can be found in rhetorical manuals or defenses of poetry to account for such swerves from social give-and-take. Aristotle's attention is too much on plot and the arranging of its supports to develop a concept of multileveled influences and receptions. Commentaries on mixed genres such as Sidney's concentrate on longer hybridizations like tragicomedy and pastoral romance. The difficulty with songs and lyrics set in plays is that the normal need to make something happen is suspended in any stanzaic or tuneful structuring of feeling. Emotion spreads out from its moment of delivery into the surrounding dialogue but not by specific urgings. Very little matters except what anticipations of melody and conventional images lift syllable by syllable into a distinctive acoustics. Despite its availability to causes (if some exploiter strikes while the chords are still vibrating), the special bracketing of the musical world places it as far from rhetoric as a singer's vow to be true until the seas run dry is from a marriage vow. Whatever phrases and conventions a song draws from predecessors and whatever generic schemata it exemplifies and universals it holds up, it is uniquely constituted in the notes as they sound. We re-create songs as fully as possible and tend to remember them fairly completely or set them aside; they are impossible to summarize and unsatisfactory in snatches, which suggests that they are more experiential than notional. The fuller the instrumentation, the less satisfactory a lesser reproduction (unless one likes a whistled Beethoven's Ninth).

This suggests that if paraphrase and abstract argument lose the portion of verse that goes into music, which in a play like *As You Like It* or *The Tempest* is considerable, the gaze of the dramatist may have trouble returning from the recital to the social exchange. Songs may advance and deepen sympathy for characters, but they are seldom helpful to our interpreting of conflicts among major ones. They are usually sung by people to one side of the chief movers—by Feste, Ariel, Amiens, Autolycus, rather than by Orlando, Prospero, Florizel. That is approximately where the playwright and the audience hold their conferences—beyond symposium elaborations of ideas, although not necessarily beyond ironic commentary on them or lyric reactions to them. The difference between a song and a marked-off aside or centripetal speech in this regard is striking. Both songs and soliloquies carry inward and make us momentarily entranced with something not subject to immediate answer, and both may venture to the verge of act. Solo speech usually comes from people obliged to act who postpone doing so until they have found the right reasons or frame of mind. It may also be inserted simply for the audience's benefit, possibly to lay bare ideas that can then be seen in operation. These are never the purposes of songs. We do not have to be delivered from their subjectivity by dialogue because they are ephemeral and authorial, not personal and purposely directed. Where the speaker of a soliloquy can be reintegrated into social discourse and bring what he has just revealed along with him, making delivery incidental to thought, a singer leaves behind part of the persona and resumes his regular character. That isolation of the moment is the song's open acknowledgment of artifice.

Songs are weighted toward performance, then, and set speeches toward information. Because of the billowing and wafting of melody and rhythm, song can override an obvious contrivance easier than lines can that are beholding to propriety. (That relation of convention to suspended disbelief is another feature of special language that does not figure in Aristotle's demoting of poetic elements.) Once we have accepted the usual sounds of poetic lines, a more startling difference is required to distract our attention than normal talk requires; in song, a still greater lyric extreme, nothing that pertains to the singing seems out of place. Formalized gesture, dance, and uncharacteristic sentiment become more allowable. The stretching of propriety affects the entire contract between performance and audience, and although neither mood nor message prevails very long, the contract does. The first song of a musical comedy opens the way for all the rest. A Puck or a Hecate would challenge the dramatic illusion more severely did we not grant the initial improbability of singing fairies and chanting sorceresses. Our difficulty as critics lies not in seeing such a distinction but in combining discrepant modes as cooperative partners or counterforces—an exaggeration of the difficulty we have in incorporating notable eloquence into statements.

If *The Tempest*'s songs appear more easily assimilated into Prospero's stage management than Amiens's into Rosalind's, it is partly because Shakespeare has them register immediately on people. Seemingly that makes our task easier by allowing a thematizing crossover between dialogue and song. Music's power to quiet disturbances puts airs to work in something of Samuel Daniel's way with meter, as a formal molding and conducting of emotion to constructive ends. In contrast, the songs of *As You Like It* tend to be show-stopping; after listening to them, the audience onstage resumes what it was doing, obviously not the case with Ferdinand beckoned by "Full Fathom Five" or wishing to live within the world of masque. That makes our task harder by marking the borders and preventing characterized motives from crossing the thematic bridges.

Despite this difference, however, the songs of *As You Like It* seem more integral (until the end) than *The Tempest*'s, the poetry of which eludes the best onstage management, even Prospero's. That reversal of expectations is again a comment on the nonparaphrasable component of both metrical and highly figurative language. If songs are not totally subject to action, perhaps both action and transported style are subject to something else that uses both. We find a clue in *As You Like It*'s assigning of lyric elements to people who can be brought to the marriage festival and a restored social order based more on instinctive likes and dislikes than on argument. The excluded parties are countervoices; if they sing, they do so to undo or complicate song. In contrast, the chief singer of *The Tempest* belongs to Puck's kind and chafes at discipline until he is allowed to escape, just when humans are finding themselves. Ariel's likes and dislikes are thus even more untranslatable into social forms than those of a Jaques or Malvolio, who if given the right coaxing could become more congenial. That Ariel's masque is broken off also says something, if we cannot be quite sure what, about the relation of action to interlude and the relation of argument to the something in song and dance that escapes it. *As You Like It* uses its exiled party and its love affairs to explore not only the festivity of songs but the functional value of literary artifice. It can do so without strain because love codes and sonnets are as rooted in the acting out of class distinctions as songs are in festivity and the perpetuation of manners and dynasties.[10] The posturing of unnatural language from Petrarchan curios to songs is as pertinent to the conduct of courtship as eloquence is to station in Puttenham. In both plays, a holiday interim crystallizes in recitations before proceeding to the communal festivities of home-going and marriage. But the songs and interludes of *As You Like It* are infused into the easy-going society that returns to court; songs and performances of *The Tempest* are copyrighted by demispirits and point toward a distinct realm of nature and the lesser supernatural. The latter stretches into the vast dissolving of castles that Prospero foresees. No one (unless Ferdinand and Miranda) takes the spirit of song home.

In *As You Like It,* place depends on one's locating an appropriate style somewhere between rudeness and foppishness. The courtly performance of lyric and song is pertinent to that task. Practicing a little at verse doesn't hurt, although Shakespeare emphasizes mostly the miscalculations and stilted formalities. Phebe and Silvius, the pair most opposite to the rough-and-ready Touchstone and Audrey, carry bookish practice to such excess that stylization begins to look unreclaimable. Implicit in their observance of protocol is a critique of formal rhetoric and its alliance with sonneteering. Touchstone's account of courtiers edging toward duels, a literally pointless dance of attitudes, makes a similar parody of matchups in salvaged honor and name-bearing. Avoiding the Lie Direct, on the dangerous side of Reply Churlish and Countercheck Quarrelsome, duelers who do not duel are more or less equivalent to lovers who do not marry. One of the dangers of preening is that sublimations—and songs and sonnets fall in that category—use up and misdirect the available erotic energy, which would be better converted into approved forms of festivity. For lovers who gnaw their quills until they are exhausted, wording a situation takes the place of enacting its next steps.

But songs and sonnets nonetheless express love's sentiment and sort lovers themselves into appropriate, matchable levels. Flanked on one side by cardboard cutouts and on the other by Jaques's pessimistic naturalism, Rosalind and Orlando have a similarly indirect but better way marked out for them that the play uses to justify the alliance of breeding, manners, and rhetorical practices. What Orlando seeks under Rosalind's guidance is a way to speak that is proper to bearing and yet answerable to passion. The path is not so obviously posted as to prevent straying. It suggests the narrow range of propriety that aristocratic demonstrations allow between stifled and crude feeling. If Orlando's poems and his love fare better eventually than Silvius's, it is because Rosalind's disarming receptiveness and critical leniency allow an advance of the courtship through them. Good humor and common sense go some way toward directing his faltering literary genius back to the subject in hand. Actually, he is easy enough to coach, since far from washing his liver "as a sound sheep's heart, that there shall not be one spot of love in't" (2.2.442), Rosalind needs merely to rid him of excess moonshine and some of his favorite rhymes. The sentiment itself she nurtures, even relishes.

It is after all sentiment that binds people together in this play, as it must if the right parties are to take to each other and have no illicit ambition left over; and romantic sentiment is one of the easier things to make common among dialogue, song, and poem. Everything comes out even: desire and object, social status and inner worth, the liking and the having. All the misfortunes that can divert a young prince (that run rampant in Calidore's misadventures or the collection of errors in Sidney's *Arcadia*) have a much reduced presence here. So do poetic forms and myths which take the most sociable and least visionary forms. Sidetracking possibilities in Touchstone and more seriously in Jaques offer a way of gauging and validating the best procedure. Sentiment moves the spirit not only in the right direction but at the right pace, timed by the stages of affective approach. Wit and training give it a way to proceed, to pay it out bit by bit, not only in poetry's formal procedures but in protocol-dominated dialogue, which despite its wit is always threatening to lapse into marked-out steps. Writing a sonnet and pinning it to a tree may be private and idiosyncratic, but commentary makes its sentiment into spendable currency: wit and sentiment together, poetry and social discourse in collaboration. Meter and the rest of poetry's sugary preservatives tone up eroticism while love's determination makes it serve a purpose and gives it the rhetorical edge that courtship requires.

To indicate something of the range of social and personal variability, Shakespeare counters each marriageable pair with the others and the sum total with Jaques. The devices that give pause to the proceedings in that arrangement are the several songs and Jaques's summary speech on the seven ages. The question with each such bracketed moment is what the usable repercussions will prove to be, whether or not the listeners gather in a message and respond to it or simply go on their way. In a play as dialectical as *As You Like It*, any contrast helps define, Jaques's no less than Silvius-

Phebe's or Touchstone-Audrey's. The momentum of the seven-ages speech (2.7.146) makes all moving passions seem the involuntary mechanisms of the biological clock. The harshness of Arden forces us to pay some attention to those ages and to crude nature as a disruptive force. Whether people resist their roles like schoolboys or endorse them as lovers sighing like furnaces, they make up a parade of vanities. As the body's clock ticks, conventions freeze people into emblems. Life goes on while duelers practice their flourishes and Orlandos carve their sonnets. Flashed in quick succession, Jaques's emblems animate a jerky progression toward decrepitude. The total life, moving inexorably toward its conclusion, exposes failures of awareness in each posture. Such emblems can be moralized and converted into moral tags, but they cannot be used to distinguish one person from another or to conclude a romantic comedy.

The speech that proposes these types is sufficiently detached to make a comment from the outside on the folly of one's trying to will an identity unbeholding to biological limits. However, it does not block Rosalind's way or even the alternatives of the other matched pairs. One reason is the atmosphere created by the songs and set speeches, together with romantic comedy's conventional immunity to crippling cause and effect. Shakespeare limits the effect of the seven-ages speech by assigning it to a relatively minor character and buffering it with counteremblems—Orlando bearing the ancient Adam to the feast, for instance, and thereby uniting youth and age in a civility that eludes determinism. Duke Senior's courteous society makes individual vulnerability to youth or age less crucial. Despite the inevitability of life's phases and the savagery of the *silva*, the exiled court puts its faith in social delights and in a perpetuation that works through name and status.

Thanks to the reigning sentiment, we are never allowed to suppose that either Jaques's cynicism or icy weather will do much damage. Shakespeare's other open-air comedies reach similar conclusions. Arden, Prospero's island, and Bohemia are places to generate song and changes of heart and then to be left behind, with some individual and social betterment in hand. The only permanent outdoor types are the sturdier classes or elusive elves and fairies. For the exiles, excursions among natural marvels may be salutary, but only if one maintains the better relations one has learned elsewhere. Whatever they acquire is not a replacement, only a supplement, which is basically what the poetry and musicality are where they do not demonstrate class-related artfulness. While seeming to resist romantic elements, even songs and set speeches that declare otherwise maintain the holiday spirit. They prompt us to ask which weighs the more, Amiens's irony or the unquenchable "Heigh-ho, the holly." Certainly Lear's "unaccommodated man" and Edgar's beggardom are kept out of sight except for the glimpses that Jaques gives of them. Nature is reduced to setting and atmosphere and denied an active function except for the serpent and the lioness it provides. Sentimental motives can be concluded logically enough in Hymen's song, as though the dramatic thrust has all along been toward lyricism in the service of marriage—the settling of sexual roles with Rosalind's return to female attire, the inheritance of the family name, the political office, the bonds of friendship among peers and of measured acquaintance among unequals, the salvaging of dignities and honors.

If a certain percentage of readers nonetheless resists the play's charm, it is not necessarily out of sympathy for Jaques's spiking of the romantic wheels. The difficulty with the collaboration between dialogue and songs is that, once the play puts aside Rosalind's wit and Touchstone's parody, the singing Hymen produces too little to replace them. Miraculous reforms and diversions flatten into an assertion that Bottom might have extemporized:

> Wedding is great Juno's crown.
>   Oh, blessed bond of board and bed!
> 'Tis Hymen peoples every town.
>   High wedlock then be honored.
> Honor, high honor and renown,
> To Hymen, god of every town!
>   (5.4.147–52)

Completing the courtship and setting up the future as renewal, this dodges the worst of Jaques's determinism by suggesting the durability of marriage and its progeny. Nor does it hurt the play's mystification of politics to have "Honor, high honor and renown" inserted as a communal form of worth recognition. We can see the dramatic point of dynasties where society is built around them, and wedlock in turn harnesses sentiment to their perpetuation. But it is more difficult to concede the constricting of lyric to bond and board. The division between poetry and drama could not be totally overcome unless Hymen's benediction reengaged the play's conflicts on another level or offered a commanding interlude in its own right. He might have done so with the discovery of some mode in which myth or psychology invoked a well-being that a Jaques could not deny or that the songs have already hinted. As it is, he is brought out of nowhere, which makes him seem an authorial prerogative of the kind that introduces the lion and the serpent. He claims to know that heaven rejoices over such affairs and remarks (to our mystification) that Rosalind has herself dropped down from there. But most of all he simply sacrifices wit to a catechism in "Here's eight that must take hands / To join in Hymen's bands / If truth hold true contents" (5.4.134–35). We do not have to look very far to see the comparative thinness of that; we need only think of Feste and Puck, the reunion of Hermione and Leontes, or Florizel celebrating Perdita's grace in a richer prespousal verse.

Prospero Explaining

Shakespeare provides further grounds for dissatisfaction with Hymen in *The Tempest,* where Prospero divides his attention among marriage festivity, the dissolving of the pageant, and the mortality of his own last phase. Eventually I want to turn the poetry of *The Tempest* in another direction, to face Milton's echoes of it and marking of a quite different poetry-drama relation in "Comus." But it is useful here to note the play's tendency to take action one way and song another as it tests intermittently the capacity of plots to fasten down not only songs but a diversity of entertainments and moral argument. Leniency toward subversion is the policy all around eventually, as Ariel is released, the criminals are let off, and Antonio is not even asked for an apology—not that he would give one.

This leniency is part of a simultaneous gathering and scattering typical of the play from the opening storm. Ariel initially captures Ferdinand's attention in two remarkable songs, for instance, that are and are not responsible to the dramatic context. Offered under Prospero's general urging but without specific instructions as to means and style, his musical beckoning suggests an initial temptation for the lyric imagination to take its own way whatever changes of mind and heart it instigates. In saying that "The ditty does remember my drown'd father" (1.2.408), Ferdinand notices the words of Ariel's first song, but only in a general way. Susceptibility to charms is natural in a romance hero, as Ferdinand shows again in his first view of Miranda and his reaction to the masque. Here he is being guided into a sentiment approvable by Prospero, but nothing like the full range of Ovidian metamorphosis registers on him. The best connections of shape-changing are perhaps not with anything in the plot but with Prospero's vision of universal dissolvings, which also stand apart from anything Prospero actually does. Such promontories look at each other above the action, which is rare for comedy to do. Ariel's conversion of bones to coral is calming, then, but if Ferdinand were in fact listening closely he would notice that it is monstrous as well as beautiful. For the audience, the metamorphosis recalls a literary tradition and patterns of change that are mythic and universal rather than character-specific. The unattached affects are augmented by musicality and find their best corollaries in the tonality of images and other devices of eloquence more attributable to genre than to those who speak or sing the lines.

The stopping of the dialogue is itself sufficient to drive mimesis toward showcase performance and to raise the distinctive singer-audience relations I suggested earlier. Nor does thematic interweaving quite catch all the song, not even with the help of Prospero's revels speech. Despite its own version of metamorphosis, the latter is opposite in meaning. Whereas Ariel imagines permanent artifacts forming out of melting flesh and bone, Prospero foresees solid things dissolving into clouds. Both are aloof meditations on mortality, but one goes in the direction of fixed, small artifacts, the other toward a massive dissolution of nature and human achievement. Each touches on the hypothetical dreaming of Caliban and Gonzalo, who think of another world while grubbing for provender and power in this one, except that Prospero is being rational as well as visionary while Ariel is being artful. Whereas Ariel's metamorphoses are marvellous, it is easy enough for Prospero to infer those distant meltdowns logically from ones closer at hand. Such metamorphosis is without magic; Ariel's requires a rare chemistry. Whether illicit or blessed, the visionary and the fantastic go too far afield to bring their several levels into playable exchange. Ariel and Prospero leave people stunned; Gonzalo is answered by mockery; the dreams of the others are mainly illicit and must be suppressed.

The relation of poetry to drama in *The Tempest* is not continuous and mutually supportive, then, but interruptive and dialectical. The critical juncture in that relation is Prospero's revelation of himself to his countrymen when he steps forward as a man without wand and cape. He thereby provides his own transition to something closer to natural language. Although his reforms have worked mostly through Ariel's illusions and songs, his explanations of them will adhere to probability, or so he says. He will not account for how splintered timbers and ripped sails have gotten repaired without shipyards and will exclude most of what poetic language has "estranged from the ordinarie habite" in these things so full of "surplusage." If Alonso got all the explanations he requested, they would have to adjust one plane to another:

> Sir, my liege,
> Do not infest your mind with beating on
> The strangeness of this business; at pick'd leisure
> Which shall be shortly single, I'll resolve you,
> Which to you shall seem probable, of every
> These happen'd accidents.
> (5.1.245–50)

Seem suggests that to get down to earth Prospero will have to improvise. Although he is not shown making good on that promise, it is unlikely that he is speaking with tongue in cheek, as Philip Brockbank assumes, or is merely dragging out the farewell-taking to delay the surrender of his powers, as Harry Berger speculates.[11] He is genuinely reduced and is willing if not totally happy to be so. Alonso himself seems anxious to exchange enigmas and mysteries for either science or religion:

> This is as strange a maze as e'er men trod;
> And there is in this business more than nature
> Was ever conduct of: some oracle
> Must rectify our knowledge.
> (5.1.242–45)

Prospero is not really obligated to mention anything beyond his own motives and their results, which will lift the play from watery depths and bring it down from stormy heights to the middle ground of social and psychological plausibility. To the external audience, however, probability cannot explain the play, and if Alonso cannot be infested with beating on such strange business, we cannot avoid it. He will be given "accidents"; we still have in mind the alluring tunes of Prospero's chief spirit, the symbolic pageantry of Ceres, and the meltdown of towers in the poet's accelerated planetary clock.

A parallel shrinkage is perceptible, if not so prominently, in Ferdinand and Miranda, whose impending union will cement an alliance between city-states. At the very peak of their wonderment they too must sail for better-known parts. The extent of that settling down can be gauged by the difference between their first sight of each other and their posture at chess. As Joan Hartwig points out, on the former occasion Prospero sees to it that Miranda's glimpse of Ferdinand reinforces what under any circumstances is likely to be a highly charged moment:[12] "The fringed curtains of thine eye advance, / And say what thou seest yond" (1.2.411–12), that is, "open your theatrical eyes and tell me what you see in this magical show." Ariel's song gives melodic supplement and brings her exclamation, "What is't? a spirit? / Lord, how it looks about" (1.2.412–13). They both suspect supernatural intervention.

In the final tableau what we see is a game that works with definite positions and limited powers. Pawns do not transgress their stations (as boatsmen do under the pressure of storms and a meddling Gonzalo); kings and queens hold positions of power; knights take brave leaps in their defense; bishops angle across the social ranks on powerful religious biases. All of which reminds us that the lovers have been thrown together all along under the rules that march their feelings to the cadence of the social disciplinarian and type of the colonialist. After assisting their first attraction, the father and duke does not excite them by marvels again until the masque; he uses his authority mostly to dampen their ardor. To some extent, the game offers the kind of relief that comedy best affords. The struggles of real kingdoms may be matters of life and death, but removal of an ivory bishop from the board requires no bloodshed even if winning is important enough to make even lovers cheat one another. In the play too, every time someone raises a dagger Ariel intrudes and converts a real threat into a cartoon confrontation. A spirit of friendly competition guides everyone to the one social combination that will work among many that are conceivable but misleading. Such an arrangement is not quite arbitrary, but it scarcely seems inevitable, not until rules become second nature and impose their own sense of probability and necessity.

Other apparent wonders and clumsier attempts at winning are undermined by comic means without requiring any special effort or the use of pinches and lures. Stephano breaks into the final assembly under Caliban's generalship with feisty nonsense of his own: "Every man shift for all the rest, and let no man take care of himself; for all is but fortune.—Coragio, bully-monster, coragio!" (5.1.256–58). In acknowledging the "goodly sight" that greets them, Trinculo and Caliban correct their odd dreams of glory, and so another phase of fantasizing is brought to heel. Like more astute members of the stranded company, they have been kept at arm's length from the better class of marvels up to that point. They then readily transfer their floating wonder to the splendid nobility that is the point of the European's glamorization of himself—just what they have been burlesquing. Here then is the real thing: civilization's flower looking splendid, at another level from rich and strange sea changes that no one makes a point of remembering. We suspect, where they do not, that beneath the newly laundered costumes there still may lurk a potential subversion, and the audience may possibly not transfer quite all the romanticism it has collected to the social imagery. Prospero himself endorses with very mixed feelings the ordinary life he has patched back together. The important part of the epilogue that follows is the recalling of the theatrical game and the moment when it too surrenders its powers, in the playhouse parallel to the banishing of once-serviceable spirits. Applause marks the end of the highly engineered drama and replaces it with the mannered relations of appreciative audience to the playwright and the stage technicians. To expect to live further in the special domain of poetic explorations and vistas would be self-indulgent. Following the model of Prospero-Shakespeare, we are apparently to accept what is, not in any niggardly spirit, but because it is worthy of allegiance. It is all we ordinarily have. Nothing is changed structurally or reformed; much is polished and restored.

To keep the outline of this competition between a realizable social order and a potentially distracting poetry as sharply etched as is conscionable, I have avoided softening the rivalry with undue complications. The argument I want to return to more fully later is not that as a work of written literature *The Tempest* fails to put its songs and other poetic and rhetorical elements to work, but just the opposite: the text as a whole and even more the performances onstage make use of those elements but in an unusually elaborated opposition to the socially possible—to the nobles returning, to a chess game that must be played with full attention if one is not to encourage an Antonio to move one time as a knight and another as a rook. Any exclusive pursuit of probable human behavior squanders the Ariel element of the play and the inset entertainments that dwell in the conjuring word. Such transcendences of the probable are precisely what Milton builds upon in giving them a permanent place to be. So too the plays that lead in this direction, such as *Antony and Cleopatra, King Lear,* and *The Winter's Tale.* We cannot pull their evasions and their subversions out of them without breaking tendrils, but neither can we quite subdue them to social mimesis and its rhetoric.

Daggers Unmannerly Breech'd

As Shakespeare's boy actor speaks lines that "Cleopatra" foresees in mockery, our attention is momentarily directed less to the historical figure he impersonates than to literature's house of mirrors. It is not merely Cleopatra's own mythmaking or histrionics that we have to consider but the enhancements that make her a household name. Recognizing the collaborative venture of historians, poets, and playwrights in giving substance to the name, the poet knows that his version of Cleopatra is a party to the hyperbole that comes with it, which she directs into a certain channel by warning us ahead of time of the squeaking impostures to come. In this respect, verbal flourishes go with the rest of an exotically costumed show that anyone attending a play called *Antony and Cleopatra* expects to see. The straightening of the crown is Charmian's last-minute adjustment before the show opens to its first Roman audience, the discoverers and publicizers of the truth. They become historians beginning to memorialize. "I'll mend it, and then play," Cleopatra says, and goes forth to the chronicles, a queen "Descended of so many royal kings."

Cleopatra's speechmaking reminds us of the powerful combination Shakespeare makes of represented character and awareness of the fictions that influence reputation. But perhaps the easier example of Elizabethan extravagance to use along with *As You Like It* and *The Tempest* is again *Macbeth*.

As we have seen, its theatricality is rendered in an unusual diction and in supernatural solicitings akin to song in their departure from ordinary idiom. A large melodramatic element enlivens the dialogue as well as the recitational poetry, which alerts the ear early with such bell-clangings as "'Aroynt thee, witch!' the rump-fed ronyon cries" (1.3.6). Although Yvor Winters complains that Shakespeare's matching of speech to a distraught and confused Macbeth renders it obscure and badly structured, primarily because it is mimetic, the problem is really just the opposite: the general practice of abruptness and vehemence again and again transcends Macbeth's state of mind. Elmer Edgar Stoll comes closer to the mark in noting the play's numerous special effects, which Shakespeare never quite duplicates elsewhere.[13]

As Simon O. Lesser argues, *Macbeth* approaches novelistic technique in moving the play's perspective close to Macbeth's own dream world.[14] But the play's initial premise is that moral and metaphysical questions can be cast as enigmas and apparitions. Harry Berger appropriately calls these "Capricious, trivial, and spiteful . . . pedants of mumbo-jumbo."[15] Macbeth's own view of them is less detached. One of his first functions is to translate the improbable into conceivable human reactions, doing within the play what the spectator does on the fringe:

> This supernatural soliciting
> Cannot be ill; cannot be good:—
> If ill, why hath it given me earnest of success,
> Commencing in a truth? I am Thane of Cawdor:
> If good, why do I yield to that suggestion
> Whose horrid image doth unfix my hair,
> And make my seated heart knock at my ribs,
> Against the use of nature? Present fears
> Are less than horrible imaginings.
> My thought, whose murther yet is but fantastical,
> Shakes so my single state of man,
> That function is smother'd in surmise,
> And nothing is, but what is not.
> (1.3.130–42)

Guided by this, we easily translate the man into a type of the tyrant, the impersonation into something resembling the Longinian sublime, and the witches into dramatic agents operating within a convention akin to that of the Greek furies. The speaker-actor of "doth unfix my hair" and "function is smother'd in surmise" becomes a riddle-making spokesman for the opening intrigue. His "Nothing is, but what is not" turns the witches' paradox into preparation for ironies, climaxed ultimately in his realization of the emptiness of power.

A second distancing factor is the social anatomy that Shakespeare carries out with both explicit thematizing and imagistic subtlety. Such ambition creates its disturbance only at the top of the hierarchy, since it is not a competition anyone can enter. The office one seizes loses its hereditary value the moment it is pulled from its accustomed place and royal pageantry yields to the struggle of passions and egos. New locutions are the product of liberated perceptions; their twist from sociability is the result of desires that have no chance of public acknowledgment.

This much any ratio of mimetic to poetic elements can acknowledge. Franco Moretti makes that breaking of forms the product of a general failing, present in a number of plays, not a specific trauma brought on by one powerful ego: "It should be clear that this Shakespearean 'poetry' has nothing 'liberating,' 'constructive,' or 'universal' about it. It is made possible by, and is identical with, the stupefied perception that cultural paradigms, abruptly defaulting, are no longer capable of ordering and guiding the word."[16] I will take up the matter of fault and defaulting as a recurrent prompt to Shakespeare's most complex poetry, especially in *King Lear*, but with respect to Macbeth, it is not at all clear that Duncan is in any way seriously to blame for getting himself killed by a demon-driven psychopath. The chief unmaking is Macbeth's of himself. At the moment of his first unleashing of horrible imaginings and sublime hyperbata, overpowered by what will be, he finds himself made nothing by the "present." The evaporation of that new name "Cawdor" is equivalent to explosive releases of energy that we never realized was in the words and a plucking of bright honor not from the moon but from covert corners of the ego. Over and above any specific undoings, he develops a signature language of lightning flashes and metaphors and proceeds to damage the capacity of that language either to work within the social bond or to make confessions that might redirect him to the ranks of the human.

As to the witches' part in the repercussions that ripple into the future, they read like a Calibanish attempt at the sublime and cause some editors to deny the authenticity of the second batch of chants altogether. As Macbeth is caught up in the initial monstrosity, however, his own conjurations loosen toward the cauldron's miscellany and reestablish sound and fury as a legitimate moral and metaphysical confusion. In support of the Elizabethan myth of collaboration between natural and social orders, the various powers of empire are usually assembled in a kind of national blazon or itemized list of naval, agricultural, and architectural achievements. Here the house of figures is ransacked for devices of upside-down extremity:

> I conjure you, by that which you profess,
> Howe'er you come to know it, answer me:
> Though you untie the winds, and let them fight
> Against the Churches; though the yesty waves
> Confound and swallow navigation up;
> Though bladed corn be lodg'd, and trees blown down;
> Though castles topple on their warders's heads;
> Though palaces, and pyramids, do slope
> Their heads to their foundations; though the treasure
> Of Nature's germens tumble altogether,
> Even till destruction sicken, answer me.
>
> (4.1.50–60)

Because this dismantling of a landscape and its monuments prepares for the murder of Lady Macduff and her son, it is relevant to Macbeth's deterioration; but Shakespeare also uses it to help the audience take in the play's judgment of a state of mind. He stretches the speech into a specimen, one among many in a play full of quotable passages. The distortions of syntax and diction conduct us toward a meeting of minds stationed at dramatic and poetic summits where the imaginative life comes forth to meet a willing audience.

Perhaps no play of Shakespeare is more committed to the deflection of words and images from normal usage. While Macbeth debates whether or not to proceed, he conjures associations that address both his weakening resolve and the play's recitational building of implications. In showing an apparent decision in the making, the "If it were done" speech(1.7.1–12) is crucial to the play in much the way the speech on the forked plague is to *Othello;* and like Othello's vacillating course, it reflects more than Macbeth's choices. Wanting kingship without murder if it could be had, Macbeth realizes the impossibility of skipping links in the chronological chain. Moral judgment is based on the inevitability of psychic as well as corporeal punishments. He touches upon free will and necessity, moral obligations, the invention of action, distinctions between the present and teleology in an unnamed "there," the tempo of events, the nature of justice, and finally— given what he discovers in this tangle of topoi—his lack of stomach for what must come back to haunt him.

Ranging beyond that array of anxieties, carried largely by the mixture of abstraction and metaphor, are other associations that we cannot be sure he understands. These extend beyond gothic atmosphere and premonition into bardlike prophecy, as the business of regicide momentarily draws upon an apocalyptic fury and reinforces propriety by suggesting murder's near unthinkability. Pity riding the air and trumpet-tongued angels have an eschatological energy that is surprising in one as vacillating as Macbeth. Were he this magnificent to others, it is doubtful that Lady Macbeth, for instance, could budge him or a mere kingship would beckon so overpoweringly. If most audiences take the discrepancy between the regicide and the poet Macbeth in stride, it is no doubt partly because they are responding to the entire play as set up in the first scene. But the poetry is nonetheless unsettling in the hovering ambiguity it entertains between the eloquent and the mean-spirited figure, and as I suggested earlier, between the actor and what he impersonates. The criminal syphons off enough imaginative power from the play to turn us a little against other claimants to power, who, apart from Duncan, have enough flaws of their own to encourage our complicity.

The play's making of a gory business into performance is especially pronounced in Macbeth's account of his reflexes after the first orgy of bloodshed:

> Here lay Duncan,
> His silver skin lac'd with his golden blood;
> And his gash'd stabs look'd like a breach in nature
> For ruin's wasteful entrance: there, the murtherers,
> Steep'd in the colours of their trade, their daggers
> Unmannerly breech'd with gore.
> (2.3.111–16)

The reason the scene lies so deeply impressed on his memory (and on ours) is no doubt much as he suggests, because of the tangible replacement of royal cloth by animal blood, emblematic of the play's frenzied tearing away of frail protections to expose severed veins and nerves. Duncan's blood is ruined royalty, his skin not merely silvery but delicately ornate in this new lace. The daggers themselves are clothed as though poised for a portrait in barbarity, breeched not only because of Macbeth's bloodbath, but as Jonson's defense of natural language illustrates, because decorum is often expressed in clothing imagery. In depicting this result of his knife work, Macbeth accidentally brings about a recoil that is difficult to calculate but is based on the audience's simultaneous decoding of several levels of the speech. At least one of these is a reminder of the costumes they now see onstage. The fact that Macbeth too is horrified attracts our complicity. But what he *intends* is a vivid image of what startled him into dispatching the attendants; what he *achieves* is a breaking of our entrancement—so viciously calculated is the covering up of one crime with another. We are appalled by his capacity to exploit feelings under these circumstances, yet find it difficult to separate revulsion toward the man who kills people from admiration for the artful story he is engineering and anxiety for one whose point of view we have been maneuvered into sharing.

All this is difficult to disentangle from admiration for an artful Shakespeare, who in exposing Macbeth's scene-making also exposes his own. We are not granted the nervous release of laughter as we are when the porter goes to the knocking. Instead we are brought very near the heart of ritualized violence and the confusion of vehemence with vivid poetry, possessed of the *enargia* that goes with hyperbole. Were we to watch a real murder through a window or through binoculars, the detachment would be similar but by no means identical, since this one appears through the shield of its articulated fictionality. Awareness of the performance from beginning to end is clearly a qualifying feature. We know the fiction will hold; the nightmare will not suddenly become ours, to stick to us for life. Although it seems real enough on one plane, then, and we know too that stabbings occur with alarming frequency, for now they are not happening. The periphrastic overkill and the quaintness of "ruin's wasteful entrance" draw the real into the sanctuary of the poetic, where reality drops some of its power over us, or rather transforms it into readerly fascination. The words are evocative but remain words, corporeal but not bleeding, breeched with gore in the mind's eye while resonant with reiterated imagery and resounding in the ear with *r*'s and the lingering hideousness of *gore*.

Shakespeare's verbal display makes use of Macbeth's invention to explore a little further the theater-world analogy until it teases us with near mystery: an impresario of Macbeth's skill can cloud the distinction between true and feigned character sufficiently to put off our passion for justice. Shakespeare can cloud it sufficiently to put off paraphrase and the using up of the poetry by interpretable motive and act. While Macbeth implicitly confesses that he murders due place and identity, Shakespeare confesses nothing restatable about politics, psychology, and fascination with creativity. We know Macbeth as many things at once: a stylization, a mirror for magistrates, one among many tragic protagonists guilty of overreaching, a go-between who filters the witchery for us into something closer to conceivable thought, and a creature of chilling fascination and charm, as artificial as a marble David or a creation myth committed to a plaster ceiling.

Part Two

Four Plays

3

Cleopatra's Phantom Marriage

> And by these hymnes, all shall approve
> Us *Canoniz'd* for Love.
> —Donne, "The Canonization"

> But to her sight
> Drawing nigh and nigher
> Its deep delight,
> The fog is bright
> And the wind a lyre.
> —Hardy, "On the Way"

> one there is to whom these things,
> That nobody else's mind calls back,
> Have a savour that scenes in being lack,
> And a presence more than the actual brings.
> —Hardy, "Places"

The Phoenix Riddle and the Posthumous Antony

Perhaps elegy's most common tactic is to summon or station at a measured distance recollected presences for which the poem is part consolation, part substitute. Even the anticipation of absence can draw upon some of its resources. The lovers of "The Canonization," for instance, predict their departure and their revival in the valedictory songs and sonnets they leave behind. By publicizing their current lovers' dying and rising and by looking ahead, Donne prepares for the posthumous reappraisals that pilgrims seeking a lost pattern will make. The strategy includes hyperbole and the sifting out of aggravations so that the savoring of one's being gone can intensify one's still being here.

The more usual way, however, is to look behind rather than ahead. In "Places," "At Castle Boterel," "During Wind and Rain," "After a Journey," and "Afterwards," for instance, Thomas Hardy looks into the ghostly past of his wife Emma and implies that putting memories into words replaces what was once "warm, real, and keen" with something both more and less than that. In "The Phantom Horsewoman" the rider hovers between art and life in simultaneously remembering and creating "a phantom of his own figuring."[1] "Figuring," like the lyre wind of "On the Way," confesses that the summoned presence is the poet's doing and a calculated blurring of the distinction between the real and the reconstituted. To a viewer prepared to see the invisible, a trope may be more sharply etched than an actual human shape, certainly than mere memory's image. Thus in "A Light Snow-fall after Frost," Hardy assigns a virtual new presence to rhyme's palpable intervention and revelation:

> The frost is on the wane,
> And cobwebs hanging close outside the pane
> Pose as festoons of thick white worsted there,
> Of their pale presence no eye being aware
> Till the rime made them plain.
>   (*CP* 695)

As the glass frames the cobweb festoons, the poet finds the web of memories close but "outside." What once was is doubled in the image, suspended in rhyme. Like snowfall on already white hair, it retells the length of a "rough pilgrimage." The result is luminescent detail, at once phantomlike and imprinted, "happening in the traces of itself," Hillis Miller suggests, traces having "the power of iteration that cannot be stopped."[2]

In their retrospective moments, plays have ample time to remember the presences we have just witnessed, which gives them the chance—if they wish to go a little past the catastrophe itself—to emphasize both loss and reconstruction. Thanks largely to Cleopatra, *Antony and Cleopatra* is remarkable for its prolonged partings and recasting. Antony's early removal gives the off-going a twofold rhythm—first his departure, recollected by Cleopatra, and then hers, as eventually recollected by Plutarch and Shakespeare. After such leave-takings, one version of their story will beget another and then another, each rendering some reasonable facsimile that varies from the postures of a fizgig to stately poses.[3]

While Donne's lovers live within range of their critics or while an Emma Hardy still lives, opportunities for such refiguring are scant because the counterchecks are too strong. The main matter that Plutarch gives Shakespeare to work upon is Antony's increasing entanglement in Egypt and loss of stature in the empire. If Octavius applies politics to love where politics does not belong, Cleopatra errs in the opposite direction. Her sailing into battles and out again is a disastrous intrusion of love's contests into military affairs. If war and love are traditionally problematic images of each other, the rift between them here is widened by rival views of greatness in a divided chivalry. Yet every slip in matters of state is a step toward a monumentality that fares better than politics does. Whereas both Octavius and Cleopatra display enough inconsistency and unprincipled behavior to spice a long chronicle, Octavius remains Octavius; Cleopatra's record is merely tangential to what she becomes. She is often uncertain about what to feel and how to present herself, but not so once she carries chicanery to a higher level and goes off to the facsimiles.

The discrepancy between act and afterthought is persistent. When Antony arrives at the monument, for instance, the departure of one of the play's two central figures might seem to call for love's genuine elegiacs. What Cleopatra issues is a parody:

> O sun,
> Burn the great sphere thou mov'st in, darkling stand
> The varying shore o' the world. O Antony,
> Antony, Antony!
> (4.15.9–11)

Like her barge entry, her "O sun" calls for a fanfare not too softly played. Her refusal to descend to give Antony the one last kiss he begs makes that doubly apparent:

> I dare not, dear,
> Dear my lord, pardon: I dare not,
> Lest I be taken.
> (4.15.21–23)

So much for love beyond measure. Nor does her secure place prevent her from maneuvering for better staging, although Antony might be thought to have earned one last flourish. The competition Cleopatra brings to the parting is not harmless lover's play; it degenerates to a politics-of-two and ends only with her possession of the spotlight. Until then, part of what empire-making means is the gaining not of security or the right to rule but of a platform from which to address posterity.

On other occasions Cleopatra sounds like an actress auditioning for the role, working up emotions that look promising for workshop development:

> Noblest of men, woo't die?
> Hast thou no care of me, shall I abide
> In this dull world, which in thy absence is
> No better than a sty? O, see, my women:
> The crown o' the earth doth melt. [*Antony dies.*]
>   My lord?
> O, wither'd is the garland of the war,
> The soldier's pole is fall'n: young boys and girls
> Are level now with men: the odds is gone,
> And there is nothing left remarkable
> Beneath the visiting moon.
>   (4.15.59–68)

If in time she eventually lifts the play into hymns we can approve, she is obviously not yet there at this point. She does turn impressively, however, from defiance of the gods to her companions. Eventually her own dying is to be shored up by her willingness to pay whatever such displays cost. Here "This case of that huge spirit now is cold" (4.15.90) is worth considerably more than the crowns, as is "Our strength is all gone into heaviness" (4.15.33). Both lines acknowledge the corporeality of an Antony who is no longer a pillar of empire.

Other Recollections

Cleopatra's leave-taking puts us in the wicked crook of a dilemma. She bases her projection of greatness not only on Antony's stature but on her dignity as half empress, half goddess. If we accept her premises and grant her reunion with Antony, the death is not tragic; if we do not, her triumph becomes just another self-delusion. It may help to remember that love's exaggerations have never been hers alone, nor dying their only opportunity. When she rebukes Antony initially with a reminder that "Eternity was in our lips, and eyes, / Bliss in our brows bent" (1.3.35–36), she is already deleting grosser elements in constructing impromptu sonnet fragments. Even so the earlier gestures are future oriented and set a tone for performances to come. The reunion must at least seem a noble illusion that idealizes the warrior-love and empress-beloved.

It also helps that much of the play's translation of historical incident into pageantry and fifth-act poetry comes as reflective commentary. Memory is a midway point, set in a lower key of plangency but amplified enough to block out some of the dissent. The recollective verse that comes before the autumnal phase serves as storage for moments to be laid out in the final rites. Cleopatra's final project is not to regain her former condition but to surpass the prankster and "do that thing that ends all other deeds, / Which shackles accidents, and bolts up change" (5.2.5–6). Retrievals of what will otherwise sink into oblivion are made easier by the linking of one incident to another in a total story frequently recapitulated. An attendant point is that strength derives from weakness. Political and military failures are a necessary part of love's liberation. If Cleopatra were less preoccupied with the stratagems that make her remarkable in the annals of love literature, she might do better in the arts of survival, but then she would not be Cleopatra. The question is not so much how deep her flaws reach as how her charm alters under the pressure of the end rushing up.

All this recollective gathering, which helps reconcile dramatic moment to lofty style, depends on the cross-referencing of places and episodes by other than the linear or causal trail of the fable. The oddly scattered, circumstantial plot of *Antony and Cleopatra* gives ample occasion for the tossing up of tableau moments, fixed in an uncommon pictorial density to be summoned for the reprise or the shackling up. One function of an eloquence that is awarded to several voices is to mark off and hold selected instants above the dramatic flow as history's monuments. The pauses are usually not greatly expanded, however, but are briefly remembered (or messenger-delivered) implantations from elsewhere. Since Antony and Cleopatra speak a good many lines about, as well as to, each other, they grow adept at bridging distances. Thinking of Antony in Rome, Cleopatra speculates about his "contriving friends" and hints at the dead man's weight and the bestriding colossus:

> O Charmian!
> Where think'st thou he is now? Stands he, or sits he?
> Or does he walk? or is he on his horse?
> O happy horse to bear the weight of Antony!
> Do bravely, horse, for wot'st thou whom thou mov'st,
> The demi-Atlas of this earth, the arm
> And burgonet of men. He's speaking now,
> Or murmuring, "Where's my serpent of old Nile?"
> For so he calls me. Now I feed myself

> With most delicious poison. Think on me,
> That am with Phoebus' amorous pinches black,
> And wrinkled deep in time. Broad-fronted Caesar,
> When thou wast here above the ground, I was
> A morsel for a monarch: and great Pompey
> Would stand and make his eyes grow in my brow,
> There would he anchor his aspect, and die
> With looking on his life.
>
> (1.5.18–34)

The stuff of drama is drawn inward here, where it meets recurrent amorous dreams. Thinking of the world as a stage for love, Cleopatra brings personal relations to the threshold of myth in a meditative daydream that gives Charmian no opening for an answer. The nostalgia increases as Cleopatra slides from the initial subject—Antony in mundane circumstances—to her other triumphs. The passage perhaps foreshadows the asp in the "sweet poison," but more important, both that oxymoron and Pompey's dying of love are apparent losses that generate a greater life. Intensifying the absence with vivid tableaux of the demi-Atlas is the poison; placing him next to her as he coaxes her out of hiding with the familiar call to his serpent is the sweetness. The reliving of the other conquests is also vivid, but they are much further off. She is now older, and Caesar is buried. In retrospect, at least from this biased and self-flattering recollection, Pompey's direct gaze upon her amplified him. The paradoxes of love thus collaborate with those of memory. Love increases the self that gives itself to another; distance then increases love's triumphs as memory retrieves them.

And so Cleopatra relives these several moments the more sweetly because they lie in the still-reachable distance. Her drift from the initial topic follows a train of associations guided by self-feeding. For added attendance it sweeps a mythological machinery into its train. The godlike sun scorches and consumes her in a personal way. With amplification comes selectivity. That her use of passion to protect Egypt politically drops out of sight suggests that, in the scale from reality to imagination, she moves toward the latter, as she often does when circumstances allow. Although for the time being, the interaction of the two keeps the dream entangled in something resembling a real chronicle, they will meet in a different balance in her later applications of sweet poison. She will then transfer what has by then become an altogether transcendent love from the past to the future and leave the poison exclusively for the wrinkled body.

When she gets Antony within reach again, she puts the portrait of the aging lover to work, using the directorial manner to guide them back to salad days:

> It is my birth-day,
> I had thought t'have held it poor. But since my lord
> Is Antony again, I will be Cleopatra.
> (3.13.185–87)

So presentable are the scenes she conjures, so ready for legend, that nothing seems to stand between the actual image and the story in the making (if one forgets the Roman armies). When messengers bring unpromising materials, she makes them go out and come in again, speeding up the revisionary memory. The actual must be emptied out before something richer and more answerable to desire can fill in. To prepare for the constancy that belongs to the title role (or co-title role if one must count the leading man), what she requires is not an Antony who is Antony again but the one she helps nature invent.

The Rest of the Supporting Cast and Antony

Only Antony and Cleopatra can rehearse their own personal separations, but they are not alone in making retrievals and emendations. Vividness characterizes Octavius's recollection of an Antony whose past campaigning is distant enough to begin looking legendary. Like Enobarbus, whose barge speech makes a specimen chronicle, that recollection measures the decline against an older glory:

> When thou once
> Was beaten from Modena, where thou slew'st
> Hirtius and Pansa, consuls, at thy heel
> Did famine follow, whom thou fought'st against,
> Though daintily brought up, with patience more
> Than savages could suffer. Thou didst drink
> The stale of horses, and the gilded puddle
> Which beasts would cough at: thy palate then did deign
> The roughest berry, on the rudest hedge;
> Yea, like the stag, when snow the pasture sheets,
> The barks of trees thou browsed. On the Alps
> It is reported thou didst eat strange flesh,
> Which some did die to look on: and all this—
> It wounds thine honour that I speak it now—

> Was borne so like a soldier, that thy cheek
> So much as lank'd not.
>
> (1.4.56–71)

Octavius protests mainly Antony's un-Roman pampering of the senses. Genuine Romans accommodate themselves to whatever they must, the harder the conditions the better. But if half of anything is what a strong mind makes of it, the same willfullness that makes a feast of tree bark may also make a demigoddess of a harlot. Both assert mind over matter. Romans will stoic self-consistency; Egyptians will the alchemical change of base matter to glorious signs.

The most prominent of the earlier insets from the supporting cast belongs not to Octavius, however, but to Enobarbus. The vividness of what he remembers proves useful to Cleopatra's confirming of the memorability of love's pageantry. Its suitability for Elysian fields is set up by that preliminary tableau enshrinement, not as merely one of many vignettes in the play but as a weighted one to be outfitted again for Cleopatra's last sailing to catch an Antony, her version of sailing to Byzantium:

> The barge she sat in, like a burnish'd throne
> Burn'd on the water: the poop was beaten gold;
> Purple the sails, and so perfumed that
> The winds were love-sick with them; the oars were silver,
> Which to the tune of flutes kept stroke, and made
> The water which they beat to follow faster,
> As amorous of their strokes. For her own person,
> It beggar'd all description: she did lie
> In her pavilion—cloth of gold, of tissue—
> O'er-picturing that Venus where we see
> The fancy outwork nature. On each side her,
> Stood pretty dimpled boys, like smiling Cupids,
> With divers-colour'd fans, whose wind did seem
> To glow the delicate cheeks which they did cool,
> And what they undid did.
>
> (2.2.191–205)

Where Cleopatra will set up a very actionlike emblem of Atlas as her own centerpiece—bestriding, cresting, turning the spheres, shaking the orb—Enobarbus presents her as a goddess ready for descent into action. At one level, his painterly image is army gossip, which recalls the play's frequent insertions of poetry in the midst of belittling contexts, in this case set up by subalterns imitating their higher-ups. The theme is taken from Maecenas, who has wondered at revels in which eight wild boars are breakfast to but a dozen people. Several times the listeners hint knowingly that duty in Egypt must be something, and Enobarbus allows as how they have learned to use their throats. Antony has played the groom they would all like to be, to the love goddess they would all like to imagine floating into their reveries. The gold enameling he casts over the throne and the water is the color of both sumptuous revel and flashback. "Burn'd" echoes "burnish'd" and reminds us that gold is fiery, fire golden, and both are the purer elements that immortal longings will lead Cleopatra to extract from the history of the sun's amorous pinching. With its loading up of qualities—"beaten," the royal purple, the perfumed winds, silver oars a little distant from the goddess and slightly lower in the metallic scale—the passage is moved by powerful but burdened and slowed-down verbs. Cleopatra herself is inactive as someone on display, but everything else surges to flute-timed strokes. The fans move not to cool a gypsy's lust but to heighten the color of delicate cheeks. The water that elsewhere makes Egyptian slime and casts up monstrous creatures floats the entire construction. None of nature's elements goes unused or unrefined. Waters patterned by the timed strokes wish not to return to irrelevant matter and become as "indistinct / As water is in water" (4.9.10–11). Just by making an entry, she is capable of implying that nothing Roman is quite good enough.

In retrospect, the progress Enobarbus describes is a visual rhetoric as well as material for her recollective poetry—a display of glamor designed to reduce a Roman power whose triumphs are merely political. But in the subliming of poetic narration, especially as read between the lines by the audience, the portrait is less a Shakespearean rhetoric on behalf of sovereignty than a guarantee of the strong impression the play requires to close the book of Cleopatra. It converts the opening scenes of the play into a legend already underway long before Philo's less flattering portrait. The final implications of its spotlighting method are not clear until Cleopatra sends Charmian for her best attire (5.2.227) and leaves her reconstructions to those who wander about the vacated stage wondering how she managed. From that final perspective, the poetic materials return toward epic, when no messenger can be sent off to Hades to check the results of "Husband, I come." If the initial descent into Antony's phase of the empire entangles love in politics (patching up Egypt's relation to post–Julius Caesar Rome), the exit frees love from further entanglements. It lifts Cleopatra's desire and its machinations out of their cramping circumstances. Assuming that her preview of Hades resembles Antony's, death becomes an onward sailing to cure what the downward one has gotten her into.

The plausibility of Enobarbus's barge narration is vouched for by the fact that his perceptions of the lovers elsewhere are open-eyed and principled, which is rare in both Rome and Egypt. Nearly as variable as Cleopatra, Enobarbus reveals what can happen to one who does not become fully committed to a projected role. His mixing of grandeur and debauchery is typical enough of Romans to suggest that he is suspended between versions of love and chivalry. He can trade hints of thievery with a Menas or banter with sophisticated Egyptians, but he never falls to railing like a Roman Thersites. He has Horatio's capacity for loyalty up to a point but can also challenge pretensions. Trenchant good sense and clipped parallelism give him, if not ascendancy over Cleopatra's showmanship, at least the right to appraise it. Just the sort of lieutenant Antony needs, we say, and therefore the sort whose choice of sage conduct in leaving Antony shows the limits of sage conduct.

From the division in Enobarbus we see more readily that Antony carries about with him several levels of response, some political, some egoistic, some capable of celebrating the vision of the barge. Without pausing to deliver such retrospective summaries as Enobarbus's, Antony suggests by distraction his entrancement in what lies elsewhere, as in carrying a piece of Rome to Egypt or of Egypt to Rome. That fracturing is causal in taking his attention from what he needs to do to brake Octavius's momentum. But self-division is also an advantage to the man whose passion has the royal object Enobarbus describes. If his military triumphs make generosity possible, the failure brought on by the floating vision (even if he sits elsewhere while others rush out to admire it) rises toward a magnanimity that the poetry expands. He is torn not just between Egypt and Rome but between the tarnished opportunities of his political career and a life of imagination fulfilled in erotic dream. To be Cleopatra's lover and create the expansive tone that love prefers, he is required to take up a certain kind of speechmaking. Although he offers a resounding preliminary in "Let Rome in Tiber melt" (1.1.33), his better contributions come as farewells.

If sifting the chaff from Cleopatra's speeches is not easy at any stage, it is not a great deal easier to follow his course toward the Hades he invents as glory's final scene. In that autumnal tone, he himself recognizes the vaporish pageant they are passing through and thus the potential vanity of any high style:

> That which is now a horse, even with a thought
> The rack dislimns, and makes it indistinct
> As water is in water.
> (4.14.9–11)

So any likeness, any troping of the lived life, can collapse. But here that touch of Prospero's dissolving pageantry sets the tone for "Unarm, Eros, the long day's task is done" and the contrast between the dreamed afterlife and the disgrace of being "window'd in great Rome." His eyes at that moment are so clear and his manner so impressive that we have no difficulty conceding his "place i' the story." But only just before, his acute sense of his own victimage drives him to frenetic extremes, especially when it appears that in spite of everything he might actually win:

> Dost thou hear, lady?
> If from the field I shall return once more
> To kiss these lips, I will appear in blood,
> I, and my sword, will earn our chronicle.
> (3.13.172–75)

By "chronicle" he means the historian's tribute to a prince, a title he can still claim. He is understandably not yet prepared to realize that certain chroniclers and poets prefer, in their subjects, tragic defeat to victory.

Unfortunately, not all the ways he is transported help Cleopatra's cause in the posthumous phase. She notices instantly when a Roman thought strikes him, and yet as Pompey and others predict, he will never be completely with them: "Let witchcraft join with beauty, lust with both, / Tie up the libertine in a field of feasts" (2.1.22–23). Beyond that absentmindedness are the outright lies that the imagination proposes and politics ambushes. Cleopatra is more resourceful in these than he, but for both of them the play's constant blending of improvisation and affairs of empire makes it impossible to separate self-deception, sociable lies, and authoritative vision. Act 3 is particularly lacking in what the poetry later extracts with selective hyperbole from the fourth act. The key change comes suddenly, when the twice-defeated general mistakenly thinks that Cleopatra has betrayed him again. In the reciprocity of the elegiac tone and the dramatic situation, it becomes more and more evident that actual place in empire must be lost that words may prevail. The dramatic means of establishing greatness will have to be supplemented or replaced by the subversions of love poetry. Whereas the dimensions that Antony announces earlier could perhaps have been earned by a return to stoic rejections, he has never really meant to carry through with that line. (For one thing, Cleopatra would have no place in it.) From the low point on, he can only move toward legend, other alternatives having been squandered. Good stars that were formerly guides have by then "empty left their orbs, and shot their fires / Into the abysm of hell" (3.13.146–47)—gleaming nonetheless *as* stars and making Hades a second realm for those who cannot hold their places. The best language of the play finally is not a language of power or of analytic choice-making, squeezed by narrow Roman ways; it is the language of sweeping self-making that uses sovereignty as a springboard to a place where the ruled become bewitched witnesses summoned by love's spectacle.

Greatness Going Off

> The cancellings,
> The negations are never final.
>   —Stevens, "The Auroras of Autumn"

Although the hymns it assigns Cleopatra have nothing of Donne's passage of lovers into saints, *Antony and Cleopatra* is nearly as concerned about the signs that lovers issue as "The Canonization," and as concerned about memorialization as Hardy. For Donne, the miracle of love's exchange at its best transcends self and other, body and soul. Having found the phoenix riddle, the lovers can intercede for others. Lest we think that love's passage from its waste of days to hymns pulls it out of the real world and appeals only to cultists, however, Donne reminds us that lovers actually extract the world's soul and keep it in essence. In a part-for-whole representation, they become exemplars rather than antagonists. Love's scene is a global stage, and its actors are presenters of a world no longer confused. If long-departed lovers epitomize country, town, court, the essence of these places too must be love (although, if so, country, town, and court seldom know it).

The reduction of Antony and Cleopatra also coincides with new phoenix selves. The world returns to them not as pilgrims begging a pattern but as an Octavius setting them up (and aside) in final tribute. Since Cleopatra is the mover as love's celebrant, prompter of Antony's worst decisions, and prime exhibit, the play considers her quite-different effects on him alive and dead. The conflict she instigates in opposing self-centered love to public chivalry is as important as the love itself. As Kenneth Burke remarks concerning those who stir things up, "dramatists like cantankerous characters," and Cleopatra does her share through four acts and part of the fifth.[4] So adept is she at stirring that she becomes virtually the voice of negativity, the power of antithesis, just the one required to convert losses into triumphs. We could imagine Burke addressing her in that office more appropriately than love-struck pilgrims (if we allow still another liberty with chronicled fact):

> Fie wrangling queen, contrary perspective
> beNiler of things Tiberish,
> you unleash lotsa charm,
> then with much ado

> move up the ladder of magnificence.
> Your consummate act is dying,
> but never fear:
> you'll arise, no neutered phoenix,
> haranguing again and again
> in the dampened eyes of global crowds.

We should distrust any promise she makes to abandon that haranguing in Hades, as we distrust Falstaff's reform. "I see him rouse himself / To praise my noble act," she remarks, well aware of her next grand entry. Her "Husband, I come" has an eagerness that portends a great scene rising in the imagination, assuming word and gesture to challenge all extant versions of Venus and Mars.

Concerning the phases of contrariety that the play actually stages, Shakespeare's dramaturgy does not lean on direct argument or theses but blends its *quaestiones* into the drama. Cleopatra's meddling scarcely has anything like a true cause or intellectual grasp of policy behind it, certainly not a moral cause, merely a succession of personal whims in evidence of a changeable will. Hence to shackle change, she must become her own opposite. Romans provide most of the impetus. Their stamp of approval on the Antony who once was and on the Cleopatra who makes a sex object of barges shows that they recognize personal dimension; but even their funeral tribute, although impressive, tends to hang midway between rhetoric and poetic. It is mostly useful for enabling the audience to exit from the tragedy with a positive feeling. Octavius does not rise all the way to the reformed Cleopatra, but then her suicide is not intended to show *him* her best side, merely to outwit and frustrate him while showing it to others. The combination of rhetoric and elegy with which he answers is formulaic in the way of speeches that precede curtain calls. It is cast in a ceremonial style appropriate to the moment when one's irritating enemies are laid out.

The point that tells more heavily against him, however, is that, where Antony loves ambivalently (whether the object is Octavia or Cleopatra), Octavius loves ostentatiously. Losing an opportunity to put a gesture to double use, personal *and* political, is an annoyance to him, as when Octavia arrives from Antony without sufficient train to make an impression:

> Why have you stol'n upon us thus? You come not
> Like Caesar's sister: the wife of Antony
> Should have an army for an usher, and
> The neighs of horse to tell of her approach,
> Long ere she did appear. The trees by the way
> Should have borne men, and expectation fainted,

> Longing for what it had not. Nay, the dust
> Should have ascended to the roof of heaven,
> Rais'd by your populous troops: but you are come
> A market-maid to Rome, and have prevented
> The ostentation of our love; which, left unshown,
> Is often left unlov'd.
>
> (3.6.42–53)

This comes from one who would have the populations of cities lean from their windows to see a caged strumpet. He undoubtedly appreciates such shows partly for their own sake, but their value is doubled by the political argument they make. Even the dust of horses' hoofs becomes a proclamation.

Antony is himself half Roman as long as things Roman are still available to him. Even when he is down and out, he can only half master Cleopatra's style, partly because every time he practices she interrupts and partly because he still hopes for Roman honors. In the defeats and betrayals of the third act, he hovers between the leader he has been and the immortal lover he dreams of becoming. He manages to be better in her absence than in her presence, which is partly what enables the poetry to work its way out of the dramatic engagement a little at a time. Whatever our judgment of him in that vacillation, losing most of his "pillar" status is preliminary to the note he strikes in response to her most provocative act:

> Eros!—I come, my queen:—Eros!—Stay for me,
> Where souls do couch on flowers, we'll hand in hand,
> And with our sprightly port make the ghosts gaze:
> Dido, and her Aeneas, shall want troops,
> And all the haunt be ours.
>
> (4.14.50–54)

This is most un-Roman and shows that he too has a taste for the decorative. If he is to make people turn their heads, it must be as Cleopatra's companion, not as a general. The Roman Antony commands by office in the conventions of a status society, this one by bearing, in the alternate realm of Virgil's underworld. Having passed beyond the giving and receiving of wounds, those who have formerly depended on his prowess will become troops of gazers, in no way harmed by the diversion. They will be an admiring citizenry unlike the populace that, as Caesar says, "Like to a vagabond flag upon the stream / Goes to, and back, lackeying the varying tide, / To rot itself with motion" (1.4.45–47). Emotion they will still feel; turbulence they will not. Unfortunately, such a glory beyond the fame of the throng would also be less tangible than anything Egypt or Rome offers, since Hades is after all merely a haunt. However sprightly their "port," lovers there remain spirits.

The quarrelsomeness of both Cleopatra and Romans who wish Antony a stoic again obviously poses a quandary for Antony, since it allows no compromise. The opposed parties leave it mostly to him to decide what conscience and duty have to do with behavior, such questions being out of Cleopatra's range and serving mostly as conveniences to Romans. He does not do badly for a time in making up a character that men can respect. Indeed, as Julian Markels points out in his defense, Shakespeare goes out of his way to make him stronger and less calculating than the Antony of North's Plutarch.[5] He remarks to Octavia concerning his apparent lack of principle:

> Read not my blemishes in the world's report:
> I have not kept my square, but that to come
> Shall all be done by the rule.
>
> (2.3.5–7)

Where Agrippa and Octavius are busy hooping and binding and keeping matters of negotiable advantage foremost, he bases social relations less on bartering than on personal loyalties.[6] We witness directly other reasons for his reputation as a leader. Much of the second act is devoted to what allies and enemies believe about him, and Shakespeare builds a reasonable case for him there before dismantling it in the third act. As Arnold Stein suggests, merely his appearing before Pompey in Rome shows a certain bearing among princes, a squaring by Roman rule.[7] Nor is he blind to his own dotage. He can cut through the light talk of an Enobarbus with plain-style honesty and moralize decisions in public council with pithy statement. Fulvia's campaign has embarrassed but not deceived him, and his apology to Octavius is manly and open. He says with some conviction that to lose honor is to lose himself. In that range of self-society relations he has basically only Enobarbus for company.

However, these achievements depend on keeping Cleopatra at a distance. His pumping up of courage in her provocative company makes even Enobarbus fear "A diminution in our captain's brain," as "valour preys on reason" (3.13.119). Keeping square with Octavia more than a day proves beyond him; within a few lines he reneges on his vow, since his "pleasure" lies in Egypt (2.3.37). There may be more to his reasons for relapsing than he suggests, but everything conspires against constancy until an honorable death is the only alternative. Although it would not be Roman to admit it, his former glory has come too much from soldierly hardship and bravado, and even then, if Ventidius is right (2.1), his subordinates have done much of the real work. But again losing respect in one sphere prepares him for stature in another. In teasing out the shift, the play puts him through not only the protracted suicide but two defeats (where North chronicles a single extended one). The first triggers the defection of friends; the second drops him further initially but leads toward the grade to the monument. The speeches that come of these defeats linger over requisitions of the past to grace the present—or would linger if Cleopatra permitted and if Antony could exclude vanity:

> The miserable change now at my end
> Lament nor sorrow at: but please your thoughts
> In feeding them with those my former fortunes
> Wherein I liv'd: the greatest prince o' the world,
> The noblest; and do now not basely die,
> Not cowardly put off my helmet to
> My countryman: A Roman, by a Roman
> Valiantly vanquish'd. Now my spirit is going,
> I can no more.
> (4.15.51–59)

In North's Plutarch, Antony says such things to console his followers. Here, although Shakespeare plants that idea, the speech depends on the example Antony has set some time ago. Judged by Cleopatra's transport, it looks underpowered.

Despite the statuesque posing of the prince and warrior, self-slaughter on behalf of love is a new factor at the fulcrum of the empire-love balance. That he does not blame Cleopatra for her feigned death is contrary to her expectations and is further evidence of the best survival of the magnanimous general. Shakespeare clears enough underbrush from around the image to suggest an escape from the worst of Romanism. Even so, one persistent difficulty is that magnanimity can shade off into public gesture until we find it almost impossible to distinguish forgiveness from the purchase of good opinion. Self-dramatization and theatricality are so built into departing greatness that even when Antony says "now my spirit is going, / I can no more" we hear it as a public announcement. (Can no more "speak," "doing" having dropped out of contention.) My assumption is that Shakespeare makes this fumbling into a first run at grand dying in order to keep Cleopatra prominently the measure of Antony's best scenes and then give her a better version to herself. Antony can then be summoned by the elegiac Cleopatra who governs the stage-managing one, who by then is more poetess than playwright's cantankerous helper.

"My desolation does begin to make / A better life"

Although Antony leaves the play in time to give Cleopatra the entire last act, his departure is prolonged, and the grade to the haunt grows steeper, indeed literally vertical, near the end. Out of the poverty of spent resources (as Emerson realized in seeing poetry and affluence as a dialectic), we generate rebirth. Cleopatra knows then that it is desolation that makes a better life. The making is tentative at first, as the lengthy withholding "does begin to make" suggests. If Antony were to die immediately, we could more easily link the stoic who drinks horse stale to the great-souled man; the dramatic structure would have command over love's (and death's) poetic agenda. As it is, to outfit him for the passage Shakespeare alters not only his place in empire but the quality of the departures he rehearses. As Enobarbus has remarked much earlier, women especially must die in their own ways, and frequently; and so Antony may as well leave Egypt, although "Cleopatra catching but the least noise of this, dies instantly." Having now great moment, she does indeed manage dying twenty times better. Although those earlier farewells have a serious as well as a farcical side, they are undercut by the gamesmanship of her sailing into battles and death announcements. The instructions she gives Antony on how to do such things call attention to copious tears and elegiac facsimiles (1.3.76–80). She makes it extremely hard for even a prolonged death scene to generate anything very stirring. Seeing the promise of his final speeches as he seems about to find the right note, she simply takes over: "No, let me speak," by which she means "rail so high, / That the false huswife Fortune break her wheel" (4.15.42–43). They both lean toward that style when no hindrance intrudes.[8]

The second run at elegy, Cleopatra's without Antony, is also clouded by her public image and its obligations, which translate until almost the end into a mix of politics, love, quarrelsome maneuvering, and legend-making. These make dying a strategy as well as an upgrading. But the more aggressive side of sexual gamesmanship melts into a new longing that rearranges the other elements. If, as Burke notes, Cleopatra's image of Antony's delights as dolphins rising "above / The element they lived in" (5.2.89–90) maintains an erotic double meaning, it nonetheless manages a semimythic scale. The last longing too is sexual, but much more than that. Always apt at impromptu, Cleopatra seizes upon circumstances as they arise and hammers them into the end she pronounces unified and right. The spirit works loose from counteractions while still using them for leverage. Shakespeare's middle-aged lovers move into that last phase not with the naive devotions of a Romeo and Juliet but with ambivalences unique to them. Plangent statements such as Iras's "Finish, good lady, the bright day is done" (5.2.192) maintain one foot in the might-have-been and keep the poems playable as drama (albeit a minor drama of confidants), voiced not as a mounting collision of major powers but as encouragement to attendants. Cleopatra's own blend of reality and imagination (or what Matthew Proser describes in the preferred Renaissance terms *nature* and *art*)[9] has little further use for power and reminds us that, although sailings into the unknown are wafted by poetry, they are dramatic in rejecting one set of values for another.

In the national epic part of the fable, Antony has had less luck and less persistence, if more scruple, than Octavius; yet Cleopatra's last performances begin with the assertion that the loftiness she sees in him has actually been there, in the struggles of ships and men. This assertion audiences have to deal with as best they can, using a sense of the age of heroes as ballast against moral judgment. It amounts to a claim that dream and fact are intimately related—that what she offers is a gloss on the active Antony: no great character, no grand dream. We can experience tragedy only through the loss of something valuable. Yet her conviction that the heroic image is justified does not alter our realization that her second world is imaginary. Its value is that although it could not survive in a real Mediterranean, swarming with Roman ships, it springs only from such a world while passing judgment on it. The potential greatness formerly overwhelmed by petty sins and grievances she now buttresses with courage and new purpose.

Our knowledge that Cleopatra is deceiving herself about the reunion does not grant us any noticeable superiority over her. To reject the dream with too great a self-assurance would be for us to draw away from a strong performer at the very moment she takes us into her confidence. We have already seen what a betrayal on behalf of good sense does to Enobarbus. The other part of her myth creation, the image of the colossus, is not entirely beyond credibility since Antony has after all been Antony. She merely contracts a new partnership of memory and imagination. Dolabella's grudging respect and sorrow that smites his "very heart at root" (5.2.104–5) are founded not in his belief but in hers, as ours must be. He is audience to the poem, knowing that he does not believe it but suspending his disbelief because the fiction shows him something the literal truth does not. In her "I thank you, sir" she takes such sympathy humbly, although perhaps too much as applause. The test of her vision, if not of the rightness of the accompanying argument, is that Dolabella neglects his mission from Caesar and drops whatever he was prepared to say about Caesar's intentions, which again demonstrates the reentry of poetry into the plot on its own terms. It must be rhetoric too, or it would not hinder the Roman advance. The result is a submission of lesser intrigues to her greater one. That so many Romans have by now succumbed testifies to the augmented life of those whom Dryden's Plutarch calls the Inimitable Livers Together (Amimetobion), whose way is "beyond comparison" except for its theatrical relivings. The greater dimension is communicable to a degree, however few its deeds have been lately.

Dolabella's skepticism is one of a half dozen potential belittlements that Cleopatra has to overcome in her blend of strategy and sacrifice, including some residual drawbacks from the real Antony himself, her own flaws, Octavius's watchfulness, and the clown who lingers. Her meeting of each of these obstacles proves the versatility of her dramaturgy and her powers of contention (if we had any doubts about them) and the caginess of the poetic instinct in meeting its interlocutors on their ground. She requires for her Elysian husband a figure who, without drawing much upon the Roman scoffer at famine, has conquered enough to afford liberality. The speech to which Dolabella responds has not just asserted such a figure but added a metaphysics to frame it. It is the closest thing to an argument she mounts, but it also shows how little argument matters. It throws a single spear of intuition and a little foggy metaphysics against thickly buttressed evidence:

> You lie up to the hearing of the gods.
> But if there be, or ever were one such,
> It's past the size of dreaming: nature wants stuff
> To vie strange forms with fancy, yet to imagine
> An Antony were nature's piece, 'gainst fancy,
> Condemning shadows quite.
> (5.2.95–100)

The "if there be" sounds conditional enough to plant doubts even in Cleopatra's mind. Nature does forge real people, not the costumed phantoms of the stage. But if that is undeniable, it is also without bearing, since her argument is question-begging. *Her* Antony is now as large as dream can make him—as rattling as thunder, as bountiful as unending harvests, as full-voiced as the tuned spheres.

Cleopatra assigns to her coming wifehood (a clawed swipe at Octavia's) an equivalent dimension, following from that nobler group the Diers Together (Synapothanumon), who make a second pact under their death sentences. She inspires other coplayers besides Dolabella to support that dimension. Yet even in transcending her reputation she neither names nor discards the personal faults that fill the file on her. Where Octavius thinks what an honorable Roman most conquers is the flesh, she reverses that stoic reduction. Her performance recalls enough of what is devious and merely human to keep the new Cleopatra much the same as the old one in "the posture of the whore." Several differences, however, sustain the sympathy toward which Dolabella guides us. She is now loyal to Antony and resolved to drop her baser elements. In her peevish moods, it has not been entirely clear why she flies from battles or plays pranks on Antony or holds back her jewels from Caesar; but her announced plans for suicide close the gap between audience and stage manager and move us into the position of privileged onlookers.

The implied rhetoric could cut either of two ways or angle off somewhere between. If the proud claiming of titles helps one die nobly, royalty earns its tragic privileges. But incapacity to rule wisely has put her in this fix to begin with, and her greatness comes from her staunchness in love fueled by otherworldliness. Perhaps the best compromise is to consolidate the political maneuvering with personal transcendence, since neither is conceivable without the other and both build upon love's new voice. Part of Cleopatra's dying well is dying in state, in public; and again the poetry, in the circumstances of its performance, becomes a concealed rhetoric in its implicit critique of smaller-minded plots and their public exhibition of lovers. Where Enobarbus goes out dispirited and alone, she is well aware of the intimates who have roughed out the rules. Charmian's straightening of her crown, the brilliant gesture that Daniel shows Shakespeare how to exploit,[10] both reasserts her queendom and readies the lifting of the curtain. Her death supports a purpose we have to concede to be better, at least for her honor and her talent as revels master, than any other alternative the play allows.

To these foils for setting off the last scene, her Cydnus entry and practice dyings are again pertinent if more distant additions. The reservations of many critics notwithstanding, her preparation for the celestial rendezvous is partly moral. The former creature of inconstancy now plays her part to the hilt: "from head to foot / I am marble-constant: now the fleeting moon / No planet is of mine" (5.2.238–40). She herself sees this as a reversal, behind which is a lesson that few other tragic heroes or heroines learn outside of Lear: not that wisdom is rooted in folly but that a better self is both discovered through loss and completes the losing. This more difficult way of honor surpasses sagacity. Cleopatra eases into it with the illusion of immortality. Whereas politicians never finish their work and one revel only leads to another, her new resolve carries beyond both and finishes them off.

Cleopatra's insight into the art of dying—or into the art of bespeaking and laying out one's dying—is perhaps not really extraordinary for one as practiced in arrangements as she has been throughout, but Shakespeare gives her exceptional orchestration. She takes her sense of consummation partly from Antony, but his farewells as we have seen are constrained by his concept of Roman princeliness. She too is concerned with what chronicles will say, but even more with how plays will mimic her, a subtle but characteristic difference. Although she has to deal with the rag ends of imperial power and what it would do with her if she survived, she carries fewer recollective burdens and affairs of reputation and honor than Antony does and more anticipation. He leaves her behind, she goes to him. Hence he is not among the chroniclers but is offstage waiting for the next play to begin. With thought of that reunion to bolster her, she gains ascendance over those disgraceful scenes that lesser imaginations propose for their superiors: "Hoist me up, / And show me to the shouting varletry?" she asks (5.2.55–56):

> 'tis most certain, Iras: saucy lictors
> Will catch at us like strumpets, and scald rhymers
> Ballad us out o' tune. The quick comedians
> Extemporally will stage us, and present
> Our Alexandrian revels.
> (5.2.213–17)

Where Antony's final speeches reincorporate Rome into the reputation one leaves behind in a still-relevant scene of power, for Cleopatra kingdoms are left to schemers. She neither succumbs to politics nor turns her back on it but simply gets the better of both it and the distorted truths of its scald rhymers.

As I noted, Shakespeare tests both her resolve and her elevation by having a clown deliver the asps. The clown tests her ingenuity and is a means to keep some cantankerousness in the final moments. She may be a master of farewells, but she does not like to waste them. Only after he has extracted three from her and actually left can she proceed with "Give me my robe, put on my crown, I have / Immortal longings in me," which comes forward all the more impressively for the delay. If dying queens can claim privileges beyond others, this one makes the instrument of death itself a final demonstration. Her address to the asp suggests a director stuck with a tongue-tied actor who ventriloquizes his part for him: "O couldst thou speak, / That I might hear thee call great Caesar ass, / Unpolicied!" (5.305–7). Through that last thorny realism and the nettled entryway to death we must squeeze the play if we are to see where, or rather how, she goes. Her address places on the fringes of lyric a satiric spirit as pointed as the one that prepares for Donne's canonizing of lovers. Having done all this, she can then virtually coast out: "As sweet as balm, as soft as air, as gently, / O Antony!" (5.310–11).

Among those whom Cleopatra leaves behind are the impersonators who put images on the boards. In the best of them, poetry gives substance to and validates the extremity of her act. It shows simultaneously both itself and the limits of the dramatic action with which it collaborates even as they separate. If we doubt that something like the historical figure actually dies and rises the same in reenactings, we can steal a page from her circular argument for Antony's reality: to have merely imagined her would be past the size of dreaming. To evoke such images the poetry must be grounded in the drama, the drama in the chronicle, and the chronicle in the stubborn traces of a real or conceivably real life, enhanced and distorted but not utterly displaced by the performance.

4

The Polysyllabic Moor and Venetian Parlor Talk

> Methinks the wind does speak aloud at land,
> A fuller blast ne'er shook our battlements:
> If it ha' ruffian'd so upon the sea,
> What ribs of oak, when the huge mountains melt,
> Can hold the mortise? ... What shall we hear of this?
> —*Othello*, 2.1.5–9

The Illusion of Choice: Othello's Duel with Iago

It is a tribute to Shakespearean dramaturgy that an actor playing Macbeth seems as men of ambition do even when speaking well beyond any man who ever stabbed a king. The nature of literary logic is to capitalize on dimensions of language we seldom encounter elsewhere. When a metaphor, as Puttenham says, wrests a word from "his owne right signification, to another not so naturall, but yet of some affinitie or convenience," new meaning generates that affinity and gathers supporting figures. "Corrigible" attracts "penetrative" in Antony's attempt to win a helping hand, and together they suggest wheeled and fortunate Caesar. As one twisted word makes contact with others, all such make up the realm of transport within which character becomes not merely impersonation but a complex of signals nowhere operative except on the boards and the well-edited page.

A heightened and condensed vocabulary carries not merely to an end but to a culmination, and it is in that directedness that a genre—a selection of tones and styles from the available repertory—works not only forward but backward from the end. The apparent Antony only seems to be deciding what to do at a given moment. The Antony of the collective readership has already done so many times; in the eternal present of the play, everyone has always already decided everything. We never quite escape the pressure of that knowing; we may experience scene-by-scene disclosures, but we also read them in the light of a whole greater than the sum we have encountered by act 3 or act 4.

This does not prevent our going along with the represented Antony or Enobarbus, since we know too the feel of their uncertainty. Because of similar experiences with contingency, we are capable of growing almost equally anxious over their choices each time we see them enacted: we still want Antony to avoid fighting at sea this time; we wish Lear would tumble to the truth a little earlier. Too forward a recognition of formal pressures hampers that serial ordeal. As Robert Ornstein argues in pursuing a confidence in mimesis, if we assign Antony's eloquence to Shakespeare too readily, we may not know where to stop.[1] Is Hamlet, too, to become Shakespeare's choral spokesman, not enacting but acting? Is Othello a puppet speaking for the play, running on schedule toward the final catastrophe? The questions are virtually rhetorical, but someone used to the paradoxes of theater should nonetheless not hesitate to answer no *and* yes. To forget either representation or formal determinism is to lose the activating energy of their union and their collisions. Caught up in the chemistry of their union are all the relations of poet to playwright and of readers to texts.

Othello makes a fair test of that chemistry. It is Iago's assignment to make Othello plausible, backing off, turning vehement in response, renewing the attack, enticing him into a participatory building of the case, and winding him up to an explosive excess of language and feeling. Iago's *rhetoric,* the language that creates the image of Desdemona as Bianca, serves Othello's *poetry,* the language of suffering rising to the tragic occasion until they become full-fledged confederates, Iago on one plane, Othello on another, but Othello bending down to Iago's for the belittling stuff of domestic betrayal, Iago rising to pretended pitches of sympathy and compassion.

Iago's crafty vehemence, Othello's pathos: they compose one of a half dozen of the most striking duets in Shakespeare. The progress from Othello's slow-paced dignity to his third-act upheaval follows a sequence of pulsations or catches and releases within a general tightening that takes Iago's vengeance from pranks to triple murder. The crucial change in Othello is simultaneously drawn by the end and pushed by psychology. Iago's proofs and demonstrations swing him from helpless suffering and attitudinizing to irreversible action. Iago's bluntness plays against a Latinate dignity that mounts in a statuesque vocabulary that shatters from its own weight:

> *Iago.* I once more take my leave.   [*Exit.*]
> *Oth.* This fellow's of exceeding honesty,
> And knows all qualities, with a learned spirit,
> Of human dealing: if I do prove her haggard,
> Though that her jesses were my dear heart-strings,
> I'ld whistle her off, and let her down the wind,
> To prey at fortune. Haply, for I am black,
> And have not those soft parts of conversation
> That chamberers have, or for I am declin'd
> Into the vale of years,—yet that's not much—
> She's gone, I am abus'd, and my relief
> Must be to loathe her: O curse of marriage,
> That we can call these delicate creatures ours,
> And not their appetites! I had rather be a toad,
> And live upon the vapour in a dungeon,
> Than keep a corner in a thing I love,
> For others' uses: Yet 'tis the plague of great ones,
> Prerogativ'd are they less than the base,
> 'Tis destiny, unshunnable, like death.
>   (3.3.261–79)

That Othello is speaking an aside suggests that we are observing a thought just now developing despite the pomp and ceremony and such circumlocutions as "declin'd / Into the vale of years" (for "old") and "knows all qualities . . . / Of human dealing" (for "knows people"), both demonstrations of "those soft parts of conversation" he says he lacks. The comparison with hawking assumes a potential wildness in wives as well as mastery in husbands. But Othello can maintain his detachment only so long before he realizes that Desdemona cannot be whistled off and that marriage is not a military order. The social axioms and generalities of a military indoctrination hang like shreds from the "forked plague" he imagines on his brow. In recoil come the resurgence of pride and the consolation that the well-born ones are doomed from the outset, such is the way of the world. Not only are we almost convinced that we see him actually sorting out the choices, but we are doubly on edge for knowing how easily such a man, trying to be honest with himself, could be spared if he would look more closely at the evidence.

    At the point at which Othello gets in sufficient disarray to commit himself, Iago joins him in vows. In their ritual pledge, the play grants feeling unusual amplitude and finishes one phase of its interweaving of higher and lower ranges. To Othello's "In the due reverence of a sacred vow, / I here engage my words," Iago answers:

> Do not rise yet.
> Witness, you ever-burning lights above,
> You elements that clip us round about,
> Witness that here Iago doth give up
> The excellency of his wit, hand, heart,
> To wrong'd Othello's service.
> (3.3.469–74)

The two of them have crossed, Iago borrowing Othello's poetic stars and sacred causes, Othello adopting Iago's degrading portrait of his wife and his plan of action. It is questionable as to who has the better of the exchange. Seemingly Iago, since he has captured Othello's nobility and turned it toward a murderous cause; but he has also gotten hold of more than he can manage and will be destroyed by it. The union of poetry and rhetoric is bastardized and temporary. The rediscovery of the true Desdemona in driving act and feeling apart again will break its hold.

If *Othello* does not make us forget the actor and the playwright in these moments of decision, perhaps nothing in drama is likely to. And yet, . . . The vow-making, like the whistling off, contains much that is neither social nor psychological and not even quite right as a plausible mimesis. We are forced to take in not only Iago's falsity and Desdemona's faithfulness but the unfolding of a plot whose every twist is designed to further Othello's agony. Iago's trick of backing off is transparent acting that can be attributed as much to good theater as to guile. When Othello says "This fellow's of exceeding honesty," the very word "honesty" (as Empson shows) marches with companions that chorus through the play. Iago works not merely as an enemy of Cassio and Othello but as a playwright's assistant who arranges illusions, gets people on- and offstage, and nudges Othello into appropriate states of mind. Othello himself may or may not be entirely creditable, but he becomes what he has to be. Seeing him misinterpret the same evidence that we are given, we are caught up in a maze of watchings and hearings in which he becomes both an audience within the play and the chief exhibit. For most of us (unless Thomas Rymer sits at our elbow), these layers of awareness do not interfere with engrossment in the apparent man making an apparent mistake. Shakespeare can count on the dramatic illusion holding as long as the pace is maintained. But a playwright so assured of the dramatic illusion can also confess his tricks openly. The performative nature of an Iago saying "I once more take my leave" would prevent anyone from rushing onstage to save Desdemona even if paying admission and settling in for a performance did not.[2]

Hyperbole

One often-noted disadvantage of reading *Othello* after the Bradley manner—with attention mostly to character and credibility, both variants of an Aristotelian probability of doubtful value for a drama whose native tradition features morality demonstrations and dumb-show interludes, allegories, and pantomimes set to "drommes and fluites"—is that all dimensions of language must then be made to serve a discernible decorum based on social position and psychological type. Allowing performative conventions and literary ambience to disappear into the imitated object loses as much of *Othello* as of perhaps any Shakespeare play, since the Othello-Iago contest proclaims its morality-pitched battle and its eloquence openly and pervasively. The play also assigns rhetorical colors at times to quite indifferent speakers. It attends to casual discourse and measures the romantic idiom of chivalry against Venetian customs and commonplace gossip.

If chivalric standards bolster Othello's high style and escalate his emotions, Iago's most natural medium is realistic social discourse. He is good at gossip: he does not merely repeat it as a raconteur or invent it but exploits it to open selected windows in less inquiring minds. He gives small increments to motives already there, brightens a flagging desire in Roderigo, and breathes new life into Othello's subsiding anxiety. Again, this is most Shakespearean and cooperative in him: if someone in the play does not identify the exact prompting that a motive needs, the play will falter. Given his prose realism and assortment of social resentments, Shakespeare does not need either the diabolical credo Boito supplies his Iago or Verdi's swelling of blissful and agonized themes. He provides the great passions of the play with social hooks and handles that can be tugged at by the subtle innuendo all around them.

Othello's conviction of Desdemona's guilt is inseparable from the parlor and the bedroom prejudgments that Iago leads him to adopt. They come forward like the *formulae majores* of rhetorical manuals, ready for an Emilia to use to hammer down a moral or for her husband to apply at a different level. Iago's technique is not to manufacture anything new but to associate Desdemona with stereotypes and an assumed general practice, thus to mobilize Brabantio, Roderigo, Cassio, and Othello according to biases requiring no real argument to trigger. Were it not for Othello's capacity to upgrade domestic quarrels and cuckoldry, Iago would generate merely a somewhat routine comedy.

Desdemona is thus the victim of two things working in tandem: preconceptions that label her and an idealism that multiplies the force of Othello's reaction. Do the collisions of small and large talk belong to differences in character, then, or should we assume that the play has an interest in language in its own right and thus in performative and illustrative character (apparent, stage character)? When the indignant Emilia comes forward to speak the truth about Othello, does she do so as a wife choosing between her marital obligations and her fondness for Desdemona or as a play-ending convention, a moral-pointing correction, a style of unsubtle sanity to counter Othello's richly warped, metaphor-laden madness?

Shakespearean drama is realistic enough to argue for the former, but as the vow-making scene suggests, it is also stylized enough to use its Emilias and Roderigos for local effects and fit them into the functional roles. Thomas Rymer's dislike of the play, the most celebrated if not the most articulate of views based on verisimilitude, hinges on how people of certain standing *should* talk and act, given the ways of the world. Complaints of the F.R. Leavis and T.S. Eliot sort are rooted in similar expectations and result in similar judgments. In Rymer's view, the play slips into fustian when after but a few hours of marriage and a few moments of jealousy Othello speaks as though from the depths of long agony:

> What sense had I of her stol'n hours of lust?
> I saw't not, thought it not, it harm'd not me,
> I slept the next night well, was free and merry,
> I found not Cassio's kisses on her lips.
> (3.3.344–47)

In feigning sympathetic distress, Iago too resorts to melodrama, but in his case obviously put on for the occasion:

> O grace, O heaven defend me!
> Are you a man, have you a soul or sense?
> God buy you, take mine office,—O wretched fool,
> That livest to make thine honesty a vice!
> O monstrous world, take note, take note, O world,
> To be direct and honest is not safe.
> (3.3.379–84)

To Rymer, such passages amuse as they attempt to elevate, because they abandon decorum in the interests of pathos, as again in a passage he saves for his greatest scorn:[3]

> O heavy hour!
> Methinks it should be now a huge eclipse
> Of sun and moon, and that the affrighted globe
> Should yawn at alteration.
>
> (5.2.99–102)

He has a point if we grant the premise: credibility cannot be the prime concern of a playwright who has someone speak of the simultaneous eclipse of sun and moon. Modifiers like "huge" and "affrighted" are neither quite self-conscious nor natural; "yawn" exaggerates the gaps of the global face, yet "alteration" remains strangely neutral for such a tearing.

One effect of this strain is no doubt to deepen and complicate character, but it is difficult for either the playgoer or the critic to establish a sequence of inner changes that would lead to just this language or is best served by it. Moreover, if minor characters rise to great heights, the character of Othello cannot be exclusively responsible for the play's excesses. To accuse of bombast "exchange me for a goat, / When I shall turn the business of my soul / To such exsufflicate and blown surmises" (3.3.184–86) or to hear pompousness in "O now for ever / Farewell the tranquil mind, farewell content: / Farewell the plumed troop, and the big wars" (2.3.353–55) would be more reasonable if huge mountains did not melt for subordinates or if parlor games and council judgments were not rhymed. Even so, one might well be meant to ask of Othello—rather than of the play—"*big* wars? So many farewells? Exsufflicate?" That Othello's frequent hyperbole, or some degree of it, also reveals character gives us a difficult task of balancing. Fortunately the matter of how to integrate romantic and plain matters (to give them shortcut labels) receives some attention within the play. Our responses are guided by a recurrent concern with hearing and interpreting and sharp juxtapositions of style that all but raise the issue of hyperbole to a thematic level. So let us see first what advice we can extract from dramaturgy in combination with the diction.

Hearings

One task clearly laid out for criticism by idiomatic and pointed talk, bounced against a highly literary style and the exotic adventures of the alien Moor, is to call upon one to define the other. But how? Perhaps a first step should be to keep the dramatic action and verse far enough apart to determine what we are combining. Such a separation is not an arbitrary exercise, since it lies at the heart of the poetic subtext's commentary on act. In calling Othello's rarified, highly metaphoric language "poetry" and Iago's persuasion "rhetoric," I made rhetoric more or less equivalent to the rhetoric of Yeats's distinction, in the comment that in the quarrel with others we make rhetoric, with ourselves, poetry. Rhetoric is the prodding language that strikes a path through social habit and accustomed judgment. Iago stirs up *Othello* as Cleopatra does *Antony and Cleopatra*, both of them tightening the screws until their plays wind up to tragic intensity, one in the disastrous undoing of a love, the other in love's projected other world. Such labels are more convenient than absolute and are not entirely applicable to the social idiom that Iago uses, although he forges it into rhetoric and lets very little pass without weaving a snare of it.

We have to be especially cautious about the rhetoric-poetry distinction when the exchange works up to its highest intensity and Othello applies his romantic repertory to the matter of infidelity before he stabs to death his own "Turkish" alienation in defense of Venice. We should not forget that he kills both Desdemona and himself on the assumption that he is serving chivalry and justice. Without exploring the murkier depths of *Hamlet* or the mad rhetoric of *King Lear*, *Othello* mixes several proportions of fiction-making and deliberation quite apart from Othello's own ear-catching glorifications of the battlefield and star-watched causes.[4] More specifically, the language of pomp, at least in the amount and intensity Othello uses it, provides one of the linguistic screens through which evidence in the trials of Cassio and Desdemona is admitted to consciousness, just when closer attention to evidential procedures would be in order. Rhetoric is seldom so intricately involved in logic and hypothesis as it is here[5] and poetry seldom so bound up in love's lyricism and its torments (the latter falling into two phases, the sufferings of jealousy and the agony of the discovered error).

Beginning with the opening street scene and Iago's method as practiced on Brabantio, the play examines the misuse of logic in street trials and public hearings. As we follow the initial interrogations, we hear the same evidence that councils and judges do, but in Othello's set pieces and narrations we also hear more. The central showpiece eventually is Iago's besieging of Othello in the third act, but in the literary game Desdemona entices Iago into playing, Shakespeare stages a lesser one, easily overlooked. That odd setup and the matching one at the beginning of the third act should put us on guard as we work toward Iago's assaults on Cassio and Desdemona.

The parlor game makes an almost open confession of its love literature contexts. Troubling to psychological readings, it raises fewer difficulties if we see it as an insertion of contrastive tea talk. It translates into triviality the courtship with which Othello has won Desdemona and the flirtation he later reads as a grievous offense. Renaissance romances, sonnets, and plays are adept at presenting the side glances that accompany such floated testings of value, reactions to which indicate whether public assessments of one's merit match one's own. Desdemona's proposal of the courtship game comes just after the impressive organ roll that marks the stormy transition to Cyprus. By a logic not so much of character and action as of metaphor and audience attunement, that scene-setting prepares handkerchiefs for their hallowed meanings and households for an elemental fury, both a justification (of sorts) for Othello's resonance:

> do but stand upon the banning shore,
> The chiding billow seems to pelt the clouds,
> The wind-shak'd surge, with high and monstrous main,
> Seems to cast water on the burning bear,
> And quench the guards of the ever-fixed pole;
> I never did like molestation view
> On the enchafed flood.
>
> (2.1.11–17)

The question is whether in some way this grand show also prepares for the parlor game in which Desdemona shuts the window not only on Othello's sea-peril but on all the terrified consciousness soon to be so prominent.

The exhibition in aristocratic language of both sublimity and manners does not fully explain the steep descent from the grand to the trivial, but it exposes a contradiction between decorous rhetoric and contests that proceed easily from polite talk to witty insult. The courtship side of chivalry is not far from swordplay in the fierce wars and faithful loves that run through Othello's mind, or for that matter, from courtroom judgment, where parlor idiom and ritualized battle are supplemented by the law. We are reminded that Othello is not only a lover and military leader but a self-appointed judge, and eventually an executioner. His fulfillment of these offices is governed by his sense either of how he will be perceived by his adopted Venice or how he should administer its values.

To underscore the incongruity between the higher and lower levels of this sorting out of place, Shakespeare has Cassio announce "the divine Desdemona" ostentatiously, as though directing a royal progress, giving further notice that the *Othello* music is not all Othello's but is built into status display and is handed out lavishly by subalterns:

> The riches of the ship is come ashore!
> Ye men of Cyprus, let her have your knees:
> Hail to thee, lady! and the grace of heaven,

> Before, behind thee, and on every hand,
> Enwheel thee round!
> (2.1.82–87)

Desdemona's testimony before the Venetian council has earned her some tribute, but Cassio's coronets have no sooner sounded here than the "riches of the ship" says, "What wouldst thou write of me, if thou shouldst praise me?" Neither that question nor her mock anger, "O, fie upon thee, slanderer!," is distinguishable from fluff. Whether or not Elizabethan knights and ladies actually talked this way, for the moment the visitors to Cyprus agree to speak romances and sonnets. Despite being a singularly unlikely gallant, Iago contributes the language that love normally receives in Renaissance blazons.

If we try to explain the transition entirely in terms of motivated character, the scene falls victim to Rymer's view of the "long rabble of Jack-pudden farce" (pp. 110–11). Modernizing Desdemona as one who betrays a suppressed erotic interest she knows Iago will take up is a somewhat desperate remedy.[6] She herself offers an almost sufficient motive:

> I am not merry, but I do beguile
> The thing I am, by seeming otherwise:
> Come, how wouldst thou praise me?
> (2.1.122–24)

But this is unsatisfactory for the Desdemona whom Cassio has announced and especially for the innocent victim the play soon makes of her. The question is not so much why she wants to beguile the time as why the *play* wants prattle inserted among its accounts of true and untrue ladies and the courtship of Othello, which draws upon the literature of adventure and battlefield. The codified interpretation of parlor rites that I have suggested points toward an answer, as does the border that Shakespeare places around the scene and the change of tempo he works through it. This is not after all the only such noisy gear-shifting in the play. Part of our sense of any scene must be the context of analogous scenes juxtaposed by likeness, contrast, or proximity. That someone hitherto understandable comes forth to speak in a foreign language strains both the delivery and the reception. People assume Iago to be "honest," for instance, until they are forced to reinterpret. Brabantio thinks Desdemona well categorized as a dutiful daughter and a promising debutante until she surprises him; Cassio is capable of passing almost instantly from a reliable lieutenant to an unstable drunk and then back again with a bucket of water over the head. The Venetian council has placed the procedures of courtship under scrutiny, stopping in the midst of a wartime emergency session to do so—quite unbelievably Rymer remarks but perfectly in keeping with the play's interleaving of personal and public exhibitions of chivalry under fire. What's fair in love comes up again in Iago's inserting of startling perceptions into Othello's contentment. In each case, protocol is tested by apparent misfittings—the debutante married to a black foreigner or the cynic expressing praise for ladies or the apparently chaste Desdemona as Bianca.

Under what precepts *should* Venetian ladies be cataloged? How shall they be styled? In constructing his blazon for a paragon (while assuming real women to be just the opposite of what he says), Iago doesn't so much fulfill as counter Desdemona's request for a civil answer. His estimate of women is obliquely relevant to the play's comparison of black and witty, bright and dull kinds, and of Bianca, Emilia, and the faithful Desdemona. But the point is less the undertone he gives courtship than his breaking off of the stilted manner with a style more typical of gossip-under-stairs throwing off its literary pretensions.

Inserting that sportive contest into the Cyprus reception, Shakespeare drives home the incompatibility of styles, as he does in *King Lear* by rhyming France's declaration on behalf of Cordelia, a tattered courtly remnant amidst Lear's demand for other formal vows. Iago can pick up the idiom of almost any game, but as he does so on each occasion he becomes more intangible and "mysterious," especially in the larger shift from trickster to tragic villain, in a plot that eventually features three murders, an attempted fourth one, and a suicide. Each of these shifts is an eruption of poorly contained passion unable to endure the discrepancy between reputed status and personal worth. With almost equal poise and lack of definition, Iago can enter Othello's battlefield talk, set up alehouse songfests, prompt seduction intrigues, and match wits with courtiers. But in every situation he enters, he stirs up trouble, turning up the volume of the turbulence for Brabantio, upping what little voltage he finds in Roderigo, awarding Desdemona a sexual energy and talent for intrigue she utterly lacks, making a brawler out of a placid Cassio, releasing a ferocious moral reserve in an otherwise half-cynical and realistic Emilia, and goading Othello into barbaric primitivism.

Even Iago's adaptability has its limits, however, and nearly everyone else is allotted only one major change. Having already gone from suffering warrior to romantic lover, Othello balks at cuckoldry. Except when drunk or whoring, Cassio sticks narrowly to his courtly training and its view of women, both compatible with the typical soldier and future governor of Cyprus. Unable to accept the role of betrayed father (father-in-law to a Moor), Brabantio simply dies, though the agitator in this case is not really Iago, who only serves as publicist, but Othello. The Venetian hierarchy is thoroughly settled into its customs and either applies ready-made mechanisms to translate one thing into another—Othello's elopement into a legitimate marriage, for instance—or expresses shock and wonder at the strange things it hears. Like Venetian society at large, it is too collectivized to be knocked off course.

As in other wit contests, Iago's skill in manipulating people consists partly in his passing from specific matters to the governing schemata that society has codified in its several tongues. As he later argues in agreement with both his urban contemporaries and literary misogynists, is it not true that in "Venice they do let God see the pranks / They dare not show their husbands" (3.3.206–7)? And is it not also true, he asks Othello, that Desdemona in particular "did deceive her father, marrying you" (3.3.210)? If so, she must be betraying him now. That is the logic of custom and the pointedness of language that penetrates respectability. Equally important to sophistry's skirmish with logic, Iago's association of words as far apart as "pranks" and "God" prepares for a further twist in logic as the husband who discovers those pranks sits in judgment on loose talk and the behavior it reflects.

Although others too bring forth packaged observations either from common speech or literature, Iago possesses not only a greater store of them but the most adept capacity to link thin evidence to causes, which can then be followed by Othello's construction of still higher causes in keeping with the heroic ethic. The parlor game, to return to it, is symptomatic of these subtle infiltrations of levels both in its departures from mimetic character and in its tampering with motives in the gray area that rhetoric usurps between reason and intuition, also in this case between logic and the wizardry of love. When Iago exits from the game by striking down the Petrarchan house of cards he has just erected, we are reminded that social and literary conventions can be given unexpected application, as they will be climactically when Othello makes his removal of Desdemona into a public service.

Othello's transcending of the courtship Iago pushes toward satire frames the other end of the interlude. In one of his better moments, the higher mode Othello carries about with him is shown to emerge not from sonneteers or from what stereotypes teach us to expect but from an impressive un-Venetian style. His importing of a different range of language into Venice and Cyprus is the play's most comprehensive forcing of the stylistic issue next to the prolonged third act. Even so, the speech he makes upon landing can also be performed as rhetorical inflation. Certainly no staging of the play should prevent it from implying another kind of formality—matching as well as contrasting to the parlor exchange. The lovers after all greet one another in public and offer a set recitation—close enough to an aria that Boito and Verdi could translate it almost intact into near-Wagnerian music. The circumstances do not permit the intimacy of a Romeo and Juliet. Yet these lovers obviously do not have the canny and ironic stage presence of Antony and Cleopatra:

> *Oth.* O my fair warrior!
> *Des.*   My dear Othello!
> *Oth.* It gives me wonder great as my content
> To see you here before me: O my soul's joy,
> If after every tempest come such calmness,
> May the winds blow, till they have waken'd death,
> And let the labouring bark climb hills of seas,
> Olympus-high, and duck again as low
> As Hell's from heaven.
>   (2.1.182–89)

This greeting underscores the guileless devotion of someone just beginning to understand how thoroughly he has changed from battlefield to love-story romanticism. Shakespeare gives the lovers prompting for that operatic note by resounding the storm motif and recapitulating the declarations of the council. Although he puts the preceding byplay to shame, Othello is clearly unguarded, and subsequent events show his command to be illusory. It is not quite parodied here, but the juxtaposition of any two styles causes the judgment to pass both ways. In the return fire from the parlor game, Othello's elevation of tone and the formality look if not inflated at least inflexible. Such grandeur could go unqualified only if the entire decorum of the work were rescaled to fit and no Iagos were around to exploit its assumptions. As it is, we are again advised to be on guard both against the prejudicial assumptions of either common or chivalric language and the distortions of the romance temperament. And we have scarcely begun to witness the apparent straight talk of Iago, the talk that gives the play its momentum and its cynical realism.

In the love duet, Othello lists no particular joys among the marital comforts he expects. That too is a kind of vacancy in keeping with a general lack of undertone and wit. It points up an insufficient sophistication in sexual matters for him to detect the difference between harmless flirtation and serious intrigue. Comic Renaissance husbands never can, but then comic characters are not driven by such powerful mechanisms. Although Desdemona addresses sexuality frankly enough before the council, the reunion turns away from the kind of byplay that would very likely have crept into the talk of almost any other Shakespearean lovers and their observers. In that respect, even their most impassioned poetry says both more and less than they intend. Othello's expression of "content so absolute / That not another comfort, like to this / Succeeds in unknown fate" (2.1.191–93) is unhesitating and resonant, but "absolute" marks an escalation that will prove dangerous to him. He repeats his comforts and content as though marvelling over them in what is simultaneously a rhetorical amplification and a sincere stumbling: "I cannot speak enough of this content," "I prattle out of fashion, and I dote / In mine own comforts" (2.1.196, 206–7). Contentment and comfort put domestic bliss in contrast to the bachelor general's hard fields, but the "fate" that accompanies those fields makes romance and stoic assumptions work better there than here. As Bernard McElroy has pointed out, Othello's former imprisonment has the effect of making love's gifts seem too fragile to last. One is *supposed* to suffer in such a world. His arias are keyed to a tragic pitch, and any experience that feeds into them must rise to it. An implicit familiarity with death accompanies that fatalism, the intrusion of which goes some way toward explaining Othello's response to Iago—as though he knew all along that some treachery was waiting for him and he for it, armed with principles.[7]

Style alone obviously cannot tell us all this, and I am not trying to make the linguistic screens so thick that we have trouble seeing the impersonations through them. But Othello's style does prepare for the emergence of a more and more vicious Iago and an extraordinary contest of levels and built-in biases. It is not as though Iago the assassin were the actual creation of Othello's nobility and Desdemona's dedication; morally speaking, Iago is the responsibility of Iago. But in another sense he *is* the product of the play's overall design and of Othello's quest for grandeur. A shrewd man of many campaigns like Iago, with his knowledge of the competition for place that leads inferiors to observe their superiors closely, is especially suited to work on blinded social predispositions. A peripheral question is whether or not a love so highly wrought could have survived the domestic translation that the other levels of Venetian talk lead us to expect. But that question we never have to answer, since Othello gets hold of wifely betrayal before married life can develop. The glimpse of tranquil days is just sufficient to make the erasure a felt loss, with something of the effect of Verdi's setting Iago before a background of innocent children's song and Desdemona's expressions of joy.

Othello's display of new domestic bliss in the Cyprus arrival heightens a number of other contrasts as well. Desdemona has less to say than her husband, but the long increase of love she expects suggests a plausible direction for maturation to take, given time and nourishment. In the offing is the unfolding of a deepened womanhood already impressive in her self-defense before the council. Cassio's elaborate courtesy has a minor place as attendance on the public figure she must also become, as a delicate interplay of private devotion and public rhetoric. Iago's rhymed wordplay and innuendo earlier and his insertion of an aside here—"O, you are well tun'd now, / But I'll set down the pegs that make this music" (2.1.199–200)—establish a secretive counterpoint to both the polite world and Othello's signature on courtship. Altogether, the scene presents open but incompatible directions for love to take through a dangerous field of associations partly social, partly literary, into which Iago begins to lob explosive insinuations. The styles form into jostling opposites that narrow in the third act, where charges and countercharges are gradually sucked into one maelstrom. The emotions of that vortex get more powerful as Othello enters the upper register of suffering and reaches for a tragic poetry that cannot be dragged completely down by the act it rationalizes provided that it comes to recognize that act for what it is.

The Courtship of Desdemona and a Double Crossing

Actors onstage do not seem to be delivering themes the way words on a page do; instead they issue biases, motives, and interpretations. In the extended exposures of reading we find actor-executed emphases growing less commanding and literary features more so. It is also true that reading, however acute and repeated, does not visualize a theme as a gesture or a set does, nor can it manage the crowd-pleasing byplay of a Polonius or the affective power of a Hecuba. Thus performance sacrifices verbal cross-reference and its specific memory to the emphatic moment and its affective momentum. The difference has a history in the estimation of probability in *Othello*, which is compelling in the theater under the dominance of serial feeling, unfolding at an accelerating pace, but in reconsideration raises troubling questions. Othello's change is chief among these. But other changes are also, if not unexpected, inconvenient to character reading and convenient for the play's movement toward a given end: Cassio's momentary change, the initial one in Desdemona that catches Venetians by surprise, and the play's taking on of seriousness as it advances from the romanticism of the newly married couple to the wit contest of the second act and on to Othello's assault.

The exchange between Cassio and the clown at the beginning of act 3 marks another oddity in that sequence. It too is a kind of interlude that plays on the entertainment-demonstration theme, no doubt appealing to those who have grown drowsy since Iago's drinking song last roused them. Both the parlor game and this episode are minor and quickly slip past us, if indeed a director stages them at all, but in retrospect they have the added importance of dramaturgic puzzles. They lack any notable metaphoric pattern or paraphrasable content, which reading normally uses to rescue lagging passages. Nor are they at all necessary structurally or remarkable in any way for setting a tone. In a play concerned with Othello's sifting of evidence, however, both comment on hearing problems. As I indicated, the first thing one notices about both transitional scenes is their contrastive function. Where the great wind of the tempest drops several leagues in Iago's command performance in the first, the windy words of the second one parody the agitation he orchestrates. It is typical Shakespearean technique to deposit several levels in the clowning variants of a paradigm.

He does so here with the concern for protocol and the thresholds between incompatible zones of value and feeling. In a bid to restore harmony, Cassio misapplies another convention of courtship. When Desdemona's expenditure of words on his behalf (an attempt to harmonize a discord) troubles her husband's ears, she too keeps at it untactfully. Once Iago has set down the pegs, one party cannot quite get in key with another no matter how sympathetic the relationship. Cassio and the musicians issue harmonies that change into discords in the passage through the window. Those harmonies arrive all noise and disturbance. The mistranslation is accompanied by intensification, the offensive music becoming a headache as Cassio's misdemeanor becomes a felony and an assumed infidelity a cause for murder. The difficulty seems to lie in specialized signals and the sensitivity to them that training nurtures. It reminds us of how often in the play noise is an irritant and everyone is on edge for tonal adjustments.

No single incident marks the change from comedy to tragedy, but Cassio's ill-timed serenade begins the act in which the play passes the point of no return. The incoming evidence begins to register well up on the scale of vehemence. The apparent comedy of the first act finds people inclined to hold to limited types of the kind that Rosalie Colie and Albert Cook label for us—vice in Iago, the courtier in Cassio, the gull in Roderigo, the outraged father in Brabantio, the helpful kinsman in Gratiano, the statesman-general in Othello, and the innocent bride in Desdemona—a collection filled out later with the maid Emilia and the prostitute Bianca.[8] Among other things these provide predictable reactions. We know that by stage convention a gull will be tone-deaf and blind to certain things; the jealous man will mistake his clues and overreact to them; the romantic heroine will amplify her lover's voice. Each such type is thus a stylistic emphasis and selectivity that the play uses to pick its way through the possibilities of ambiguous statements. What people hear and react to becomes motive for act; what they miss is left to the marginal exchange between playwright and audience, some of which joins the poetic subtext. By the end of act 4 all the types of *Othello* have assumed sinister functions. Neither Othello's marriage nor Cassio's drunkenness would be of sufficient magnitude to predict the change were it not for the play's suspicious edginess. For two acts, Iago is mainly an opportunist who does not appear to have Othello's total ruin in mind. Othello's later vehemence fulfills the promise of his earlier poetry, which awakens the ear to large dimension as it reaches for another pitch, as though in the passage he encounters a magnitude of suffering implied earlier, not by anything he has done but by the poetry. What prepares for and marks the critical turn, then, is stylistic as much as causal and suggests that what conducts the play forward is a policy imposed on hearing, a transformation enroute of music into discord.

The reception of Desdemona is the critical case. In pursuing Othello's perception of her through several stages, Shakespeare allows her very little direct influence, especially from the third act onward. After her sympathy toward Othello's suffering (a masterful tuning of one personality to selected data from another in the romance key), she is singularly without either argument or poetry except for the willow song. She is simply unable to translate what he says into what it portends. She finds him issuing what seems mere noise and understands the fury but not the words themselves. That disengagement heightens our uneasiness at the momentum Iago and Othello generate without check from her, since when the false image is strangled the real Desdemona will die. Any solid evidence or genuine obstruction could break the trance and upset the timing Iago must maintain; but so locked into irritation is Othello that nothing can make him hear or see the other sides of what is presented to him. He eventually stifles her attempt to pray in the play's most blatant unhearing, although he cannot stifle the "Commend me to my kind lord" that comes so forgivingly and weakly from the dead.

Presumably imagination and susceptibility to the adventures of others work the initial transformation, and Othello's narrative on that change renders the play's first account of truly attentive listening. Far from notes turning sour in passage, Othello's words ride a romantic conveyance full of supplementary meanings. Desdemona's imagination, the receiving amplifier, is somewhat specialized. It enables her to see something in Othello's outdoor life and is akin to his own flight from reason (if beyond it in generosity and compassion). But it too is unarmed by wit and does not help later to defuse his misperceptions, as Rosalind's capaciousness or Hermione's reason might have. The very idealism that generates the romance leaves her unalert to warning signs. When she finds herself under siege, even Emilia's coaching cannot bring her up to dramatic parity. In leaving the others behind them in their escalating nightmare, Othello and Iago close off a private world governed by the suspicious reading of evidence and drag her into it. She is still talking in the original style of innocence, still trying to receive the rest of the world on the wavelengths that bring in stories of rescues from pirates.

The mood of her interlude music in the willow song sets up even as it delays Othello's entry into the bedchamber and prepares her for meek passivity by providing a substitute for rejoinder. It suggests that, when dramatic exchange breaks down and what two people say becomes an irritant, the recourse borders on solipsism. The song's sad romanticism suggests a taste for the exotic that in retrospect comments on her initial attraction to Othello. Insofar as it is premonitional as well as retrospective, it fixes attention on the victim and frames Othello's rage. Such a song underscores the frailty of romance and its ballads, and Desdemona thins to a wisp in it, even as the music works on the audience to generate pity. Shakespeare goes out of his way to stifle exact parallels between the word and her plight and thus to limit the applicability of the song. Whereas Desdemona is caught between Emilia's pragmatism (which weighs infidelity against its rewards) and a jealousy that judges by a rigid idealism, the subject of the song is the victim of a philanderer, crushed in the common way by a cynical lover whom everyone understands.

Desdemona's initial transformation, which comes before the play opens, was apparently the product of a similar susceptibility. Much of the first act concerns reactions to the difference it has made in her. To Brabantio as the inflexible *senex,* social forms seem nature itself. In the light of the Moor's impact, however, those forms are clearly too narrow to grant even a modest maiden freedom of imagination. She tried to incorporate a new commitment into the framework of her breeding:

> My noble father,
> I do perceive here a divided duty:
> To you I am bound for life and education,
> My life and education both do learn me
> How to respect you, you are lord of all my duty,
> I am hitherto your daughter: but here's my husband:
> And so much duty as mother show'd
> To you, preferring you before her father,
> So much I challenge, that I may profess,
> Due to the Moor my lord.
>   (1.3.180–90)

The formality of "noble father" and "do perceive" announces her allegiance to hierarchy and decorum, as does the loading up of honor diction in "respect," "lord," and "duty." Forcefully but dispassionately put, such discriminations apply the brakes to Brabantio's runaway assumptions, no less by the formality than by the message. They compose a public rhetoric without resorting to the plangency that chivalry often assumes when its standards are assaulted. She is not sorry for what she has done and does not assume the breach to be irreparable. Duty remains duty, honor honor. The capturing of the very life and education Brabantio has given her for "the Moor my lord" is witty without parading its cleverness.

Desdemona does not go into detail, but we can imagine reasons that even a dutiful daughter would not confide her feelings to Brabantio or a public council. The precedent of her mother's marriage clinches the case. The only complaint left to Brabantio is the racist one Iago has worked upon, which he chooses not to elaborate here. Required to explain a little further, she is again as persuasive in evidence as she is formal in style:

> That I did love the Moor, to live with him,
> My downright violence, and scorn of fortunes,
> May trumpet to the world: my heart's subdued
> Even to the utmost pleasure of my lord:
> I saw Othello's visage in his mind,
> And to his honours, and his valiant parts
> Did I my soul and fortunes consecrate.
> (1.3.248–54)

The talk of heroines in love contributes the consecration, honor, and valiant parts and the somewhat weakly emphatic "Did I my soul." But showing through these is a tougher common touch. The confession of sexual submission, the recognition of "downright violence" to her upbringing, the well-assessed cost in terms of father and family show that she has considered her decision and will stick to it. Her consecration goes some way toward satisfying protocol while respecting privacy and scanting her violation of filial trust. The answer to Iago's otherwise telling parallel between her deception of her father and her likely deception of Othello is clearly implied to any rational and trusting mind: to take a suitor is no violation of her obligations. In the one case, her character, though altered in the public eye, can be trumpeted to whatever prepared hearing such things find in the world of gossip; in the other, a transfer of affections would require a quite different kind of concealment and a subtlety that she lacks. The distinction is not particularly fine, but it gets lost in Iago's maxims about courtesans and romantic fatalism and in Othello's rush to conclusions. "I saw Othello's visage in his mind" is the anchor line. It locks into a simple declarative sentence the powerful reception of what she regards as the total person.

The most tangible sample of what has worked the change in Desdemona is Othello's reconstruction of the courtship, which has much in common with ballads and a little even with the willow-song sentiment. Although his narrative has been frequently interpreted, I will cite it at length as part of the play's first formal hearing and as a love story to set beside the blazons Desdemona commands and the ballad's conventional betrayal:

> ... I spake of most disastrous chances,
> Of moving accidents by flood, and field;
> Of hair-breadth scapes i' th' imminent deadly breach;
> And being taken by the insolent foe;
> And sold to slavery, and my redemption thence,
> And with it all my travel's history;
> Wherein of antres vast, and deserts idle,
> Rough quarries, rocks, and hills, whose heads touch heaven,
> It was my hint to speak, such was the process:
> And of the Cannibals, that each other eat;
> The Anthropophagi, and men whose heads
> Do grow beneath their shoulders: this to hear
> Would Desdemona seriously incline;
> But still the house-affairs would draw her thence,
> And ever as she could with haste dispatch,
> She'd come again, and with greedy ear
> Devour up my discourse; which I observing,
> Took once a pliant hour, and found good means
> To draw from her a prayer of earnest heart,
> That I would all my pilgrimage dilate,
> Whereof by parcels she had something heard,
> But not intentively. I did consent,
> And often did beguile her of her tears,
> When I did speak of some distressed stroke
> That my youth suffer'd: my story being done,
> She gave me for my pains a world of sighs;
> She swore, i' faith, 'twas strange, 'twas passing strange....
> She loved me for the dangers I had passed,
> And I lov'd her that she did pity them.
> This only is the witchcraft I have us'd.
>
> (1.3.134–69)

Nothing in this narrative suggests precisely the kind of rhetoric Iago professes to hear in one who with "bombast" has turned aside Iago's "three great ones of the city" (1.1.12–14). Though "insolent," "idle," and "antres vast" are unusual, no witchcraft is evident in them. The language is that of Greek romance made into fireside yarn. If anything is obscure about it, it is Othello's interpretation of the different invitations from Brabantio and Desdemona and what their initial interest was. "It was my hint to speak" and "pliant hour" sound as though he required no great urging. His eagerness to "dilate" could mean that he began to love Desdemona or that he relished the spellbinding power of the telling. Certainly both parties are open to unusual adventures. The focus of the council too is supposedly not so much on the substance of Othello's autobiography as on the method of courtship and whether or not its spellbinding played by the rules. In any case, for once listener and performer were attuned to each other, and we glimpse the meeting of minds that susceptibility prepares and language enables. Having listened critically while the outer audience listens to the listening, the council decides that if Othello was beguiling it was in innocence at first and within the permissible calculations of love later. Everyone except Brabantio can be brought to understand the game—the invitations, the way love grows and supersedes filial relations, and the way life in the deserts excites the imagination of a Venetian maiden.

Yet the narration is far from being the transparent window of the mind that Desdemona takes it to be. The ways and means of representation rule out as well as bring in. Othello gives each image its heightening adjective—disastrous chances, moving accidents, imminent deadly breach, vast antres, insolent foes. "Idle" is what desert become if one personifies their inertness and projects human affairs into them. The charm of the speech comes largely from the strength of such qualifiers and from an occasional rise in style, as in mountains that touch heaven and the greedy ear that devours discourse, both typical animations. As a man of disciplined action, Othello balances broils and repose. He notes shapes, postures, and actions as he has noted Desdemona inclining to hear and returning to hear more. But his noticing just such things and not others slants the narrative and may be a danger to him in the proximity of Iago. If he has encountered a Cressida or a Thersites, he does not take notice of them and like Hector might not recognize them.

Othello is one of the notable participants in Shakespeare's continued dialogue between heroic traditions and the idiom of romance. He inserts a literary performance into a volatile Venetian situation that can itself make use of such a chivalric figure in its present turmoil. How is one to imagine Othello's manner working its enchantment on such sage and serious listeners? As the dramatic re-creator of his own narrative, he includes a sufficient man-of-the-world poise and acting ability to impress a group that has already seen enough of his judgment to make him its military chief. That the moment is agitated helps open the Venetian doorway to an alien, but the Duke's response suggests that Desdemona has not been abnormally vulnerable to spellbinding. His conclusion that "I think this tale would win my daughter too" sounds like a guide to our reaction as well as a comment on the credibility of her change. The secret no doubt lies partly in the combination of adventure and aftermath, as the original stir of Othello's life and its first presentation passes into a retrospective mode suitable to urbanity. Othello puts the excited ordeals of the past through the syntax of retrospective calm, recast as recitation. The lived ordeal and the new love thus return as echoes. But the calm is by no means stagnant: Othello would naturally be struck by the vast stillness of the desert as he would be by the quiet of a maiden never bold and the promise of a permanent tranquility. These stirring events mark the crisis of the biography and the transmitted energy of the narration.

Like the rest of Othello's narration and its focus on dangers, the account of how love has grown sounds modest by comparison to the garish illegality Brabantio suspects. Not until love is threatened do we see how much more it contains. "Pity" is the closest permissible emotion a maiden could express; that word comes from a neutralized vocabulary that screens off sexual attraction. Othello in turn is not one who can love only what is devoted to him (as some critics maintain). Having been induced to love, he discovers later that not to love breaks down the new self he has garnered up, here set out for judgment. Each has risen to the other in moving toward the style of the Cyprus greeting, the style Othello cannot go back on when Iago engineers the triangle. The authenticity of what Othello describes is partly confirmed by Desdemona's loyalty to him under trying circumstances. In tying "her duty, beauty, wit, and fortunes / In an extravagant and wheeling stranger" (1.1.135–36), as Roderigo picturesquely puts it (as though he has heard firsthand of men whose heads sprout from their chests), she has swept past the differences between the stranger and the debutante. Having done so, she discovers that neither past training nor current affections tell her what to do next, when domestic comedy and romance slide into baffling accusation and sidewalk pantomime.

Social Unease and Othello's Initial Hearing

Othello's first establishing of a tone comes in response to Iago's attempt to capitalize on any uncertainty he may be feeling about Venice by playing up his accusers and feigning an impulse to stab them nine or ten times himself. Othello's "'Tis better as it is" tells us that he is not too easily excited and forces Iago to start over again with a comment on Brabantio's "scurvy and provoking terms" (1.2.7). Where one might expect anxiety in an alien who may have offended an adopted society, Othello maintains a statesmanlike demeanor not easily reconciled with his later instability. His second response uses the standard vocabulary of chivalric reputations and a rhetoric somewhere between public address and confession:

> Let him do his spite;
> My services, which I have done the signiory,
> Shall out-tongue his complaints; 'tis yet to know—
> Which, when I know that boasting is an honour,
> I shall provulgate—I fetch my life and being
> From men of royal siege, and my demerits
> May speak unbonneted to as proud a fortune
> As this that I have reach'd; for know, Iago,
> But that I love the gentle Desdemona,
> I would not my unhoused free condition
> Put into circumscription and confine
> For the sea's worth.
>
> (1.2.17–28)

It is just such speeches that critics use to expose the soldierly pose. The language is marmoreal and self-congratulatory, and its reduction of Brabantio's racism to spite lacks something in perception. However, one would expect Othello to concede the case, and nothing truly condescending toward Iago appears in his reply. Although he realizes that people exchange favors, the word "services" is without a hint of bargaining. We get a fuller notion of what he means by both service and reputation when he recalls his defense of Venice against the "turban'd Turk" (5.2.235) and turns his hand against himself. Even in the first act, however, we can see that he is not timid in backing a preconception. That readiness shows in the certainty of the opening speeches: "I know," "I fetch," "I have reach'd," "I love" (although the latter is seated in a somewhat complicated conditional tone). "Circumscription" and "confine" mark narrower boundaries than his breeding and his adventures prepare for, but in weighing the life of the open field and sea against a cramping domesticity, he has fully accepted the cost.

Since no one can claim stature apart from society, Othello's concept of service, along with the stiffness of that concession, marks another side of his vulnerability. Unlike a Donne or an Antony, he does not think of sacrificing position to love, nor does Shakespeare give him an intimate language of feeling free of its public settings. To be compatible with a career that depends upon assigned posts, the marriage must be acknowledged by the state. He regards himself as thoroughly *of* society. His native royal siege was obviously not the same as the hierarchy he now serves, but he has held it back as a trump card against criticism and can play it now. If his language hovers somewhat awkwardly between self-defense and pomp, as though he were already before the council, an Elizabethan would appreciate the careful gauging of place and lineage and the fact that concern for reputation in an alien society is not a vanity in an older warrior unlikely to start over again elsewhere. What a confession to a close friend might have evoked is left for the imagination; Othello has nothing of the range of loose conversation in Hamlet's lower register.

All told, the situation is strained and uncertain in generic signals. The postponement of "put" in the last sentence, the ornateness of "provulgate," and the suspension of sentence parts suggest an inflexible man using dignity as a shield, but justifiably under the circumstances. It is worth noting that people in Shakespeare's histories who speak in the archaic terms of royal siege, chivalric pride, and fortune (Troilus, Richard II, and Hotspur) are more susceptible to a fall than those who speak more incisively and perhaps hold back a little. But in these and the other early speeches, Shakespeare does not go so far as to suggest pompousness. He merely gives sufficient hints of a stage performance to qualify the integral self with performance selves and to suggest that Desdemona's reading of the mind is incomplete. Any such frailty that we spot we can be sure Iago will also, since he is commissioned by the play to identify blindness and aggravate differences. Given the passions that are eventually stirred in Othello, we come to realize that, like the eruptions and the music that changes on the way through windows, he is volatile. Altering one layer alters others. For the moment, the chief apparent dangers are his failure to recognize differences among forums and his basing of self-defense on a reserve of credit that he takes to be assured. Other aspects of vulnerability are left between lines in what we overhear of greatness more or less as Desdemona does, "by parcels and not intentively."

Although any assessment of Othello's initial standing can be accused of overlooking evidence if it does not take into account other speeches, such as the surprising summary of his parts, his title, and "perfect soul," I'll pass by those that seem to argue for much the same version of his dignity and his failure to engage different levels of conversation. We can see clearly enough without them that in everything he does except judge Desdemona he assumes a valid showing of inner worth, simply received for what it is. If that confidence is too close to Troilus's belief in truth's simplicity and Lear's belief in public speeches, the first act nonetheless allows it to proceed unchecked. Because his soul is "perfect" (trained to enact truth), he has made progress with those who judge him and believes that this case too will find a sympathetic hearing. But with so much deliberate obfuscation coming from Iago and some prejudice in the Venetian view of foreigners, he cannot count on an accurate reception.

Othello himself is an untrained listener who becomes the chief examiner in the crucial cases and proves to be the greatest destroyer of truth's simplicity. No one is more dedicated to single-minded loyalty than Desdemona and no one less capable of accepting her version of it than he. That amounts to a stylistic double cross: he coaxes her into accepting his large dimension and then allows that dimension to be recaptured by Venetian gossip. In its native province of social opinion and scanty evidence, reputation stands somewhere between the actual self and its casual perceptions abroad. He is singularly ill-equipped to operate in that half light. Like the formal dignity of his diction, the special order of metaphor bears upon his capacity to render judgment when the offense strikes close to home and prompts associations that defy logic. An early indication of these metaphoric links hovers in the command,

> Keep up your bright swords, for the dew will rust'em;
> Good signior, you shall more command with years
> Than with your weapons.
> (1.2.59–61)

The tone must be peremptory to counter Brabantio's "Down with him, thief!" But the context does not explain the full resources of the language, which uses distilled wisdom as a shortcut to moral ascendance. The speech's dew and bright swords make it another of those that in performance give us a full-voiced personal presence but in reading reach for associations from further off. "Bright" and "for the dew will rust'em," while adding nothing substantial to the statement, open to view the motives of his assailants and their poses as such, so that in reading we become aware of the mockery of postures.[9] Othello in effect is recasting the players in this Iago-arranged farce in more appropriate parts, halting one playlet to initiate a more modest and civil one.

As a professional warrior, Othello does not fight over trifles. He is capable of building up causes, but only in what he considers justifying circumstances. His two remarks thus subordinate military to civil values and advise a behavior in keeping with a gentleman's code, which he crystallizes in the maxim and decorates with the proverbial twist. Indeed, in reverencing age and position, he is almost more Venetian than Venetians, as he is later in defending marriage and taking action against himself as an enemy of the state. The addition here is the aesthetic attachment to sparkling swords, in both the adjective and the figure, which makes them so visibly a part of the soldier's glory. Suspended in air, the bright swords set up an expectation for use that receives further attention in the farewell to battle, the weapons that Iago maneuvers Cassio into wielding (before he turns them against Cassio himself), and the instrument of Othello's self-slaughter.

The associations of that first line, however, range beyond any reinforcement of Othello's scorn for ostentation or compressed saying. We can only wonder about their origins in a mind that also makes skin into alabaster and finds magic in handkerchiefs. If these likenesses are akin to genius in skipping past logical thought, they also operate beyond Othello himself in the signals from author to reader having to do with the tarnishing of bright things. Failing to heed that metaphoric weight hinders us from seeing that Othello's nobility and monstrosity are opposite sides of the transport based in metaphoric category-crossings. The image is like an unexpected note dropped into a sequence; it alerts the ear to like deviations from tonal regularity still to come. In taking in the momentousness of such phrases, we again find it hard to attribute all the resonance to Othello, although it fits well enough the idiom Shakespeare assigns him. Othello's language not only sets him apart from other tragic heroes in Shakespeare but suggests that, despite his present judiciousness, such a man will never sift carefully through moral confusion or be at ease with "What wouldst thou write of me?" and serenades by Cassio.

Rendering Judgment

As Heilman and others have helped us realize, Othello is not at his best in sentencing Cassio, Desdemona, and Iago.[10] We need not entirely drop our reservations about the Venetian council to see that its rendering of a verdict sets a higher standard. In a play that deals in gross deceptions and errors, the most telling thing about the council is that one has to labor to unearth its dubious assumptions, whereas Othello's are obvious to everyone. His important decisions are practically all the products of haste. He misjudges Iago, Cassio, and a Desdemona whose truth is so obvious that it should take overwhelming evidence to dislodge it. His verdict on Cassio ("never more be officer of mine") is unsettling both in its severity and in the short-circuited course he takes to it. One important witness (Roderigo) is missing and another (Iago) commits perjury; Cassio is not self-possessed enough to know what has happened and thinks he is guiltier than he is. A sounder judge would have dropped the "never more," which comes from offended dignity and the romantic idiom. Since a court-martial is not totally different from normal deliberations, we might expect investigation and reasoned argument; instead Othello issues the edict of a field commander setting an example. His misreading of the Cassio-Bianca episode is more serious. Shakespeare prepares for it, or has Iago do so, as carefully as he leads Troilus to spy upon Cressida. In Othello's mind Cassio and Bianca substitute for what Iago cannot present directly without the "tedious difficulty" of showing lovers "bolstered." Seductiveness provides one legitimate likeness, but whereas in Bianca it travels the street, in Desdemona it is unaggressive and is meant to attract only one man. The difference is again not a subtle one.

An avalanche of crumbling forms and assumptions follows from these misjudgments, which undermine foremost Othello's command of himself. He has not much more than said "Fear not my government" than Iago realizes that "trifles light as air / Are to the jealous, confirmations strong / As proofs of holy writ" (3.3.327–29), in demonstration of which Othello returns distraught and issues one of his absolutist proclamations:

> Avaunt, be gone, thou hast set me on the rack,
> I swear, 'tis better to be much abus'd
> Than but to know't a little.
> (3.3.341–43)

The balancing of *much* and *little, abused* and *knowing* looks precise, but the measured phrases and the "avaunt, be gone" mark a passion grown melodramatic. Other statements, all of them notorious in Othello criticism, practice an odd combination of formal dignity and disturbance, as in "I had rather be a toad," cited earlier, and in the similar outcry later:

> But there, where I have garner'd up my heart,
> Where either I must live, or bear no life,
> The fountain, from the which my current runs,
> Or else dries up, to be discarded thence,
> Or keep it as a cistern, for foul toads
> To knot and gender in! Turn thy complexion there.
> (4.2.58–63)

Thus might say the preacher or Job, if his sufferings, too, were domestic. Dungeons are obscure, and to live on dungeon vapor is to lose the fame that goes abroad as reputation. Honor is the nettle. The "current" of the second passage has not yet reached the power of the Pontic Sea, but Desdemona as a fountain of life is virtually Othello's flowing forth of mind and heart, his visible emblem. Both images realize that bottling up and imprisoning lead to festering; both read like manifestos halfway axiomatic. Although the mind that fastens upon them is not the same as the one Desdemona describes to the council, its plunge into the grotesque is not totally out of keeping with antres vast and majestic mountains. It has simply been infiltrated by Venetian suspicion and the defense of private property.

The sustained note of Othello's farewell to war gives an even clearer measure of his tendency to skip links in the evidential chain. Let us consider it at greater length and juxtapose it with Lear:

> O farewell,
> Farewell the neighing steed and the shrill trump,
> The spirit-stirring drum, the ear-piercing fife;
> The royal banner, and all quality,
> Pride, pomp, and circumstance of glorious war!
> And, O ye mortal engines, whose wide throats
> The immortal Jove's great clamour counterfeit;
> Farewell, Othello's occupation's gone!
>
> (3.356–63)

Readers often take this plangent note as unmistakably "Othello," as indeed it is when we set it beside anything from Macbeth, Hamlet, or Lear. Hamlet's meditative subtlety and aggressive wit are less hypnotic in meter and parallel in structure. Macbeth's guilt and awareness of his deep offense to the natural and the social order give him a more introspective turn and bring us much closer to his point of view than we get to Othello's, which stands a little apart on its pedestal. Lear's association of disillusionment with lust is akin in its obsession with adultery but nothing like in style:

> Ay, every inch a king:
> When I do stare, see how the subject quakes.
> I pardon that man's life. What was thy cause?
> Adultery?
> Thou shalt not die: die for adultery! No:
> The wren goes to't, and the small gilded fly
> Does lecher in my sight.
> Let copulation thrive; for Gloucester's bastard son
> Was kinder to his father than my daughters
> Got 'tween the lawful sheets. To't, Luxury, pell-mell!
> For I lack soldiers.
>
> (4.6.110–20)

Neither Lear nor Othello allows the drama to proceed by its usual exchanges at such junctures, and Lear too has said farewell to grandeur in solo styles. But Lear's outbreak moves in shorter bursts and does not wind up rhetorically. His diction punctures sentiment and manages to be copious without Othello's amplitude or altitude. Concerned ironically with a lost chivalry that in some kingdoms makes being the head of state worthwhile, it is close to dark comedy. Mixed into his rebuke is a social conscience bothered by inequality. His contrasts sharpen into antitheses under the animal concretion of his imagined circumstances. His no longer being a king who sentences and pardons is a reflection less upon himself than upon the citizenry, two daughters and a son-in-law in particular. The distinction between lawful children and bastards hangs on a relatively fine moral point that one would not imagine holding much interest for Othello, whose one suspected case of betrayal is quite enough. The skittish nature of Lear's thought makes it difficult to follow, but despite the crooked trail of associations he adheres to his obsessions: the identification of wealth with obscenity and the incompatibility of either virtue or rationality with lust.

Although Othello's thought is even more preoccupied with the erosion of chivalric conduct and loss of masculine dignity, it does not advance where metaphor leads in this instance but states a theme and amplifies it. Othello too links status to pomp, but for him pomp has a lingering appeal cherished in the energetic adjectives. It is obviously not to be dismissed with "take physic, pomp." Camp followers may sully it a little, but they keep to the fringes. It is less diction than meter and syntactical parallelism that sustain the speech, and less any particular stylistic trait than simply the performative stance and its cadence. The peculiar thing about the regulatory devices in this cherishing of the military sublime is the way in which they raise anticipations that are formally satisfied despite the disruption of thought. Nothing similar happens in Lear's unevenly paced thought and its flashing of emblems. Othello's cumulative force is put to use to engage our feelings even as it keeps a considerable distance from dialogue. Under the sway of the repetition, we proceed to the next point ahead of the speaker and wait for him there, as we would in anticipating a rhyme pattern or the dropping into place of *loci communes*. We are reminded that audiences sometimes interrupt arias to applaud.

Othello's other misjudgments are minor compared to his penchant for size and dimension and drumming of feelings. His dispatch, courage, and personal honor are good military and civic virtues ordinarily; they become dangers here. Thus almost without further frailties or tragic flaws, the play can rely on virtues to be sufficient. But the issue of character is rendered virtually mute by the fact that if Othello were as judicious as Solomon we would not have a tragedy. A truly suspicious, not merely a jealous, man would have squirmed loose rather than wind up to madness and break onto the high plane he eventually reaches.

His grandest aria, "It is the cause," brings him to the next-to-last phase of poetic heightening. Motive and character obviously underlie the judgments it harbors, but again Shakespeare assumes a different hearing in us than in

116   Transported Styles in Shakespeare and Milton

Othello listening to his own self-justification. It is the most deliverable of his speeches and the one that most directly offers noble reasons for wife murder:

> It is the cause, it is the cause, my soul,
> Let me not name it to you, you chaste stars:
> It is the cause, yet I'll not shed her blood,
> Nor scar that whiter skin of hers than snow,
> And smooth, as monumental alabaster;
> Yet she must die, else she'll betray more men.
> Put out the light, and then put out the light:
> If I quench thee, thou flaming minister,
> I can again thy former light restore,
> Should I repent me; but once put out thine,
> Thou cunning pattern of excelling nature,
> I know not where is that Promethean heat
> That can thy light relume....
>   I must weep,
> But they are cruel tears; this sorrow's heavenly,
> It strikes when it does love.
>   (5.2.7–22)

Based on the mistaken Desdemona in whom Othello sees the cunning pattern (both nature's best art and someone clever at betraying husbands), the speech travels all over the universe and spins out among stars, life principles, and justice. It pauses on an aesthetic observation of white skin, as though by smothering rather than stabbing he could put it in a grave without marring it. His sensuous gentleness and his will to choke spring from that ambivalent love and the twisted high-mindedness of "else she'll betray more men," as though the world's honor were in his keeping. The poetry lifts confusion into theatrical proclamation, working partly by rearrangements of syntax and unusual diction secured in the slow pace.

From the point of view of someone trying to juggle dramatic action and playhouse eloquence, such a speech is as right for the formal moment as it is for one whom we catch devising smoke screens of words. Even while what Othello must do occasions the speech, speech delays act and offers reasons for his not doing it at all. To the audience, that such a man could murder now appears possible. We remain attracted to the Othello that could still be, who holds back because he is not totally debased, and are set on edge by the Othello who now becomes a lethal weapon. Such divided perceptions do not blend but struggle as contraries, and it is the poetry that suspends them. Among other things, Othello reestablishes the regret necessary both to his self-deception and to the pathos that is shortly to spring from it when he judges himself. This is after all the speech not merely of a plausible, pathologically evasive wife-killer but of someone gifted by Shakespeare for tragic ironies the play can now proceed to harvest.

Another principle of poetry-action relations is also discernible in this critical moment. As Norman Maclean observes about dramatic form unfolding in poetry, the great tragic speeches in Shakespeare are not usually directly applied in the midst of act, but anticipate an "impending tragedy" or are "assimilations of the event after its impact, like scar tissue after the wound."[11] This is a valuable insight, and we can build from it a sense of the opposite pull of motivated act and bardic vision. Separating word and deed is after all a regular pattern: Hamlet thinks and soliloquizes and then goes on to act (much later); Lear pauses to construct his prison idyll; Cleopatra prepares her exit elaborately, although in this case the instrument of suicide allows her to talk all the way through her application of it. Similar patterns are less common in comedy, but Prospero stages the masque interlude, breaks it off, delivers his comprehensive revels speech, and then finishes his work. Stage people stop and recite or sing and dance, all the while lifting what they do as an ensemble into gratifying readability. Words heighten the intelligibility or the complexity and ambivalence before allowing the impact of the deeds. Poetry tends toward contemplative ends, but what it works upon is act and spectacle. As these head relentlessly toward conclusions, their articulation comes in the interstices.

As long as the poet is content, the partnership thrives. Deeds come with contracted speech, as Maclean continues, because "the immediate moment of tragic impact is [itself] a contraction—abdominal, in the throat, in the mind impaled upon a point" (pp. 111–12). The reason for this difference between the language of punctual climax and language before or after is not so much that to talk and to do are incompatible as that words come forth as the retelling of experience, as its simultaneous making and undoing and its assimilation into consciousness. The telling "carries off" the deed in more than one sense: transforms it, claims it as its own, and finishes it or confuses it. It steadies the will and the nerve in some cases and then reacts to having done so, all the while (for the audience or reader) weaving a tapestry of allusions. The directions of transport are both horizontal (back and forth across the borders of the stage and traversing the gaps between dramatic moments) and vertical, as transfigurations and sublimings of the perceptions that the play as communique offers its audience.

As I indicated, Othello is both judge and criminal, hence the keeper of standards and their victim. Here again the question of hearing is complex. Emilia's judgment is harsher and more reliable than her husband's, but her word too is far from definitive within the stylistic contrasts the play trains us to hear. It serves mainly to set off the eloquence of "It is the cause" and the greater torments of Othello as he comes to the same truth about Desdemona. Emilia has a built-in resistance to romance as well as evasion and sees both Othello and Desdemona through Venetian practice. She alone, among characters who are not merely functional, is without marked elevation or flexibility. The cost of her morality is lack of shading and dimension. That too, like Desdemona's earlier judiciousness, makes for a counterstyle that is useful to the play's comparative idioms but is defective in itself. It speaks, in its place, as a disclosure of Othello's error; but it is not suited for a choral comment on the range of perceptions and misperceptions that carry Othello from "'Tis better as it is" toward "to die upon a kiss."

In his compression of prosecutor and victim in the aftermath of the great irreversible act of the play, Othello himself makes a self-judgment, but it is not much more definitive than the ones Shakespeare stations around him. He has never been strong in introspection or articulate about either love or justice in the abstract. Classifying himself among those who love well but not wisely is as far as he ventures into judicial maxim, and as Jared Curtis argues, whatever one means by loving "well," it is not necessary to love unwisely merely because one loves intensely.[12] But Othello's desire for justice is by no means a veneer to cover jealousy or confusion; it is vital to his suffering and the would-be Solomon element of his eloquence. No other passion except the ones for military life and for Desdemona equals the one he has for strict accounting. When people are not what they seem, he cannot wait to set matters straight, which is commendable on some occasions, self-destructive on this one.

As his critics maintain, one difficulty has been all along that judgment in his hands does not sufficiently accommodate ambiguities and human foibles, partly because whatever comes within range he translates into the categories of his "occupation." Like Coriolanus, Lear, and Richard II, he overspecializes in the mode implanted in him by fetching his life "From men of royal siege." Although we cannot blame him for not using his last few moments to delve further into the flaws, we might wonder at his refusal to recognize at least the salient point—jealousy's twisting of his feelings and the desperate need to end his anguish with murder.

Othello Impersonations

Othello takes his exit in keeping with openness as he understands it, acknowledging such of his faults as he sees. If the chief safeguards against the warp of private perception are the reasonable judgment and the common wisdom of open hearings, affairs of the heart are not ideally suited to these safeguards, which may be partly what loving unwisely means. Love is nothing that others witness with perfect sympathy. It overvalues the beloved and is inherently hyperbolic. Its language slips past rhetoric, which assumes a persuadable audience, into a lyric that in its rapturous extremes forgets all audience. The speech that finishes Othello's story maintains the grace notes and oblique movements that have characterized his authoritarian manner. But a difference is now noticeable. Despite having been "perplex'd in the extreme," he stands in a relatively clear light, free of the murky passions Iago has raised. Although afflicted by the melting mood that "Drops tears as fast as the Arabian trees / Their medicinal gum," he is also brief. His demeanor toward the state is respectful and resigned, which is not unexpected. It seems the time to end the *beguilement* of words, perhaps his greatest susceptibility next to belief in appearances and the frailty of contentment. The final sentence, punctuated by action, reconnects speaker and hearer and allows nothing to detour the judgment that honor dictates.

But as I suggested, that final self-estimate is not any more his to render than it is Emilia's or Iago's. Nor is judgment necessarily more certain in any witness than Desdemona's reading of noble bearing in the mind. It finally belongs to the audience as the witness of all hearings, the observer of styles and reader of poetry, an ultimate court of appeal. Unfortunately, the audience of any actual stage performance is in the difficult position of having to locate the man behind the actor and decide on the relation of the impersonation to the entire literary business. If the nature of presentations and of evidence is more than usually problematic in *Othello,* it is not only because of the special nature of its evidence, where style selects what bears witness and worms its way into the causal chain, but also because of Shakespeare's use of scenes as demonstrations of the evidential process. We are meant to observe Iago's directorial job in making Cassio an unconscious exhibition and to see Othello mistaking staged shows for truth. In place of the Desdemona who is a figment of his imagination we see the true Desdemona. Most of all, we hear the fuller message of an extremely dense poetry.

As such external jurors, apt listeners are offered some extra certainties and some comparative means of judgment that characters lack who stand forth and take their turns rendering judgment, especially if we come to the play from other treatments of love, war, and jealousy. Whereas in *Troilus and Cressida* chivalric assumptions do not survive the onslaught of Cressida, Diomedes, Ajax, Achilles, Pandarus, Proclus, and Thersites, no such pervasive bestiality troubles *Othello.* The deeper flaws reach barely beyond Iago and Bianca, with some traces in Roderigo and Emilia. We have reason to think that Cassio will become a decent if not terribly imaginative governor. Emilia dies loyal to the truth and to Desdemona, which puts her in the company of Kent and Charmian. Othello's view of war is professional and his devotion to Desdemona is praiseworthy next to Antony's conduct of battles and relations to Fulvia, Octavia, and Cleopatra. He is wiser in matters of government than Lear and less inclined to despotism. He is more self-deceived than Hamlet but stronger in resolve. Despite the ravaging Turks who roam abroad, we do not get a sense of armed evils ready to flood through any crack he mistakenly opens. Rather than reinstating a questionable heroics and a bloodletting honor as Fortinbras does, the senior Venetians stand outside the closeted nightmare, ready to close it down. They model a quietly pragmatic oligarchy of "most potent, grave, and reverend signiors," dull, every one perhaps, but not oppressive.

The Othello whose eyes are finally opened must dispose of a monstrous self who has acted cruelly, unwisely, and vehemently. But we can perhaps be more merciful. What the poetry coaxes us to do is distinguish between potential selves that "Othello" could have played (given what the metaphors suggest) and the self that actually performs. That distinction between what is and what could be is not much like anything we apply to real people who lack the opportunity and the skill to create supplementary selves in the resources of poetry. The alternatives include the shadowy figures of Othello's narrative past and intimations of a self whose love of Desdemona causes part of him to resist killing her. These intimations belong to a play of mind behind which lies the something we call authorship. Contrary to his initial views of reputation, the fuller creature of that well-orchestrated language can never be pinned to gesture and act. The Othello of "I'll not shed her blood, / Nor scar that whiter skin of hers than snow, / And smooth, as monumental alabaster" (5.11.3–5) reveals a fastidious reverence that almost to the last we hope to see take another direction.

From the possible impersonations that a richly poetic script can proliferate (like battlefield kings sent out to confuse the enemy), a given performance allows just one to be rendered with sufficient force to carry out a plausible action. Given what the plot instructs him to do, Othello cannot salvage much of what appears in "Put out the light" and cannot finally abide a schizophrenia of noble and monstrous selves. The play's tragic regret lies not only in the error he makes and the pain it causes but in those potentials, denied to the caricature of the jealous husband he becomes. Even critical display must leave many of the possibilities somewhat dim and unmeasured if it is not to give them a misleading prominence. They derive from the supplementary meanings of figures and from echoes of Shakespeare's predecessors and source texts, from Elizabethan cartoon Moors, and for twentieth-century readers from the play's stage history and the history of criticism. The last of these is in a sense extraneous, but no reader comes to a text without presuppositions, and many of the possibilities the play now contains for us come from the wealth of statements about it. The more we work collectively at translating the text into social and psychological coordinates (locatable in either the Elizabethan or the modern world), the more we shore up its status as text, until it becomes a showpiece, problematic and equivocal in direction but rich in overtones.

Othello's language never becomes the star-gazing poetry of a Richard II or Troilus, nor is it extravagantly inventive in the manner of a Berowne. If anything, it predicts the extremity of Lear (without the idiomatic poignancy and the self-realization that comes with Lear's more extended suffering) and the absolutism that Antony and Cleopatra claim for love. *Othello*'s differences from *Antony and Cleopatra* in this regard are nonetheless broad. Cleopatra is the subtle courtesan that Othello only suspects Desdemona of being. Although equally as taken with the unhoused condition of the warrior as Othello is, Antony does not sacrifice the grand scale in turning from war to love. He hopes until the very last moment to have both.

Having said this, I find the discrepancy between word and act in both plays, and in *Lear* as well, troubling. Adjacent moments give us the plunge of the knife or application of the asp and the grand style, or give us Lear's loss of power and discovery of authentic eloquence. But as the words fly up, the realizable social or domestic world collapses, if only momentarily in *Othello*. That is surely a comment on the visions that a society—no doubt any society—is prepared to allow. In these terms, the tragedy hangs upon the combined belittlement that act brings and the grandiosity that poetry makes us see, if not quite trust. The combination makes Othello simultaneously both stoop and rise to murder and Cleopatra abandon one world for another. Othello is not given Cleopatra's hope for a better setting, nor can he be awarded Leontes' sixteen-year reprieve to work through his jealousy to a restored life. After drumming up an almost equal ferocity, Leontes after all settles for redeeming confessions of error and family renewal; Othello has to carry on against those inclinations of a redeemable character. In some ways even Lear has it better, despite the proliferation of his enemies and the fact that his pomp and glory are destroyed not by an illusion of betrayal but by the real thing. The reason is that he is not himself guilty of the final death he grieves, and his relation to Cordelia has after all been restored, if only for a moment.

Othello never has such a moment; he is alone in death except for the thought that by killing himself he becomes a dutiful citizen again. *King Lear* begins and ends by questioning the truth of anything resembling copious speech but submits its critical juncture—that reunion of father and daughter—to (arguably at least) an impressive eloquence. After showcasing noble speech throughout, Othello ends with nothing left to say. He has no second world, having collected all romance and everything sacred into a Desdemona who might have justified his highest encomiums, who instead gets severed from his idealism long enough to have it turn against her and against him. His error finally has been to withdraw his poetry from her, insinuate it into the mistaken motives of a harsh justice, and be left with nothing to arouse it or give it to, and so on to an abrupt, unreflective self-slaughter. The society he leaves behind has had the alien element ripped out of it and shows little promise of rising again beyond the level of its customs and platitudes.

5

Words of Command, Words of Suffering in *King Lear*

>*Lear.*   O most small fault,
>How ugly didst thou in Cordelia show!
>Which, like an engine, wrench'd my frame of nature
>From the fix'd place, drew from my heart all love,
>And added to the gall.
>   (1.4.275–79)

>*Kent.* A sovereign shame so elbows him: his own unkindness,
>That stripp'd her from his benediction, turn'd her
>To foreign casualties, gave her dear rights
>To his dog-hearted daughters, these things sting
>His mind so venomously that burning shame
>Detains him from Cordelia.
>   (4.3.43–48)

Parabolic and Tragic Beginnings

King Lear's fairy tale of the foolish old king and his daughters three is set up for demonstration, if not quite so pointedly as *Mankind* and *Wit and Science* are.[1] Although it launches generic codes on one of their roughest voyages and stages a great number of deflections from both psychological plausibility and parable form, it does not pile up so many deterrents to its announced patterns that we totally lose confidence in our capacity to see what probably will happen. It advances to the several quietuses of Edmund, Goneril, Regan, Oswald, and Cornwall with enough likelihood to salvage moralized purpose, its choppy crosscurrents emphasizing all the more the forward movement that knocks us into them.[2]

Shakespeare can count on the fairy-tale structure itself to raise specific expectations. Because the heirs of the old king are daughters (rather than a Porrex and Ferrex), husbands are being selected to rule with them, and as Elizabethans who remembered the courting of the virgin queen were aware, male suitors bring unsettling potentials with them. Hence the initial attention to Cornwall, Albany, Burgundy, and France. Shakespeare sets the group up in contrasting pairs, one (Burgundy and France) in keeping with the fairy-tale style, the other (Cornwall and Albany) developing in some complexity later. The fable is evidently to be built not merely upon tensions among the three daughters, or between them and a father who extends the father-daughter relation to the king-subject one, but also upon differences of character within paradigm situations. Loyalties to family and state normally come at different times in childhood and adolescence, but they overlap enough in kinship dynasties to be mutually reinforcing. Here the daughters are put in a bind when paternal loyalty is made a test of the right to inherit. Something has to give. Once Cordelia has said that explicitly, we assume that the other two must also realize it but are concealing their ambivalence, which is both the storybook way and the likelihood under a probable psychology.

As to the husbands, a good son-in-law like France can ease the father-daughter problem by disappearing from the play, but Cornwall, turning against his benefactor, is a major contributor to the splintering that follows. That sufficiently reinforces disruptive energies (along with Edmund's forceful self-serving) to escalate the evils of parable into those of tragedy. Albany eventually offers to surrender his share of the rule, once his wife is out of the way and the old king seems durable; but for some time he pursues an ambiguous course. If he sides with the Lear-Cordelia, Gloucester-Edgar alliance, he could conceivably salvage something from the wreckage. But for all we can tell initially, he too may fall in with the opposition. Certainly one possibility left open by the initial setup is a ganging up on the old king. Either little by little, by subtractions from his dignity, or all at once by armies, he is likely to be elbowed aside. Seeing his stiff arrogance, we can predict that he will provide all the impetus such a ganging up needs, provided that the factioning (which we can also almost count on) holds off long enough to focus a collective enmity. One of the graver fears the fable eventually taps is that natural, demonological, and psychological furies will so break down a state weakened by the misgovernance we see at the outset that it will unleash not merely a war of children against fathers but of nature against humankind.

But thanks to the sturdy morality of Kent and the fondness for each other that Cordelia and Lear reveal before they smother it, much more than a disintegrating kingdom is implied in the initial fable. Love is not entirely evident since it goes unvoiced, but skilled acting has no trouble showing it in the excessive disappointment the father and his favorite daughter show toward each other. Filial affection too, then, is converted into a piece of unfinished business possessed of its own momentum. Had Lear been prepared by any former distrust of Cordelia, he might have responded with moderation. His surprise vouches for their past and thus in a sense for their future. The loosening bonds between him and the other two will compose the first phase of his complicated journey back to her. He obviously has much room for repentance and change, which may include renewal. Leontes is much further gone in anger and unwisdom, yet he can be administered to and turned around. A foolish old king will necessarily remain old, then, but nothing forces him to remain foolish. Such growth is less typical of symbolic parables than of tragic protagonists, and it must be paid for; but it is not ruled out by the principles of development we detect in the opening speeches.

Indeed, if Lear is to become a sympathetic figure, he must learn certain things. As his three daughters take one or another path to alleviate the bind he has put them in, he may recover sufficiently to open the doorway to romance. He may head also toward madness, a distinct possibility given the vehemence of his curses. Or he may develop further weaknesses that make him merely pathetic. In the latter case, he would arrive at the catastrophe without passing through reconciliation, although not accompanied by any lasting triumph of his enemies, an unthinkable alternative from any angle. If he is given anything like a philosophic cast of mind and a second chance, he will no doubt generalize about humankind and fate in the Renaissance way, with apothegms and advice, which put poetry to the service of rhetoric as we come to expect it from Hamlet, Othello, and Macbeth. In any such developing sophistication, the audience can be played upon by a variety of social and generic habits—many of them set up to be reversed—and as it turns out tragic education is what Shakespeare chooses to emphasize.

Still further resources for prediction lie within the audience, which Shakespeare plays upon by setting up foils. When Lear finds open to him the very narrow and difficult way back to Cordelia, the pattern of the lost and recovered child serves as an enticement against which the death of Cordelia is posed. If forgiveness is the benefit of reconciliation, Lear's loss of a kingdom and security is the price he pays. These must be stripped aside to remove the safety nets of office and prestige and leave him with *only* her. The inner worth of the cantankerous king and of the daughter who redeems the general curse thus finds its reward not in vengeance or in the survival of status but solely on its own terms, in the reuniting of one inner worth to the other. That sort of reunion maintains a foot in romance and fairy tale, but what follows capitalizes on it to shift to victim-oriented tragedy. The language of recognitions and reestablished bonds gives way to that of suffering.

Most critics agree that Lear's earlier address to the wretches, the exchanges between him and Cordelia in their reunion, and finally the several reactions to Lear's and Cordelia's death come in an improved language quite different from the initial rhetoric. The final phase is marked by the contrast between the sentiment and the victimization. All the later swerves from the normal rhetorical currency of the realm are as necessary to the play's balancing of its books as the painful deaths of Gloucester, Cordelia, and Lear. That the families of the first scene are reconvened as dead bodies in the last, showing no further interest in the spoils to be gained by speechmaking, is just as the initial contrivance has anticipated.[3] Because this is after all, even in the tragic phase, still partly a realm of story-telling, some such ironic restaging of the initial group is entirely in order, if not precisely foreseeable. We recognize its formal rightness in retrospect. Now mute, the ensemble makes the preceding Lear-Cordelia reconciliation all the more important as the climax expression of recovered sentiment. If on the first occasion Lear plays with the authority of kingship and fatherhood, on the last he is totally without these but has the more powerful authority of the worst of agonies.[4]

The Course Through Alternatives

I anticipate the final effect partly to get at what the opening allows and the middle selects for development. What follows the silhouetted future of the first act is not merely the crossing of one pattern by another but disconnections between scenes and the rough progress of speeches, often thoroughly disrupted sentence by sentence. Rewards may accompany good speeches as Lear says, but only so long as the initial rules obtain and everyone agrees to play by them and so long as speech still commands act. When those rules break down, no secure power succeeds them, which means thereafter that very little proceeds as anyone plans, whether the planner has good or bad intentions. The sequence of surprises that follows is what makes it seem that the play is bent upon deconstructing itself. When critics document the play's unlikelihoods, they point to the interim scramble and eventually to the seemingly gratuitous manner of Cordelia's death.[5] Explanations of those unlikelihoods that depend exclusively on motives result in more and more enigmas and tend to reduce the play to dark comedy.

Certainly a babble of styles accompanies the fits and starts and gives some credence to George Orwell's irreverent remark that much of the play is spoken by half lunatics.[6] Although the disorders of language are most prominent in Lear's and Poor Tom's speeches (both full of side entries of feeling), problems with coherence begin with Gloucester's play on "conception" in the first scene and remain until Lear's final bewilderment over injustice. The play questions not only motives but the usual means of expressing and ordering the family and the state, together with the ways and means of romance, tragedy, the morality play, and pastoral that often endorse them. Lear's confidence in the authority of imperative speech would not be unjustified if this were another kind of play. Kings throughout Shakespeare and his contemporaries speak like civil analogues of cosmic rule and go unharmed. But such confidence in the king's vicegerency is based on assumptions that are belied by the context here:

> Meantime, we shall express our darker purpose.
> Give me the map there. Know that we have divided
> In three our kingdom; and 'tis our fast intent
> To shake all cares and business from our age,
> Conferring them on younger strengths, while we
> Unburthen'd crawl toward death. Our son of Cornwall,
> And you, our no less loving son of Albany,
> We have this hour a constant will to publish
> Our daughters' several dowers, that future strife
> May be prevented now.
> (1.1.36–45)

The purpose clause gives the proceedings apparent wisdom: "*that* future strife / May be prevented now"—prevented in an act of saying designed to head off incipient trouble in three competing heirs. Without the continued support of the office that Lear gives away, however, words become merely words. His own "constant" will lasts only a minute. Nearly everyone in the play has similar difficulties in trying to direct the future. Kent calls for the gods to bless Gloucester for his kindness (3.6.5) just before Gloucester's eyes are put out. Regan decides that they have blundered in letting the eyeless Gloucester go about raising pity, and Edmund sets forth to finish the job; he never sees Gloucester again. Indeed, most of the plans hatched by Goneril and Edmund and by Regan and Edmund go astray, but their downfalls come too late and are attended by too much negligence to produce the desired end. Edmund's order for the assassination of Cordelia and Lear is only half carried out before the revoked order too is half successful. Generic patterns do not hold any more firmly than the patterns of the well-ruled society. Cordelia's army stands prepared, moved by love, not "blown ambition," and such armies in literary texts usually win; this one is quickly defeated, which shows that battlefield fortunes cannot be counted upon to make up for political blunders. Still practicing the language of regal command in what would normally be clarifying and settling moments, Albany announces in the Lear manner, "we will resign, / During the life of this old Majesty, / To him our absolute power" (5.3.298–300); but the language of "boot," "addition," "merit," and "honours" has been discredited both by Lear's assignment of boot and honor and by the suffering of wretches.

Some of these reversals again have as much to do with convention and Lear's development from rhetoric to lyric as they do with plausibility. The basic types are the foolish *senex*, good children outcast, good counselors unheeded, connivers, and wise fools; their instruments are maledictions, prophecies, riddles, and sentences. All such types lose or alter their normal functions except the good daughter. Lear appears to be giving way to a surviving young generation but clings tenaciously to the "name and all th' addition" of kingship and ends by surviving his children, if not by much. The good counselor Kent, even while demonstrating integrity and loyalty, behaves foolishly and turns honesty into impolitic aggression, almost totally undoing the sententious good advisor figure. The chief conniver, Edmund, reforms and matches (for a moment) the good brother in generosity and apparently sincere feeling. Fool holds to more or less recognizable offices but disappears as though his role had been cancelled.

These shifts in type and other signals are a good share of what makes it difficult to follow the initial motives through the middle. Fool, the least irrational of the three mad commentators, translates the pillaged kingdom into riddles, ironic songs, and upside-down prophecies. Edgar's initial concealment behind Poor Tom's vexing concreteness places the common logistics of food and shelter in a demonized landscape. Although his invented autobiography includes a commentary on vices and is interspersed with instruction ("keep thy foot out of brothels, thy hand out of plackets, thy pen from lenders' books, and defy the foul fiend" [3.4.96–99]), his sayings do not ordinarily offer usable advice except for the counsel of patience. In the focal characters of the middle acts, then, reason has little power to prevent the further breakdown of the family and the state and is of not much more use in the repair phase. The encrustations of habit must be broken before anything better can emerge, and the breaking is felt as degradation rather than liberation or analysis.

Although many of Fool's apparent enigmas are translatable into advice, his wit is sufficiently obscure to prevent our satisfaction with it. Nothing promising emerges from it except the devaluing of personal worth, a preliminary to whatever better self Lear will eventually discover. The wisdom-in-foolishness that he applies to Lear's imprudence is vivid with analogy, which carries beyond the mere enumeration of catastrophes to visionary panoramas:

> When priests are more in word than matter;
> When brewers mar their malt with water;
> When nobles are their tailors' tutors;
> No heretics burn'd, but wenches' suitors;
> When every case in law is right;
> No squire in debt, nor no poor knight;
> When slanders do not live in tongues;
> Nor cut-purses come not to throngs;
> When usurers tell their gold i' th' field;
> And bawds and whores do churches build;
> Then shall the realm of Albion
> Come to great confusion:
> Then comes the time, who lives to see't,
> That going shall be us'd with feet.
> (3.2.81–94)

Despite elements of common wisdom and utopian thought, Fool undoes the usual purposes of counsel with cynical twists and an anticlimax. His mock prophecy is belied by an *adynata* (a string of impossibilities) that carries everything to extremes, with a touch of Puttenham's *merismus,* a paradoxical "distribution."[7] It varies its parallels by countering expected goods turning evil with a few anticipated evils turning good. Feet should be used with going, but in this kingdom going will be used with feet, as though distances were invented that feet could move. The future keeps down to earth like the style, which moves near the apocalyptic only to stumble. That descent of a normally more high-flying device parallels what is really on Fool's mind, namely, evil daughters seizing kingdoms while former kings live in hovels. Scolding permeates Fool's riddles, and when they twist away from that advice-to-monarchs function they lapse into the pathetic. Here the juxtaposition of second comings with increases in the local crime rate upends propriety while exposing paradoxes as just that, not profound tools for uncovering actual causes and cures. In its confusion of future and past, the conclusion, "This prophecy Merlin shall make; for I live before his time," breaks the dramatic illusion and reminds us that the play comes well after both Lear and Arthur. It reduces the prophet to the choral moralizer. Our chronological sense too is spilled; all is now process and middle without a promised end except for what we still intuit as the necessity of ruin and the anticipated reunion.[8] That gives rhetoric nothing to work toward and leaves poetry without a cathartic release or a tangible vision. Fictions, prophecies, and matters of historical chronicle are so thoroughly mixed that all times reveal the same sins and starved hopes.

The song that precedes Fool's prophecy (a Folio afterthought) also savors the unpredictability of large causes, but in this case in a lyric mode that foreshadows the childlike element of the repentant Lear. It inserts a pausal melody reinforced by epigrammatic sentence. Fool's scolding and rhetoric's reformative thrust are diverted into the attitudinal display of the performer, who more or less transcends the moment in a combination of Mother Goose and traditional ballad:

> *He that has and a little tiny wit,*
>   *With hey, ho the wind and the rain.*
> *Must make content with his fortunes fit,*
> *Though the rain it raineth every day.*
>   (3.2.74–77)

The undone logic mixes Lear's disastrous abdication with the lighter tone of Feste's song in *Twelfth Night*:

> *And when I was and a little tiny boy,*
>   *With hey, ho, the wind and the rain,*
> *A foolish thing was but a toy,*
> *For the rain it raineth every day.*
>   (5.1.398–401)

The logic of both songs is ruffled by the diction and the syntax and reduced to secondary importance next to the plangent longing for more innocent days. Either melancholy intrudes in Feste's playfulness or some comic fragment has strayed into Lear's realm to confound the generic signals still further. Both versions of the song have in common a sentimental pathos, which is a passing mood in *Lear* and a concluding qualification in *Twelfth Night*, a kind of coda sobriety to deepen the festivity. "Hey, ho," ordinarily a ballad heartiness, mixes oddly with the general gloom and the fury of the storm scene. If fortunes *were* really fit, the rain would ease up now and then, even for the witless. But foolishness, being very inventive and flexible, survives unexpected turns; rationality, which has only one or two correct ways to proceed, is shattered by bad luck and blatant injustice. It is appropriate for boys to make light of foolishness in the comedy of Feste or in their nursery days, then, but for an aging Lear the absurdity reaches deeper and the repercussions hurt worse. Although his sudden shrinkage of brains is not responsible for England's rain, he has managed the social equivalent.

For the audience, Fool's play with proverbial wisdom is an early stage on the way to tragic victimage and a better variety of childlike sentiment. The Lear of the middle comes to a similar pseudo-apocalyptic realization when he commands the moral world to be set straight by divine vengeance, as though inner turmoil found external correspondences in storms and the dreadful pudder of the gods. Lear's third-act itemization of sins looks for criminals at large—quantities of them he assumes—whom he apostrophizes from a little deeper into madness than Fool, determined to have justice troop scoundrels off to their appropriate punishments:

> Let the great Gods,
> That keep this dreadful pudder o'er our heads,
> Find out their enemies now. Tremble, thou wretch,
> That hast within thee undivulged crimes,
> Unwhipp'd of Justice; hide thee, thou bloody hand,
> Thou perjur'd, and thou simular of virtue
> That art incestuous; caitiff, to pieces shake,
> That under covert and convenient seeming
> Has practis'd on man's life; close pent-up guilts,
> Rive your concealing continents, and cry
> These dreadful summoners grace. I am a man
> More sinn'd against than sinning.
> (3.2.49–59)

Fool's grand prophecy and the magnitude of Lear's "Rive your concealing continents, and cry / These dreadful summoners grace" reach toward a range of reference that the play tries intermittently. The fiercer evil becomes, the more it opens the way to the eschatology that Lear will eventually put in a finer tone. The general ruin never comes, however. Although cataclysm is supposed to be followed by messianic triumph, we have no indication that it will be, either here or in Lear's later assertion that he will stay with Cordelia until time's end. Despite Gloucester's initial fear that late turmoils predict a final upheaval, the cycles give every sign of continuing. Whoever is in goes out; whatever is on top spins down again. It is true that evil has an inherent disintegration that undoes individuals, but the end of rage, at least of Lear's, is not a final ringing down of the curtain, merely frustration.

Lear takes this judgmental note in complete oblivion of speeches addressed to him, which points up the breaks he makes with dramatic connection in his urge to dictate or recite on a heroic scale. Ironically, one who assumes that men and gods pay attention is talking to himself again in this case. His tantrums and Fool's prophecies have the peculiar status of vignettes. They would not escape dark comedy if a recuperative force were not available through Cordelia's return, which comes independently of anything they do except to get themselves cast out and helpless. The difficulty at that late moment is that new beginnings can find a place only in the imagination's second world, with no chance of materializing. Actual happenings are small, human, sordid, and if they are to be remedied it will not be on a grand scale but in quiet reconciliation and admitted error, in the language of personal confession. The sooner Lear gets over suffering on a cosmic scale and down to Fool's earth, the sooner he will be ready for "I am a very foolish fond old man," "I fear I am not in my perfect mind" (4.7.60, 63), and "Pray you now, forget and forgive: I am old and foolish" (4.7.84). The factual content of those and other statements belies their force and their capacity to replace gnomic riddles with the gestures of the old man bowing to the forgiving daughter.

These toned-down clarifications and touching reversals of "Hear, Nature, hear!" come from a mind that has dropped off to sleep deranged and awakened partially restored, although still unsettled. Behind its tentative exploration of a new tone and lines of affection between estranged parties is a reservoir of implied family history that collects the biography of the king into moments of self-exposure. As his best poetry (except for the broken eloquence of his final suffering), the lines Shakespeare gives him in the reconciliation establish a small sanctuary and a simple order of moral perceptions. As part of Lear's continued illusion of powerful allies, that style drops the nonsense of Fool's prophecy but maintains vertical connections of a noncommanding sort between victims and powers somewhere above.

But before examining the reconciliation itself let us back up to Lear's attempts to court daughters one and two, the parallel dramatic business. Lear becomes painfully conscious that he has lost authority not merely as king but as a speaker when even the most authoritative phrases, uttered in the most forceful voice, cause nothing to happen. His realization of that weakness grows when he finds Cornwall and Regan calculatedly slow in hospitality, in imitation of the "weary negligence" Goneril's servants have already shown. He appeals to Gloucester with all the force a royal "would" can muster:

> The King would speak with Cornwall; the dear father
> Would with his daughter speak, commands, tends service:
> Are they inform'd of this?
>
> (2.4.101–3)

The word "speak" reiterated in altered syntax and delay should, he assumes, pound the ear with sufficient force to drive out obtuseness, especially with its complied synonyms and especially coming from one who has been told that he is everything. But very little of nature or custom backs up the call of this father to that indifferent daughter, and nothing survives of the king's commands to his hidden allies. He may not realize yet that water wets and frail bodies are not ague-proof, but it is clear that the house of a potential friend has been requisitioned and become one of several that close their halls and kitchens to him. Given those telling gestures, which signal the redefinition of all houses and their titles and privileges, what he has left is the threat of noisy hammerings:

> bid them come forth and hear me,
> Or at their chamber-door I'll beat the drum
> Till it cry sleep to death.
> (2.4.117–19)

This is as pointedly phrased and as full of spunk and idiomatic clarity as a cranky ex-tyrant can manage, but it is totally empty. As Regan reminds him, "Nature in you stands on the very verge / Of her confine" (2.4.147–48), although she may not know how many the ways—physical, verbal, psychological.

Still under the illusion, or pretended illusion, that Regan at least does not mean such things and that he can play one daughter against the other, Lear tries a last rhetorical rush before the second act brings him to the end of one alternative. He makes it emphatic that he is not rash—that in the character of the judicious king he still weighs, assesses, and discriminates and will recognize with a father's praise such merit as he can locate. He curses only when driven to it. Any courtly system depends on such recognitions of merit and on what gentility acknowledges as the continued standing of one party with another:

> No, Regan, thou shalt never have my curse:
> Thy tender-hefted nature shall not give
> Thee o'er to harshness: her eyes are fierce, but thine
> Do comfort and not burn. 'Tis not in thee
> To grudge my pleasures, to cut off my train,
> To bandy hasty words, to scant my sizes,
> And, in conclusion to oppose the bolt
> Against my coming in: thou better know'st
> The offices of nature, bond of childhood,
> Effects of courtesy, dues of gratitude;
> Thy half o' th' kingdom has thou not forgot,
> Wherein I thee endow'd.
> (2.4.172–83)

Although this is a little like coaxing down a snarling wolf, memory can at least reconstruct ceremonies that hearken back to the original call for eloquent speeches, as though beginning the public commitment again, less the two ungrateful ones, Goneril and Cordelia. But the hearkening back begins to look futile as the old days move as far off as myth. For his own sanity, he must assume that offices and bonds remain in force and that only the sway has changed. But if they were still effective, there would have been no bandied words or closed doors to begin with. The insults have not been accidental. The blunt answer to his lingering hope for resurrected illusions is another piece of advice, "I pray you, father, being weak, seem so" (2.4.203), a lesson in matching appearance to truth from one who has seized every chance to separate them.[9]

From this point on, Lear has in hand only the fragments of the systematic rhetoric, grounded in the authority of those who assign signifiers their traditional powers—arranged, bequeathed, blessed, or used to curse. Even plainness has only dubious value. The eloquence of misery will bear little resemblance to the wisdom literature Fool draws upon or to the folktale symmetries, although in retrospect the latter forecast this particular futility as the ironic overturning of the initial commands. As John Baxter suggests concerning plain axioms generally, Shakespeare ordinarily defines "the law of our nature" by them, the law that presumably, when all's said and done, has been demonstrated. Where such a style manages to reach beyond reason's distilled precepts into intuition, it usually makes that intuition too "a triumph of condensed rationality."[10] Here, however, neither the containment of evil nor the issuing of maxims is very closely related to the tragedy of Lear and Cordelia. Whatever relation language is to have to social or moral norms, which are always more assumed than prominent, it cannot reunite lawful authority and compassion. Practically all Shakespearean plots, whether in comedies, histories, or tragedies, look first to institutional power to see if it is steady, or, if not, what can be done about it; now nearly finished with his forced diagnosis, Lear discovers the arbitrariness of traditional defenses.

It would be a logical time for him to turn to the third daughter, as the symmetries of the opening suggest that he will, but the severity of the parting says not yet. The maledictions he has heaped upon her lead to extremities of derangement that urge a protracted working out rather than an emblematic shortcut. Falling back on that nursery of old age would weaken both healing forgiveness and tragic repercussions. In a halting of pace, Lear's vehemence first turns against itself and then opens the door a crack upon the madness to follow:

> No, you unnatural hags,
> I will have such revenges on you both

> That all the world shall—I will do such things,
> What they are, yet I know not, but they shall be
> The terrors of the earth....
>   O Fool! I shall go mad.
>   (2.4.280–88)

Coming from Lear, such a device can be a crafty appeal for pity. But this hitch in the indignation is no doubt as genuine as bluster gets. The beginnings of a curse and the terrors of nature break from syntactical hold and scatter. The desire to reform his daughters comes to an abrupt standstill. He must now take another direction, his stumbling toward unaccommodated man having left him stripped of sentence and rhetorical powers as well as dignities.

Before he can find a language to give and to render heart, the chief business of dynasty-recognition romances, Lear must learn the vehemence not of rage (strategic or otherwise), but of compassion. This is a commonplace among those who hold that the play's middle reeducates him, and I assume its general validity despite his relapses. But the tyrant we first see undoubtedly thinks of his abdication as charitable, since leaving the throne early will let his children prosper. His desire to shake the superflux to wretches also needs to be scrutinized closely for hairline fractures between rhetoric and poetry:

> Poor naked wretches, whereso'er you are,
> That bide the pelting of this pitiless storm,
> How shall your houseless heads and unfed sides,
> Your loop'd and window'd raggedness, defend you
> From seasons such as these? O! I have ta'en
> Too little care of this. Take physic, Pomp;
> Expose thyself to feel what wretches feel,
> That thou mayst shake the superflux to them,
> And show the Heavens more just.
>   (3.4.28–36)

Although still in the grand style and still condescending, his acknowledgment of general suffering comes as a new realization. It edges across the boundary between self-deceit and genuine realization of error. Its solitude and helplessness lie beyond the comfort of the voicing itself. The investigation of injustice, the psychology of authority abused and lost, and the imagery of clothing and houses are all beyond Lear's own comprehension. The piety and residual belief in the heavens are incidental to an injustice that will prey on him henceforth and extend the play's anguish. The language is clearly of another order from that of the original speech contest and its maledictions, not just because it builds upon compassion but because it captures the complexity of an arrogant man bowing repentantly. For all his altitude and habitual dignity, Othello never manages anything comparable; and for all his subtlety and inner probing, Hamlet never really escapes the claustrophobic inner family. A fairy-tale stereotype could not absorb so many blows without shattering. The windowed raggedness and unfed sides do not fully counter the grandiosity of "superflux" and of kings standing for heavenly powers, but to his credit, Lear is often graphic where suffering and vice are involved and is growing more aware of castle-wilderness discrepancies and the entire spectrum from pomp to degradation.

The telling point, however, is less the raising of compassion to self-lacerating intensity than the fact that it is too late for Lear to change the condition of wretches. He may reverse his long neglect of them, but they will remain wretches, their numbers swollen by a former king and his followers. The only active recipient of reform is the speaker himself, who has no reason to think that charity demonstrates anything about the heavens or the king's vicegerency. He speaks as a once important man, will go to prison as just such a one, and eventually howl as one. The Lear who proves crucial to the tragic effect is more elegiac and regretful than this one but equally beyond taking care of anything he has formerly slighted.

Schemes for Self-Making and the Discontinous Middle

It is an understatement to say that affairs are not well managed or sufficiently understood in the sorrowful kingdom of Lear. Some ideas have little chance to work out to begin with; others are tripped up by accident in a realm with a sizeable quota of randomness. The wretches who weigh on the consciences of Lear and Gloucester have been overlooked for scores of years. (Nothing has been done for them by play's end and apparently nothing will be.) Cornwall is eliminated by a servant as the side effect of a gratuitous cruelty. The moments tick off while Edgar tells the touching story of his father, until the time to save Cordelia has expired and another promise has been aborted. The more improbable arrangements sometimes succeed the better. Edmund's initial forged letter has everything against it but works anyway, as do Edgar's disguises. Gloucester comes to see a discrepancy between Edmund's casual begetting and what he is, but neither he nor Kent has any way of knowing initially what desperate ventures into theology the adult Edmund will force out of them. Edgar too props up such barricades as "Who alone suffers, suffers most i' th' mind, / Leaving free things and happy shows behind" (3.6.107–8), which must pass for understanding where other interpretations fail. The counsel of patience in "ripeness is all" is a more applicable stoicism, but patience too does not provide explanations, merely a quieter endurance.

That schemers fare no better than Gloucester and Lear is of more comfort to justice-seeking playgoers than it is to Gloucester and Lear themselves. They form or anticipate alliances only to discover that no diplomacy or trickery can repair the social order they themselves have rent asunder. Edmund gets himself in so deeply with the two sisters, their husbands, his brother, his father, and Lear that it would take several expertly timed deaths to extricate him. Failing to tame Lear or to hunt down Gloucester, Goneril and Regan stumble into their graves in a half-comic pursuit of Edmund. Their opponents sometimes do better, but not as they anticipate. Edgar, as the most active dispatcher of messages and arranger of confrontations, succeeds in exposing Goneril and defeating Edmund, but not in saving his father. He sets up the cliff-top deception to cure Gloucester's despair when a better means would be to tell him who he is and what has happened. Some of these misfirings reinforce the self-destruction of the criminals; others set up Lear's questioning of justice and our continued questioning of causes and consequences.

Together with the fairy-tale opening and reassembled group at the ending, a reiterated comic business that risks laughter in the wrong places, and an opposing and balancing of characters that is elaborate even for Shakespeare (France-Burgundy, Cornwall-Albany, Kent-Oswald, Edgar-Edmund, Fool-Cordelia and Fool-Kent, Lear-Gloucester, Goneril-Regan/Cordelia),[11] these halted sequences and miscalculations expose the machinery of the plot and Shakespeare's dramaturgical choices. Does Shakespeare mean thereby to probe the nature of a dramatic action and let it utterly break down before reconstituting one or two personal relations on new ground? Is he concerned as in *Hamlet* and *Othello* with the mishandling of evidence and the crippling lack of disinterested rationality?

The parallel between Iago's ocular proof and Edmund's auricular assurance suggests that the readability of evidence does in fact matter, especially if Lear himself is still testing the evidence of Cordelia's breath when he dies and Albany commands people to "see, see" without giving them the capacity to do so. Considerable emphasis in the second plot falls on secrecy and exposure. Edmund follows up the foolish king's call for impromptu displays of feeling with a challenge to custom worked through intrigue. The divulgence of Edgar to Edmund finishes one pattern of proof and has the effect of conventional recognition patterns. However, the discoveries that weigh heaviest concern the limits of power, not what it is that Edmund comes to see or Albany's fellow survivors fail to see. The main plot hinges less on proof than on public display, which suggests that not what is true but what form an assertion takes and what effect it has are what count. We are not much in doubt about the true nature of Goneril and Regan or the worth of Cordelia. Lear is chided into recognizing them early and has probably never been as deceived by them as he seems at first. He *is* deceived by the disguises of Kent and Edgar, but not to any serious complication or preparation for disclosure. As Albany recognizes at the very end, he still "knows not what he says, and vain is it / That we present us to him"(5.3.292–93), as though the preparations for unmasking fizzle except for the recognition of the true Cordelia. Edgar's revealing of his identity to Gloucester is not presented onstage, so that one key realization of who is who fails to reach maximum dramatic impact after we have been teased with it off and on for three acts. Shakespeare chooses instead to dramatize Gloucester's discovery of Edmund's treachery, and even that is submerged in the pain of the blinding. The one person Lear truly needs to recognize he already knows well enough at one level. Although what one sees and understands informs what one says and how one says it, then, the play concentrates more on questions of command and effective speech than on truths—on *oratio* rather than *ratio*.

One difficulty that confronts both those who would do and those who would philosophize is that the roots of power lie beyond whatever ocular proof one locates. Gloucester makes the play's first run at vague piety in predicting events from extraordinary evidence. Because a plague of overturnings goes against providential care, they seem dark portents: "These late eclipses in the sun and moon portend no good to us: though the wisdom of Nature can reason it thus and thus, yet Nature finds itself scourg'd by the sequent effects.... We have seen the best of our time: machinations, hollowness, treachery, and all ruinous disorders follow us disquiet to our graves" (1.2.106–20). Edmund follows with a version of self-making that is less a counterargument than simply an announcement for the audience's benefit: "The excellent foppery of the world" and our seeking causes in fortune rather than in "our own behaviour" cause us to "make guilty of our disasters the sun, the moon, and stars; as if we were villains on necessity, fools by heavenly compulsion, knaves, thieves, and treachers by spherical predominance, drunkards, liars, and adulterers by an enforc'd obedience of planetary influence; and all that we are evil in, by a divine thrusting on" (1.2.124–31). He is more right than his father, or less wrong, but a philosophy of self-initiative does not explain; it motivates. It is excellent both for dismantling custom and for a play that sets about removing the social props from Gloucester and Lear.

As Edmund's own fate suggests, retribution much as Lear demands from the thundering gods lies in wait as one consequence. Indeed, Edmund's undoing is uncanny: toying with the hearts of women, he is accosted by a righteous husband; a stager of scenes and manipulator of evidence, he is trapped by his former dupe; a forger of letters, he finds the evidence against him a genuine letter. Even where he gets what he wants, contradictions abound in his justification. Ironically, the very title he covets as Gloucester proves his undoing when the chivalric code that goes with it traps him into dueling. If his mind were as generous and gallant as Edgar's, he would not be scheming; if nature were truly his goddess, he would not work a breach of natural affections. But nature does not in fact provide the trappings of Edmund's preferred world of low-cut gowns and furs. The final irony will be that in accepting Edgar's chivalric challenge he not only rescinds these declarations but forgives Edgar because Edgar too is noble. The conscience that emerges in his desire to perform a last good deed finds him trying to finish as the respectable citizen Edgar would want him to be. But the completion of the Lear-Cordelia story breaks off his reform. One pattern cannot be worked out without stifling another. His death is tossed aside finally and with perfect justice in Albany's "That's but a trifle here" (5.3.295).

Any attempt to trace inceptions through to disclosures is hampered not only by the proliferation of causes but by the number of orders that provide the ground for predictability. I identify at least six such orders, each exploited at one time or another not only by rationalizers onstage but by critics: individual desire guided sometimes by reason and compassion, often by the kinds of self-concern and psychic energy that Edmund champions; the family with its built-in cyclical changes in power and balance of good and bad children; the political realm, which incorporates all these and has its own institutional transitions when kings falter; nature or the creaturely world of elements, a force in its own right and a symbolic projection of individual and social turmoil; the supernatural; and artifice, ranging from rhetoric to disguises and performative roles. These are not all sources of motives, but no one of them can proceed very far without taking up the others. The family and state provide molds or structures for psychic energies. Nature and the gods can be either forms or sources of energy and are particularly indeterminable, since they do not announce themselves. Artifice calls on form and generic practice and is inseparable from social custom. All these have their own rates and directions of change—Lear's aging, his daughters coming of age, the state changing at the top, nature's seasonal vicissitude, capricious gods playing with mortals, and overall the governance of the playhouse parable and ironic sequencing of segments in the tragic unfolding. In terms of priority, individual motives can be preempted by family, family by state, state by nature, nature by gods, so that any tracer we put on causes is likely to jump from more definite to more complex and indeterminable levels.

This profusion of orders is not unique to *Lear* or even to Shakespeare, nor does it necessarily add up to confusion. Each order has its rules and its share of the play's symmetries, and indeed on the model of modern theoretical physics it could be that the appearance of confusion is due to hidden symmetry or as yet undiscovered relations. We can see the equivalents of gravity and electromagnetic fields in the moral laws that send villains tripping over their own devices. These work with some observable regularity. What we cannot account for are the weak or strong forces that hinder a rescue or enter as though from a fifth dimension. It is nonetheless a frequent Elizabethan practice to draw simultaneously upon several levels of justification and assume their collaboration, as in "To Penshurst," for instance, Jonson finds both nature and providence supporting the Sidneys from outside while learned mysteries of arms and arts govern from within. The social order surrounding the country estate cooperates willingly with both the outdoor and the indoor orders. Genealogy is associated with a benign topography and its produce. In most apologies for orthodoxy, providence has something to do with patrimonial continuity or discontinuity and thus with poetic symbol-making and the intentionality of correspondences. Since the cosmos is designed for human use, what nature does must also be intended, as much where it is punitive as where it blesses.

Lear has helped make his own world unaccommodating by summoning nature and the gods to the father-king's curse and breaking down the delicate order of priorities and relative powers. The question is whether he disrupts a valid relation of the several spheres or accidentally exposes the fallacy of their collaboration. Whichever is the case, not only do the several orders not combine to set upright again what he has knocked over, but wretches make evident that the elements, social neglect, and possibly the gods have for some time been cutting off the flow of benefits to those who most need them. Jarred from lifelong habits of thought at a difficult old age, Lear finds himself beyond nature and society in what seems a wasteland of randomness, just where his inattention has put the majority of his kingdom all these years. Dire as the breaking up of the civil order is (and the death of Cordelia soon becomes), however, the play would be much darker were it not for his recognition of a surviving kinship with his subjects and his daughter. The greatest symmetry of the play—the parting and reunion of parent and child—holds long enough to set the repentant king emblematically at the feet of the true inheritor, the one who bases her bond on heart and head as well as genealogy. This says little or nothing about what would make a logical political settlement or a theology, but it does speak to the reintegration of individual ego and close kin. It suggests that, whatever else one loses from the bounty of nature and social dignities, one can live within the family bond, the source of the most compelling order, the one most assaulted by the two sisters and Edmund.

Although analogous and intertwined, the play's several spheres are distinct enough to blur that familial reconnection, and the combinations are complex enough to render it temporary. One realm never collaborates with another upon command. It is doubtful with respect to Lear's prison idyll, for instance, that even a reunited father and daughter generate sufficient piety to give any special access to the mystery of things, as Lear's "*as if* we were God's spies" (5.3.17) confesses. The prophecy that "He that parts us shall bring a brand from heaven, / And fire us hence like foxes" is immediately proven wrong, since all it takes to separate them is a captain with hungry mouths to feed. The aloofness from social and political turmoil is also immediately given the lie. To dispense with any of these orders or their combinations is inadvisable to say the least. Edmund thinks he can excise social custom and ties of blood and follow merely the promptings of desire, but both the retribution he suffers and his reform (upon hearing of the reunited good son and father) show that he has not rooted out the decencies of kind or kin.

That the play intends to test what happens when individual spheres of influence are set in conflict is indicated by Lear's conflation of kingliness and fatherhood in the dynastic transfer; that it intends to keep them in turmoil is suggested by their lack of collaboration at the end in the withdrawal of individual will from the responsibilities of rule, the weakened fabric of the state, the limp passing of comments in dialogue, the continued vagueness about where the gods come in, and as always the undermined force of sayings and moral propositions. Edgar announces support for a privately responsive language that does not seem likely to issue commanding principles or new laws or even to speculate further about the nature of nature. Presumably none of these realms falls within "what we feel," which is reductive in its allegiance to pathos and the abandonment of what we think, what we act, or what we speculate. The language of feeling under the burden of sorrow would no doubt be appropriately elegiac and lyric, but no illustration follows. Lear has voiced a good deal of what he feels, quite loudly at first, with bursts of insight and moments of madness in the middle, while continuing to question everything about the social, natural, and supernatural orders all the way to "Why should a dog, a horse, a rat, have life, / And thou no breath at all?" Whereas rhetoric offers a language to champion a given order and sometimes a language of reason to link orders, poetry becomes finally a matter of suffered consequences, not a system of correspondences and orthodox topoi to link the several orders and use one to argue for the others. Dialogue literally makes nothing happen when Albany tries to transfer the rule that everyone once connived to get.

Even while he hopes for a return of the old royal and familial orders, shored up by nature, providence, and proclaimed individual subscriptions, Lear begins to realize that they cannot be argued for very broadly. He never quite understands rhetoric as part of a power game or a social artifice that teaches acting skills like those he puts on the boards initially. The give-and-take in which he finds himself caught up requires reverence for custom and respect for social codes. In desperation he attempts to put that primacy of customary standing as an argument that will be valid apart from nature's indifference to it:

> O! reason not the need; our basest beggars
> Are in the poorest things superfluous:
> Allow not nature more than nature needs,
> Man's life is cheap as beast's.
> (2.4.266–69)

This amounts to a confession that at least three orders are splitting apart, the familial one that should honor fathers, the social one that should honor kings, and the natural one without honors. The roots of his claim run deeper than he realizes, since identity is learned and depends on the reflected esteem of others. If he cannot have privileges legally, his status as former king and current father should guarantee them by the practices of courtesy. When his offices leave him, he has virtually no identity to put into a social idiom. He has accelerated the breakdown of civil exchange with such peremptory commands as "Let me not stay a jot for dinner: go, get it ready" (1.4.9.), which give Goneril the excuse she needs to exaggerate their differences. It is Goneril too who speaks a self-serving truth—but nonetheless a truth—when she remarks , concerning his decision to brave the elements, "'Tis his own blame; hath put himself from rest, / And must needs taste his folly" (2.4.291–92). With some help from a well-meaning but officious Kent, Lear does increase his own discomfort by falling back on nature, which he immediately tries to make into the portents and hurled weapons of the gods. But a mark of the complexity of the questions raised in transfers and breakdowns of dynastic power is that his bitterness is justified, since both Regan and Goneril harp upon his weakness and tie their "sharp-tooth'd unkindness, like a vulture" to an old man's heart. That they too have their rights only shows how little value reason has in dealing with conduct that has lost its footing in any consensus.[12]

As to asking forgiveness and seeking the entirely new way of heartfelt humility, if he learns that way in Cordelia's restored company he refuses to acknowledge it in the exchange with Regan:

> Ask for forgiveness?
> Do you but mark how this becomes the house:

"Dear daughter, I confess that I am old;
Age is unnecessary: on my knees I beg
That you'll vouchsafe me raiment, bed, and food."
(2.4.153–57)

With such scathing ironies he sees family roles either reshaped to fit a charade or sinking beneath the weight of a nature that ages and starves people without pity. Once nature and institutions are broken apart like this, artifice reassembles the fragments according to who has immediate possession of a territory or a title and can pass out the subordinate roles. Not incidental to the concept of a supporting cast, we recall that Lear was setting up nice distinctions in tying his original gifts to courtly display as though a phrase in the realm of manners earned a river bottom here or a forest there, in nature as economics.

We judge a force by how condensed and energetic its particles are. Though Shakespeare shows no great numbers of people marching to war to champion either side, he does indicate the ambiguous positions of retainers and courtiers caught between parties and undecided as to who possesses what rights and powers. No one has enough independent diplomacy to forge a new settlement among the unleashed egos, and no hope is extended for a return to mannerly exchange or a rhetoric that can actually command gods and nature to bless or curse one's progeny. Albany is still making an attempt to command the collaboration of alien orders near the end in returning the monarchy to Lear and awarding positions to Kent and Edgar. His taking Lear's side against his wife earlier is evidence of the inner pull of something like custom and decency—social virtues internalized as personal duty. But that is not a strong enough partisanship in a latecomer to head off the foreseeable end of the two in whom custom and decency are strongest and position weakest.

One result of so thorough a scattering of powers is likely to be a period of solipsistic inwardness or withdrawal, and again Edgar's notion of speaking what one feels, not what one ought to say, may be taken less as a first step toward a cure than as a sign of privacy seeking a way to come forward as though in a kind of maimed confessional used as a social opening. To say what one ought to say is after all to be guided by custom and ceremony, by manners. A workable balance of sincerity *and* role-playing would allow acknowledgments of both audience and inner truth, assigned social roles and inherited or trained worth. It would still elicit a speech that says one thing while hinting others, in the constant coding and decoding that is civil conversation. Edgar's rhetoric of feeling is likely to be flattened in that confessional mode or lapse into the bluntness of Cordelia's opening speeches, the play's first serious signs of withdrawal, as one who is naturally dutiful and cordial is forced to speak to herself about what she feels and cannot adjust to what she ought to say. She speaks something less than her full feelings and something different from a tactful evasion of the issue, her integrity having been threatened by the overly rough pull of family and state. In the wake of Lear's tragedy, the rhetoric of command and the language of felt connections still look very far apart. If what one feels depends on what one sees, does it include a share of Lear's resentment toward the selection of rats to live and daughters to die? Relief that at least the worst is over? The middle has spilled out consequences in an open field of such possibilities without moving toward a reforming collective energy or new collaboration of the several orders. The best relations, the ones that make the tragedy tragic, will have to be lyricized apart from, rather than in the midst of, society.

Lear's recognition of a surviving kinship with Cordelia is tellingly couched in the continued motives of abdication, which clear away sufficient debris from the motives that link individual status to the social order to allow a different Lear and Cordelia to emerge. The play finds its main recompense in the value of that personal bond shorn of the usual institutional environment. Lear does not find a workable exchange in what he proposes to Cordelia, not even in "we'll talk with them too" (5.3.14–15). The give-and-take he proposes would be a demonstration of manners without the status he went mad trying to keep. Where the still powerful king has spoken in astonishment at violations of decorum, this more appealing figure marks the passing of all connections between merit and station.

The Ending and Lear's Double Kenosis

Whatever motives we concede to Gloucester for going to Dover to find a cliff or to Edgar for leading him there, plot parallels urge us to look at the surviving Gloucester primarily for what complements Lear's restoration to Cordelia. Both fathers awaken in a different mood, and in the normal symbolism of death and rebirth that awakening extends a promise. Renewal *is* what we get in the recognition, in both figures—recognition of which offspring are good and loyal and which ones treacherous. But the journey of each is also to remoteness from the castle world's dynastic properties. Keeping Gloucester alive and outcast sets up another reunion as well, with Lear, the symmetry of which requires that Edgar stay unrecognized longer than we might otherwise expect him to. The interview is between the two lost ones before their relocation in the good graces of forgiving children, while they can still measure each other's misery. Both that interview and the reunions themselves build up the sentimental and didactic side effects of outdoor ferocity and add to the play's commentary on injustice, seen now as a gathering point for several collaborative evils.

A further cross-referencing is the disintegration of Edmund's relation to Goneril and Regan. In that respect, both plots reinforce lifelong as opposed to fleeting attachments of the kind that begot Edmund and remind us that, beside injustice and very much parallel to it, fornication is now Lear's theme. To attribute these advantages of timing and balance to the interworking of the mixed orders would be risky, since no compelling psychological, divine, or social mandates keep Edgar from revealing himself or cause the detailed parallels between the two fathers. Indeed, to look for probable as opposed to artistically demonstrative behavior in any of the key confrontations of the last two acts would be akin to reading the opening scene as though it were not a demonstration, and the concluding one as though it were not its structural rhyme. *Lear* never lets us forget for long its playhouse contrivances. A tightly integrated dramatic ensemble would demand a society or a social subset able to maintain its bonds. As it is, passivity, ineffectual words, silence, and individualized poetry give the fragments of society their compelling moments in groups of two or three suffering in comparative isolation.

The course that sentimental attachments take in both the Gloucester and the Lear plots straightens out what has been diverted by the original forced show of feelings and moved by undercurrents that pull Lear and Cordelia toward each other in the three acts of betrayals. Expression depends on give-and-take and the self-evident value of filial love. When love's exchange flourishes for a moment, it has nothing further to do with justice. The destruction of Lear and Cordelia raises anew the questions that Edmund's self-interest dodges in calling on Machiavelli. Such questions as why the good perish, always unanswerable, are asked again not to lead us into further speculations but to intensify the loss. Reasons for the assassination of Cordelia are removed by the subtraction of anything that Edmund would gain by it. The future state too is largely irrelevant to it.

We need perhaps to be explicit at this point as to why arguments for divine retribution should be put aside in the punishment of the wicked and the reunion of Lear and Cordelia. To push for a show of force from that sector over and above the others would raise unanswerable questions about the slaughter of the good and the timing of accidents, and it would divert attention from the direction-giving errors of the others and from the motives of their heirs. The parallels are set up to facilitate the anatomy of self, family, and state.[13] Where Lear draws upon piety, it is on his own authority, which is as dubious as his calling upon nature and the gods to sterilize his daughters. At the same time, saying that the vicious meet their ends by the inner logic of their own crimes sets a precedent difficult to turn off when Cordelia's end is in question. Even Lear's earlier grief over losing the name and additions of kingship has to be rethought in the wake of his heavier sorrow. The first loss could be deserved, but not the second, although both are the repercussions of his initial mistake. The latter is the last in a series of ironic turns that can be sorted into four phases: the devotion between father and daughter assumed at the outset, followed by the first reversal and the long-delayed reconciliation, and finally the culmination in Lear's uncertainty about Cordelia's death. These phases are dialectical and contrastive and thus illustrate in the plot what the pairing of characters sets forth in the agents and instruments. If the structural focus is the initial wounding and the fifth-act healing, the stylistic one is the drama-rhetoric-poetry relation. The disintegration of negotiable relations thus frames the only bond that reaches very far into lyric. The anatomy of folly in all these balanced contrasts probes the social and psychological center while the reunion is being withheld, until the slate has been wiped clean and can be reinscribed with a new language.

To return to the beginning of this repercussive chain: Cordelia as a dutiful daughter is in most respects opposite to her sisters and Edmund, and the introductory Lear is opposite to the concluding one. The framing makes the sisters Cordelia's foils again at the end, where they are unobserved, unmourned, and slain by their own malice—in short, unable to contribute the slightest fraction to the tragic effect except by contrast. Having put themselves forward as claimants to power while their sister goes toward obscurity, they recede as she returns to center stage. Look at these two and at that one and the way of the text becomes clear in broad outline. It is not even obscured by Lear's final vacillation or the various ways one can take the dismay of the survivors. All the more to show the pieties of brotherhood and loyalty to fathers, Shakespeare adds Edmund to scoff at the virtues of Cordelia and Edgar and pay for it, as we have the glib art initially to set off the speechlessness of true love and then its poetry—a contrast made prominent by Cordelia's "Love and be silent" and "Love's / More ponderous than my tongue" (1.1.77). The language of the reunion corrects all faulty or incomplete versions of the filial bond, even Edgar's bond to the blind Gloucester, since that reunion is compassionate but unknowing on one side.

Actually, Cordelia even at the outset speaks twice as many words as her sisters combined (until the latter are closeted at the end of the scene). The difficulty is not the lack of words but words not graciously applied to her father's request and thus not usable as a ritual prolonging of the affection. Lear has a considerable investment in the "nothing" that brings about the first turn, which sets up a language of disowning calculated both to motivate and to retard the reowning. Let us sample it again with the dialectical stages and the misuse of links among the several orders in mind:

> Here I disclaim all my paternal care,
> Propinquity and property of blood,
> And as a stranger to my heart and me
> Hold thee from this for ever. The barbarous Scythian,
> Or he that makes his generation messes
> To gorge his appetite, shall to my bosom
> Be as well neighbour'd, pitied, and reliev'd,
> As thou my sometime daughter.
>
> (1.1.112–20)

The legalistic will-making of the opening statement carries over into this strident undoing, which makes barbarity a religious rite and sweeps away bonds of kin and kind, the supportive sanctions of family and state, the measuring of devotion by gifts of house and home: this sometime father would as soon dine with cannibals as see again this sometime daughter. The point with respect to predictive form and the collaboration of plot and poetry is that, because the wounds are inflicted by an eloquence sprung from passion, they must be healed by a superior eloquence sprung from renewed feeling. The movement of events is governed as much by the linguistic subtext as by anything we can perceive through it. By psychic economy as well as formal logic, the wounds inflicted by passion must be healed by renewed feeling.

Shakespeare follows the initial set of contraries with mock trials, wit contests, interviews, and the riddles of the upended kingdom. The value of the repaired father-daughter bond is set up almost point by point in parodies of Lear's nursery, the sisters' reduction of "kindness" to a minimal roof, and then the removal even of that. By the end of the second act, Lear has abandoned dignities and by the end of the third has discovered his unreciprocated and helpless compassion for the wretches. His silence about his misbehavior toward the one who redeems the general curse is broken only in the reunion itself but is then amply disposed of. Thus when that relation too is destroyed in the last phase, the causes no longer have anything to do with the internal flaws of the opening. The final Lear and Cordelia have their own previous behavior as a foil and make their mutual recognition a reversal as well as a restoration, a reversal in manner, emotion, and speech. This sequence of ironies is finished by the forced separation of father and daughter as political victims just when they are most closely bound spiritually, which drives the final wedge between social rhetoric and the poetry of familial sentiment. Both the reunion and the catastrophe finish patterns: the two sisters have accidentally strengthened a bond they wished to sever; the restored bond is too authentic to be further damaged by misunderstandings but is even more vulnerable than before because Cordelia and Lear are so ill-suited for power. Virtually the dying gasp of a residual malice kills Cordelia. By then, through the process of cleansings, Shakespeare has removed all interfering emotions: we cannot lessen the grief of Lear by hating Edmund or by championing further causes. We have been encouraged to devalue social exchange only to find that the bargain between an intimidating Edmund and his hireling is sufficient to complete the final stage.

According to this reading of the play's weights and measures, the link between the reunion and the catastrophe has to be especially tight, and the dialogue Lear proposes in the prison speech must serve as prelude to his final outburst. The reasons are similar to those that make his curses and removal of blessings prelude to the better exchange. Despite all the absurdities and misleading gestures of the final act, indeed because of them, Lear's addresses to Cordelia alive and dead are locked together as the fullest building of the play's language and the plot's interior, affective logic. Whether the drama empowers the poetry or the poetry advances the drama, they are inseparable, not as act and interpretation or as speech enforcing deed, but in a squaring off. Onstage listeners become almost as much audience to Lear's appeal as we are. Insofar as they are drawn into the Lear-Cordelia exchange, reduced to a second-world portrait of its permanent form, they must be drawn out of their own purposes and engagement of the places they have schemed to get, much as Edmund in hearing the narrative of his father's death succumbs to the sentiment he had thought to get beyond. The pathetic or elegiac Lear is by now doubly emptied—as a king no longer capable of rule and as the former father no longer full of curses. This new Lear finds a sanctuary in Cordelia when he has given up expecting one. Other attempts to understand the world—other rhetorics, aphorism, apocalyptic prophecies, loftiness—are thus more or less beside the point in the reversal constituted by "Let's away":

> We two alone will sing like birds i' th' cage:
> When thou dost ask me blessing, I'll kneel down,
> And ask of thee forgiveness: so we'll live,
> And pray, and sing, and tell old tales, and laugh
> At gilded butterflies, and hear poor rogues
> Talk of court news; and we'll talk with them too,
> Who loses and who wins; who's in, who's out;
> And take upon 's the mystery of things,
> As if we were God's spies: and we'll wear out,
> In a wall'd prison, pacts and sects of great ones
> That ebb and flo by th' moon.
> *Edm.* Take them away.
> *Lear.* Upon such sacrifices, my Cordelia,
> The Gods themselves throw incense. Have I caught thee?

>He that parts us shall bring a brand from heaven,
>And fire us hence like foxes. Wipe thine eyes;
>The good years shall devour them, flesh and fell,
>Ere they shall make us weep; we'll see 'em starv'd first.
>Come.
>
>(5.3.9–26)

Unlike other pastoral retreats, Shakespeare's ordinarily promise the autonomy of a group, with messengers from outside to keep them aware of their remote boundaries and distinction. Thus in Arden, Prospero's island, Bohemia, and the rest, an exiled group keep in touch with the political world. Here the court, a place of gilded butterflies, is in almost every way opposite to the walled-in sanctuary. While its members seek power, these two, if they follow Lear's instructions, will scorn it. Where society's members are numerous, campaigning, and governed by vicissitude, where society harbors aristocratic privilege and prepares for the return of those who are out, they will be intimate, reach into the protective eternity of the gods, and practice the ceremonies of courtesy. Their exchange will derive from the opening ones but will be purged of stratagems. The consciousness of the father will drop its authoritarian note or be rewritten as caustic satire and apocalyptic imagination, still engaged in the spectacle of ruin but not immersed in it, using it in fact as a conscious sacrifice of one way to another.

In making the cell and the castle world so antagonistic, Lear uses nearly a dozen parallel conjunctions in a highly paratactic and rhythmic compiling of unsubordinated, equally fulfilling activities gathered under the powerful new "we" that constitutes this kingdom of two. Their cell will be a perfect topography for the shutting out of all alien matter and the admitting of merely news of such, none of its ferment. The possibilities spill out one by one as they occur to him and generate a rejuvenation of the kind that we are reminded sometimes flares up in literary deaths just before the final closing of the eyes. Lear is often unquenchable in anger or in enthusiastic anticipation of the honors he is to bask in, even at times in the recording of hellish suffering on the wheel of fire; here his energy goes into improvising a quite different kind of chivalric honor, trapping Edmund meanwhile in his villainous role and leaving him only the language of blunt command. The contrast works more against Edmund than against Lear, and Lear uses it as a springboard for a second level of affirmation that includes still more defiance, the trait most in evidence between the earlier and later Lears.

Shakespeare sets off this reconstructed bond, which virtually makes them canonized for love, with the lost "name and all th' addition to a king" and with false expectations and dashed hopes. Only fondness counts. Those who are without an equivalent loss, as Edgar realizes, have not suffered so much or spoken so well. Indeed, those without an equivalent bond have virtually nothing left to say—have had in fact nothing comparable to say from the outset, so unsatisfactory are other sets of mind imbued with the struggle for power and deeply penetrated by rhetoric. Edgar is notably lacking in such speech even to Gloucester, which is perhaps what saves him in the odd economy of a play that permits ascendance into lyric only when roots in power are plucked out and the affectionate heart is crushed.

But a lyric countermovement based on destroyed place admittedly does not go far enough in explaining the apparent chance of the last stage of the Cordelia-Lear story, at least not to the satisfaction of anyone bent on salvaging rationality or a broader community of survivors. The difficulty with moralizing is that it tends to trivialize both the restored relationship and its destruction. Indeed, probably the play's most encompassing irony next to the undoing of Lear-Cordelia in the very moment of their reunion is the defeat of philosophy and eloquence by spectacle. The final display is the speechless Cordelia and the incoherent Lear, whose wordlessness underscores the fragility of the previous lyric. The dead Cordelia and the distraught Lear invalidate the most recent runs that Edgar and Albany have made at Puttenham's "gnome" or "sage-sayer,"[14] which is no more than we expect from what we've seen of temporizing. This is not to say, however, that the assassination of Cordelia also invalidates the imaginative other world of the prison speech, which is Lear's way of making up for a grievous error by dreaming what he would do, given the chance. Injustice too puts a premium on the bond it proposes and thus on the unattainable might-have-been. The final spectacle needs that proposed ceremony to arouse sympathy for a figure whom the play has kept at a distance from us.

The prison speech includes its own counterspectacle to match the carrying in of Cordelia's body and the earlier give-and-take. In the gestures Lear proposes, character, thought, diction, and spectacle would be rejoined in a panoramic immunity to time. The ritualists would become wise, indifferent chroniclers of secular power, in on "the mystery of things." As it is, actual spectacle breaks loose in its most brutal form, having found its prime target not in who's still in but in their victims. Shakespeare has already given the shattering of ceremony and propriety shock effects in Cordelia's initial surprise, the stocking of Kent, and the plucking out of Gloucester's eyes. He does so with renewed force in the depositing of the bodies in the circle, not arranged this time around a contested throne but disinherited and most dead. These visual incidents, especially the last, are staged with too little detachment to be assimilated into ritual or to be sanctified like holy sacrifices. Gloucester's speech upon being blinded, for instance, does not convert bleeding sockets into symbolic pageantry. The recognition he is given of Edmund's villainy is virtually passed over with "O my follies! Then Edgar was abus'd. / Kind Gods, forgive me that, and prosper him!"—after which, although Edgar does survive, the kind gods allow Regan's "Go thrust him out at gates, and let him smell / His way to Dover" (3.7.90–91).

Lear's carrying in of Cordelia is heralded by "Howl, howl, howl" and ends with his notoriously difficult "Look on her, look, her lips, / Look there, look there!" (5.310–11). Most critics conclude (in the wake of reactions against Bradley) that the recognitions accompanying these outbursts are without redeeming consolations. So they are if we hold that the visionary Lear is set up not to put a premium on tragic sympathy but to be further tormented. If Lear actually thinks she lives, the discrepancy between his knowledge and ours complicates that sympathy with irony and reminds us of his other mistakes. If he is gesturing toward proof of her breathlessness (a possibility I find hard to rule out), his suffering takes an agonizing final twist and uses the last few words merely to gesture toward a mute spectacle altogether lacking in the liveliness of praying and singing and telling old tales. Either way the dramatic spectacle is not softened by eloquence but recalls the other phases of the father-daughter relation. Ironically, the lyric that ascends to the sanctuary is designed for dialogue as well as for more highly wrought benedictions and prophecies; Lear's final address to Cordelia looks like dialogue but is directed to one who cannot respond despite his refusal to accept her silence.

Whatever Lear's gesture may suggest about his state of mind, for the audience Cordelia's speechlessness points up the end of communication, bad or good. It is appropriate for the play to finish its anatomy of acts and words with such a gesture—enigmatic beyond deciphering but nonetheless charged with meaning as the conclusion of the language subtext (except for Edgar's concluding admonition). In unmatching merit and fate, the numerous deaths drive home the isolated value of imagination's kingdom, which in the grace of the redeeming daughter eludes social embodiment and transcends it in the hypothetical place. Imagining the idyll makes the two good citizens better sacrificial victims; their victimage guarantees the sanctity of the personal bond. Nothing otherwise escapes hazard and malice. Were Cordelia to walk out of prison and welcome Lear to her kind nursery, any audience that has caught the tone of the play and the force of its best verse should feel cheated, not merely of the victimage that tragedy cannot do without but of the paid-for reunion, by the confirmation of the worst by the best and of the best by the worst.

In sum: the play's attention to the cross fire of poetry and drama dislodges Lear's initial idea that eloquence goes with social dignity and authority. Shakespeare subsequently undoes all other versions of mastery and power and their public idiom, so calculated to spoil the expression of sentiment and heartfelt worth. Although the poetry of confessed filial devotion has *authenticity,* it has no *authority,* or even a martyrdom to offer up to a higher cause. It merely guarantees the closure of an affective form with a definitive ironic loss. The most crucial revelation of the play—the voiced, no longer hidden relation of fathers to their reclaimed children—comes when it cannot be paid for any further or (in Lear) spoken for any more feelingly. Since Albany, Kent, and Edgar cannot rise to an equivalent sentiment, they are not allowed to speculate further about what has gone wrong or about how to understand the play's several orders. Nor are we encouraged to think about what might happen if the gods were aware of heartfelt desires or if society learned to remodel itself on the love of kin. A well-founded new state would only attenuate tragic emotion in liberalism.[15] If in most tragedies we see what is as what has to be—if particularly in sacrificial tragedy we take the carrying off of victims as a purging of rampant egotism—Lear's unanswerable "why" and Cordelia's silence leave the tragedy untranslatable, leave it in the spectacle of ruin and the stilling of its one-to-one address.

6

Going Between in *The Winter's Tale*

> both your pardons,
> That e'er I put between your holy looks
> My ill suspicion.
> —*The Winter's Tale*, 5.3.147–49

Romance and Politics: Speaking Daggers

Perhaps having enough built-in strangeness and wonders to provide the overall ambience of romance without needing a great many flourishes, *The Winter's Tale* takes relatively few extended poetic detours outside of Bohemia. It gives its reunions—its climax incidents—a prominent place in a realizable social accord. The more obvious intrusions of the unbelievable—largely from a bookish world of romance—are Leontes' two reversals, Apollo's oracle, the wondrous bear-eating of Antigonous and the storm-perishing of his crew, the exact timing of the opening of Perdita's fardel, Time's interlude, the prince-meets-foundling fable, and Hermione thawing into motion. To such adventurous elements the play adds Autolycus's wheeling and dealing in comic ballads, the dance of the twelve satyrs, Florizel's protestations of love, and Leontes' asides, the latter two being contrasting versions of love's extremes. The exceptional in style is assigned primarily to soft hearts and sentimental moments or used as a foil to these.

For the rest, the key events of *The Winter's Tale* come more without than with eloquence and are set off more by structure and incident than by style. The key point here is that no unrealizable desire beyond the reclaimable order of Sicilia is housed in a subversive poetry. The play seems committed to reconstructing what Leontes has torn asunder. The events themselves, however, sort out roughly into diptych opposites that are not easily combined. Both settings, Sicilia and Bohemia, are foreign countries that alert us to figurative leaps and abrupt turns, but Bohemia is clearly the more exotic of the two. Leontes' initial misperception is largely domestic, and his kingdom returns to stability once he does. In between, the concerns of romance show in the disruption of one plane by another, again more by act than by word. What the abruptness and the contrasts bring to pass is a revision of perception, which begins on one level and drops or leaps to another. No evidence of identity and status, for instance, can be transparent where innocent byplay has the supplementary meanings Leontes sees in every gesture in the second scene, or where Apollo renders judicial opinions. Camillo's duplicity with Polixenes, Paulina's later hiding of Hermione, the pretended diplomatic mission of Florizel and Perdita, and the disguises and trickery of Bohemia suggest that the jealous king is not altogether wrong to expect revelations that make ordinary things suddenly startling. It is as though catachresis and far-fetching were forced into the ordinary through a dramaturgical policy of estrangement, without troubling the surface of the otherwise decorum-governed discourse that convention assigns to kings, courtiers, and shepherds.

The structural crossing nonetheless has a few stylistic repercussions worthy of our attention. Besides the chiastic linking of the familiar world and winter's tales, the play gives each component a limited linguistic range that puts it in contrast with the others. Sicilia ranges from madness (at the dangerous extreme of idiosyncrasy) to Paulina's shrewish judgment. Bohemia ranges from Autolycus and the shepherds to the voice of authority in Polixenes and of love in Florizel. Sicilia looks initially as though it will hold to courtly elegance and diplomacy, but because of Leontes' error it immediately fails to do so. As the inserting of Polixenes among the shepherds indicates, Bohemia also has rough edges to go with its romance wonders. The play's few markedly poetic passages and most of its fairy-tale elements belong to shepherdom. Yet Bohemia too maintains decorum, especially in Polixenes and Perdita, and sets formality against the clown, the old shepherd, and Autolycus.[1]

Even while Bohemia is still a long way off, we know that something is decidedly not right in the Sicilian combinations of high protocol and stress, as in this stiff appeal to Leontes:

> Beseech your highness, give us better credit:
> We have always truly serv'd you; and beseech'
> So to esteem of us: and on our knees we beg
> (As recompense of our dear services
> Past and to come) that you do change this purpose.
> (2.3.146–50)

The trial issues other such fossilized statements, such as "Hermione, queen to the worthy Leontes, king of Sicilia, thou art here accused and arraigned of high treason, in committing adultery with Polixenes, king of Bohemia" (3.2.12–14), and so on in the way of lawyers and judges bent upon making dire things bureaucratic. Despite Leontes' banishing of normal relations and disenfranchising of urbane language, only Perdita is actually forced out of her element for any length of time, and even she does not sacrifice decorum. Indeed, *The Winter's Tale* is noteworthy among Shakespeare's comedies in making its two realms "brotherly" despite their obvious differences. It supplies a Bohemian way to contribute to Sicilia's cure and to bind the two together. By keeping to the higher ground of manners, Perdita maintains her eligibility for the return, even as her role as shepherd queen contrasts to her mother's hosting. Within the stratified order of royalty, counselors, proper heirs, and shepherds, the gentle hearts of romance look for common sentiment among the ranks until the play can find a way to integrate its scattered parties. The additional question raised by the restoring of the royal mother, her daughter, and the king's friend is what to do with the extra dimensions of language that come with the Bohemian adventure. When people return to their Sicilian relations, do they assimilate that adventure? Does shepherdom leave an imprint on Perdita? What does Autolycus as maverick bring to the reunion?

Delegates and Representatives

To answer such questions about carryovers from Bohemia requires attention to conveyances and intermediaries. In its testing of styles and means of representation, *The Winter's Tale* joins a number of plays in which those who serve others are not limited merely to carrying messages but serve as catalysts and advocates. Indeed, Shakespeare's presenters are generally as varied and intricate as the language that stands between one consciousness and another. As Robert Egan, Thomas Van Laan, and Bertrand Evans have shown, most plays have one or more people who double as stage managers.

They arrange small playlets and demonstrations for onstage audiences, who lag behind the external audience in recognition.[2] These presenters may manipulate appearances to better their own positions, as Iago does in maneuvering an invented Cassio and Desdemona into the shapes Othello is used to seeing, or as the honest Camillo does in ushering Florizel to Sicilia and sending Polixenes in hot pursuit. Or they may serve with compassion and disinterest. But whatever their intent, they cannot help distorting what they present and suggesting that second- and thirdhand accounts accrue the advantages of compressed rhetoric and the disadvantages of lost real presence.

The difference in *The Winter's Tale* is the number of interferences between issue and reception, beginning with the talk of diplomats in the first scene and Hermione's surrogate wooing of Polixenes, extending to Florizel's lying to everyone within hearing, and ending with Leontes as marriage broker. The function of narrative in that wholesale purveyance is to make deliveries to relative outsiders, screened off from the primary evidence. The play obviously has a considerable investment in copies and diplomats, since it puts so many relations through some medium or other. Even a forceful oracle requires priests, messengers, and translation into events before its truth registers. More prominent at several key phases, as first Leontes' and then Polixenes' ambassador and later as Florizel's counselor, the shuttle Camillo serves the plot by a good deal of independent maneuvering. Further beyond direct accountability are Apollo's priests, who lift Leontes as abruptly into an awakening as he has fallen into jealousy. Paulina serves mainly Hermione but does so ironically in the second phase, by misrepresenting her. Both she and Camillo are double agents as well as playwright's helpers. Camillo's part in the final reunions returns Perdita to her family and sets Florizel up as a link between the kingdoms; Paulina's brokerage reunites the long-separated royal parties. Neither requires further help from the supernatural or theurgic powers beyond what is implied by Apollo's foresight. Both work toward transparent mediation and the redirected eye-contact of holy looks. Shakespeare not only stakes a good deal on such presenters to bring forth restored identities but implies that go-betweens are dispensable once they have served.

That presumably goes for the play's presentation through actors and the phenomena of theater as well. Certainly the outermost case of the vehicle or conveyance is the play itself, the audience's access to the playwright. Who learns what from whom and through what code is important to the freedom the play claims to put information forward in whatever mode, at whatever time it pleases, as in declaring its likeness to old tales. Not to believe what is represented is as risky as being taken in by disguises and subterfuges. Leontes' stubbornness in refusing to credit his wife's truth and the oracle brings about the death of Mamillius, which makes truth a force to be heeded. The play's claiming of its dramaturgical privileges and its making the stand-betweens so prominent account for several of the intrusions. The bear and the tempest destroy Antigonous and his crew not because justice calls for punishment but because the tale requires that news of Perdita not get abroad for sixteen years. The statue returns to life and ends Leontes' contrition too late for him to salvage the lost years or the lost son but in time to fulfill the oracle and complete the reunification. In making such tangible displays of the ways and means of representation, such plot devices are joined by Time, who reminds us of the story's romance origins and reportorial narrative. Without pretending to be a character in the usual sense, this splicing agent links Leontes' two phases with a particularly synoptic representation. Story summary figures in the last act as well, especially in the narration of Perdita's rediscovery, which stresses the unbelievable and the unsayable: "You lost a sight which was to be seen, cannot be spoken of," one messenger tells two others: "I never heard of such another encounter, which lames report to follow it, and undoes description to do it" (5.2.43, 56–58).

The distinction between fully presented episodes and abridgments is related to the difference between the live contacts of holy looks and delivered messages. Although the trickster Autolycus deceives the eye as well as the ear, narratives are suspect by comparison to what the eye sees. Neither the statue nor the shepherdess-queen reveals herself immediately. As Paulina remarks after setting up Hermione's return as a miraculous resurrection: "That she is living, / Were it but told you, should be hooted at / Like an old tale" (5.3.115–17). Seeing *is* believing finally, whatever the delays and the inherent incredibility. Everything depends on how perception is manipulated, and on that score Paulina is as much a fabricator as Autolycus, or as Leontes thinks Hermione is. But she is also devoted to making good on her delayed revelation. After lying about Hermione's death initially and maintaining the deceit an exceedingly long time, she brings forth convincing proof of a mother's devotion to her lost child and alienated husband. The restitution of the kingdom depends largely on that convincing settlement.

Courtship and Diplomacy

The little of the verse that does go markedly beyond ordinary speech approaches wondrous events and mystification by a means less aloof than oracles and closer to what stirs the blood in springtime. Love's intimacy finds its place where strangers cease to be strangers and enter the lifelong "interchange of gifts, letters, loving embassies." In that respect, love is the personal side of suspended disbelief and clinches the contact of minds at each end of the holy looks. It is also present, in attenuated versions, in other unions of subject and object. Florizel and Perdita are the prime case. How Shakespeare conceives of their mending of courtly protocol through lyric interjections will perhaps be clearer if we recall Romeo and Juliet and the Renaissance sonnet or the less noteworthy talk that love issues in more limited plays like *The Changeling*. In the latter, for instance, Alsemero's more rationalized love, even next to Florizel's comparatively restrained style, is quite matter of fact:

> 'Twas in the temple where I first beheld her,
> And now again the same; what omen yet
> Follows of that? None but imaginary;
> Why should my hopes or fate be timorous?
> The place is holy, so is my intent:
> I love her beauties to the holy purpose,
> And that, methinks, admits comparison
> With man's first creation, the place blest,
> And is his right home back, if he achieve it.
> (1.1.1–9)[3]

Despite *The Changeling*'s own variety of styles from mad talk to terse sobriety, Middleton and Rowley allow very little complication in Alsemero himself. Here he quickly sets aside omens without letting them build ominously and registers the potentially mythic expansion of Eden as little more than a commonplace in the formal weight of "that, methinks, admits comparison." His moderation fits a play that is initially "without displays of virtuosity," as N.W. Bawcutt remarks, although it accelerates into a spectacular disorder later.[4]

The Winter's Tale too has its careful calculation but uses it to interfere with and contrast to the language of sentiment. What Leontes' suspicion breaks down (besides the family and the political order) are displays of manners such as Camillo's to Archidamus and Hermione's to Polixenes. His paranoia questions any supposition that what people say is transparent. As nearly everyone's negative, Autolycus renders that subversion less harmful, and Perdita replaces it with a trusting charm. But before the play delves into love's paranoia and its lyricism, it gives us a sense of less high-powered penetrations of mannered and attorneyed disguise. Impulsive sentiment is after all in conflict with a good deal in the play that is functional in the restored as well as the initial social order. That even the stuffy diplomacy of Camillo and Archidamus in the opening scene is not totally unusable is at least arguable despite its corridor tedium. Camillo has a sound concept of the vast distances and winds that blow between realms, and he concludes his initial theme-setting for the play with an acknowledgment of providence that hints of Apollo's directorial function:

> Since their more mature dignities and royal necessities made separation of their society, their encounters, though not personal, have been royally attorneyed with interchange of gifts, letters, loving embassies, that they have seemed to be together, though absent; shook hands, as over a vast; and embraced, as it were, from the ends of opposed winds. The heavens continue their loves! (1.1.24–32)

Courtly diplomacy works just well enough here to suggest the niceties of "attorneyed" royalty and to set up its counterparts in the old shepherd's hosting, which accommodates outsiders and visitors while remembering bygone days. Camillo mixes the pedantry of "as it were" with poetic fancy in imagining an overcoming of absence through traveling representatives. His theme is thus basically affection's empowering of embassies and overcoming of distances. He is himself part of the ambassadorial mission, this very moment strengthening ligatures while representing Sicilia to us as well as to his corresponding lord. He and Archidamus combine the offices of royal entertainment with an observation of lifelong friendships and familial affections. That they manage to suggest an opera buffa is due both to the constraints of custom and to the expository functions of the messengers the play sends to lead in the principals. If their urbanity is evasive, it is not because it impersonates or feigns but because sincerity in any great amount is alien to it. We naturally grow suspicious of a language this unwieldy, used to describe sentiments that powerful and enduring. As bystanders, these two doormen to the action are at too great a distance from Leontes and Polixenes to prepare us for their sudden falling out.

In that respect, events are not predicated on "mature dignities" rooted in affection but are set up as abrupt explosions. The forerunners themselves generate a growing suspicion that what they say is questionable and that what they herald is not what they themselves expect. Even as Camillo remarks that "The heavens continue their loves!" we are put on guard; otherwise, why the protestation? Archidamus's reply, "I think there is not in the world either malice or matter to alter it," suggests that malice or matter soon will. When we hear of Mamillius's great promise and the kingdom's future dependence on him, we have reason to fear for his life.

It is natural to prefer the talk of lovers and Autolycus's singing to this, but Sicilia is after all not Bohemia and will not be even with the infusion of new life. Shakespeare uses formalities to come at familial relations from the periphery and to set parties at a measured distance. Even so, entertainment at court is clearly overburdened. Acknowledgments of worth can neither be altogether excluded from sentimental bonds nor promote them, as we see eventually in Leontes' welcoming of Florizel and Perdita and the betrothal of Paulina to Camillo. (These engagements also limp through formalities, although they are at least moved by sentiments that the play honors.) They illustrate an intangibility of diplomatic language that has a bearing on the breach between Leontes and his wife and friend. In Hermione's assigned task in convincing Polixenes to stay longer, the sensitive relation of Sicilia and Bohemia is even more veiled than it is in the diplomats. Remoteness and manner go together; the true feelings of the two kings at the center are obscure, even to themselves. We do not know what if anything Hermione's graciousness conceals.[5] Courtly manners obviously enable one to pretend to feel even what one actually does feel. The simplicity Polixenes describes in his childhood would produce rustic stumbling if it were carried past a certain age.

Some of what is driven underground by propriety is suddenly released by Leontes' "too hot." That outbreak of insane jealousy (I assume that's what it is) likewise conceals as much as it reveals. By definition it misconstrues evidence and assumes a broken trust. Shakespearean mad talk ordinarily has the look of riddling foolishness and compressed wit. In keeping with its abridgment here, Leontes' citation of evidence is crammed with metaphoric concretion. What Paulina calls his "weak-hing'd fancy" (2.3.118) is mired in bawdy imagery but at the same time is a radical departure from common sense. Extremities of vehemence carry well across the border from answerable dialogue to poetic excitation:

> Thou want'st a rough pash and the shoots that I have
> To be full like me: yet they say we are
> Almost as like as eggs; women say so,
> (That will say any thing): but were they false
> As o'er-dy'd blacks, as wind, as waters; false
> As dice are to be wish'd by one that fixes
> No bourn 'twixt his and mine, yet were it true
> To say this boy were like me. Come, sir page,
> Look on me with your welkin eye: sweet villain!
> Most dear'st, my collop! Can thy dam?—may't be?—
> Affection! thy intention stabs the centre:
> Thou dost make possible things not so held,
> Communicat'st with dreams;—how can this be?—
> With what's unreal thou coactive art,
> And fellow'st nothing: then 'tis very credent
> Thou may'st co-join with something; and thou dost,

(And that beyond commission) and I find it,
(And that to the infection of my brains
And hard'ning of my brows).

(1.2.128–46)

Sensing in others the danger of fantasy and emotion in league, he joins them unknowingly. "Affections" penetrate to the center of one's being and raise one above ordinary. "Coactive" and "fellowing" are sexual metaphors let loose upon the evidence. If adulterous love breeds bastard heirs, the mind communicating with lustful dreams breeds nothingness. The more Leontes tries to escape that realization, the more it jerks him back to the image that "stabs the centre." The sentences either break off or entangle him in the exclamations and questions of paratactic narrative—*and* thou dost, *and* that beyond commission, *and* I find it, *and* that, *and* hard'ning brows. The interruptions mark an uneven engagement of mind and evidence, as the parentheses bracket small retreats and enclosures of self, of voice turning inward. Often marks of Senecan abruptness, they carry here to a solipsistic extreme and pull the imitation of thought loose from fact.

Throughout this anxiety-ridden meditation, Leontes is obsessed with the problem of reading, with what is "credent" and with likeness. He pushes likeness to the limit in a run of metaphors—the rough pash and horns, the eggs, costumed actors, fickle winds and running waters, and loaded dice. In his view of signs, all things betray the forms that logic and custom give them, yet leave their unmistakable emblems stamped on the foreheads of their victims. As suddenly as he couples odd things together he divorces them, making all reality a dream that "fellows" nothing. Nothing is what it seems; nothing is what he has, what words name, what hopes for fidelity and perpetuity come to. In like fashion, because winds go where they wish and waters form and unform, it is almost futile to name them. What he believes he witnesses is thus untruth in epitome, in the very things that are closest and supposedly best known to him. His jealousy is as bizarre as Othello's, but because the evidence has not been dangled before us as Iago's is we cannot approach his interpretation very sympathetically. Like Mamillius we are left outside the door that in his quick retreat he closes behind him.

Whatever our doubts about Hermione's intent, neither the jealousy nor this distraught language can be seen developing in the dozen lines Leontes speaks before the outbreak. The impression we get from his berating of Camillo later (1.2.267–96) is that we have stumbled into a long-smoldering suspicion in a basically unpresentable private world. Lovers skulking in corners, horsing foot on foot, wishing clocks more swift, sighing, and kissing with inside lips sit vividly in his eye and abrasively on his tongue. But we see only the disturbance and its after-the-fact narration, not the evidence itself. This too says something about unreliable narration, screening intelligence, and the collapsing of reality into abridgments. Eventually it says something about the go-betweens we *can* trust. To undo them totally amid their possible ambiguities would be to unravel the play as Leontes unravels all "fellowing," because of what he takes to be an ambiguous wife and her "loving embassies." The language of madness thereafter sits so densely between the king and all who take their cues from him that no one can continue in an accustomed role toward him. The audience too must let him go his own way and hope to pick him up later.

By contrast, Polixenes' appraisal of the situation, once Camillo has explained it, is understandable and seemingly accurate:

> This jealousy
> Is for a precious creature: as she's rare,
> Must it be great; and, as his person's mighty,
> Must it be violent; and, as he does conceive
> He is dishonour'd by a man which ever
> Professed to him; why, his revenges must
> In that be made more bitter.
> (1.2.451–57)

That Polixenes is formally precise points up the command that a genteel style maintains over a nasty business—a Ciceronian style of matched clauses and well-weighed alternatives. A courtly manner bordering on the ornate is obviously not completely helpless even in urgent matters. The first two acts may leave suspended the question as to just how more intimate relations will buttress the state when younger lovers enter, but we know from the incorruptibility of Leontes' associates that rational minds are capable of interpreting conduct and judging sentiment by its manifest behavior.

Courtly and Rustic Styles

Except in a few scenes in which relationships are not clearly one thing or another, *The Winter's Tale* is relatively sure-tongued in matters of address among social levels. If the interview between Archidamus and Camillo raises minor difficulties as an initial thickening of the barrier between parties, however, the maneuvering of Camillo and Polixenes over Camillo's desire to leave Bohemia raises more awkward ones. The first introduces by ironic inversion the breakdown of Bohemia-Sicilia relations; the second plants the impulse for the return to Sicilia and introduces the festival that will assemble those who return. But in doing so it glances at a second obstacle that will take some time to remove, Florizel's rebellion, carried out behind his misrepresentation of himself to the shepherds. What is ostensibly at issue in the interview is Camillo's exile and homing instinct, as he begins to feel the tug of another timely diplomatic mission, and of heartstrings for a lost homeland. The relation of king to counselor is neither quite brotherly nor distant, which is perhaps why the scene betrays its narrative seams, as when Polixenes remarks about that fatal country Sicilia, "prithee speak no more; whose very naming punishes me with the remembrance of that penitent (as thou call'st him) and reconciled king, my brother; whose loss of his most precious queen and the children are even to be afresh lamented. Say to me, when sawest thou the Prince Florizel, my son?" (4.2.20–26). Camillo should not require so elaborate a reminder of Sicilia or need to be told who Florizel is. But the audience requires information and must be made to realize Polixenes' attitude toward his earlier misfortune. The conciliatory tone opens the way for the Perdita-Florizel match once Perdita is recognized; the word "brother" suggests that, whatever the new relation between the two countries becomes, it will remember the older one.

Despite all this, Polixenes does not inspire us with confidence in courtly formalities. This voicing of information and illustrative attitudes in the relations of kings and counselors makes both speakers momentarily authorial puppets. The flattery that Polixenes applies to Camillo screens off feeling, as does "prithee speak no more." A similar stiffness will soon be wielded against Florizel and insert problems of state into the pastoral interlude. The introduction of Florizel as a question mark is appropriate, however, since he is assailing a custom that keeps him from Perdita and will later be used to unite him legally to her. Meanwhile the sorrows of the past have been too much lamented to be really fresh and so have passed into formula. That dulling of sentiment too must be overcome; Paulina and Leontes are working at it in Sicilia and will find an effective prod in Perdita and Florizel as returning replicas of their parents. In Bohemia, anxieties of a lesser magnitude have crowded aside the ones Leontes stirred sixteen years ago. Phase two, the reassembling, is thus tentatively announced by an apparent trouble that proves not really to be one.

The brief exchange of Polixenes and Camillo does not make all these announcements by itself but is part of the transition from the apparent tragedy of Sicilia to Bohemia. Shakespeare uses the last part of the third act and beginning of the fourth to get the old events concluded and the new ones underway. The stitching at the center is especially prominent. The most critical phase, even before we hear from the shepherds or watch Polixenes and Camillo step from the pages of romance narrative, is the arrival of Antigonous on the seacoast of Bohemia as a commissioned agent or kind of caught-between. As Leontes' arm, Antigonous is a functioning reminder of the mad first half. He is privileged as the instrument of forces beyond comprehension in the mending that converts malice into good fortune. And it is he of course who sets the lost one down within Florizel's field of vision. In that ambivalent office of destroyer-deliverer, he too is an authorial convenience from the pages of romance. A kind of transporter who must negotiate the gap, he is metalepsis incarnate, a bridger in a causal chain that shows little care for probability. He simply shows up in the right place and is yanked away before he can return. He has heard the oracle's verdict, but because he believes half-heartedly in Hermione's guilt he is closed off from the ironic truth of the oracle's concluding sentence. He thus goes off partly incriminated and vaguely deserving of his fate, which allows us to imagine providence in his misfortune as well as in Perdita's delivery.

That he is qualified for disaster does not necessarily speak to the manner of his removal, but his startling exit is again not only timely but talelike. Coming at the juncture between the catastrophe and the comedy when any misfortune less than tragic can be shrugged off, the clown's tale of his becoming dinner to a bear gives his death a lighter tone than Mamillius's has, more in keeping with the merely threatened ones of Polixenes, Hermione, and Perdita. Heretofore we have had seriously designed murders; henceforth harm is subordinated to make-believe. Likewise, the audience up to now has received bad news with the secondary shock that comes of its being delivered simultaneously for on- and offstage reception. We have stayed abreast of Camillo's and Polixenes' plans to escape, but any advantage we have over Leontes is short-lived. He has already sent for the oracle before anyone learns of it, and like him we have no idea what the messengers will produce. Paulina does not share what she knows about Hermione, which is crucial to the surprise of the play's final revelations. From the fourth act onward, however, the audience is privileged to know who is who and what each thinks. Antigonous's errors in reading his dream are part of the shift. We see his error with respect to Hermione and perhaps dimly suspect along with him that mysterious forces have brought Perdita to this shore. The more marvellous the foundling story, the less it surprises us and the more it confirms what the generic clues lead us to anticipate—namely, the virtual certainty of the lost one being found and thus of Florizel extricating himself.

Autolycus

Sandwiched between the interview of Polixenes and Camillo and their arrival at the festival, Autolycus completes the transition from still another outside perspective, this one delivered in an aside. As a trickster, salesman, and quick-change artist in complicity with the audience, he runs interference for the deceptions to follow—Florizel's, Perdita's, the old shepherd's, Polixenes' and Camillo's, and Paulina's. When messages need delivery, he does not carry them swiftly as the offspring of Hermes should but looks for what will promote villainy. Concerning what he has overheard in the hasty caucus of Perdita, Florizel, and Camillo, he remarks, "if I thought it were a piece of honesty to acquaint the king withal, I would not do't: I hold it the more knavery to conceal it; and therein am I constant to my profession" (4.4.680–82). The Bohemian episode ends with his declaration "let him call me rogue for being so far officious; for I am proof against that title and what shame else belongs to't. To him will I present them" (4.4.840–42). He is obviously better for the delay than a more expeditious messenger would be. His change of clothes with Florizel transfers the mantle of the dubious messenger to the prince, who then goes to Sicilia as a diplomat pretender. That too is a delaying tactic, since Florizel's and Perdita's identities must become known at the same time to consummate the prophecy and subordinate the heiress to a male inheritance. The same costume change brings Autolycus to the one piece of stage business he does manage to carry out, the deflection of the old shepherd and his son from Polixenes to Florizel, in whose company they finally produce their evidence and surrender their prize.

So prominent is the roguish improvisor throughout the rescuing of Perdita that nearly all phases of the transporting of Bohemia to Sicilia are influenced by him. He is a comprehensive negative that proves the better status of nearly everyone else. Some of his offices give him a share in Perdita's springtime vitality. As a coentertainer in disguise, he is a kind of secret sharer with her as well as with Paulina. As an ex-courtier, he offers a variety of masking and lyric to counter the young lovers. In his way of greeting the spring, bird song prompts the surging of red blood, new thievery, and "tumbling in the hay":

> *When daffodils begin to peer,*
>   *With heigh! the doxy over the dale,*
> *Why then comes in the sweet o' the year,*
>   *For the red blood reigns in the winter's pale.*
>
> *The white sheet bleaching on the hedge,*
>   *With hey! the sweet birds, O how they sing!*
> *Doth set my pugging tooth an edge;*
>   *For a quart of ale is a dish for a king.*
>
> *The lark, that tirra-lirra chants,*
>   *With heigh! with heigh! the thrush and the jay,*

> *Are summer songs for me and my aunts,*
> *While we lie tumbling in the hay.*
>
> (4.3.1–12)

If we happen to feel that Sicilia could use some of this animality to upset its insularity, Autolycus deflects that feeling in lightning-rod fashion. Perdita's version of spring and Florizel's eye for her natural grace can then come forth unsmutched by tirra-lirra chants. The promiscuity that Leontes thinks he detects as the underside of courtly concealment is alive and well but lives elsewhere. A likeness to Perdita thus swerves close and veers off again. Though she herself feels compromised by her borrowed flaunts and holiday tasks, Autolycus "represents" her only indirectly, in the dialectical way of things that seem adjacent but prove not to be.

If Malvolio makes Puritan sobriety the enemy of festivity in *Twelfth Night* and Jaques dampens it in *As You Like It*, Autolycus does just the opposite here in setting up the gaiety of the shepherd festival. Its opposite is the entertainment that Camillo and Archidamus discuss in the first scene and that Hermione belabors in persuading Polixenes to extend his visit. Autolycus is the only one among the outcasts to possess a spirited musicality that gives devilment a rhythmic life. Although he falls well within human powers, he supplies something like the unruly element of Puck in *A Midsummer Night's Dream* or the demi-puppets of *The Tempest*. Although overpowered by the solemnities of Paulina's music and the supernaturalism of the oracle, he is akin to them in withholding secrets. His infiltrating of the festival is in the manner of showmanship rather than an alternative anyone would choose. That Bohemia shares his truancy does not imply guilt by association even though for the time being a similar radical freedom gathers in Florizel, his co-maverick.

Messengers and other connectives are meant to serve a system, an order. Above all the play's arrangers, Autolycus has no acceptable framework within which to work or any desire to find one. Accordingly, after the recognition scenes when others settle into appropriate places, he is still outside looking for chances. Everyone else who has secrets shares them with at least one other in the subdrama of confidants, where information enters the dramatic exchange quietly: the clown and the shepherd know of Perdita's finding; Perdita knows at least something of Florizel; Camillo and Polixenes plot together; Hermione and Paulina share the secret of Hermione's survival. Even Leontes has attempted to make a confidant of Camillo; he parodies the confessor situation in talking to Mamillius and ultimately finds a wiser dialogue with Paulina. Autolycus confides only in the audience. While he watches and waits, others move toward reunions.

Even so, as the parallels with Perdita suggest, disposing of him is not easy.

The release he provides from Sicilia's claustrophobic suspicion and stuffiness must be introduced in such a way as to transfer its spirit but not its culpability. The beyondness of musical gaiety provides a transfusion detachable from character. Any such truancy is especially engaging coming after Polixenes has assumed the policeman's role. Desire to play at being a scoundrel is akin to the desire aroused earlier by memories of boyhood in Polixenes and Leontes, frustrated in them by the weight of kingship. All that and jealousy are swept aside by "With hey! the sweet birds, O how they sing!" That Autolycus sings alone is a clear signal that no rival society (such as the tavern group in *1 Henry IV*) will become a permanent roistering group. Others on the fringe such as the old shepherd and his son are allowed to be transportable supplements to the courtly world that Polixenes and Leontes can eventually bless. We are no sooner enticed into casting our lot tentatively and unseriously with the rogue singer than Shakespeare counters the subjectivity of song with a confessional soliloquy that moves us back a respectful distance. That Autolycus is a courtier down and almost out sets him even further outside as one who thinks that "beating and hanging are terrors." We may not foresee how fortune will treat him when it guides Perdita to Sicilia, but we might guess that one so enterprising will be left to fend for himself. What he lets us in on are interludes and sketches designed to promote small transfers from other pockets to his. His ballads are forms of self-advertisement.

The craft of Autolycus in other phases of gulling puts him on the renegade fringe, in contrast, for instance, to Paulina's setting up of music and art for the benefit of the audience. But it does incorporate him into the play's stress on artifice and the art-nature relation as taken up by Polixenes and Perdita. The courtly manner is much less sporting, but its proposals and counterproposals do offer some negotiation between individual wish and policy. It is a social craft, a craft in the service of service. In contrast, the handiwork of Autolycus links gamesmanship to gainsmanship. The deference toward superiors that he lacks goes against a filtering down of dignities through the ranks of language and the hierarchical governing of give-and-take. The only roles he passes out are for victims and for audiences to his showing off.

Perdita and Florizel

In contrast to the confessions of this fellow deceiver and onetime associate, Florizel speaks openly on some things. Although he too is a performer, he develops a relationship that is erotic and sentimental before it is political. As long as he is not who the shepherds think he is and Perdita is not yet

Leontes' daughter, he remains irresponsible, but in the world of romance love's dreams are reconcilable eventually with a highly articulated social structure. Without knowing it, Perdita is given the task of rescuing both the gaiety of springtime festivals (from Autolycus) and the good breeding (from the overseeing fathers). Everything Autolycus celebrates as the property of healthy people in a good season (with targets of opportunity everywhere), she translates into attitudes of respect. She is uneasy with their gamelike aspect. If the sexual attraction and the hosting rigidify into formalities like those of the opening scenes, propriety will cost too much. There could still be some chance, in the context of Sicilia's sickness and Bohemia's paternal authority, that we could be thrown back to Autolycus.

Perhaps the best immediate compromise between ceremonial respect and the stirrings of spring, however, is struck not by Perdita herself but by Florizel's love lyrics to her. That compromise is helped out by her speech in distributing the flowers and by the two dances—of shepherds and shepherdess and of the "men of hair" or Saltiers with their "gallimaufry of gambols" (4.4.325). Eventually Shakespeare will require another tonal transition to the solemn joy that Paulina arranges. Although accompanied by music and ritualized by an elaborate setting of places, that mixed feeling is to be set up not as an entertainment or holiday diversion but as the climax of the oracle. It will be entrusted to pantomime and confined to a few directorial words. Here Shakespeare concentrates on the construction of a love bond that can be used as liaison and as a model of what Leontes and Hermione must recover in the crossing of youth to age and of wonders to the therapy of long reflection and repentance.

In making that crossing, the play imports at least three dialects, the ornamental freshness and energy of the lovers, the private frankness and public concealment of Autolycus, and a rusticity that borders on malapropism. (Two of these importations find no close equivalents in the traffic between the court and the outdoor resources of *A Midsummer Night's Dream, As You Like It,* and *The Tempest,* which take love back and leave the rustics and recalcitrants in the wild.) The chief healing bond of the play is the one between the lovers; and once Perdita is recognized, it encounters no hindrances in reception. Love's sentiment answers both rusticity and Autolycus's freewheeling enterprise while benefiting from the rural setting and its festival. Staying close to the soft hearts of romance, its language bears little resemblance to ordinary idiom. Serving up generalizations with each flower she hands out, for instance, Perdita is both an expounder of commonplace topoi and a herald of her own restoration, since as Polixenes concedes, "Nothing she does or seems" in that mannered deportment "But smacks of something greater than herself" (4.4.147–48). "Great" refers of course to social stature, and "smacks," though peculiar in this company, is effective.

Perdita's grace and beauty are authentic, and something must be smack right about breeding if the discovery of a birthright is to justify the emphasis the play gives it. She lands straight in nature, in a solid character, not something put on for the occasion.

In accord with that breeding, but far from blunt, Perdita's opening speech is as formulaic as anything in the play. Long before anyone but Camillo thinks of the return journey, it links Bohemia's ceremonial politeness to Sicilia's and sets a tone for reunions that allows no backslapping or giggling Mopsa:

> Sir: my gracious lord,
> To chide at your extremes, it not becomes me—
> O pardon, that I name them! Your high self,
> The gracious mark o' th' land, you have obscur'd
> With a swain's wearing, and me, poor lowly maid,
> Most goddesslike prank'd up.
> (4.4.5–10)

This standoffish talk is out of Lodge, Greene, and their Italian and Greek predecessors but is sensitive here to a social difference made edgy by Polixenes' presence. Perdita puts the flowers and the symbolism she assigns in terms of courtly heraldry. Their propriety combines nature's blossoms with rhetorical flowers and literary schemata, uniting raw materials with the best of forms.

Perdita's brand of courtesy is nonetheless not as ornate as Florizel's. The latter combines syntactic inversions, emphatic verbs ("Do give a life," "did print"), subjunctives, and formal similes with a refreshing frankness, all of which contrasts to the sportive sexuality of Autolycus and the insanity of Leontes. Florizel's metaphoric richness represents not merely a parallel extreme but a sensuous opposite to Leontes' spider-infested nature. His declarations of love—his most impressive contributions to the play's spectrum of styles—are richly metaphoric:

> were I crown'd the most imperial monarch
> Thereof most worthy, were I the fairest youth
> That ever made eye swerve, had force and knowledge
> More than was ever man's, I would not prize them
> Without her love; for her, employ them all;
> Commend them and condemn them to her service,
> Or to their own perdition.
> (4.4.373–79)

By having Polixenes bait Florizel into this, Shakespeare heightens anticipations on several fronts and prepares for an exposure that opens the way for his return. If the audience onstage does not receive him in quite the spirit he deserves, it is because given the clandestine situation he cannot speak unambiguously to known listeners. Polixenes and Camillo are waiting to pounce; Perdita is uneasy about his deception as well as her costume; the old shepherd is half in the past with his lost spouse; his son is never more than half present at a given time and is having trouble, his father says, getting from adolescence to adulthood.

The plainness of *The Changeling* is again instructive. Whereas Alsemero in confessing his love speaks to himself, Florizel speaks for all the earth and heavens to hear, overrunning the line, compounding and adding, building runs and parallels, and working toward a climactic balancing of *employ, commend,* and *condemn,* the latter showing an affiliation with the wit of the earlier comedies. The offstage audience may guess that a father bent on making his son toe the line will be a little softened. But even if he is not, the demonstration of skill in sonnet manners identifies a romantic hero likely to win the lady. It is after all through sentiment luckily delivered by the right son to the right daughter that the ailing state finds the blessing that comedy adds to the oracle's promise. We should not underestimate the atmospheric effects of that alliance with love lyric. Once it inserts typical rituals into the pattern of contrasts, the rest of the pieces fall into place. The Sicilian affair is as beholding to Florizel's discovery of Perdita as the politics of Bohemian succession is, almost as beholding as it is to the repentance of Leontes as guided by Paulina. Florizel models a ceremonial way for the play to turn inward for sincere feeling and outward for its insertion into diplomatic missions. Rather than letting transport escape into subversions or into the realm of the gods, his lyricism refocuses passion in the narrative business of heirs and foundlings.

So spirited and full of good health is Florizel's speech that it is readily distinguishable from the other styles of courtiers at their craft and from Autolycus's doxy songs, as is the noteworthy outpouring addressed to Perdita herself. In the latter, also virtually a performance piece, love lyric comes forward to make prespousal affection an unrecognized diplomacy:

> What you do,
> Still betters what is done. When you speak, sweet,
> I'd have you do it ever: when you sing,
> I'd have you buy and sell so, so give alms,
> Pray so, and, for the ord'ring your affairs,
> To sing them too: when you do dance, I wish you
> A wave o' th' sea, that you might ever do

>   Nothing but that, move still, still so,
>   And own no other function. Each your doing,
>   So singular in each particular,
>   Crowns what you are doing, in the present deeds,
>   That all your acts are queens.
>   (4.4.135–46)

Perdita's self-expression through speech, singing, praying, and ordinary affairs triggers this run on the rhetorical storehouse. Its tribute to grace must be based in royal inheritance since Perdita's manner cannot have been learned. By comparison to elaborate Petrarchan devices, Florizel avoids excessive prettiness while using "so" and "to" to tack feeling up in view. The marketplace buying and selling reminds us of Autolycus as traveling salesman but again distinguishing between matters that are unlike except for one or two points. The singularity of each act fulfills desire each instant— or would if one could remove the wish. That residue of desire is what empowers the listing of the acts and keeps some futurity in the balance. The longer a deed takes and the more rhythmic and repetitious it is, the more it holds off the cessation of presence. The more too it mediates between the thing seen and the thing possessed. Florizel's point is that Perdita's artfulness does not pull away from nature or coerce its materials into emblems against their will. It is fully the product of "present deeds," or nature converted into intuitive act. Art does not make character; character makes art. Poetry does not look away from, but directly upon, enactment, which has come in from its distant narratives and imagination's ideal realms to fill the moments of the stage. In a play with so many things to doubt, the truth of feeling is nailed down by the conversion of potential courtship rhetoric into a poetry of eloquent symbols, whose "natural" fulfillment is the language of queens.

That Shakespeare has Florizel court Perdita in front of Polixenes acknowledges a continued conflict between passion and social forms. Something depends on the hearer as well as the speaker. The real presence of an ideal is not enough by itself; the beloved must enter a contract with enduring rank and breeding if the lover's ideal is to be shared. While the lovers are still in limbo, we are not allowed to forget that *The Winter's Tale* is concerned no less with propriety than with sentiment, indeed with their common ground. Polixenes comments on Florizel's style with a "fairly offer'd," and Camillo on his sincerity with "This shows a sound affection." Both acknowledge the youthful enthusiasm, although "sound" is less accurate than "spirited" would be. But that acknowledgment can do no more than show the stirring of emotion. The elders are not ready to put aside preconceptions, nor is Perdita herself. Much of the festival scene is concerned with a standard of manners adjustable to soft minds and gentle hearts and thus with sentiments put into dialogue to finish the work of healing.

Like Alsemero, Florizel has large blind spots, but where Alsemero's faults lead to greater and greater disillusionment, Florizel's are curable under the forgiveness that romance awards. No one would hesitate to say that his indifference to his position deserves a paternal jolting, but the lyrics that love extracts from him promise the restoration to Leontes of his lifelong friend as well as his daughter. In such a reunion, private dreams as expressed in poetic speech find a place even in a conservative order unwilling to change its formulas. What the lovers want, the state needs. Their wishes merely have to be worked into diplomatic reception, beginning not with Polixenes, who is not in a pliable mood, but with Leontes.

Different Styles for the Judicial and the Marvellous

This inventory of Bohemia's chief transportable elements should help us with the fifth-act reassembling of social and stylistic components. But the spectrum is not complete without two further components, the law and the diplomatic assignments of the returnees. As to judicial language, it is under duress from the moment the chief magistrate goes mad, and it draws all special pleading into the maelstrom until a higher judge, Apollo, issues his stern verdict. In *Othello* magnitude and vehemence, which can serve either poetry or rhetoric, are so much Othello's own property that Desdemona finds no opening for reasonable disclaimers. With little idea of how to mount a case for her self-defense, she escapes into the picturesque willow song. When Othello in high-minded public zeal talks of killing her, she defends herself simply with "heaven, / Have mercy on me!" (5.2.33–34). In Hermione's more vigorous self-defense, Shakespeare gives a prominent momentary place to forensic rhetoric. The consciousness that Hermione articulates can be recollected by Paulina in reeducating the king and preparing for the play's rewards and punishments.

The appropriateness of that keying of sentiment to justice is evident in Leontes' misappropriation of the court of law as a weapon to finish off an affection that hangs by a thread. Although the trial itself seldom draws much critical attention, it underscores the contentiousness that Leontes introduces into Sicilia and is picked up in Polixenes' harsh sentencing of Florizel, Perdita, and the old shepherd—again in sentiment threatened by a misinformed, stern justice. These two negative cases argue for the mutual reinforcement of sentiment and status upheld by true character, which is on trial in both cases. While not disputatious in the way of *King Lear* or possessed of *The Tempest*'s thematic stress on dangerous rebels, *The Winter's Tale* is noisily rhetorical in its own right. What is offered to the court is the legal version of a representation of self through an arguing persona, either one's lawyer or oneself serving as self-advocate, as in effect the one actual felon of the play, Autolycus, does before the audience.

Reason should have its day in such presentations quite apart from Apollo's definitive judgment from afar, but as Hermione realizes, her credibility in self-defense depends on ethos or character. That is precisely what is at issue:

> mine integrity,
> Being counted falsehood, shall, as I express it,
> Be so receiv'd.
> (3.2.26–28)

"Integrity" in this case means marital fidelity and love as professed. It is inseparable from the queenly offices defined for her by a patrimonial system now thoroughly wrenched into tyranny. Despite the futility of her effort, she mounts a spirited defense before acknowledging that Leontes speaks a language she cannot understand or refute and that, as she says, "My life stands in the level of your dreams." As in *Othello,* Shakespeare's point is partly that trials are no better than presiding judges or their values. Perhaps implied in that, however, is a score against forensic rhetoric itself, which carries too little conviction compared to more heartfelt or more clever kinds of speech. The best Hermione can do is appeal to a higher witness and deposit among the play's styles her matching of Leontes' legalisms. The model is useful mostly in a besieged state, but it shores up the integrity until reinforcements arrive, first in the blunt message of the oracle, then in the image of the parent in the child. It also fills out a middle range of formal talk shared by officially arranged marriages and diplomatic missions.

At the level of the oracle, both in judgment and in riddle, another kind of judicial language comes to the edgy place where poetic justice makes contact with romance, where politics takes on justification in a mysterious way that parallels the smack rightness of Perdita. Apollo's timely verdict prevents Leontes from plunging as totally into disaster as Othello does. One of the curious omissions of the play is any articulation of remorse to match the prompt and unequivocal judgment. But the play is not finally much interested in grief, either in Leontes' over Hermione or Paulina's over Antigonous. Restored to a sense of proportion, feeling an obligation to make his subjects happy, the magistrate shuts off the latter with "O, peace, Paulina! / Thou shouldst a husband take" (5.3.135–36). If further disturbances can be averted like this, it is because the source of justice and the cure of madness are as far beyond logical explanation as the king's derangement itself. The far transport required to fetch the cure is matched by the authority of the return message-bearing. One sends off a courier or sends away a daughter, and both come back to the castle world as though from outside.

Bohemia's contribution to the restored Sicilia is immune to both the derangement and the rigors of justice, although it echoes each in Polixenes and Florizel. If as monitors of the shepherd proceedings Polixenes and Camillo jump in with a sternness resembling Leontes', their function is to delay, not to prevent. The softening of judgment and return of what has been lost are already showing their overall reversal of the autumnal mode, which barely edges up to regret in Florizel's pretty speech. When moral and diplomatic talk has its moments again, it practices on the fuller company from Bohemia. It also reflects a greater sorrow (in Leontes' lost years and lost son) than any familiar language has so far. The judicial element blends in without further notice in the rightness of new or restored bonds and sanctioned betrothals. The finding of what has been lost is the other face of justice turned merciful and includes the rediscovery of Hermione, who can now offer rather than receive mercy.

Even in the final recognitions, however, festivity is dampened by the transition from one generation to the other—as spousal festivity is not dampened in the unravelings of *A Midsummer Night's Dream, As You Like It,* or *Twelfth Night.* The poetry of Florizel and Perdita is not resumed in the recognitions, which receive very little verbal elaboration. That in itself is unusual. One might expect the reunion especially of a mother and a daughter or husband and wife to be amplified. Instead, the older Hermione encounters her younger image somewhat unemphatically. Together with the status of some of the Bohemians, lingering ghosts qualify the dramatic present and capitalize on Florizel's "might ever do" and its awareness of temporality. No society can totally defeat the tendency of the present to deteriorate; while institutions are renewing themselves, individuals are always abandoning them. On the positive side, Florizel and Perdita are not uncurtained playing chess and bickering good-naturedly over moves and rules.

Shakespeare makes several dramaturgical decisions in concentrating on the unveiling of Hermione. His interest lies in reactions from both close in and from the margin and perhaps in the quite different places of dramatic and narrative modes. To pursue narrative very far here would carry us out of the way, but its abridgments have a place at the far end of the spectrum from the subjectivity of powerful soliloquies and inset lyrics. Its function is to set up dialogue and holy looks as the instruments of demonstrable bonds bringing the accrued privacy of the interim to bear. That poetry is largely missing, especially of a highly associative, inner sort, helps assure the validity of dramatic openness for those who are close. The transported rustics are used mainly as foils, which subordinates far Bohemia to immediate

Sicilia. The festivity of sheep-shearing gives way to recognition. The shepherds, in thinking they have gained more than they actually have, use terms that would be appropriate in some circumstances but amount to an unconscious parody of family reunions here. That proves what we knew all along about social distance being gauged by differences in idiom and like minds being on the same linguistic wavelength:

> *Shep.* Come, boy; I am past moe children, but thy sons and daughters will be all gentlemen born.
> *Clo.* You are well met, sir. You denied to fight with me this other day, because I was no gentleman born. See you these clothes? say you see them not and think me still no gentleman born: you were best say these robes are not gentleman born: give me the lie; do; and try whether I am not now a gentleman born.
> *Aut.* I know you are now, sir, a gentleman born.
> *Clo.* Ay, and have been so any time these four hours.
> *Shep.* And so have I, boy.
> *Clo.* So you have: but I was a gentleman born before my father; for the king's son took me by the hand, and called me brother; and then two kings called my father brother; and then the prince, my brother, and the princess, my sister, called my father father; and so we wept; and there was the first gentle-like tears ever we shed.
> (5.2.127–46)

Thus they join the ranks of gentle hearts and the weeping joy of romance but in a parody form. They show clearly that only those who are possessed of dignity and elegance can wring the most out of such occasions. The vying for priority, the issuing of challenges, the "sirring," the puffing up leave the courtly birthright immune from serious invasion. The titles "brother," "sister," "father," "princess" betoken proximity and the fullest presence one party can have to another on a lasting basis. When the same names are awarded to newcomers, we recognize them as the results of momentary enthusiasm, awarded as a prize for services now finished. The Perdita who learns about her true mother and father is kept aloof from that batting around of titles. We may suspect that she will maintain affection for her foster family and that Leontes and Hermione too will honor them in some way. But appropriate distances will nonetheless be maintained. The restored cordiality of Leontes and Paulina and the shedding of "gentle-like tears" find an authentic place only in the romance. If a trace of anything similar has appeared in Bohemia, it is in the old shepherd's remembrance of his lost wife—not as a parody of Leontes-Hermione in this case but as a human touch that shows similar feelings on different levels.

The main showing of Hermione comes in spectacle rather than in argument. In ceasing to be a statue, the wronged woman becomes transparently herself, not all at once but as though arriving out of a mirage as a goddess might. Doing what she can to make the proceedings hieratic, Paulina stresses the artfulness of an image that substitutes for the real thing. The moving, warm Hermione is simultaneously a wonder to those who have believed her dead, a restored character, and an actress raising art to the impact the play demands. One of Shakespeare's most remarkable testimonies to the fulfillment of keen desire, she ends Leontes' long penitence and the breach between justice and sentiment. One or two questions remain concerning just how natural affection, nurtured in Bohemia, now stands, or how such a dramatized presence is served by the narrative cited in the play's title and inserted by Time's summary. Even for those who are not readers of such texts as *Pandosto,* references to winter tales and their marvels establish the likeness of the dramatized incidents to storybook material. That has the lingering effect of an almost unbridgeable distance, as though all this were happening in a dream. Despite its showing of the dream stepping into reality, it carries a trace of the unbelievable. In balancing restorations with the longer chronicles of two kingdoms, Shakespeare mingles joy and sorrow. Bohemia complements Hermione's rescue from obscurity with Perdita's, and complements Leontes' delight in a restored daughter with Polixenes' delight in a son no longer rebellious. These are the forward and prominent satisfactions.

The Young Ambassadors and Bohemia's Other Contributions

The survival of Hermione heads off the sort of mistake Lear makes in demanding the total loyalty of his daughters. Unlike Cordelia, Perdita owes nothing to her father and yet replaces the heir he has unintentionally slain (or induced Apollo to sacrifice). For sixteen years, Paulina has shuttled back and forth between husband and wife without delivering messages, guiding Leontes' consciousness in directions she can control, as in using reminders of the lost queen to cut off his interest in remarriage. Whereas in *Pandosto* the reproduction of the wife's image in the daughter pushes an unknowing Pandosto toward incest and suicide, Paulina removes that danger here while gaining stature as midwife to memory. Her change in bearing comes at the end of the third act and is well matured in the fifth by her role as spiritual educator. She takes the lead not only in moralizing but in heading off a patchwork restoration. Leontes places himself in her hands by a more or less formal agreement that makes her an approved broker. The kingly "we" of his "We shall not marry till thou bid'st us" (5.1.82–83) and the trueness of "My true Paulina" grant her that standing office. Where light courtly talk earlier has had something to do with Leontes' outbreak, the new language of king and confidant makes amends at an appropriate level, simultaneously stately and intimate.

Leontes' best demonstration of that combination, however, is not in Paulina's company but in his greeting of Perdita and Florizel. As an emblem of flowery chastity and gracious welcome, Perdita in effect infuses natural courtesy into mannered Sicilia and in some mysterious way, like a linking of mythology to social deportment, releases Hermione as spring releases winter. As another hostess, Perdita has not come on in any flirtatious way that remembers the initial misunderstanding. She stirs no jealousy, and when she steps out of the holiday role, we notice little difference in bearing. Her likeness to Hermione extracts from Leontes a mixture of affection and surprise and lifts the dialogue of host and diplomat to the verge of lyric:

> Your mother was most true to wedlock, prince;
> For she did print your royal father off,
> Conceiving you. Were I but twenty-one,
> Your father's image is so hit in you,
> His very air, that I should call you brother,
> As I did him, and speak of something wildly
> By us perform'd before. Most dearly welcome!
> And your fair princess,—goddess!—O, alas!
> I lost a couple that 'twixt heaven and earth
> Might thus have stood, begetting wonder, as
> You, gracious couple, do: and then I lost—
> All mine own folly—the society,
> Amity too, of your brave father, whom
> (Though bearing misery) I desire my life
> Once more to look on him.
> (5.1.123–37)

Leontes' recollections of Hermione temper his wonder over these two with regret. The word "hit" for the offprint, an echo of "smacks," suggests both the solid reality and the exactness of the simulacrum. "Brother" comes forth naturally, as it has earlier from Polixenes, and "wildly" smuggles into the kingly state the little piece of Autolycus everyone is allowed. (If a hint of homosexuality lingers there, Shakespeare quickly passes over it.) The small outbreak in the "alas" puts a minor catch in the fluency to go with a sufficient reminder of the obsession with images of fathers to make the new style a distant echo of the turbulent one of the first act. But much of the loss that causes that echo is about to be repaired, and the play wants some recapitulative regret as part of the narrative of far-off places. If official functioning and affectionate lingering now seem stylistically compatible, it is partly because so little authoritarian justice and solipsism remain. The one parenthesis here reaches inward to private feeling only to bring it forth for confession.

The multipurpose counterpattern, Autolycus, is also useful in the realigning of romance kinships, close and intimate among true relatives but measured and respectful in the adopted peripheral family. As a subtle artist and ballad writer, he parodies the authorial claim that old tales tell the truth; at the same time he helps bring an old tale down to earth. He parodies the concealments of Camillo and Polixenes and has a hand in the foundling story. The unveiling of the after-all-true Hermione, the play's last demonstration of intimacy, is untouched by him, but the disclosures he misses nonetheless incorporate something of his spirit. The teasing out of the moment gives Paulina's unveiling some small likeness to his subterfuge as well as to Perdita's borrowed flaunts. (One imagines Hermione feeling somewhat odd holding still and pretending to be marble while Paulina, now the go-between as circus announcer, finishes her preparations.) Something gamelike such as we first see in the Hermione-Polixenes relation creeps into the apparent wonder, which turns out to be no wonder at all. As Paulina's sixteen years of deceit now reveal, misrepresentation can be an indirect route to truth. Autolycus in contrast has no such warrant. The play's goal is apparently to dispense with huckstering once the outer audience is in a position to see the inner one confirm all that representation can—the oracle, the true heirs, the renewed affection of wives and friends, the awarding of the second chance that Othello and Lear do not get. As the stage empties, we assume an assured future. If the story surrenders again to narrative, it does so not in the adventurism of romance but as time's fulfillment, recapitulated and relived in the aftermath.

It is difficult to gauge with any exactness the contribution Shakespeare has wrested from the lyricism of Bohemia, but the play's excursions beyond ordinary idiom conclude in a sustained high decorum that reinforces the restored dynasty, which no longer stifles or misconstrues its affective bonds. *The Winter's Tale* is like other plays in requiring some way to *administer* the extraordinary. Consequently, the plot manages to consume most of the lyricism in relocating the main elements of renewal. It does so by consigning the outward excursion to one phase and allowing a full treatment of the return, an unusual tactic in Shakespeare's second-world comedies. Lack of such a demonstrated reinsertion of the second realm is much of the problem elsewhere, when the courtly company retreats to places not totally serviceable to its ordinary round of intrigues, marriages, and struggles for power. Childlike charms, fairy folk, magic, Falstaff's rotund charm and wit, Autolycus: these play renegade to heirs apparent and have little place in the restored order. Their language varies from prodding satire to robustness to lyric, and their mental states range from calculated assault on ruling powers to individualism and comic defusings.

The romance comedies represent that outreaching in less drastic forms than the tragedies. Othello's love of pomp and glory has something to do with escalating jealousy into a high cause; self-importance makes Lear intolerant of interference. Were Antony and Cleopatra shrewder and less prone to setting love beyond reckoning, they might juggle their commitments and salvage a place in the empire; as it is, their desire must be fulfilled beyond the reach of Fulvia and Octavius. In contrast, Prospero has already absorbed one important personal lesson by the opening of the play and does not try to dwell permanently with spirits when it is over. When all's said, he does not want to inhabit a new-world paradise, nor does anyone else in the European entourage. All of them land on the island against their wills and leave at first opportunity. He may not be entirely content to divest himself of godlike powers, but that he is willing to do so reveals a different Prospero than the one we see in the disciplinarian who calls Miranda his foot and pretends to think Ferdinand virtually Caliban's double. Unfortunately, the world itself is insubstantial, and because nature cannot be permanent, no hold on it or representation of it can be final either. Looking up from the close work of staging, the playwright finds his theater "floating through clouds, / Itself a cloud." We can see in Stevens how that goes, as the visionary imagination

> leaps though us, through all our heavens leaps,
> Extinguishing our planets, one by one,
> Leaving, of where we were and looked, of where
>
> We knew each other and of each other thought,
> A shivering residue.[6]

One of the remarkable features of *The Winter's Tale* is that those who go to Bohemia return with so little loss. But the reunions do bring a diminishing of the exotic and the poetic that *The Tempest* acknowledges more fully, even if it does not trace it into a dramatized image of the court before and after its travels. Autolycus, Perdita, and Florizel, the primary voices of the other place, are subdued in Sicilia, and of course the innocence of the past is lost along with the promising son. *The Tempest* merely asks us to examine the moment of leaving. It has more to say, or to suggest, about the diminution at that point and about the poetic subversions of plot. When Milton's Ludlow masque looks through *The Tempest*'s widening division between the drama and the poetry, it sees a radically different second world and advises a change of emphasis in the first world from problems of rule and status to problems of morality. The guidance in both comes from a revised Ariel, a Spirit-delegate concerned with conduct and its bearing on an ultimate placement that is not an island sojourn but the final point of it all. Hence "Comus" suggests no equivalent in the reunited Egertons to the Shakespearean marriage plot or calling in of fairy resources to bless a social arrangement. Taking note of these adjustments first from *The Winter's Tale* to *The Tempest* and then in the reversals of "Comus" is thus of some importance in our assessment not only of the uneasy relation of poetry to drama but of relations between a representable social reality and attendant—or transcendent—spirits. In Milton, life here and now qualifies or disqualifies us to follow where no play can go, not by citizenship engaged in the relationships that dialogue develops but by our plugging into the resources of inspired songs and charms that serve as conduits between worlds.

Part Three

Going Beyond

7

The Tempest's Capable Spirits
Vanishing, Milton's Ascending

> *Where the bee sucks, there suck I:*
> *In a cowslip's bell I lie;*
> *There I couch when owls do cry.*
> *On the bat's back I do fly*
> *After summer merrily.*
> *Merrily, merrily shall I live now*
> *Under the blossom that hangs on the bough.*
> —Ariel, *The Tempest,* 5.1.88–94

> *Whilst from off the waters fleet*
> *Thus I set my printless feet*
> *O'er the Cowslip's Velvet head,*
>   *That bends not as I tread.*
> —Sabrina, "Comus," 896–99

> *To the Ocean now I fly,*
> *And those happy climes that lie*
> *Where day never shuts his eye,*
> *Up in the broad fields of the sky:*
> *There I suck the liquid air*
> *All amidst the Gardens fair*
> *Of* Hesperus, *and his daughters three*
> *That sing about the golden tree.*
> —Spirit, "Comus," 976–83

Emblems of Other Worlds and Journeys to Two Ends

One of the striking things about the apprentice Milton is his ambitious assimilation of materials from all directions—philosophy, music, science, literature, and current history—and the Ludlow masque is a prime exhibit. Spenser, Shakespeare, Jonson, and recent masques furnish some of the models; Neoplatonism gives much of the substance, especially of the brothers' parts. Its quasi-allegorical mode provides hooks to pull these and other threads through the narrative and extends the context of interpretation not only to specific sources but to ideas receiving renewed application in the debates of the 1630s over festivity, country, and court. The moralizing of song and dialogue makes the masque's local region a paradigm case for these issues. The materials of the debate extend beyond anything traditional masques, or for that matter most plays, allow. But despite its explicitness on many things, it leaves the connecting of Platonist and Christian matters to social, natural, and ethical ones largely to our own devising. Poetry's collaboration with drama depends on how we manage that task and on the separation of the two chief realms, Jove's and England's.

In accord with the latter realmic separation (which masques usually put in terms of floor-level and upper settings), Spirit's journey has one destination and the odyssey of the Egerton children another. I want to focus chiefly on it in negotiating the turn from *The Winter's Tale* and *The Tempest* to "Comus" and in suggesting Milton's solution to the bard's parting of ways with the playwright. The site of the Earl of Bridgewater's "new-entrusted Scepter" (35) is the logical end of the children's perplexed path through "The nodding horror" of the woods, as though to say that the adolescents of the family assume their place not when they reach a certain level of training or puberty but when they prove their virtue. Yet the virtues of rejection—continence, chastity, virginity—do not mesh all that well with the arts of governance implied by the tribute to the Earl of Bridgewater and masque commemorations of magistrates. The extreme youth of the three Egertons rules out any very direct application of their self-denial to social or political matters. True, Milton makes token gestures toward an application of morals to manners in having Lady voice a distaste for drunken villagers. But she also associates incontinence with "lewdly-pamper'd Luxury" and is glued to a seat not in the forest but in a sumptuous palace—just the kind of place that the sets of Inigo Jones usually glorify.

Negative virtues are the property of a psyche or soul in which strict conscience watches over temptations amidst England's fruitfulness, which is more Comus's concern than Sabrina's or the Earl of Bridgewater's. Pursued as rigorously as Lady suggests, virginity under these conditions is more likely to be disadvantageous than useful to dynastic themes. Comus's own perception when he sees beauty going unobserved and nature being "strangl'd with her waste fertility" (929) is that Lady is not combining body and spirit but rejecting one for the other:

> Beauty is nature's coin, must not be hoarded,
> But must be current, and the good thereof
> Consists in mutual and partak'n bliss.
> (739–41)

To counter the social "dear Wit and gay Rhetoric" of Comus-cavalier, she talks in terms of saintly rapt spirits and the "flame of sacred vehemence." What the masque leaves out, then, is adult life, where politics, marriage, and estate management could apply Comus's polished wit and natural bounty.

That the masque leaves the temperate virtues unapplied to breeding is vaguely comparable to Puritanism's gap between spiritual and political reform.[1] Certainly hindsight from *Paradise Regained* and from the attempt of the saints to reconcile civic and spiritual concerns suggests that the hiatus is more than superficial. Milton's treatment of magistrates in the treatises of the 1640s is limited to the bearing they have on Reformation issues and the freedom of conscience that goes with them. In the Old Testament kingdoms he applies as models, right worship is the deciding factor in a national wellbeing that is governed providentially. Thus after intestine wars, the free grace of God, granting a new covenant, "didst build up this *Britannick Empire* to a glorious and enviable heighth with all her Daughter Ilands about her." The campaign against "hiereling Curats" living at "the rate of Earles," as Milton puts it in *An Apology Against a Pamphlet*, implicates civil reform in ecclesiastical reform.[2] What *is* the relationship, we are thus pressed to ask, between governance at the provincial and national levels and trials of virtue? What do politic virtues have to do with private ones, as Spenser might have phrased it?

Similar questions haunt Prospero's treatment of Caliban and Miranda, when Caliban's barbarism (which takes the form of an angry attempt to rape Miranda) gives Prospero a pretext to enslave the presiding resident of the island and to maintain a paternalistic vigil over his daughter. Caliban is of course dreaming when he plans to people the isle with Calibans. But Comus is less naive. His "Hail foreign wonder" and "I'll speak to her / And she shall be my Queen" (264–65) show some craft as well as admiration. The temptation he offers is for Lady to assume command of the abundant resources. Her answer is to deny the relevance of anything having to do with economic or sensuous man. Spirit and Sabrina do not indicate how they look upon nature's goods or the arts of civilization, and Milton does not develop any pointed social commentary from their authority. Although Spirit would bless Sabrina with a small empire, that repayment in goodwill is incidental to her freeing of Lady. It is merely a kind of farewell saying similar to Lady's own wish for heavenly status for Echo if Echo will find her brothers for her. The translation of the virtuous to heaven that Spirit promises will leave everything lesser behind.

One index to a possible compromise between the high saintly ambition of Spirit's prologue and epilogue and the poet's concern with matters of conduct might be found in Spirit's services to the family as the shepherd Thyrsis. The difficulty with looking at those services is that they are either a fictional part of Spirit's disguise or topical (in reference to Henry Lawes) and hence somewhat disjointed. The disguise enables Milton to avoid dealing directly with the family's recognition of him: we know that he is not Thyrsis and therefore not beholding to the noble peer, but by the time his fellow players know it, they too are merely part of the audience. Nor does Milton have them answer the invitation to follow.[3]

The question as to which realm claims the masque's chief loyalty and how public behavior bears on individual salvation goes back to Spirit's own initial confusing image of the world. Compared with the "Regions mild of calm and serene Air," earth is a dim spot where one strives to keep up "a frail and Feverish being." Hard upon making that assessment, Spirit notes the "old and haughty Nation proud in Arms" and the several well-governed quarters of the "Sea-girt Isles," richly laid in sapphire crowns—all in patriotic terms that resemble Carew's and Townshend's. We can only puzzle over the double standard into which the masque plunges even before the question of alternative destinations comes up. At the other end of the masque, depending on how long the triumphant dance goes on, the festive mood is either truncated by or fades into what dampens it by comparison in Spirit's second odyssey.

To debate such issues openly, Milton shifts the emphasis of the middle from the display features of emblematic masque to description and dialogue. In the Neoplatonist principles of Elder Brother, virtue guarantees the successful passage of the soul. But if anything necessary to chastity's survival depends on the family or the presidency, the brothers ought to address that issue as well. Instead, they take up the neutralizing of Comus. Whereas Caliban is not after anyone's soul and has numerous confederates in folly whose goal is to overthrow Prospero, the Earl of Bridgewater is never at issue with Comus. Lady is not being held hostage for bargaining purposes.

The Predecessors

Echoes of *The Tempest* in "Comus" suggest that Milton separates the soul's ultimate goal from civil themes and upbringing to avoid the even more radical division of Prospero's limited goals from his longer-range vision. To explore the Puritan alternatives requires a new Ariel and a new heroine. If the weakened Prospero abandons his spirits near the end of a life devoted to esoteric studies, "Comus" does not force anyone to sever connections with the greater region of spirit. (Such helpers grow more and more instrumental in Raphael and Michael, until it is Christ himself who aids feeble virtue in *Paradise Regained.*) But it is not merely *The Tempest*'s journey from and back to the court that "Comus" reconsiders. Milton undoubtedly has recent masques in mind as well. These too do not worry the issue of authority; they simply assume a workable union between the social order and individual virtue, as modeled in the elite. This allows them to eschew argument and dramatic conflict. The nationalism of Aurelian Townshend's *Albion's Triumph* and Carew's *Coelum Britannicum,* for instance, assumes an easy association of the current court with heroes and gods. Carew's Mercury links Juno with Henrietta, Jove with James. Influence passes the opposite way one might expect, from men to gods, as James induces the gods to expel strumpets and pagans from their starry places. Filling the vacancies this creates among the constellations (which have contained enough monstrosities to fill seven antimasques) requires all the historical eminences of England, Scotland, and Ireland. When Hedone (pleasure) argues that she is the end for which everyone strives, she too is displaced, and pleasure is made the useful servant of human reproduction, which guarantees still more generations. Such dynastic bridges between private chastity and the commonwealth are beside the point in Lady and Sabrina, the latter being immortal in her chastity and the former clearly among those who will follow Spirit's final invitation.

Carew and Townshend are pertinent not because Milton attempts anything similar but because they open to view further differences between the Ludlow masque and its Ovidian, Homeric, Shakespearean, and other sources, differences that can be identified partly in structural terms.[4] *The Winter's Tale, As You Like It,* and *A Midsummer Night's Dream* are cyclical in issuing from and returning to the court. In masques, antimasque elements give way in the final dance, an equivalent relocation, as social and divine grace are established in visual patterns under overhead emblems, with a generous allotment of planetary and sidereal influences. The implication in Shakespeare is usually that lyric excursions among elfish powers are useful indirectly to governance, which is tested but not seriously undermined in Arden or the Athenian woods. The image of nobility is shared by the several social levels and sanctioned by the romantic plot. Ferdinand and Miranda, for instance, are nurtured on that image and aspire to it, and even Caliban is impressed by it. Implicit in the relation of the ducal ruler to the second world is a potential dilemma, however. If the governor does not venture where lovers go, desire and invention might run loose or Caliban might succeed in his vile projects. If he does venture, he may restrict the exploration of desire, as Prospero rides herd not only over Caliban but over Ferdinand. Even Ariel, a reasonably willing servant, seeks gratification among his blossoms as soon as he can escape his master's demanding schedule. To exploit him without stifling his animation, Prospero must give him a reasonably free hand as to means. He is of course quite willing to grant the union of Ferdinand and Miranda in due course. But the normal state in Milan or Naples will have to get along without spirit helpers. The discipline of the state and the family under paternalistic heads is restored, not replaced or made over, after the wildland excursion.

Doctrine and Experience

Spirits and angels in Milton travel between heaven and the historical arena where every moment is a trial and has an influence on the outcome. The provoking of the contests themselves falls to Dalila, Satan, Comus, and other dramatizations of error. For the most part what they test is not the validity of doctrine as expounded by the heavenly visitors but its application to given crises and the secular order. In "Comus" the younger brother finds his confidence ebbing and his feelings edging toward panic at the thought of his sister helplessly lost in the woods, but his essential beliefs remain unshaken in the assuring company of his older companion and the visiting spirit. Lady sings to find comfort and fights her way through anxieties to supreme confidence, also partly confidence in descending helpers. What steadies all three youths are both principles of conduct and faith in the watchfulness of heaven. The main articles of belief are stated unequivocably before the drama gets under way.

The effect of that early insertion of a stable framework is more the conditioning of tense moments than a loss of drama (an arguable point that I will return to in the last chapter). Spirit's opening narrative demonstrates that his native realm has a full file on Comus and cannot be deceived by him. Even in his disguise as Thyrsis, Spirit maintains Orphic powers of great strength and with "his soft Pipe and smooth-dittied Song," "Well knows to still the wild winds when they roar, / And hush the waving Woods" (86–88). From within the woods, however, the perspective is more obscure. The storms suggest something like Comus's metamorphoses, with wind as temporality, the natural changes of which are speeded up and mythologized by black wizardry. Certainly nature on its own is inclined to lapse into chaos under Venus, the mysterious goddess-dame whom Comus beseeches only "when the Dragon womb / Of Stygian darkness spits her thickest gloom" (131–32). As the pitched battle in the middle realm between the dark and the starry threshold draws feelings this way and that, Lady is pulled into a murky light where things "in wavering Morris move." Where Ariel's tawny sands and wild waves are greeted by ceremonial courtesy and controlled by aristocratic grace, Spirit does not appear to her or actually put his Orphic powers to use. Except for her own voice and chaste footing, the woods yield only the sounds of swilled insolence.

At that level, feelings may stray further than the certainties of doctrine suggest. When Lady asks

> O where else
> Shall I inform my unacquainted feet
> In the blind mazes of this tangl'd Wood?
> (179–81)

the discrepancy between the woods as seen from Spirit's perch and the woods as seen from within sets up the impelling movement of both journeys. It also divides the poetry into two levels, one serving lyric monodies and their woodland description, the other serving the ascent to tiered realms in the visionary mode of the epilogue, which has several anticipations. When a thousand fantasies "Of calling shapes and beck'ning shadows dire" throng to Lady—as they do also to the wood-stranded ladies of *A Midsummer Night's Dream*—she finds reminders of unassailable virtue in faith. Hope helps her composure, if not her position. What she most accomplishes in this realm of confusion is a change of attitude and a consolidation of inner strength, which "ever walks attended / By a strong siding champion Conscience" (211–12). What she actually sees before her is "pure-ey'd Faith, white-handed Hope" and the more applicable "unblemish't form of Chastity." The first two support the third and pertain to what the soul eventually requires for its eternal destiny. To keep from adopting substitute satisfactions, chastity is what it needs now. Whether these costumed presences are also seen by the hypothetical audience that readers of the 1637 text suppose (the passage was not performed in 1634) or are present only to the imagination could be a question of some importance for the drama-poetry collaboration. But the main point is surely that Lady sees them at the crucial moment of her doubt. From that point on we assume that she will pass the test. She is given what seems a concrete vision applicable to self-rule. Milton thus saves the audience too from deeper doubts and "blind mazes."

It is difficult to say whether virtues create the opponent who forces their demonstration or a certain kind of enemy brings forth certain virtues. But together they form a dialectical system. The oddity in "Comus" is that the rescue is not the doing of Lady's three virtues, or even of Spirit finally, but of Sabrina. Her coming forth skews Milton's relative unconcern for local governance, bringing it nearer the traditional masque or the masquelike Shakespeare. The implication of Milton's later trials in *Paradise Lost* and *Paradise Regained* is that secular empire is mainly a hindrance; the implication of "Comus" seems to be that the rescued youths have a social phase to get through and must honor their regional commitments. Their chief ally is a nymph who does not herself rule anything beyond the river but helps fend off hostile spirits.

Through a Wall Darkly

We need at some point to isolate the function of art in the apprentice's complex twisting of his sources, partly because it is featured in *A Midsummer Night's Dream*, *The Tempest*, and masques, and partly because it figures in most of Milton's own probings of poetry's power before and after "Comus." It is featured in the masque as well, but without the usual genius of the wood or lyric speaker to take responsibility for it. Songs, dances, rites, and thematic emphasis on shepherd piping and charms weave several arts into the debate at the center and suggest that argument must be armed not merely with truth but with apt expression and melodious form, Milton's usual assumption being that the poet and musician in collaboration are better than either separately.

For Shakespeare, the wooded place or island is a theater of illusions as well as a place to be ruled. The struggle between poet and magistrate, imagination and reason, complicates the outland-court contrast. In *A Midsummer Night's Dream* he has Theseus associate the poet with madmen and lovers and does not strike him down because of it. He thus suggests that it is reasonable to find men and women of imagination deranged by their moonlight misperceptions and needing to be awakened. At the same time, it is Shakespeare himself who invents Titania, Puck, and Oberon. What the imagination fosters primarily is erotic desire, but what it leads to under the guidance of reason and custom is festive nuptials and the performances that grace them. Marriage is obviously a sociable way out: it blesses desire while taming its extravagances and ends plots happily by promising dynastic renewal. Whatever has gone wrong recently can go wrong again, but the same genealogical principle that set the generations at odds also proposes the truce between them. However free-ranging one's licentiousness, mate selection guides it into acceptable forms.

The journey into a second realm is meanwhile very like the audience's excursion into the theater and submission to a potentially subversive illusion. Although *A Midsummer Night's Dream* does not allocate charms to forest folk, equivalents to a serviceable and momentarily moral Ariel, neither does it have an equivalent evil to contend with. Egeus complains of the amorous beguilement that has afflicted his daughter, but the play equates that beguilement with a curable mooniness, always alive and well in the young. It is not collected into any pointed malice, certainly not into a Caliban or a Comus:

> This man hath bewitched the bosom of my child.
> Thou, thou, Lysander, thou hast given her rhymes,
> And interchanged love tokens with my child.
> Thou hast by moonlight at her window sung,
> With feigning voice, verses of feigning love;
> And stolen the impression of her fantasy
> With bracelets of thy hair, rings, gawds, conceits.
> (1.1.25–33)

The opposite of that bewitched singing is religious devotion. Egeus gives Hermia the choice either of following paternal advice or of chanting "faint hymns to the cold fruitless moon" in a nun's habit (1.1.73). With no men around, nuns use songs to carry themselves off in pure imagination; the "fruitless" moon is known to be just that by the lack of generative love.

The question comes down to a degree of sublimation and domestication. That Hermia neither obeys her father nor becomes a nun finally is a reproach to Egeus (and would possibly be to Lady's sage virginity were she and Milton older and Comus not the only alternative). By implication, one function of the poet in *A Midsummer Night's Dream* is to promote and celebrate nuptials, thus working out from under both the father's curse and the forest's demonology. Whereas Ariel has supreme power in spellbinding to counter the flaws of Alonso, Sebastian, and Caliban, his less service-minded predecessors lead people on for reasons of their own. Titania's "contagious fogs," "rheumatic diseases," distempers, hoary-headed frost, and other inhibitions of fertility derail the generative process. But to make marriage nonetheless a comprehensive blessing still in contact with its original erotic dream-promptings, one of the fairy kind turns up to comment on visions "no more yielding but a dream" and make amends for the entertainment as one of them.

Bottom's play provides another line of defense against runaway fantasy, a defense that *The Tempest* consigns to the farcical subplot of Trinculo and Stephano. It parodies among other things the dense symbols that crop up in the imagination's productions. Take Wall. As Pyramus complains, Wall sits in a dark terrain where impenetrable shapes block out the light, just as Bottom's tedious brief scene keeps promising to show a story but never quite does, being all presentation and medium, no message, it too no more yielding than a dream. In that fantastic realm Wall himself becomes the beloved object of address, as though an animated force from *Alice in Wonderland* rather than an overrated piece of stage carpentry:

> And thou, O wall, O sweet, O lovely wall,
>   That stand'st between her father's ground and mine!
> Thou wall, O wall, O sweet and lovely wall,
>   Show me thy chink, to blink through with mine eyne!
>   [Wall *holds up his fingers.*]
> Thanks, courteous wall. Jove shield thee well for this!
>   But what see I? No Thisby do I see.
> O wicked wall, through whom I see no bliss!
>   Cursed be thy stones for thus deceiving me!
>   (5.1.175–82)

Shortly thereafter Thisby does put in an appearance through the chink, which both lovers kiss in substitution for the lips they cannot reach. Having then discharged his part, Wall may exit. The problem is not that stage walls are simulacra but that as plaster props they are much in the way and threaten to express nothing beyond themselves except by the generous allowance of a tolerant viewer. Theseus's defense of such fictions comes from one who is looking only for something to beguile the lazy time. He has so low an opinion of poets that anything halfway amusing will serve. In that opinion he is later echoed by Prospero's belittling of *The Tempest*'s masque and belief that the true likeness of the imagination's pageantry is the metamorphosis of all mutable things. The removal of the representational means, like the discovery that the statuelike Hermione is for real, edges the audience somewhat closer to the actual world and disarms the imagination. When Theseus is upgraded to Prospero, and Puck to Ariel, Caliban and his crew replace Bottom as objects of ridicule. Unlike Bottom, however, Caliban has a plan of his own, and to counter that subversion among others, the puckish figures must be given extra power, range, and discipline. Dreams do not come from the wild interior exclusively but are sometimes planted by Ariel as part of Prospero's mind-policing. In the skimpier romance that Prospero watches over, dreams do not figure at all.

I dwell on this because some of the momentum toward "Comus," which generously echoes *A Midsummer Night's Dream* as well as *The Tempest*, derives from Shakespeare's own self-revisions. In harnessing and dismissing its spirits, *The Tempest* confesses both the rigorous demands the dramatist must make of the poet and their ultimate parting of ways. Milton's Spirit has benefited from Shakespeare's second thoughts about fairy kinds and about how to turn the charms of verse to constructive use, but Milton also realizes that for his purposes the rethinking of Puck goes only halfway. Spirit must complete his closed-circuit journey down and back as the delegate of an unquestioned authority. Like Ariel, his songs have power, but he ranges further and has no local demispirits to confuse his calling with that of the genius of place. The power to resist the Severn's natural blessings and lower supernatural thus does not come entirely from within the region. Assuming that the spirits one commands are a sign of the service one expects to perform as a poet, *Spirit*'s willingness to help reveals *Milton*'s intent to have the sacred invade the place of Comus and speak directly to the Egertons.

But speak to them not about their identity as Egertons. To repeat the main point: whereas Prospero summons Ariel to celebrate a betrothal and prepare for the unmasking of the rightful duke, Spirit summons a well-laved and purified defender of chastity in Sabrina. Returning to the darker setting of *A Midsummer Night's Dream,* Milton suggests that the forest, a traditional place of confusion and soul-testing, belongs partly to Jove and is penetrated not only by Spirit this one time but by stellar light habitually, although not profusely. It binds musical charm to virtue, if somewhat unwillingly. The island with Ariel and his crew may seem in some ways more attractive than Naples under Alonso, which makes it difficult for Prospero to accept his limitations, but the visitors do all return; Milton's forest is not to be abandoned, although Comus continues to run loose in it. The implication in *The Tempest* is that the theater of alluring song has accomplished its reformative task. The audience sends off the performance by hailing Prospero and Shakespeare simultaneously. The implication of "Comus" is that, whenever virtue needs help (which will no doubt be often so long as forests and palaces are inhabited as they are), similarly combined resources—heavenly, artistic, philosophical—will be necessary. The poet looks as far off for help as he can see.

Secular and Divine Glory: The Substance of the Debate

If one danger of the moonlit forest of *A Midsummer Night's Dream* is that it encourages the runaway imagination, Milton's Lady, caught in a similar place, calls not only on Echo and a far-reaching music but on debating skills and school exercises in rhetoric. That she does not need a Theseus or a Prospero to speak for her suggests Milton's willingness to assign the guardianship of the moral order to one strong-minded advocate. That reliance on debate is not unusual in Milton. Before proceeding with the visionary level of "Lycidas," the uncouth swain pauses for the broadside against a corrupt clergy; both epics define their issues in confrontations; much of the dialogue of *Samson Agonistes* brings ethical and theological terms to bear on the narrative. All these make the *Areopagitica* assumption that the mind will choose wisely where issues are brought into the open.

Another indication of Milton's departure from his sources, and perhaps an indication also of the pressure of the contemporary rethinking of secular and sacred relations, is the view of empire he assigns to Spirit. As I suggested, Comus corules the forest. What exactly the state of the Athenian forest or Prospero's island will be when the invasion ends is difficult to say, but no comparably permanent evil is likely to take them over. Caliban has prior claim to the island and will probably get it back. Granted that Prospero justifies the position O. Mannoni gives him in *Caliban and Prospero* (and perhaps even Roberto Retamar's condemnation as well)[5] and granted that he behaves like someone determined to rule while he can, the chronicle of Prospero begins with his abdication in Milan and ends with his return. The island interlude is only a middle stage where he assumes certain duties. It is climaxed by the renunciation of his special powers. Even with the enslaving of Caliban and disciplining of Ferdinand, the island is as much a stage as it is a piece of the new world. Prospero plants no crops but does serve as the playwright's assistant and magician in getting the show on and off.

Comus's skill in the arts of the masque and his migration not only from Homer to Milton but from nation to nation suggest that he too is at the root of empire. The dark rites of his Venus worship and specious stellification are more than hedonist rites; they are a rival mythology, in support of his version of hegemony. He makes a lateral transport from Homeric sources through the fields of Spain and France, across the channel, and—in no way elevating or improving on the works of his mother—installs them in these drear woods. That he therefore represents a considerable legacy is more than sufficient reason for the masque to look for another literary ancestry and perhaps begin looking also outside national boundaries altogether. But again, one of the strategies of Milton's poetics is to recover the very imagery one thought discarded and to deflect it from social to moral emblematics. For instance, the heroic virtues that he mocks among the tournaments and Olympic games of Hell he can salvage once the argument has removed their corrosion. He reassigns them in a higher mode to angel legions and the apocalyptic fury of Christ on the chariot. Even the sloth of Belial and the Homeric wrath of Moloch could be said to reappear in the repose and wrath of the divine being. Thus what is corrupt at one level, once it has passed through the alembic of scriptural refiguration, is reinstated on another as revelatory emblem. In that passage, it severs our connections with secular realms and reaffirms our eschatological destiny. The chief use of debate is to remove the tarnish and make the rescue possible.

In that light, the entire satanic empire is reactive and conservative in reinstating the confusion of poetic emblems and rhetoric it inherits from Elizabethan forerunners. In Milton's view, it is emptied of the true father's attributes as they appear in the true son. Imperialistic epic is consigned to a limited phase of literary history. As "Comus" too illustrates in Sabrina's recovery of the magical chant and Spirit's epilogue delights, almost any topos, style, or kind can slip and slide back and forth between poetical and rhetorical uses, depending on who gets hold of it. Lurking behind even the worst of emblems may be a model of reform that can make better use of it. Indeed, what else but the perception of a surprising kinship in Lady's song inspires Comus to his enthroning of her? His usual tactic is a more Circelike debasement of victims. For this once he is inspired to emulate the "express resemblance of the gods," much as his starry rites pass momentarily from hedonism to the higher sin of idolatry. The Venus that his worship contaminates turns up baptized in Spirit's epilogue, as though she too shared in the cleansing of the classical legacy. For Milton the litmus test for the legitimate use of figures whether of love or power is fairly easily applied: the proper use belongs to parties whose virtue is a given, whose intentions are holy. That they are elect they show by their choices.

Such an elevation of tropes and figures has risks, and rather than take Milton's upgrading entirely at face value, we need to consider what new rhetoric may be unintentionally concealed in it. The privilege of saints after all was shortly to extend to the overthrow of a king and his prelates, though perhaps we shouldn't anticipate that in reading "Comus." Marvell, looking at both himself and Milton, associates such holy enterprises with spiritual overreaching, especially in the poet of "The Coronet," who in hoping to weave a chaplet "As never yet the king of Glory wore" finds the speckled serpent twined within it. Flowers are "transported" there from rhetoric's source books and from former courtly pastorals. The holy diadem is clearly an upgrading of the poet as well as the tribute he offers. The very attempt to use flowers for such purposes brings in its wake the realization that any writing is an egoistic assertion. The "never yet," an "exceeding" phrase, is poisoned at the root. Marvell fears something similar in reading Milton's most ambitious effort:

> When I beheld the Poet blind, yet bold,
> In slender Book his vast Design unfold,
> *Messiah* Crown'd, *Gods* Reconcil'd Decree,

> Rebelling *Angels,* the Forbidden Tree,
> Heav'n, Hell, Earth, Chaos, All; the Argument
> Held me a while misdoubting his Intent,
> That he would ruine (for I saw him strong)
> The sacred Truths to Fable and old Song,
> (So *Sampson* groap'd the Temples Posts in spight)
> The World o're whelming to revenge his Sight.
> *(On Mr. Milton's Paradise Lost)*

Even in second thoughts, Marvell grants that "None will dare / Within thy Labours to pretend a Share."

Milton's tribulations and enemies are more active and exterior—more political—than Marvell's. His strategy concerning spiritual pride, which he too recognizes (at least in Eve), is a defensive one, namely, to make the quest for secular glory still worse and focus mostly upon it. The more glittering and impressive the foe, the more otherworldly Lady or Christ is driven to be. Virtue's task in "Comus" is simply to get beyond the hedonism of the palace and the crudeness of the woods. If Lady is not to go too far on her own, that requires compromises with the aristocratic values of the traditional masque. The two journeys appear to provide an answer in that the promise of the second one defines the limited achievement of the first. The most the combined efforts of the three children can accomplish—and even that with the help of grace—is to free Lady. The rest is promised by Spirit but not offered. What Sabrina manages with her combination of cool translucent chastity and riverbank towers is the allowance of an ambiguity that avoids both spiritual assertion and contamination by lesser ambitions. When the noble masquers dismiss lesser ones for the final dance, they do so less as a model of superior manners and bearing than as a spiritual elite who have freed festivity from the stigma of Circe without necessarily making it the exclusive property of social prestige.

That meritorious elite recalls Jonson's *Pleasure Reconciled with Virtue* and the visibility that virtue gains from patterned dance, except that "Comus" offers very little connection between virtue and the actual form that festivity takes. Concerning that, however, Milton is not reluctant later to show even saintly multitudes and angels in well-designed song and dance. The only adequate consolation in "Lycidas" finally is the solemn masque of saints. In *Paradise Lost,* angels spend their days, Raphael says (in describing their masquelike choreography),

> In song and dance about the sacred Hill,
> Mystical dance, which yonder starry Sphere
> Of Planets and of fixt in all her Wheels

> Resembles nearest, mazes intricate,
> Eccentric, intervol'd, yet regular
> Then most, when most irregular they seem.
> (5.619-24)

Comus and his crew are not far away from a similar intricate homage to the stars, all the more to tempt those who lack disputational help in identifying the difference—who might be tempted to combine imperialism with apparent piety. But that is precisely his worst trait: he presumes to know how to invoke sacred powers and bring them down to the forest. He pretends to have found the secret to the union of starry gods and splendid palaces, much as the traditional masque claims for its sponsors. Milton is less sure of such immanence than he is of eventual transcendence, which lies well beyond visible historical fields.

Ariel-Spirit

Milton's departures from *A Midsummer Night's Dream* and *The Tempest* are prominent not only in the second itinerary but in the kinds of allies that gather and the appetites they combat. The terrain of Shakespeare's two-world comedies spans adjacent forest and court realms, not lower and higher ones, on the borderland of civilization where civil order meets savagery, dreams meet waking perceptions, and illegal designs meet their corrections. Ariel uses his helpers mainly to entice Prospero's captives toward the moment that in a masque would be the hinge, when the relation of upper to lower stage becomes operative or when what has been behind rotates into view. Here we are given voiced recognitions instead. Hanging somewhere on the edge between realms, Alonso is confused by what still seems more mystery than revelation:

> I cannot too much muse
> Such shapes, such gesture, and such sound, expressing—
> Although they want the use of tongue—a kind
> Of excellent dumb discourse.
> (3.3.36-39)

Ungoverned appetites are a mark of the primitivism that Ariel's pantomimes help purge. They extend beyond the natural to the civilized man. The supposition is that, once an excellent discourse has worked, endorsements of titles and places will follow, as they do even in Caliban, and that they are a sufficient goal.

Whereas we are privy to Prospero's plans from the beginning and know the unruly types that must be controlled, even the best-informed mortals in the Ludlow masque can only guess at the devisings of Comus, who seizes the initiative. The unlocatable gateway to the second journey is matched by indefinable powers that threaten to keep it permanently hidden. Since his subversions are not aimed at authority, authority is not of first importance to Lady's rescuers. Spirit does, however, chart some levels of delegated rule in the prologue and knows the relative powers of the forest's inhabitants. A related difference is that, whereas Ariel's highest ambition is to resume his residence in summer blossoms, in effect merely to go back to the natural source of the rhetorical flowers that grace his poems, Spirit pursues a mission that he not only understands but fully endorses. As a shepherd singer himself, he has in common with Ariel a disengagement from the grossest nature; and as infiltrations of island and forest, both of them are nature's tangents. Their respective powers hinge on that implication in a topography and in the tangible dependence of powers of expression on natural imagery. Although a creature of air primarily, Ariel is by no means assigned exclusively to sun or stars, nor does Prospero associate himself with a stellified realm. The applied charms of *The Tempest* use a full spectrum of imagery from naturalism to animated myth and from fire and light to bog and ocean.

Ariel's first song, for instance, beckons its listeners into a dancelike ritual that tames wild waters at the shoreline:

> *Come unto these yellow sands*
> *And then take hands:*
> *Courtsied when you have and kiss'd*
> *The wild waves whist.*
> (1.2.377–80)

The metrical procession lays out stages of courtesy by which things strange to each other are joined and made a harmony. The waves are calmed as though in the final phase of an initiation ceremony that awards residence to visitors as they are gentle and can combine nature, art, and manners. By that ceremony of greeting, the new beginning settles quickly into an intimate and delicate friendship. In contrast, Spirit is not given to materializing out of thunder as though a force within nature, and he has nothing to do with curtsies and kisses. As Thyrsis he commands the winds and by implication the vatic afflatus that plays gently through Ariel's songs. That Spirit also explains and moralizes along with the philosophical Egertons keeps him within range of positive reason and converts what might have been a vague pantheism into a project-defining, problem-solving morality. More explicitly than Ariel, he knows what it means to leave his native element to render help, although he does not tell the Egertons about it.

Ariel has powers far beyond those of his opponents and runs Prospero's errands more or less willingly, but his literary associations are closer to Drayton's than to Spenser's moralized fairy realm—closer to imagination than to allegory harnessed to humanist service. He commands an imagery less of emblems than of Ovidian transformations. Like Spirit, his main weapon is music, which together with the enacted pictures of excellent dumb discourse goads the conscience into dealing with a dubious past and insinuates divine charms into the nonverbal graces of melody and rhythm. For reasons that lie near the heart of his appeal, he is often quieting even while enticing. To Caliban and Ferdinand, he acts as a tranquilizer; to others already embroiled in evil, he stirs things up further. Like Caliban, he would apparently not be much interested in ethical fine points and matters of social rank if he were left to himself. But as Prospero's stage manager he at least heightens consciousness of these things if he does not instruct or argue. (Detailed education is left to Prospero and has already left its mark on Miranda and Caliban before the play opens.) Ensnared by what is not even his best music, his entranced audiences go to stations quite different from those they would have selected on their own, until "the charm dissolves apace" and "morning steals upon the night, / Melting the darkness" (5.1.58–60). Some of the mystery dissipates with that dawning.

Whereas Spirit comes down mainly to coach others in the countercharms that virtue needs where the straight way is lost, Ariel is initially more like a sergeant-at-arms, a master of active verbs agitating people before he calms them again. The tempest he raises is an assertion of sheer power attended by a flickering sublimity. It looks like the doing of sea gods transported by rage but as we are quickly told is the artfulness of the magician and his agent making up for a past passivity toward a cruel Sycorax and an usurping brother:

> I boarded the king's ship; now on the beak,
> Now in the waist, the deck, in every cabin,
> I flam'd amazement: sometime I'd divide,
> And burn in many places; on the topmast,
> The Yards and boresprit, would I flame distinctly,
> Then meet and join.
> (1.2.196–201)

Close to the genius of Longinian sublime, Ariel materializes Prosperian ideas, which righteous vengeance vents as wrath. Ariel is also the attendant spirit of what springs up between Miranda and Ferdinand, a direct incursion into the workings of desire as a musical fellow of Cupid. As kissing waves into gentleness indicates, he has other such infiltrations as well. That side of him reappears more in Sabrina's printless grace than in Spirit, although Spirit's own power too is curtailed. Overall in both Spirit and Sabrina, the restraining of ambition and appetite leads somehow to the eventual escape from mortality and the heavenly cruising of the epilogue, which perhaps has something to do with the transformation of Shakespeare's ceremonies of the shoreline into Sabrina's laving rituals.

These Miltonic changes of the Shakespearean spirit amount to a transcendentalizing of materials and apportioning of extrahuman powers to a task in hand. Whereas Ariel is commanded by a ruling authority whose aim is the restoration of family priorities within view of the audience, Spirit is the agent of an invisible realm, not yet an angel or bringer of Holy Light or even a Protestant instructor like Raphael and Michael. That he knows the calm of the heavens bears more upon the return journey and the general encouragement of those who would follow than upon the lore he needs to organize the resistance and summon Sabrina. Most helpfully to the masque, as a member of a court beyond courts, he can judge the fraudulence of Comus's starry worship and tell us its history. As a shepherd, he is immune to the forest's confusion, although apparently not able to lead others directly out of it. How he manages is up to him, which puts him in the Ariel business of extemporized manipulation, minus the thunderbolts and harpies. What he seeks to do is bind into one concerted force all the resources of ethical philosophy, herbal lore, and song that reside in the lower realm and contribute to a moralized and emblematic poesis. Both helpful spirits are eventually released, but as I suggested, Ariel's departure with elves "that on the sands with printless foot / Do chase the ebbing Neptune" leaves Prospero himself reduced; having done away with the internal pageant master, Milton cannot himself be abandoned, whatever the implication may be of Spirit's leaving the Egertons behind. Rather, the most ambitious side of the poet asserts itself in the passage through the gateway to celestial realms, which he is privileged to know about and to describe.

In keeping with these changes in the magus-controlled Ariel who administers to romance sentiment, manners, and government, Milton's concluding focus on Spirit's return recalls the opening and celebrates the collecting of blessings at a high level of erotic grandeur. Before that recovery of Comus-like splendor, Spirit joins his service to Sabrina's, and from one perspective the two together make up a more complicated substitute for Ariel. They set up the notion of idealized realms whose next higher form is the garden of

Adonis and whose completion is Jove's palace. A genius of watery place "Sprung of old *Anchises'* line," Sabrina is to be the patroness of a culture that, unlike the starry court, will thrive in full view:

> May thy billows roll ashore
> The beryl and the golden ore,
> May thy lofty head be crown'd
> With many a tower and terrace round,
> And here and there thy banks upon
> With Groves of myrrh and cinnamon.
> (932–37)

Like Elizabethan analogues between the realm of grace and the realm of Eliza, this empire opens up a long-range view to supplement the epilogue's. Clearly not an invitation to soft pastoral or noncommercial shepherdom, it places the prophetic image within the British setting of the "old and haughty Nation proud in Arms." Inasmuch as Sabrina receives this domain for having been purified, social health depends on spiritual health.

Yet this realm *is* hers, or will be, not that of crowned heads. It seems less political than moral and places her closer to the saints than to Henrietta Maria and court ladies. Its shimmering on the edge of the mythical is partly what points us toward the epilogue, where Cupid and Psyche lie beyond presentation. They do not descend to the stage in the costumed exhibits of nobles, as Carew might have had them do, but dwell within a literary sanctuary. Ovid and Spenser sponsor their celestial rendezvous, which is not agricultural or even architectural and gardened, as Severn's terraced lands and groves will be if Spirit's hope is realized. Their etherealized love contrasts both to the chaste dynastic marriage of Miranda and Ferdinand and to the eroticism of the Garden of Adonis. Spirit's last service is to direct desire to that level. That has the effect of defining besieged chastity as a virtue for *interim* woods and palaces, not forever. Perhaps his greatest service, however, is simply to ignore the potential conflict between the towers and the region of the golden tree so that a connecting passageway does not have to be specified.

The epilogue moves far enough from both *The Tempest* and Spenser's garden to suggest again the intervening masques as texts that in some sense specialize in the bridging of social forms and mythological figures. Jonson's Mercury in *Pleasure Reconciled* is about halfway between Ariel and Spirit in linking social status to its supports. From the higher mountain, but limited and without specific instructions or enticements of his own, he is neither a political reinforcement nor an otherworld spirit. The grove of Comus sits at the foot of the mountain Atlas, the top of which does not extend beyond our seeing. Besides being a "plump paunch," Comus is a master of practical (not magical) arts who shows necessity to be the mother of invention. In place of magical powders tossed in the spongy air, Jonson gives him the plough, flail, mill, furnace, and wheel and makes him responsible for both festivity and the productive labor that precedes it, the benefits of which extend through all the social ranks. As we might expect from the eaters and drinkers of "To Penshurst" and "Inviting a Friend to Supper," what rescues pleasure and appetite is less temperance than knowledge, with the help of which pleasure can be subordinated to virtue, once the belly, in Jonson's words "the truest clock i' the world to goe by," has been satisfied. Skill in deciphering pleasure's labyrinth comes from "wit" in Daedalus's song and is manifest in the measure of the dance, the wisdom of feet. Pleasure is not to be hounded by any of Virtue's legions (although a cue from Hercules makes the grove of Comus vanish and establishes a better choir in place of the foot-thumping crew). Earth is overly fruitful but not evil; the cup of Hercules offers the drink that thirsty heroes earn as their reward. The opposites are thus less extreme all around than Milton's but more explicitly cosmic than Shakespeare's.

The Ludlow masque shares with *Pleasure Reconciled* some of its questions about prosperity and folk festivity. It has no interest in Jonson's food-getting and harvest and not much (as I have been arguing) in civil rule, but a great deal in the agents of occult power and divine intervention. Until Spirit describes Sabrina's future groves of myrrh and cinnamon, no one has much in a positive vein to say about consumable nature, arguments for which Milton has awarded to Comus as the concretizing of magical charms. Although Lady's defense of an ascetic life and young Lord Brackley's of an undefiled soul are extreme, what replaces them is neither Ariel's harpy banquet nor Jonson's disciplined hedonism, although the latter may seem to be reflected in the "sweet entranc't" Psyche and the extraction of Youth and Joy from her side. The reveling "spruce and jocund Spring," the graces, the balmy cedars, and the "purfl'd scarf" of Iris are sensuous in a decorative rather than a productive way. Milton thus transports hymeneal rites to the middle distance, somewhere between Venus's eroticism and the soul's marriage to the bridegroom. There love lingers in the masque's final teasing emblem, remote in the prophetic dimension of poetry that converts all the former participants into enraptured listeners.

Despite the introduction of Cupid and Psyche just in time to salvage an edenic or "L'Allegro" element even for "Comus," Milton's condemnation of Comus's stake in Neptune's realm prevents any compromise between consumption and continence. To concede the necessity of consumption would be to concede also the need for an informed and applied political and economic sainthood whose task would be to oust Comus from his palace. Mortal remains are dregs to Elder Brother, and in at least that much he not only goes uncorrected but is supported by Spirit's view of the "smoke and stir of this dim spot." The smoke no doubt comes from fires to keep one warm, and the stir from the industry that even Sabrina's small empire will have if it is to produce and supply the towers. But after the vision of Sabrina's beryl and golden ore, the woodland remains a "cursed place," a gloomy covert that urges pilgrims to seek "holier ground" before Comus returns. It is difficult to listen to the prologue, Lady's defense of virginity, and the lengthy discussion of the brothers without feeling that Milton stands behind a good deal that they say. To do so too confidently and openly would be to suggest a metaphysical mechanism by which virtue leads directly to spiritual transcendence, which would take us totally out of the reach of home fires and industry. It is not clear that Milton really wants to do so, or just what he does want.

Nature in Caliban-Comus and Miranda-Lady

To rescale an operation already as large as Prospero's and as lively as Jonson's, with their storms, excellent dumb discourse, pageantry, pinched Calibans, and roistering Comuses, requires unusual confidence in a young poet by no means certain as to what a Protestant poetics can salvage from the literary past or what politics its moral interests argue. I have not assumed a systematic or entirely consistent revision of sources in "Comus," rather an allusive touching upon them, a tentative first run at an association of social, natural, and supernatural forces. That contact of things Puritan with things Elizabethan may or may not allow an alliance based on continence and moral discipline. Perhaps as much depends on the Egertons of the realm as on the poet. In any case, evidence as to such an alliance is at best tenuous. Anything that remains of similar size and social orientation in the echoes and allusions is likely to look disproportionate. Even the epilogue rescue of a Spenserian fragment takes some stretching, which is the price Milton pays for placing several localities in a single narrative. Whereas in Shakespeare no one is expected actually to achieve the transcendence that a Lear or Cleopatra dreams about (certainly not to follow the departing Ariel), Milton's heavenly visitors usually hint at a more or less chartable course.

If "Comus" does not say at what point the second journey begins to matter, "Lycidas" and the epics make death the critical gateway. What precedes is stoic waiting, with patience as the sustaining virtue—patience more than hope—and thereafter the rest of heroic martyrdom, in total, Michael says,

Faith, Virtue, Patience, Temperance, and Love or Charity, "the soul / Of all the rest" (12.584–85). Foreseeing that individual mortal end (as opposed to the apocalyptic one that in *Of Reformation* brings the collective equivalent) means something to the quality of interim spiritual life. The uncouth swain is allowed to hear the unexpressive nuptial song that Lycidas joins. Adam and Eve know that a higher paradise lies in the offing and what they must do while they wait. Christ (in *Paradise Regained*) rejects a broad spectrum of substitute glories.

Given such glimpses of the end from within the trial, the ratio of dramatic to poetic elements must be scaled differently. No moment or exchange maintains a merely natural or social orientation. Lady and her two brothers are initiated into discrepant domains that must somehow be connected if they are to finish either odyssey successfully; yet the masque retains much of the topography of *A Midsummer Night's Dream*, *The Tempest*, and the masques. What Shakespeare and Jonson offer is a dense locale populated with good and bad demons who brush up against symbols already at several removes from Homeric and Ovidian antecedents.

Nature's ambiguity requires that a good deal in both "Comus" and *The Tempest* be sorted out and discarded. Certainly *The Tempest* too does not make an enthusiastic endorsement of the natural condition. Caliban is treated roughly from the outset. The grubbier aspects of his love affair with earth are abandoned in the exodus of nobles from the island, as are the gratifications of Gonzalo's utopian project and Ferdinand's love of the glittery world of Isis and Ceres. A workable middle-level management of city resources in Milan no doubt avoids the extremes of idealism and the primitive, or so it would seem from its past and future dukes. Consequently, anything that runs counter to Prospero's plans must be either reformed or excluded from the marriage and the political settlement. The schemers, who seem to themselves only a knife thrust away from power, are never really a threat. In that respect the play, like "Comus," is as much demonstration as drama. Prospero speaks no more than the truth when he says "My high charms work, / And these mine enemies are all knit up / In their distractions" (3.3.88–91). Perhaps no other Shakespeare play risks so many unequal contests. As men draw swords to commit murder, Ariel heads them off; as Ferdinand raises an arm to defend himself, Prospero freezes him into the cartoon role he designs for him; Caliban and his confederates have no notion how to proceed and no future as revolutionaries. They look dangerous and under ordinary circumstances might be, but not this time.

Like the lack of dramatic engagement in *Pleasure Reconciled*, whose parties succeed each other onstage almost like acts in a variety show, this ritualizing of conflict is partly the result of Shakespeare's making characters into emblems. It also has to do with the powers of artificers. These are in-between, neither celestial nor natural, bridging imagination and intellect. *The Tempest*'s spellbinder is never challenged by Stephano-Trinculo drinking songs, although Caliban absorbs some of Ariel's poetic gift as part of his course in linguistics. Ariel in turn has a touch of Caliban's earthiness, a matter, from this perspective, of chemical and spiritual arts reaching into baser elements as their expressive agents. Air and earth are not equivalent to good and evil or even the refined and the crude, as critics are tempted to think. Generation, youth, age, and harvest can escape Calibanish crudeness if they join the better version that Ariel stages in the masque and hints in the songs. Peasantry and plowmen have a place; savages do not. What must be rejected are fingernail harvests and besotted rebellion, the latter being more dangerous in courtiers than in sullen sailors and drunks.

In this respect, Comus is formidable as a master of revels empowered well beyond Caliban and beyond Jonson's speechless emblem of Bacchus and harvest. That increase in force has a metaphysical rather than a social authority and summons the songwriter and poet to their educational tasks. If Caliban can be forgotten in Miranda's return to civilization, Comus we expect to have an eventful future—as he does in Satan. Together with his associates, he has already had an eventful history. The fault lies not in nature but in Comus's appropriation of it and in the arts he applies to it. He possesses a descriptive amplitude that enters the labyrinth of the ear and speaks softly of every "Dingle or bushy dell of this wild Wood, / And every bosky bourn from side to side" (311–14). Where Caliban's taste runs to drinking songs, Comus is fascinated by voices and heavenly harmonies. In both, monster nature is supposed to be tameable by something like Stevens's substitute for Orpheus, the third girl in "The Plot against the Giant" who whispers "Heavenly labials in a world of gutterals." The witch mothers make an illicit use of resources, but Circe is an adept enslaver of men whereas Sycorax has captured only Ariel (that we hear about) and is no longer present to assert the claim of her offspring to the island.

Caliban's dream of luxury includes enough Ariel-induced harmonies to prepare for his capitulation to Prospero. Despite his susceptibility to "Divine enchanting ravishment," which he relishes for the wrong reasons, Comus is unfit for service except as the herald of Satan and idol-worshipping Philistines. Caliban's choreography of groveling and bog wading supplements Ariel's printless grace and the in-between dance of harvesters (which Jonson concedes to Comus and his crew). His curses suggest a topsy-turvy Orphic power or Circe-like enchantments reduced to childish impotence:

> As wicked dew as e'er my mother brush'd
> With raven's feather from unwholesome fen

>   Drop on you both! a south-west blow on ye
>   And blister you all o'er!
>
>   (1.2.323–26)

Comus can chant such curses more eloquently and make them work. Caliban's parentage adds the witchy monstrous and the fantastic to what could otherwise more legitimately be taken as a version of the new-world savage, which he is, but not exclusively. What prevents *The Tempest* from being a colonizing and merely politically conservative play finally is the attractiveness of both its naturalism and its demi-elves, which represent a romance element native to imaginative fictions. All the more reason, from Milton's viewpoint, to think that, despite a less decisive separation of realms, Shakespeare's localities draw apart as irreconcilable attractions, whereas his own—arranged by loose analogues between Sabrina's realm, Cupid's, and Jove's and by the forward thrust of continence toward the postponed promise—might conceivably hold together as a single enterprise in two basic phases of the soul's growth.

Equally important to the bridging of primitive and improved or transcended nature in Caliban-Comus and Ariel-Spirit is the naturalism of the young ladies. Granted, "naturalism" is precisely what Milton's adolescent Lady resists, but she must at least try to define it. The forest itself would allow no alternative even if Comus did not spring forth as the agent of its confusion. Caliban finds a model for a naive range of charming words in Miranda, who is no less corporeal than he even if she puts her relation to authority in better order and adds beauty, intellect, and virtue to bodily grace. That feminine image of youthful enthusiasm is unmatched in *Pleasure Reconciled* but contributes to pleasure reconciled in *The Tempest* once Ferdinand proves himself a proper suitor. In that respect Miranda stands more in opposition to Sabrina and Lady than in anticipation of them except in verbal charm, which in "Comus" first announces the potential accord of nature and heaven in Lady's wishful echo song.[6] Both Miranda and Lady seek a countervoice or "original response," not the mocking echo of their own. Lady expresses specifically a wish for an answer from her own kind, not the masculine other voice of Eden. What she gets of course is not a Ferdinand, the friendly objectivity of nature, the return of her brothers, or even a celestial echo that would bring nature into partnership with heaven. What she gets first of all is Comus. The call to Echo is ordinarily a first stage in the development of erotic desire, if not the provoking of debate. Lady is caught in a perilous moment of outgoing in which every path seems wrong, the one that leads to the safety of the Egerton household having vanished momentarily. Certainly Milton will not have her awaken to the delights of love and courtly splendor or retreat to narcissism. Nor is her rescue by Sabrina allied with these in any marked way.

Both Shakespeare's and Milton's young ladies are poet's assistants in justifying beauty as a stirrer of motives for possession. They are part of the romantic plot, if Comus making passes at Lady and Caliban attempting to rape Miranda qualify. While Caliban is still a puzzle to himself, Miranda teaches him his own meanings. When he would "gabble like / A thing most brutish," she shaped his grunts into articulate sound (1.2.358–60), without quite making him into a Petrarchan suitor. Something of that female Orpheus is attached to Lady for a moment but is quickly converted into the less-winning resourcefulness of debate. Milton's women generally stir up more commotion than Miranda does, Lady working a reversal of Comus's initial plans and both Eve and Dalila tampering with male devotion to God. Miranda is protected by an active father and good demons; on her own initiative Lady turns aggression against her besieger until her allies arrive. This self-possession, once her moment of fear and doubt is quieted, we can interpret as either the product of Puritan contentiousness and belief in reason or as simply a requirement of the masque's teaching. In either case it identifies an empowered viciousness in nature that underlies the urgency of the greater voyage.

I have hinted at Caliban's contribution to Comus and how short he falls of being a composite necromancer and demon even with Sycorax as a mother. But in several other respects he is surprisingly close to the rudimentary genius of place whom Milton usually assigns the job of collecting "samples" and diagnosing "what the cross dire-looking Planet smites, / Or hurtful Worm with canker'd venom bites" (*Arcades,* 52–53). That is the figure, descended from Eve as gardener, who in "Il Penseroso" is armed with book versions of botany and chemistry and rightly spells "every Star that Heav'n doth shew, / And every Herb that sips the dew." Although possessed of nothing approaching Prospero's magical lore or Ariel's embodiment of the lyric spirit, Miranda's tutorial Caliban does claim to have taken to the task of putting the heavens and the island into nomenclature, which gives some credence to his odd reciprocity of bogs and stellified language.

In that claim, he parodies the adamic figure whose fresh beginning is without either civilized habits or native wisdom—who has remaining mostly the degeneracy and a little of the autumnal mode. Paradoxically, what the primitive natural man illustrates is how alien nature has become from its own best forms. Its elements deny easy harvest. They also deny easy accommodation to the mind's desire for names and intelligible symbols, which is one reason that Prospero has devoted so much of his life to esoteric studies. An urge for poetry comes to Caliban not only in Miranda's company but whenever he dreams. Early in the play, he shows at least the rudiments of social reciprocation:

> When thou cam'st first,
> Thou strok'st me, and made much of me; wouldst give me
> Water with berries in't; and teach me how
> To name the bigger light, and how the less,
> That burn by day and night: and then I lov'd thee,
> And show'd thee all the qualities o' th'isle,
> The fresh springs, brine-pits, barren place and fertile:
> Curs'd be I that did so!
>
> (1.2.334–41)

He is intellect struggling to free itself from barbarism and bring classification to things already familiar to sight and touch. As Stephen Orgel points out, the agriculture he practices is without tools and engines.[7] In guiding Trinculo to nature's bounty, he becomes not only a poor spiritless Adam but an Ariel parody, echoing the gestures of songs. He is not an infiltrating light or tangent force of metaphor on the surface of objects where mind meets substance but a pair of hands digging in:

> I prithee, let me bring thee where crabs grow;
> And I with my long nails will dig thee pig-nuts;
> Show thee a jay's nest, and instruct thee how
> To snare the nimble marmoset; I'll get thee
> To clustering filberts, and sometimes I'll get thee
> Young scamels from the rock. Wilt thou go with me?
>
> (2.2.167–72)

In the courtesy of this, we should not overlook the vehemence of the earlier and less gentle "curs'd be I that did so," which is like Satan's recoil into the siege of contraries. It suggests a failure of lyric apostrophe just when place beckons the mind to unite with created forms and perhaps move from mere naming to lyric. That may remind us that Lady too lacks the immediacy of Eve's creaturely address. It will not do to sentimentalize Caliban merely because he has stirring dreams and squatter's rights to the island. Whether we like it or not, Shakespeare gives him criminal impulses, virtually no sense of right and wrong, and none at all of *vestigia dei*, which Comus does have in a perverted form. The advance of mind and language is stopped short in his prickly vegetable and insect items. His kinship with Miranda and forerunning of the two Comuses nonetheless show in his conversion of sight and sound to primitive science and in his reaction to a splendidly outfitted mankind in the last scene: "O Setebos, these be brave spirits indeed! / How fine my master is!" (5.1.261–62).

This is Shakespeare's main point and again a signal for Milton to detour once Comus has made a similar gesture in hailing Lady. That happens early enough to give ample opportunity to develop the idolatrous side of Comus's worship and to recast the cultivation of nature in terms Spirit bestows on Sabrina. If living in a natural state does not free Caliban from slavery to appetite, ceremonies based on status and on civil conversation might. Rival ceremonies cannot do much for Comus, who has his own. Nature in itself is thereby made no better or worse for Milton; it is merely the confusing, potentially beautiful, always ambiguous scene of the trial. Inner merit, not nature's redemption or its use, brings assistance and justifies the music and dance that are devoted to chastity's triumph. Nature's last function in recalling the Garden of Adonis is to parallel the blessings of the saints mentioned in the opening lines. To map the way toward other groves and other streams will take the progress of "Lycidas" through the realm of the overwhelming sea to apotheosis and the progress of humankind from Eden to the end of waiting.

City and Country Entertainments

Although both "Comus" and *The Tempest* concern discipline and moral conduct amid natural bounty, the festivity of both texts suggests that it is possible to overstate their rigor, especially the restraints Shakespeare's not always sweet-tempered magician imposes on Ferdinand and Caliban. Each text eases up in its own way even while warning of the dangers. The junctures at which they do so reveal something of the relation of rites of passage to poetry and of governance to social class. Comus is the paradigmatic case of cultic overdoing, of excess given all the fervor of initiation ceremony and membership recruitment, outfitted with worship, magic, and the arts. His own rapture, however, or at least a new phase of it, begins when he hears the Echo song and breaks out in adjectives and adverbs:

> Sure something holy lodges in that breast,
> And with these raptures moves the vocal air
> To testify his hidd'n residence;
> How sweetly did they float upon the wings
> Of silence, through the empty-vaulted night,

> At every fall smoothing the Raven down
> Of darkness till it smil'd.
>
> (246–52)

The compliment to Alice Egerton's singing and Lawes's music is probably meant to stand, even though Comus is reminded of his mother and her "Sirens three" and the good times they had in making swine of travelers. He is stirred to "exchanged words," as Cicero calls such devices of transfer as "empty-vaulted" and "vocal air," and to catachresis (or abuse). The entire inserted lyric is animated enough to bed down the raven night and make it smile like an innocent child. "Testify" rises a notch in transitive power from the more usual "testify to" and brings the song close to the manifesting of truth that holy scriptures undertake, just the sort of idolatry Comus performs with starry choirs and ancient goddesses. A good deal is obviously being twisted and displaced in his music appreciation, which in his family normally goes with the culling of baleful drugs and the handiwork of those who as they sing "take the prison'd soul, / And lap it in *Elysium*" (257).

To this example of why restraint is necessary could be added Ariel's dangling of banquets and other enticements before the senses. The airy splendor of inserted lyrics in both texts comes laden with an abundance not only of Calibanish delights but of blossoms and "odorous banks that blow / Flowers" of mingled hue. Since we are supposed to be entertained by them, the texts themselves, with all their costumes, dances, vocal arrangements, and images, are the worst offenders if such things are truly bad for us. The question to ask may be the bearing on moral law of releases of desire. Especially in "Comus," some of the poetic enrichment comes as a surprise from the abuser of words, at least the quantity and high status of it, accompanied by the energy of dancing troops and nature pouring "her bounties forth / With such a full and unwithdrawing hand,"

> Covering the earth with odors, fruits, and flocks,
> Thronging the Seas with spawn innumerable.
>
> (710–13)

The corresponding bounty in Ceres' masque and Caliban's imagery is not really disciplined on the spot, as William Bowden suggests that it should be.[8] It is allowed its uncritical moments and local triumphs and has much to do with the recurrent success of the play, perhaps more than its plot does. As David Lindley notices, Ariel's song of summer freedom, for instance, comes after Prospero has called for solemn airs and qualifies them. Like Caliban's "No more dams," it reads like a spontaneous personal overflow.[9] Those unreproved pleasures suggest a poetic supplement to the social wellbeing of the betrothal and the subdued rebels and thus a release of song from the dramatic functions it has had to perform and a continued disparity between Ariel and his spirit-dampening master. In that respect, Ariel's singing, like Autolycus's, is one of a kind with Shakespeare's other funnelings of energy into free spirits. Miranda's and Caliban's exclamations recapture the wonder of glittering social models and might lead to a greater sense of accomplished initiation and membership in a community if Prospero did not counter that excess too. It is his melancholy savoring of the autumnal mood, more than the rigor, that overmatches the festivity, both in its amplitude and in its digression from the business at hand.

Where it is allowed to go unchecked, bounty prompts three kinds of responses in both "Comus" and *The Tempest*: the desire to consume it, the desire to replicate it in symbols and allegories or simply to celebrate it, and the logistical or social desire to organize and distribute it, the last of these much more prominent in *The Tempest*. These are vastly different means of possessing. The failings of the subversives fall in all three categories—gobbling up, representing, and "sharing" by conspiratorial seizing. In a play filled with "sanctimonious ceremonies" and rites, Caliban's consuming, representing, and redistributing, to take seemingly the most hopeless example to go with Comus's comprehensive one, have to travel some distance from his teaming up with Stephano and Trinculo to get to anything acceptable. Far from divine enchanting ravishment, his songs are rough chants on the order of "Flout'em and cout'em / And scout'em and flout'em" (3.2.119–20). As to social logistics and redistributions of goods and power, what he proposes to do specifically to his forbidder (while stealing his magic and his daughter) is unfriendly:

> there thou mayst brain him,
> Having first seiz'd his books; or with a log
> Batter his skull, or paunch him with a stake,
> Or cut his wezand with thy knife.
> (3.2.86–89)

The object of all this violence is to control the larder by mastering what protects it in the current hierarchy, which is stingy in its apportioning and overbearing in its social organization. What Caliban reduces to foot-stomping metrics and crude gratification is the more civilized stabbing that an Antonio would have Sebastian apply to Alonso. Antonio's aim too is to exploit the social order for his own gratification. Nature after all enhances the uses and attractions of power and is partly what the fuss is about for both Caliban and for Comus, despite their enthusiasm for the company they come across. Much of what Caliban says and does performs a loutish turn on custom, speech, song, courtship, service, agriculture, and leadership, each of these a phase of the public order and its shaping of individual desire to the available objects. Although the play's humor is not as broad or as well witnessed as that of *A Midsummer Night's Dream* and is never so startling as that of Antigonous pursued by the bear, the absurdity of the contrast between lower sedition and higher sedition, and the contrast of both of these to Prospero's magisterial command, makes the discipline easy to apply. When the aggressors ease up, however, the guard can relax as well. All along Prospero has managed (through Ariel) by coaxing and song as well as by beatings and pinches. That the most misshapen knave of all can get from battered skulls to "How fine my master is!" is a tribute both to him and to the image he finally acknowledges. Eve's "The Serpent me beguil'd and I did eat" is not more winning to Milton than Caliban's "I'll be wise hereafter" to Shakespeare. Both bow to the undeniable power of the paradisal bestower and forbidder.

If Caliban's last speeches grope toward a better idea of service and of ennobled nature than he has managed before, they do so in the context of mercy's tempering of justice and Prospero's overall cure of the contention that began with Antonio's treachery and explodes anew in the sailor's back talk at the beginning of the play. Once the noble image and the external discipline have departed the island, we might doubt that Caliban will wander through his berry patches and say, as Adam does, under this tree he "Stood visible, among these Pines his voice / I heard, here with him at this Fountain talk'd"; but he will presumably not be as he was before Miranda taught him words and Ariel gave him dreams, both extensions of Prospero's gentler side. His glimpse of another world has been too compelling, and again it has been partly of liberal goods accompanied by art and pageantry. Dream representation, in collaboration with airs, doesn't so much translate riches into ornaments as heighten their physical appeal:

> Be not afeard; the isle is full of noises,
> Sounds and sweet airs, that give delight, and hurt not.
> Sometimes a thousand twangling instruments
> Will hum about mine ears; and sometimes voices
> That, if I then had wak'd after long sleep,
> Will make me sleep again: and then, in dreaming,
> The clouds methought would open, and show riches
> Ready to drop upon me; that, when I wak'd,
> I cried to dream again.
>
> (3.2.133–41)

Where Caliban merely marks the presences and records the emotion, Comus's rhapsodies to nature and to the something holy within the ravishing singer are better armed with intellect and readier for misapplication. But both are captivated and respond with their own answerable eloquence. Ariel might well have planted these particular dreams of our universal primitive delight; but beyond receiving them, Caliban requires language to reissue them and gain self-consciousness concerning his own reaction. That improved sociability is what Miranda has taught him, along with basic science. Caliban may own the island before the invasion, then, but he does not know how to double it and repossess it in narrations of its resources. He is a monster clearly ready to be undone by heavenly labials or at least ready for a gentler model than he finds in his stern enslaver, until he comes at last to see the nobility of the European overlords. The better image of nature, the master artisan and distributor, at that point becomes part of the lyric dream.

It is not a totally different Caliban, merely a more westernized one advancing from one level of delights to another who opts for clemency and makes it almost conceivable that the change will take. Whatever optimism he allows, as we last see him he is undoubtedly awakened from the dream and knows that proper service lies in laying everything he has at the feet of well-clad apparitions. He is now perhaps as much an image of the overcome beast in them and in us as an identifiable new-world savage. (The latter after all did not have to be taught a first language.) His flirtation with poetry suggests that the play's contrast is not only between romance and a realistic development of character (as Howard Felperin suggests)[10] but also between a lyricism of dim intuitions and this more initiated attachment to the noble company. As to the management that citizens of Milan and Naples show in that company, what matters to it is less plantations than social forms. Titles and manners come first; economics follows. Getting a fuller sense of the coincidence of manners and status is one benefit of journeying to the far edge to see Caliban and coach him into orthodoxy and away from his tendency for enslavement to the Trinculos and Stephanos.

That Milton is less inclined to put the poet at the disposal of social forms does not make him oblivious to them; it merely shifts the balance from manners and their expression in festive rites to what he regards as the final cause of human form, which is not genealogy but the express resemblance of the gods. It is really this that Comus discovers in Lady through the vocal airs. His debate with her casts him in the role of sophisticate in charge of confusing that first priority. It suggests as an antidote a combination of plain living and spiritual calm, no matter on what social level, reinforced by the issuance of argument, airs, and lyrics. As John D. Cox points out, court and country cross in Milton's way of seeing them.[11] I take these to be rival proportionings of manners and goods, with goods dominating country ways, and rituals and forms city ways. The categories also cross in *The Tempest* and in intervening masques, but with a preconceived preference for sophistication and with more debased opposites in crude rustics and demons (Jonson's Comus again excepted). The lower classes of *The Tempest* must be forlorn and inept to team up with Caliban, whose idea of courtship appears all the more ridiculous by comparison to Ferdinand's. Like Florizel, who has Mopsa and Clown as foils, the heir apparent to Naples encounters a country-raised but well-born maiden *in* but not *of* the country. (The country-city groups in *A Midsummer Night's Dream* and *As You Like It* are more complex, with sophisticated foolishness traveling into the forest to encounter there rough-hewn counterparts and fairies in charge of weather and harvests.)

Spirit's vertical range and his family service as Thyrsis-Lawes comment not only on regions above and beyond the wood but on the shepherd tradition, another line of "country" forms that has to do with the mastering and representing of nature. Virgilian pastoral is a way of translating Arcadia into codified courtesies and Orphic tamings of the wild without drawing upon urban luxuries or class distinctions. Neither *The Tempest* nor "Comus" makes much of that pastoral, but they do recognize the option and its resemblance to the naturalized songs of Ariel, Lady, and Spirit. Sabrina's descent from Anchises suggests still a third side of imported civilization to match the others, hers more architectural than musical. Although it includes luxury, it places less stress on provincial dynasty and its contribution to nationalism than river regions do in Drayton and Spenser. As in the Orphic power of Thyrsis, moral behavior guiding from within takes precedence over the possession and use of resources.

Comus's roaming of Spanish, French, and English lands puts a counterculture in transit toward the same vicinity as the negative of all these—an inverted Virgilian shepherdom, a rival source of the performing arts, and the life of balls and revels within sumptuous architectural piles. He is thus the perpetrator of a range of bad forms and misappropriations. As I suggested, that he also possesses potions by which the express resemblance can be changed "Into some brutish form of Wolf, or Bear" (69–70) makes him more dangerous than Caliban and his clay-footed comrades, who have no access to the book of magic and not a very winning collection of chants and charms. His skill in magic, in fact, gives him something of Prospero's magisterial command and suggests a comprehensive inhumanity spread out over the threefold division of Ariel, Caliban, and Prospero.

It is the chief business of such a demon of feral images to cover the divine analogue with fur in a dreamlike monstrosity beyond mere deformity. His range from forest to palace offers a different festivity for every company in the celebration branch of his command. In his high spirits the masque reassesses the folk gatherings of "L'Allegro" and "Il Penseroso"; in its powerful ancestry and demon intent, it looks forward to contrasts on a larger scale

The Tempest's Capable Spirits Vanishing, Milton's Ascending 215

between pandaemonium and heaven and between Israelite and Philistine notions of holiday, both of which have dropped most of the city-country associations of the thirties. All these topographies and their local inhabitants suggest that to live in paradise surrounded with riches is not enough. If the spirit is to dwell in those riches, it must draw them into the inner chambers with rhythmic words and recited images and discover in them intimations of their origins.

How rustics are mannered is thus not the chief difficulty Milton sees in the propensity for good times that overlaps holier raptures, nor does he associate incontinence with the primitivism of Calibanish violence. Slit wizards and staked paunches fall outside Comus's tactics, and the "loose unlettred hinds" that Lady hears and Younger Brother thinks might find her are the very distant sounds of "Riot and ill-manag'd Merriment." When Spirit renders his variant of the Circe myth (44–45), he calls attention to a particularly Reformation and Platonist interpretation of the reverse motion in metamorphosis, the motion of the inner self toward crude nature. As an indulgent moment of make-believe bestiality, a similar change is usually expressed in the costumed dances of the masque that reflect its ballet origins. Hence "Midnight shout and revelry / Tipsy dance and Jollity" (103–4) must be rigorously excluded in the initial stages if their cadences are not to break down the barriers.

To lessen the loss of leaving the island in *The Tempest,* some of Ariel's summer freedom must brush off and become partly political in the satisfactions of the marriage plot. Forbidden equivalents to that freedom have been cast as escapist and criminal self-gratification. Judgment here too is partly a matter of knowing who opts for what. As I suggested earlier, any set of plans and any momentary whim are illicit if Prospero cannot endorse them. The play has more misadventures and schemes ill laid than either *A Midsummer Night's Dream* or "Comus," which gathers its evils into one consortium. Most of the countermotions marked for discard are founded on misperceptions of the social order or desire sprung loose from legitimate form. They begin on the ship of state sinking under inadequate leadership and continue until the ship and its obedient crew are ready to sail again. Antonio and Sebastian are given just enough rope to hang themselves. The atmosphere of change and freedom encourages Gonzalo's utopian blueprint, which enlarges the social imagination without giving it feasibility.

Although harmless in itself, that scheme is typical of attempts to liberalize the free spirit in all phases of life, when to Prospero it belongs only to special occasions and more to symbolic presentations than to actual life. Trinculo provides a basic reason that all such projects fail simply by being himself and knowing the rest of the citizenry: "They say there's but five upon this isle: we are three of them; if th' other two be brain'd like us, the state totters" (3.2.4–6). Those with brains in *The Tempest* recognize the possibilities of self-satisfaction within a system. It is dangerous even to pursue esoteric delights beyond the reach of responsible rule, as Prospero has in preferring the power of the magus to that of the duke. His error is obviously of a higher order than his brother's or Caliban's and reaps undeniable benefits for the duration of the play, but what he has learned of magic can be used only for reformative purposes.

Ferdinand's dream of Miranda, in contrast to the aborted hopes, *is* achievable because it fosters what society needs and falls into an acceptable romance pattern. Caliban's desire to people the island is its farcical inversion, just as his tiptoeing toward Prospero's cell translates social revolution into myopic clowning. The defining contrast for Milton is between Comus as Lady's suitor and the mythological lovers, Venus and Adonis, Cupid and Psyche. Shakespeare sets out to fulfill the genealogical imperative, somewhat chastened in the aftermath of the broken-off masque; the game of chess has nothing of the riches of Ceres in its stiff pageantry of bishops and knights. Milton's mythological pairs, presented in a passage he might not have written later in his career, reintroduce the holy rapture Comus feels for Lady and perhaps the song-induced ecstasy of the poet of "L'Allegro" and "Il Penseroso" at a level that prefigures the unexpressive nuptial song.

The poetry of abundance and of gentle metamorphoses that infiltrates the island's atmosphere and Caliban's dreams is also a reconceiving and repossessing that in the masque rises to myth. But in Shakespeare's case that ascent is temporary. Although it extracts from Ferdinand the desire to live entirely within the symbolic pageant, the elegiac poetry that follows is a means of simultaneously representing and letting go. The representing finds corresponding sublimations (in "Comus") in Venus and Adonis and in Sabrina; the elegiac note is unnecessary, thanks to the eternal summer Spirit vouches for. *The Tempest*'s discrepancy between Prospero's extended vision and the earthly possible is hinted even within the masque by Ariel's association of Ceres with images not only of fertility and bounty but of rocky shores and forlorn bachelors, which represents a sterility that forms no part of either Comus's or Spirit's consciousness (and of course no part of Eden).

Prospero's eventual reduction to merely administrative powers is also anticipated by the elegiac note of the sweetly sad Ariel, whose own aim is solitude and whose imagery suggests the escape of the riches it presents. Eyes that have become pearl no longer see; bones made into coral no longer move. Within the natural process from spring to fall, the harvest is only part of the story:

> Iris. *Ceres, most bounteous lady, thy rich leas*
> *Of wheat, rye, barley, vetches, oats, and pease;*

Thy turfy mountains, where live nibbling sheep,
And flat meads thatch'd with stover, them to keep;
Thy bank with pioned and twilled brims,
Which spongy April at thy hest betrims,
To make cold nymphs chaste crowns; and thy broom-groves,
Whose shadows the dismissed bachelor loves,
Being lass-lorn; thy poll-clipt vineyard;
And thy sea-marge, sterile and rocky-hard,
Where thou thyself dost air;—the queen o' th' sky,
Whose wat'ry arch and messenger am I,
Bids thee leave these. . . .
Approach, rich Ceres, her to entertain.

(4.1.60–75)

Cold nymphs and dismissed bachelors balance the copiousness. In the way of poetic indirection and tonal modification, they perhaps reflect upon marriage, a little chilled itself in Ferdinand's cheating at chess. If a poll-clipt vineyard is halfway to civilization, a rocky-hard sea-marge stands further off. Nor is what Iris lists any more immune to long-range dissolution than the palace and temples, which constitutes an admission that the victory over nature in either city or country is as temporary and partial as the herdsman's and farmer's over pastures and fields. Rainbows are as fragile as Caliban's dreams and Gonzalo's fantasies.

It would be pressing too far to associate the autumnal note of *The Tempest* with tragedy, although a similar note is sounded in Macbeth's "my way of life / Is fall'n into the sere, the yellow leaf" (5.3.22–23). Yet even if no drastic emptying of "honour, love, obedience, troops of friends" awaits Prospero, the large-scale cancelling in the revels speech and the discarding of powers are unusually somber for comedy. Where Jaques banishes himself from the restored dukedom and carries off most of the countersentiment of *As You Like It*, Prospero's pessimism is less easily remedied. In contrast, the Miltonic agents of visionary splendor point the way to a permanent marriage of the something holy within to what best fulfills it. They are also moral teachers who know the origins of the express resemblance and what matches the soul to its glory. They can combine obligation with delight and reconcile eventual freedom to interim discipline. In Spirit's intermediate place, although Venus and Adonis are somewhat inactive and saddened by Adonis's wound (usually a sign of the yearly vegetable cycle), *celestial* (!) Cupid "Holds his dear *Psyche* sweet entranc't / After her wand'ring labors long," having apparently earned that repose by the journey he too has taken from Greek and Roman precincts. Nothing forbids the access of the virtuous to such a realm.

In sum: what Kerrigan calls the "apotheosis of narcissism"[12] in Milton's epilogue makes self-indulgence no longer forbidden. The west winds that stir the imagination come laden with balmy smells. Chaste fertility comes without labor or mingled sterility but represents a departure from both the sources and from Lady and Sabrina, the latter being limited to emergency help for ailing herds and imperiled virgins. Lyric celebration (as opposed to charmed summoning and echo-song beseeching) lies amid narrative vision and escapes from woods and palaces. Both Ariel and Spirit move very close to allegories of poetic genesis, but Prospero has to abandon the romance of interior paramours when the play comes to its epilogue; Milton only begins to disclose such a romance at the corresponding point of the masque. The result in the latter is a reconnecting of the dramatic rites of passage to bardic poetry. Shakespeare's forbidding of visionary gratification puts Prospero the governor in the spotlight. Although the former magician does not frustrate anything very worthwhile in the Gonzalos and Antonios, that restriction of himself dampens the festivity. In what becomes literally a dispirited play, his curing Caliban and Antonio of their lustful itch has little carryover in his own mood. What the Egertons have accomplished does have an effect on the victorious dance "O'er sensual Folly and Intemperance," even if for all this I have not succeeded in saying how far that first joy leads toward the second. Certainly the Ludlow masque renders a reverse belittlement in its reassessment in the light of the dance around the golden tree. Milton does not allow the juxtaposition its full logic, since to do so might undermine the triumph more than he wants and suggest a disconnection where we are perhaps to be only a little put off, not utterly baffled or disheartened. He is not prepared to say just yet that vatic gratification is antithetical to what moral effort gains here and now and so passes without noticeably altering course straight to the "additional saying" (*epi-legein*) to match the opening fore-saying, with its true servants on their "Sainted seats."

8

Holy Signs and Songs

Truth indeed came once into the world with her divine Master, and was a perfect shape most glorious to look on. But when he ascended, and his apostles after him were laid to sleep, then straight arose a wicked race of deceivers, who, as that story goes of the *Egyptian Typhon* with his conspirators, how they dealt with the good *Osiris,* took the virgin Truth, hewed her lovely form into a thousand pieces, and scatter'd them to the four winds.

—*Areopagitica*

Patrimony and Forms of Drama in This Second Eden

Although a matter as complex as Milton's apprenticeship and refurbishing of things Shakespearean—a case in point of Puritan rethinking of things Elizabethan and Jacobean—does not lend itself easily to summary and goes through several phases and adjustments, I want to insert a synoptic attempt here for the sake of orientation and then devote the rest of this chapter to the sorts of reading that contributed to Milton's reshaping of genres and tracing of their origins. Armed with the theory of representation and signs that he and others draw upon, we can turn in the next chapter to specifics in texts other than "Comus" and their compromises between drama and bardic transport. Milton's predecessors sometimes put in an appearance through allusion in such compromises. Translations of classical texts also figure in it. As John Hollander points out, those who professed to be men of letters in the Renaissance made one vast transumption of such sources. What models in any genre mean to Milton is bound up in that large enterprise of reclaiming, as it is for most of the major figures from Wyatt to Pope.[1] But the conditions of allusion and rewriting obviously change once a poet has English models in front of him, especially such dominant ones as Spenser, Shakespeare, and Jonson. Arthurian and Italian romances after the 1690s have to be seen through Spenser; Catullus, Martial, and Horace through Jonson; and so on.

In the Shakespeare-Milton relation (as in the Spenser-Milton one), succession is a second-generation reaction skewed by generic differences, observance of specific occasions and contexts, and personal style. Concerning the second of these, the issues of the 1630s are the more important inducements for Milton's reconceiving of masque elements; unfortunately, they are also the most intangible. One can only conclude that however well-delegated Jove's rule is in the "Imperial rule of the Sea-girt Isles" (21), however Spenserian the river kingdom of Sabrina's "lofty head" and the new Garden of Adonis, Milton's ambition is not satisfied by the usual masque rhetoric in praise of noble houses. His celestial Cupid, Psyche, and their offspring (eternal Youth and Joy) go well beyond *The Tempest* in rewarding well-tried virtue on its own and freeing it of English locality. Whereas Ariel's masque keeps sensuous revels under constraints by denying Venus a place, Milton lets imagination range into uninhibited desires, as though his real teacher in the epilogue were Colin Clout piping to the buxom, mirthful Graces. Some imaginative effort thereafter goes to reinstating the winds and flowers of Spirit's jocund spring in other settings in "Lycidas" and eventually *Paradise Lost.*

Despite a keen eye for the stress fractures of Elizabethan and Stuart institutions, Shakespeare uses dramatic forms not to prepare for such a permanent shift of place but to probe the issues of place and power and return to kingships or dukedoms in better health. Breakdowns in authority are nearly always destructive and seldom lead to anything better, despite a coexisting regret that even the best workable state excludes the idealizing imagination or makes it look fairylike in Ariel, or foolish in Gonzalo. He is consistent in this conservatism from beginning to end. As Ruth Nevo points out (following Northrop Frye), the softer elements of his earlier comedies as modeled on Roman New Comedy are teleological in the sense that they move toward the satisfying of gentle hearts secure in their affections, claiming positions appropriate to breeding and merit.[2] Position and merit together, never separately. At the point of unmasking in *As You Like It,* Hymen's festivities make courtship serve that restoration, as it normally does. Jaques's recalcitrance leaves him outside, where he is likely to stay. Marginality in some, subordination in most, and evasion in everyone are the requirements of the life of excellence so defined. The reverential treatment of mate-selecting sentiment marks a Shakespearean change in the comic emphasis of Plautus and Terence, who expend their energies less on the pairing up and the dodging than in raking wit back and forth across the insensitivities of parasites, fools, idealists, braggarts, and critics.

Shakespeare's English plots differ somewhat from Roman and Greek ones in validating authority, because neither Rome nor Athens has houses of Lancaster or York or can prescribe an elder-son succession. That Antony and Cleopatra have no inheriting issue makes love a truancy, not a serviceable courtship. Thus the idealizing of the state as a silent partner in love affairs is lost—perhaps one reason that the Roman setting encourages problem plays and tragedies rather than comedies. Cleopatra's children are no danger to Octavius, who threatens to murder them only in order to prevent Cleopatra from depriving him of his public triumph. Rome itself prefers politically arranged marriages. That separation of the military or administrative aspects of chivalry from erotic ones not only drives the political-military Antony from the Egyptian-reveler Antony but plays havoc with the concept of a fulfilled private dream gaining public recognition in the combination of fierce wars and faithful loves that Elizabethan neochivalry liked. It perhaps has something to do with reducing Antony's festivity to debauchery and projecting the afterlife he does. In the real world, dramatic dialogue, shadowed by political responsibilities, cannot entirely shake the envious lowering of the blatant beast; in Hades, lovers can promenade openly.

That the entire visible state is absorbed in struggles for power in *Julius Caesar, Coriolanus,* and *Troilus and Cressida* makes us appreciate all the more the capacity of the comedies and histories to restore authority wherever they find a solid genealogy and a consensus. Henry V's courtship of Kate comes as an afterthought and scarcely shows the commitment or abandonment of an Othello or an Antony, but it does suggest a reinforcement of the king's reign by nuptial comedy. A fuller romance makes it possible for Ferdinand and Florizel to have both their kingdoms and their chaste young ladies, who bring courtship in from its more circuitous wanderings. The lovers have grace and ardor enough to inspire lyricism, however short it falls of Ariel's and Prospero's magnitude. The magic and the marvels also expose the imagination's escape from an exclusive social identity and offer a critique of Prospero's and Polixenes' firm fatherly judgment.

Poetic excursions are difficult to bring into line with the plausibilities that drama prefers. They add a dimension to the critique of ideologies that get their chief voicing in the dramatic cross fire. Octavius and Cleopatra reveal each other to be suspect and incomplete, both by explicit analysis and by a contrast in style. Even when such parties pay tribute to each other, they are not necessarily reconcilable. Octavius on behalf of the dead Antony falls short of Cleopatra on that same enigmatic figure, she rising to lyric, he merely to imperialist rhetoric:

> The breaking of so great a thing should make
> A greater crack. The round world
> Should have shook lions into civil streets,
> And citizens to their dens. The death of Antony
> Is not a single doom, in the name lay
> A moiety of the world.
>
> (5.1.14–19)

Cleopatra's diction has a comparable infatuation with "world" encompassment, but *her* world, when it gets installed beyond the reach of this one, gives her a personal investment we do not detect in Octavius's funeral oratory. We suspect that Octavius does not mean half of what he says and is imagining rising tiers of filled senate seats.

The Origins of Genres in the First Eden

We can only speculate from such things as the political tracts, reflections of *The Tempest* in "Comus," and the awarding of a small empire to Sabrina just what Milton saw in this division between projected desire and the social arena. Or for that matter what Milton might have felt about Shakespeare's awarding of eloquence to Macbeth's ruinous energies, Ariel's restless desire for freedom, and the transcendent yearnings of Lear. But he himself grants the poet and the epic narrator privileges over the dramatist by way of conclusion-making and access to a country beyond politics. He insists upon the latter almost from the very beginning of his concept of the poet. He is obviously not so willing to bypass the state in the prose-writing interim and makes a serious attempt to put rhetoric in the service of a moral elite. The millennial fervor for a time made it seem as though the visible state could become an equivalent to the visible church, which for Milton does not exclude a range of cultural enrichments. An ideal Christian commonwealth depends on an educated citizenry that knows its classics as well as the Bible. What sets such a state apart from "Hunnish and Norwegian statelines" (in *Areopagitica*) is polite "wisdom and letters." It is not clear that even Christ in *Paradise Regained* goes entirely back on that article of faith. That Englishmen are not Goths and Jutlanders depends (in 1644 at least) on a humanism that in its openness risks the proliferation of heresies but roots them out by debate well informed by tradition.

Classical learning is not sufficient in itself, however. What Milton uses of it reinforces a community of scholars, whom he imagines contributing to a civil edifice the perfection of which "consists in this, that out of many moderat varieties and brotherly dissimilitudes that are not vastly disproportionall rises the goodly and gracefull symmetry that commends the whole pile and structure."[3] The function of rhetoric is not to close ranks but to put wayfarers such as Lady and champions of refutation such as Christ and Abdiel on the offensive in a fallen world, to reclaim it from obvious error. Mimetic drama serves by throwing opponents together under conditions that educate both the combatants and the readers; dialectic serves drama by raising serial incidents to illustrative status and moralizing them. Any chronicle episode a representation takes up, even from the Bible, remains less interpretable in its source than it becomes after the dramatist has disclosed the detailed relations among plotted incidents, types, and ideas. As to the principles that underlie that collaborative effort of rhetoric and dialectic: the genealogy that counts most to Milton's dramatic contests is the one that passes from *the* father to the son-word. A portion of their dominion goes to first parents and in damaged form to their progeny, among whom arguments are likely to be specious. But in Milton's scheme of things, that danger is overcome by the visibility of the son on the pinnacle in *Paradise Regained*, where within history itself he renews Adam, corrects Eve, and reinstates the father's image.

Origins

This retrieval of authority in its roots is primarily what gives the bardic poet his sharpest deviation from most classical and many English predecessors. It places the origin of genres in the circumstantial recoveries of the word, planted mostly trouble-free in Eden, to be relocated only with sifting and sorting thereafter. For Adam and Eve as its least-hampered adaptors, stimulants for invention come from turns of the edenic clock and from visitations that insert into human language matters from far-off. I will reserve some of the details for the next chapter, but it is useful here to have the main principle of derivation before us, including some negative variants. When Satan hits upon warfare to counter angel hymnody, for instance, what he discovers is the aggressive status-claiming of Homeric rhetoric. The moment warmongering breaks out in heaven is the same unsettling moment that the hierarchy is jostled, the hierarchy as a chain of authority and a conduit for the passing on of the father's goodness. By means that Ezekiel and the Book of Revelation suggest, Christ on the chariot then converts into apocalyptic symbolism the epic that has adopted the mass expressions of phalanx and cannon. Christ thus unwrinkles deceit by a kind of supertrope, and we get a hint of seventeenth-century Puritanism surveying history plays, tragedies, Virgilian epics, Spenserian and Italian chivalric romances, and medieval tales of Arthur, and deciding that behind the chivalric displays of these national literatures lies a misconstrued dream of glory that fixes its love on banners and the rhetoric of status.

Before the fall, edenic genres have more peaceful beginnings and make no use of parody. The love language that Adam and Eve invent comes in response to morning and night and to spiritual growth. Eve's confessional autobiography (the first of its kind except for Sin's negative version) leaves its narcissist beginnings behind and proceeds to the discovery of dialogues. Thereafter until the fall, Eve addresses lyrics to her "Author and disposer" within the general elaboration of a mutuality that so far is their only "state." In setting up transitions to next moments, she keeps both the local hierarchy and her origin in view. Knowledge fairly easily keeps pace with sensation and new experience. Thus in asking Adam about stars at the end of a kind of Petrarchan blazon (the first of *its* kind too and as Milton's logic goes the purest and best), Eve gives evening talk a rapturous but controlled pace. Adam incorporates science into his response and while laying out their domestic labors and studies makes it not only increasingly apt for personal relations but a way to command abstraction. His talk with Raphael (in a symposium format) employs accommodation to get beyond Eden without ambition-inspired transport.

Milton thus discovers the source of several genres in the flow of the moments and encounters they develop between two or more compatible but quite different minds. He asks the reader to place each distinct emergence into a whole that reveals itself momentarily and partially, on the move, so that whatever seems dramatic is also implicitly visionary. To understand anything local is necessarily to understand its source and its purpose. Instrumental and efficient causes are applied types of final causes. Each form or mode is relatively satisfying and complete in its place but only partial in its requiring of adjacent kinds and moments to establish its limits.

Rather than becoming totally discrete, the genres of Adam and Eve assemble combinations that subsequent literary tradition will fragment. They conceive the diction of georgic alongside that of pastoral, for instance, and finish the creation in garden labor as a type of works and days. Whereas *The Tempest* makes both the labors of Caliban and the dreams of Gonzalo and Caliban into detours that the social order will eventually leave behind, in Eden nothing need be lost. Later episodes echo earlier ones. Even though any lower form is defective by comparison to a higher one, it is analogous and related. It calls down analogues that in turn lift it up. Thus divine love (as it passes among angels or between the divine father and son) is echoed in less perfect form in the human variety; Adam in looking at Eve in Book IV is not turning away from God but reenacting the meeting of minds portrayed in Book III. An aubade comes with morning; as day blends into evening it yields to evening song; evening then leads to sleep through Adam's mini-lecture on stars and tomorrow's work, and on through the marriage rites, all full of celestial echoes. The particular night we observe it, sleep brings Eve's dream, a moonlit and illusory insertion into Eden's repertory of one of Satan's misrepresentational modes, in an enticing rhetoric disguised as lyric apostrophe. Night then passes to morning by way of "Awake / My fairest, my espous'd, my latest found" and its correction of the satanic greeting ("Why sleep'st thou *Eve?*"). But what Adam's aubade anticipates and recalls primarily is another range of high spousal relations and summonings, ultimately perhaps the wedding of bridegroom to soul and the apocalyptic call to the awakening dead. Besides the marriage of Eden, it reveals the range of marriage in its meetings of minds, including the presence of the divine mind in those it chooses to inspire. As morning orison follows aubade and Eve's second autobiographical narrative, the relation of one mode to another follows from the restored day, having been temporarily threatened by moonlit adventurism and novelty.

Both the experience and the mode of representation are cross-referenced as words repossess act and assimilate it to other planes of existence by analogy. Insofar as some of the comparison moments are fallen ones, the genres develop a long-range dialectic, polarized in the extreme as God against Satan. Some dramatic unease creeps into even peaceful exchanges. Although none of Eden's complementing of celestial modes need be lost, the full story of origins includes the second phase of inventions that turn against the source. In Book IV, Adam is already making gestures toward Book IX, when pompousness will trip him up and prompt Eve's imitation of the satanic withdrawal. The new dialogues of the last three books are a direct result.

These moments of invention imply an interpretation of literary history that sets Shakespeare into place alongside Ovid, Virgil, Spenser, and others who fail to look all the way to origins. Whatever the reliability of the Synoptic Gospels themselves, both the materials and the forms Milton uses for them must be lifted from archaeological ruins and reoutfitted for the composite epic. It is difficult to say just when Milton saw the necessity of comprehensiveness if any given incident was to be properly interpreted, but it is clear that a driving totalism governs the partnership between dramatic or narrative incident and the highest choral poetry of visionary sainthood. What strikes Marvell about *Paradise Lost* in this regard is the sheer size of the undertaking in getting from distant beginnings to the present: "Where couldst thou words of such a compass find? / Whence furnish such a vast expense of Mind?" One might well ask. Most likely Milton's decisions concerning vocation and poetic styles came in a prolonged series of partial realizations until the idea of tracing them to their foremost beginnings took root and diverted him from early ideas about Arthurian romance. Even in the earlier poems, each outing takes up the special task of getting from its specific occasion—the birth of Christ, the inauguration of the President of Wales, the death of Edward King—to placement in an overall order that can only be encapsulated or flashed on the screen as a framing limit. Milton also shows the careerist having difficulty assembling a literary ancestry at those crucial moments.[4]

The most critical dramatic unveiling in Milton next to Eve's fall and the revision of modes that attends it, and the most critical juncture between dramatic event and its far extensions, is Christ's on the pinnacle in *Paradise Regained*. That manifestation of obedience to the father's will replaces the somewhat ill-defined genius of the shore in "Lycidas" and the Ludlow masque's manner of having heaven stoop to feeble virtue. Satan's goal is to hasten and direct Christ's rise from obscurity to his prophesied mission; Christ's is to accept an upgrading of his progress toward the messiahship when it is offered by the only party capable of completing the course. The progeny-relation that Satan seeks carries back to the father's presenting of the son to the host and may recollect the command to Adam and Eve to multiply and hold dominion, since Christ is among their offspring too. This particular son, being foreseen by prophets expecting a Davidic king, follows by direct descent from the fathers of Israel as well as from Mary, daughter of Eve. In a sense he also descends from his satanic rival, whose attempt to grant him an empire defines a better patrimony by a worse. Satan's command "now show" (show your origins and your mission) thus brings to its historical moment the sweep of history that Michael previews. Given the father that the son best expresses, no showing forth (not even this one) can be wholly adequate; but it can go some way toward establishing what divine glory is not. The climax revelation lifts the dramatic trial to its completion in panoramic narrative and choral lyric. Given Christ's eschatological dynasty, the privileges of Israel as a chosen nation are declared past even as they are fulfilled as predictions of gathered saints and readers, the latter of course the chief beneficiaries of disseminated gospel and inspired brief epic.

Whether or not Milton is any longer thinking of Shakespeare, a contrast between them may be in order to finish this synoptic contrast. One of the more powerful unveilings of the final product of status-strife in Shakespeare is Henry V's "I know thee not old man," with its proclaiming of monarchical allegiance to Lord Chief Justice and rejection of the old Adam. Henry's coronation finishes a pattern anticipated remotely in earlier plays and more immediately in the current one. The recognition scene announces a kingship cleared of encumbrances and associates temptation with chivalry twisted into the patronage of cronies, which Falstaff has rushed into town to capitalize upon while the moment is right. With that devil father and Henry IV both out of the way, the new Henry is free to blend into the monarchy. The audience of Henry's rhetoric is both the older English nation that stands represented with him on the stage and the Elizabethan state, prone to see itself in historical terms. The national memory now has something to cling to, as does the idealizing imagination seeking not exactly a golden age but an epic of greater swordsmen and just leaders, the first joined by the prince in Part One, the second just now finding their model.

If the goal of the prince's strategic announcement is eventually further conquest in the fields of France, the goal of Christ's is the presence of the father both now and forever:

> whether thron'd
> In the bosom of bliss, and light of light
> Conceiving, or remote from Heaven, enshrin'd
> In fleshly Tabernacle, and human form,
> Wand'ring the Wilderness.
>   (4.596–600)

As an expressive form recovering the integrity of divine revelation, Christ, complete in himself, redefines the terms of address and all preceding genres, with their lesser salutations, lyrics of place, epic challenges, and georgic labors. Milton's showing of the hero is thus inclusive, where Shakespeare's is social and nationally specific. Milton's hero complements his source without replacing it. But Shakespeare's is also unquestionably dramatic, and much of Milton's drama dissipates in the ritualizing of the conflict. Concerned with spanning first and second worlds, the desert encounter cannot really make it seem that Christ is in danger of failing and turning humankind back over to the false oracles and empire-makers.

I cite the two examples partly to get at that difference, which is typical enough to stand for other moments and to suggest the rhetorical leaning of the Shakespearean situation and the choral leaning of the Miltonic one. The dominance of the political office is obvious in the prince. Few protagonists in Shakespeare have less outside their leadership than Henry V, and perhaps none has so expendable a second world as the prince's taverns. This is not to deny that the heir apparent picks up a vernacular vocabulary from his subjects and gains a shrewd flexibility from his travels through the ranks, but these are dialogistic resources, not something to be stashed away in a corner of the mind and dreamed about in private. They help diagnose kingship and equip it; they do not redirect its energies.

Extractions from the Bible and Their Reapplication

The co-opting of individual desire by a greater design is typical of Milton's spiritual discipline from at least the sonnet on his twenty-third birthday onward. At the same time, it is the design that promises the fullest satisfaction of desire. The question is whether the ending is given such prominence that the interim is undercut and loses all contingency. No very complete answer can be derived from *Paradise Regained* or "Comus" by themselves, but the concluding moral formula of the masque ("If virtue feeble were / Heaven itself would stoop to her") does offer counsel. It allows first initiative to moral effort, if only because virtue must be proved feeble before heaven stoops. The problem is that if virtue proves to be strong it does not require help; in peril it always receives it. The outcome is certain either way. "Stoop" I take to be ambiguous, but neither of its meanings—the dropping of a bird of prey to its quarry or the bending down of a kindly help—lessens its power. Both the pervasiveness of these questions and their inseparability from Protestant positions on faith and works suggest that we take a route that passes not only through "Comus" but through Milton's *Christian Doctrine* and related commentaries on the relation of civil to religious issues.

Christian Doctrine is especially advisory on the efficacy of works and indirectly on the threshold between drama and visionary poetry. Without denying that the will of God is the first cause of all things, including the assignments one draws within the arena, Milton does not equate divine foresight to necessity: what happens "according to contingency and the free will of man, is not the effect of God's prescience, but is produced by the free agency of its own natural causes."[5] To make predestination not "altogether of grace" and thus dependent "on the will and belief of mankind" would be "derogatory to the exclusive efficacy of divine faith" (p. 925); but the doctrine of salvation by grace alone applies only to election, not to all the worthwhile causes and interim acts men may perform. None of Milton's protagonists is concerned with merely that minimal self-rescue. While Samson waits for the Philistines to be seated in their collapsible temple, he develops his relationship with his people, settles a score with Dalila, and intimidates a giant. In that respect, the blind poet and the blind Samson are parallel in rewriting the "Comus" formula, as though to say, as Donne reduces it, "Therefore that he may raise the Lord throws down" ("Hymne to God my God, in my sicknesse"). The ways of being thrown down are legion and may be dramatically vivid. Partly for that reason, Michael's listing of virtues for Adam (still very new to such things) includes active ones. Adam is surely better equipped for the wilderness thereby than Lady is with merely faith, hope, and chastity.

Even with good and bad works, however, self-initiative may not seem very extensive in Milton by comparison to what ambitious people strive for in Homer or Shakespeare. Also beyond reach are most of the punning, rhythmic repetition, parody, bawdy play, courtly wit, and sophisticated banter that fill Shakespeare's plays, not to mention the kind of progressive self-making that Henry V undertakes. And because the idiomatic and ornate vernacular is missing, so are many a devious turn of mind. Lady is not capable of seeing the many-sidedness of nature that the passage from Ariel and Caliban to Sabrina and Comus suggests, nor does Milton put her in a position to discover it. But if Milton's speakers and dramatic characters choose among a limited number of options, they also choose a long-range purpose, often under severe duress. The beginning poet, for instance, awaits his calling with apprehension in "How Soon Hath Time," and the mature writer is still doing so in "When I Consider." Neither has a specific mission or a way to find one. Because of that doubt (variations of which affect nearly all Milton's speakers and protagonists) drama is salvageable even if it must become the inward drama of self-discipline and even if eventually it must give way to the narrative framework.

The ratios of poetry, rhetoric, and drama shift as the initiative and the temptations do. The choices hinge on the relationship between opportunistic egoism and specific applications of divine will that are discoverable only within the trials themselves. Even before the fall, Adam must exercise his full component of intellect and feeling to interpret what he has and define what he doesn't have. When Adam wants company, God prompts him to argue for an end already foreknown in heaven. He is the stronger in self-understanding for having to clarify the difference between his incompleteness and God's self-sufficiency. He hits upon forms of dialogue both less strenuous than the one in progress and more available to the growth of the self in partnership with someone else. If his election of Eve is inevitable given the source text, it nonetheless reads like discovery, as the inevitable fall reads like tragedy. As William Kerrigan and Gordon Braden show, the courtship of Eve itself is dramatic and seemingly could turn in other directions—and soon does.[6] Adam's confession to Raphael that love unsettles one's equilibrium acknowledges the pressure of contingency even in one of relatively sure instincts:

> but here
> Far otherwise, transported I behold,
> Transported touch; here passion first I felt,
> Commotion strange, in all enjoyments else
> Superior and unmov'd, here only weak
> Against the charm of Beauty's powerful glance.
> (8.528–33)

The repetition of "here" and "transported" and the parallelism of "behold," "touch," and "felt" are devices of vehemence. They reflect the hammering insistence of this pleasurable sensation. Given the fall, the first man and woman must pursue that disturbance much further, into another kind of vehemence—accusatory, guilt-ridden, and prone to rake up the past. Far from being a course railroaded by the known plot, then, Milton makes it seem the invention of novel circumstances, as the several genres of Eden are. Eve's wish for more autonomy takes its significances from an upsetting of the balance of self-sufficiency and mutual dependence. It tests the capacity to stand alone and brings the fateful realization from Adam that he cannot. On her part, that wish seems a whim, but we know from accumulated pressures that it is more than that. The fall has every trademark of avoidability in the options both have—but also of probability, gaining momentum from influences entering on the spot.

Accommodation

The question of works, the success or failure of trials, and the point toward which dramatic lines converge on the greater vision are all inseparable from the efficacy of divine manifestation, which Milton makes crucial to all midway complications and impelling motions. Any completed heroic act, joined in mid-course by providence, expresses more than the protagonist's own volition. The conversion of event into sign is typical of a sizeable body of seventeenth-century commentary, especially on biblical events. A curious instance of the ironies of surprising divine presence crystallizes for Herbert, for instance, in the name "Mary": "How well her name an 'Army' doth present, / In whom the *Lord of Hosts'* did pitch his tent!"—not Mary herself or the historical setting or the events of the biography that begin with her, merely the lettering. The respelled name confirms the dictum of "The Flower," "Thy word is all, if we could spell," the poet's equivalent to faith-alone doctrine. The pointed past tense of "Did pitch" describes both a singular episode and an archetypal Lord of warring angels and saints. The endorsement the speaker voices in the "How well" adds to that gift of language an enthusiastic appreciation of its great-in-small reversal of decorum: the lettering is paltry; the meaning is huge. Without the visual and aural splendor that ought to accompany such majesty, the speaker has only the idiom of tenting to put between the sacred and the commonplace. The entire exclamation speaks to a period of comparative ignorance before the speaker tumbles to the full meaning of letters. His course has been dramatic even if the statement itself is lyric.

Herbert's "Beautie and beauteous words should go together" allows another alternative in the assumption that before the fall Adamic language was worthy of its moments and that gifted poets may recover the right spelling of some things. When Second Brother rhapsodizes in "Comus" (prematurely as it turns out), "How charming is divine Philosophy!" he catches the enthusiasm that accompanies the pleasure of notable truths well phrased. A few moments later, his sister, in fending off Comus's "false rules prankt in reason's garb" (759), relies upon the full voicing that goes with right causes: "I hate when vice can bolt her arguments, / And virtue has no tongue to check her pride" (760–61). When reason is reinforced by a store of wisdom and eloquence, good is thus doubly protected: by sacred truths and by the charms of forceful expression. Besides Lady and her brothers, Comus too recognizes the uplift these bring and confesses that what he hears from his opponent is "set off by some superior power" (801). When well put, wisdom breaks through flimsy argument; it converts debate into something less investigative than declarative. The question becomes more or less academic whether the words are inspired from beyond or are one's own.

What both Herbert and Milton look for in trials are tangible signs of an authoritative word from beyond. Reason's task is to inform the judgment on that issue, rhetoric's to counter bolted arguments. The contribution of an inspired poetry is less clear when it puts wisdom into fable and makes signs part of an overall narrative invention; but as I indicated, most of Milton's major performances begin in specific occasions. Seated within them, the investigative reason labors to disclose their logic. As Milton remarks in a familiar passage in *Areopagitica*, friends of the reclaimed Truth must roam the world to gather her scattered pieces. When Truth's master once again molds those pieces "into an immortal feature of loveliness and perfection," they will include a reassembled natural world. In the interim, as Truth's friends search they will no doubt argue, and the treatise asks for relief from censorship that they may do so under optimal conditions.

The Preface to the *Christian Doctrine* shows a conciliatory willingness to draw upon predecessors in the collecting of scattered truths despite their "affected display of formal sophisms" and erroneous inferences. Given the vastness of the story and the many ways that individual moments have of obscuring their design, beliefs must be the products of lifelong study.[7] Where the poet connects kinds in a system, his collaborator, the explicator, connects issues under headings such as "Of the Divine Decrees" and "Institutions of the Sabbath and of Marriage." Bringing together the passage and commentaries that bear upon it, his method is a "winnowing and sifting of every doctrine." Anyone suspicious of enthusiasm would find nothing very alarming in that scholarly procedure, which makes *Christian Doctrine* a tissue of quotations. Since such a scholar does not campaign for innovation in belief or propose new knowledge, it seems doubtful that "the prophet who narrates [his] poem," as William Kerrigan maintains, "attempts to become a major instrument in the continuing revelation of the Word of God," not if the revelation is of what was never before seen or set down.[8] In reading both sacred writing and the book of nature, the poet finds truth already established. Milton may claim Mosaic privileges and add sacerdotal functions to them, but a poetic adapter of sacred passages presumably runs no greater risk than someone who tries to translate them into discursive commentary.[9] All readers require personal conviction if they are not to rely upon an ecclesiastical packaging of doctrine. The Reformation turn from ritual to preaching depends on the assurance that wisdom, not only about salvation but about civil and religious policy, is discoverable. What the poet adds is narrative and dramatic amplification to make his teaching concrete. If poetry is to be as forceful as rhetoric in winning and keeping converts, it must not merely claim inspiration but must argue and explain. So plentiful are the modern builders of the reformed "Temple of the Lord" in their "brotherly dissimilitudes" that compared with the seventy elders they are legion: "all the Lords people are become Prophets," as *Areopagitica* could still boast (p. 556). They take many branches but stem from one root. The branches are the result of the occasions of history; the root is the single providence inscribed in occasions closely scrutinized.

The strength of the teaching function, which applies universals to troubleshooting tasks, is difficult to assess out of the context of the 1640s, but Milton's desire to develop a scriptural poetics based on styles from familiar to high—united with classical lyric, epic, and dramatic forms—is unquestionably ambitious. Given the confessional nature of the autobiography that precedes Milton's catalogue of kinds from divine pastoral drama to lofty hymns in *The Reason of Church Government*, it is difficult not to concede that he means what he says about the "inspired gift of God rarely bestowed." But the pedagogical practice that shores up that talent is nonetheless readily available and minutely applicable. Perhaps even more important than talent is the conviction that teaching too is guided by the spirit that "from the first / Wast present." That expressive forms vary in their initial distances from unaccommodated truth opens the way for the poet's increments both to the biblical repertory of forms and to the sacred reuse of classical forms. Although the final word on tragedy as the fall of great men may not be found in those who do not associate that fall with the Eden story, a Greek chorus does suggest what can be done with it. When tragedy turns to the apocalypse, where ruined majesty goes beyond fallen kings and almost beyond conception, catastrophe is carried to the limit.

Even in the midst of saying that, however, Milton drops into the tone of the common expositor and combines the bard with the textual critic. The excavation of paradigmatic moments bears directly on his conviction that all moments count and prompt their own generic entries. To extract the revelatory potential from a classic text or to reuse its form requires the same diligence that amplifying or clarifying a biblical obscurity does, only perhaps a little more. In its placing of biblical genres in the foreground, *The Reason of Church Government* goes significantly beyond Sidney's uniting of poetry and rhetoric in laureate exhibitions. Something similar happens with the concept of magnific odes, impressive in Pindar and Callimachus but surpassing in the prophets: as appreciation of their subjects lifts the listener, their critic appraises judiciously the "very critical act of composition." The seer and the comparatist expounder are almost one, at least brothers. The poet must learn to interweave dramatic and lyric moments and to cross-reference the analysis of ordeals in their parts and awareness of the ends they serve; the exegete must learn to associate this episode with another that "ten leaves off doth lie" and reinforce the delights of revelation with the labors of scholarship.

Applying biblical genres to new situations must be preceded by a reading of the complete text, then, which in practice usually means illuminating one passage, possibly obscure, by means of others that are clearer. I want to explore a little further the context of that reading technique in order to suggest that much of Milton's revision of predecessors is prepared for him by a climate of absolutist thought pinned to Protestant Bible reading. What Herbert hints in that regard in the Mary anagram he expands in "The H. Scriptures (2)," with the added twist that the speaker's own destiny is the chief matter to be discovered among the text's configurations. The associative or "recipe" principle resembles Augustine's view of scriptural readings in which not only are doubtful passages controlled by others but all reading is guided by charity. Milton adopts both principles—the charity and the connectedness—in *Christian Doctrine* and again in the divorce tracts. What is notable in practice, however, is that the scattering of passages is not easily overcome. The question as to what constitutes a valid parallel and how it gets planted in the mind of one expositor and not in another grows more sensitive as more and more readers strike out independently. The proliferation of sects calls attention to the likelihood that no single reading will be compelling even to reasonable minds. What Herbert's critical reader seeks is not only the general pattern, which he knows he cannot recover in its totality, but also, and primarily, assurance of his own destiny, which he can discover. Even there the attempt causes a hint of sorcery to creep into the art of reading, which resembles herb collection and astrology.

The doctrine of inner light that Milton's seer draws upon lessens the problem of individual variance, at least from the standpoint of the inspired reader himself, although it aggravates it from the standpoint of other readers who are given inadequate proofs. In "Of Prophecy" John Smith tries to avoid the disadvantage by distinguishing legitimate, reason-guided inspiration from the fantastic imagination. Platonism tells him that truth is aloof and abstract, but he also realizes that the "rude and illiterate sort of men" need to understand the things necessary for their salvation, hence figural accommodations of a cruder kind: "Truth is content, when it comes into the world, to wear our mantles, to learn our language, to conform itself as it were to our dress and fashions," even if it has to speak "with the most idiotical sort of men in the most idiotical way." [10] The poetic sort of idiot speaks in vulgar figures and has God "riding upon the wings of the wind" or "sitting in heaven, and the like" (p. 174). Differences between visions and dreams, between the comparative obscurity of Mosaic revelation and New Testament illumination, and simply between powerful intellects and impostors, occupy much of Smith's critique. A coincidence of reason and inner light is required to give truth the right mantle without obscuring it.

That is one common way out of the dilemma of variant readings in the seventeenth century. It does not fully address the discrepancy Herbert notes between deciphering "all" the constellations of the story and applying two or three specific passages to some particular destiny. Exegesis may take either of two forms, abstraction made evident by induction and deduction, and particular providential intent made evident by extraordinary events. The chief way of combining them is to examine the language and the event closely for their typological implications and to suggest that the individual incident falls into a type. Lancelot Andrewes is a meticulous worker of that method and especially adept at bringing together the biblical example and the current moment. His reading of the nativity scene, for instance, joins divine to human nature at the historical point when types and their accommodated expression can be seen to yield to the antitype and its revelations. That reunion of detail and overall plan is then made parallel to the incorporation of the present into the past. In juxtaposing the signs that interpret the divine birth with the songs that amplify them, Andrewes spirals down into the heart of dramatic progress and back out again. If for Milton the divine birth not only occasions the "Angel Choir" but requires the young poet to translate an angelic mode into a form suitable to his own emergence, for Andrewes participation is more remotely that of the reader. He pays particular attention to the approaches to divine presence from several removes and to the kind of spiritual and intellectual equipment needed to open up the text from a distance. That a Christian mode is often paradoxical is due to the "puffing up" of the world's great, which lowers the divine sign to meanness. "For their lifting up . . . was he brought thus low" in a "*signum vobis,* for us." [11] Had the Lord come in full resplendence, "that had been no sign"; the sun eclipsed is different, not the sun shining (p. 81). What appears to be Christ's distance from his source becomes through his humility an accommodation in an upside-down context—an implied countermanding—and hence a rhetoric embedded in catachresis.

Andrewes's audience stands at two further removes from observers of "the childe swadled, and layed in a cratch," in the "scandal of the cratch." It approaches first through the sermon and then the text. Each component of that multilayered situation requires its own consideration, including initially the ranked orders of angels, the day star that signifies faith risen in hearts, and the swaddling clouts. If an interpreter finds some inadequacy in these signs and is still bothered by their lowliness, Andrewes reminds him that the "cratch" is a sign of the cross, the last and greatest of Christ's hard beds and the epitome of humiliation—on the verge of a great triumph. The less glorious, the more: divine presence is *perfected* in the weakness of its signs that makes the human drama possible (p. 83). To find Christ by any means is all in all, and "All is, in the thing signified. . . . Be the sign never so simple, the signatum it carries us to, makes amends. *Any* sign, with such a signatum" (p. 112). Any sign is therefore a figure of transport, a conveyance that can be lifted from the text to the sermon and from firsthand witnesses to seventeenth-century participants.

Similarly in explicating John 20:11–17 on the resurrection, Andrewes finds an empty grave a paradoxical signifier, looking into which is equivalent to searching in the literal letter for the spirit. Only after the practical interpreter has translated the allegory and found the meaning of the word does he "partake of the mystery." Balancing the divine presence in signs against the absence we would have without them (in a Whitsunday sermon of 1611), he weighs Christ's going, at the other end of the biography, against the Comforter's coming: "no *impedit,* without an *expedit:* no *abeam,* but a *mittam:* no going away, to bring a loss; but a coming too, to make a supply" (p. 629). If these statements sound much like the modern play with absence and presence, they do in fact bear a resemblance, but with the usual medieval and Renaissance twist: what reason and perception cannot produce, faith does. The abyss between the pitifully inadequate sign, the "scandal," and the logocentric power Christ brings to bear is crossed by both miracle and consensus. The common type of the redeemer does not need to be proved again and again. Andrewes's task is the lesser one of showing its emergence to a new audience in the unlikely letter. As to preaching, that too depends upon a simultaneous going and coming, filling and emptying of the sign-graves it uses. Without Christ's actual departure, there would not only be no ascension and no completion of his meaning but no recapitulation in new teaching, which gets back to faith by laborious stages of exegesis: "no preaching, neither; for, that is but a letter that killeth, except the Spirit come too, and quicken it" (p. 632). The authority of the sermonizer is granted and cancelled in the same instant. Its highest ambition is to disappear into the act of reading, as the character of the speaker blends into the typical character of the evangelist or imitator of Christ.

Andrewes has less to say than Milton about the singing that accompanies the nativity and its sermons, but when the "whole Queer of heaven" makes melody on the occasion of the sign's issuance, he supposes that too to mark the spirit's presence, translated this time not into paradox, in preparation for the abolition of authorial wit in the realization of truth, but into harmony "to couple low and high together," "to sing away the sign; to make amends, for the manger" (p. 109). This spirited participation constitutes a second assault on the gap between low sign and high signified. Thus as one learns to find the child intellectually, one also salutes him with "words to praise God" (p. 78). One is to do so somewhat differently in reading this particular event than in reading others, because by interposing itself between Old and New Testaments the birth comes at a moment of clarified definition to which transport comes naturally. The purpose of recapitulation is both to reenter the discovery and to make a ritual demonstration of it—a yearly reminder of a realization long ago acknowledged and passed down to scholarship and custom.

That Milton's moderate variety and brotherly dissimilitudes in *Areopagitica* are not altogether euphemistic for warring sects is suggested by the broad agreement among Protestants as to the certainty of meanings to be derived from a close reading of the text and optimism for their influence. What remains when that reading has done its work, however, is often further waiting for specific applications to one's own calling and the generating of still other historical episodes. The interpretive work can never be finished until all episodes are connected. Dramatic moments may conclude in revelations that weave them into the whole, but they are followed by still others. Even Milton's apparently definitive showing forth of the father by the son in the desert leads not to the establishing of the final kingdom but to further acts of teaching. If the scriptural version of the trial were sufficient, *Paradise Regained* would not be necessary. Even if it were, its application to the moment might require the initiative of the poet or exegete as its sponsor. It is not so much the discovery of truth's perfect shape in the text as its reconstruction from within the complexities of moments that is the difficulty. The seer is on safer ground than the dramatist in somewhat the way that Spirit's epilogue in "Comus" can be much briefer and more confident than the story of the woods.

9

Kinds and Moments of Plot

> With what delight could I have walkt thee round,
> If I could joy in aught, sweet interchange
> Of Hill and Valley, Rivers, Woods and Plains,
> Now Land, now Sea, and Shores with Forest crown'd,
> Rocks, Dens, and Caves; but I in none of these
> Find place or refuge; and the more I see
> Pleasures about me, so much more I feel
> Torment within me, as from the hateful siege
> Of contraries.
> —Satan, *Paradise Lost* 9.114–22

Contention Mixed with Song

The debates of "Comus" are the first of Milton's serious handlings of moral choice through copious discussion, and as we've seen, he arranges the supporting elements of the masque around them. The customary way to move from one phase to another in a masque is to bring groups on- and offstage separately—opening a hole in the side of a mountain to let dancers out or floating a cloud down and depositing a deity or seating a dignitary at floor level or slightly above. The changes of scene can be ironic and the movements perverse, as when dancers move grotesquely or belly gods ape their betters, but the choreography does not try to articulate the choices. In contrast, "Comus" integrates songs, drama, dance, and thematic labeling by carrying argument across the borders between media. It suggests that ideas can assume several guises so long as they are all served by language. As Milton reminds his opponents in the remonstrance against Smectymnuus: "true eloquence I find to be none, but the serious and hearty love of truth: And ... whose mind so ever is fully possest with a fervent desire to know good things, and with the dearest charity to infuse the knowledge of them into others, when such a man would speak, his words ... like so many nimble and airy servitors trip about him at command, and in well order'd files, as he would wish, fall aptly into their own places."[1] "Comus" is a demonstration of some confidence in truth and its nimble servitors, if not quite an equivalent confidence.

Just how powerful the combination of allies may be is nonetheless open to question. The immediate respondent to Lady's song is moved but not reformed by it. What a worldly self desires here and now finds a strong counter-rhetoric and a great deal of energy in Comus and *his* nimble servitors. Coming near the front end of the contention between the "stye" (this pinfold earth) and the "starry vault," Lady's song is a kind of stopgap measure that uses mythmaking and embroidered streams as an alternative to doing something about a fearful situation. Milton's readers are expected to work resourcefully from descriptive panorama to song as the masque proceeds toward the debates at its center. The object is obviously to infuse knowledge by explaining as well as by enacting underlying concepts. George Smith's sketch of the symmetries of "Comus" shows its structural care in placing the main contest between Comus and Lady.[2] Immediately inside Spirit's rendering of a greater cosmos in the outer framework come the dances of Comus's crowd and the noble masquers, the most conventional of the masque elements. Inside these are the songs of Lady and Sabrina, which in turn bracket Lady's meeting with Comus and the dispersal of Comus's crew. Innermost are the brothers' philosophical discussion and Comus's temptation of Lady, one in a symposium mode, the other in gay rhetoric refuted by a stern Puritanism.

In Smith's view, the emphasis falls on entertainment even in the debates, and the succession as a whole is designed to show off the virtuosity of the Egerton trio. It is well to remember, however, that Thyrsis-Lawes speaks and sings many more lines than the children and finishes the masque virtually by himself. Beginnings and endings are also emphatic. They reabsorb the philosophizing back into myth and into the narrative of the second journey. In retrospect, that reabsorption raises questions about the effectiveness of talk by itself, especially when Lady threatens to unleash her Orphic powers and shatter Comus's magic structures over his false head (799) and merely remains seated. It is difficult to see what the debate settles when the final counter to Comus's charms is magical incantation from someone summoned by esoteric formula. The most magisterial lecturer in philosophy, Elder Brother, is least able to match words with deeds. This does not make philosophy "mere moral babble," as Comus pretends to think, but it does loosen the alliance between words and power.

Where powers from one level do manage to engage others, airs and magic seem to open the windows. If we reach Lady's stichomythic exchange with Comus after several modal adjustments in pursuit of thematic lines, by the end, in working back out again, we find the argument being converted into ritualized demonstration, into song and dance, and finally into Spirit's peculiar travelogue ecstasy. If at the center comes definition through dialectic, at the extremes comes a vertical movement required by the vista that reaches from the woods to Jove's realm. The masque opens and closes the growth of the children with regions beyond either their line of vision or ours. While they prepare to go on with whatever comes next for young English men and women, Spirit breaks loose from the inner boxes. Yet these phases and transformations of the argument cannot be left discrete if the masque is to hold together. Each must be permeated by the others, so that argument sets up song and song infiltrates argument. Ideas transported across the borders must remain somehow much the same ideas, but as they go they must carry new increments in the way emergent genres in *Paradise Lost* remember and translate each other in the growth of the human psyche.

The use of argument between songs and dances has no exact precedent in *The Tempest,* and indeed it is difficult to locate close precedents for Milton's combination of act and contention, the typical form of Miltonic trial. The earlier example of "L'Allegro" and "Il Penseroso" follows a generic blueprint remotely like Shakespeare's in *Love's Labour's Lost* as it moves forward by the forming and altering of opinions. After exploring several angles of the battle of the sexes, Shakespeare concludes with a sung debate between spring and winter. As modal translations, the songs retreat from the affairs of court to those of landsmen and shepherds, as though to an outside and refreshing perspective. In the lower ranks, the taunting of cuckoos is blatant and simple compared to the sophistication we have just witnessed:

> Spring. When shepherds pipe on oaten straws,
>   And merry larks are plowmen's clocks,
> When turtles tread, and rooks, and daws,
>   And maidens bleach their summer smocks,
> The cuckoo then, on every tree,
> Mocks married men; for thus sings he—
>   Cuckoo,
> Cuckoo, cuckoo! Oh, word of fear,
> Unpleasing to a married ear!

> Winter. When icicles hang by the wall,
>   And Dick the shepherd blows his nail,
> And Tom bears logs into the hall,
>   And milk comes frozen home in pail,
> When blood is nipped and ways be foul,
> Then nightly sings the staring owl—
>   Tu-whit,
> Tu-who, a merry note,
> While greasy Joan doth keel the pot.
>   (5.2.913–30)

Even as these lyrics replace the antics of Holofernes, Armado, Berowne, and Moth, their elbow-nudging references to adultery and the tricks that men and women play maintain the game. But the merry note and the milk pails also soften the contrast and direct attention elsewhere. A cuckoo for an Elizabethan is a shortened euphemism, scarcely felt as a misnomer because of its frequent use, even though the connection between actual birds and adventurous women would otherwise be remote. The frozen pails and staring owls are less likely to disappear into their emblematic meanings. Cold hands and recently warm milk (now freezing) assert themselves physically and simply. Having let the characters overhear and mock one another throughout and ransack the language for still more ways to say virtually nothing—and having failed to quiet them even with news of the death of the Princess's father—Shakespeare puts them in place with this display of native English, compressed into the metrical shape of "Then nightly sings the staring owl" and "Dick the shepherd blows his nail."[3] Without having to say anything directly, he shows common sense having its way in native eloquence.

    That "L'Allegro" and "Il Penseroso" are similar in looking into English countryside and cottage materials before going on to antique pageantry and haunted streams suggests that Milton has an eye on mock debate. But he uses the contrasts between mirth and pensiveness to generate movement in a quite different direction. Shakespeare ends with an arrested balance and exits to a realm the play has not heretofore considered. The result is an unexplored juxtaposition of social levels, sets of values, and literary fashions. Milton dissolves the debate in a futuristic chart for further growth that leaves behind the realms of the plowman and the shepherd. Opposites in neither the play nor Milton's twin poems are really ethical polarities of a kind that would interest the writer of "Comus." (Spring is not winter's opposite, for instance, merely an adjacent season.) The softened contrasts of the poems are looser in their parallels and more elaborate in imagery than moral or philosophical argument is. All along, the different intensities and levels of mirth and pensiveness call for different literary modes. One complication is that much of what the speaker encounters comes from books rather than from observation. Both "L'Allegro" and "Il Penseroso" presume a stock of kinds and topoi among which the speaker conducts his search. The poems see the possibility of better alternatives, so that one's thumbing through the pages and walking the landscape produce not chance encounters but an index of choices. A purposeful direction through those materials would begin to arrange them as illustrations. The principle of increase prevents the itinerary from bending into a circle that would simply renew each day and limit the poet to models available in the plowman or in Plato, Jonson, and Shakespeare.

Milton will later deepen the threats and penalties for wrong choices; but a curious discontinuity shows even in "L'Allegro" and "Il Penseroso" in the opportunity that music and art present at their respective climaxes. Hearing the melting voice and discovering the hidden soul of harmony in "L'Allegro" and being dissolved into ecstasies in "Il Penseroso" spring one loose from the senses. Although ascent is anticipated in "Il Penseroso" by the Muses that "in a ring / Aye round about *Jove*'s Altar sing" and by the Cherub Contemplation who soars on golden wing "Guiding the fiery-wheeled throne," those are points of transcendence that coincide with modal shifts to a higher art. Where Shakespeare's two songs implicitly criticize the witty life of courtly love while setting their sophistication against country life, Milton frees artifice from manners and makes it the instrument of vision. The mock debate for him is an instrument of correction and rising, lyric release replacing the nightly "Tu-whit" with high anthems. Not even Philomel's sad song or the warbled Orphic lay that "Drew Iron tears down *Pluto's* cheek" can be said to prepare for those anthems. The chief resource of the mock debate is not its threading of logic through the accumulating resources of mirth and melancholy but its figural revision, its discovery through inspired gift of what storied church windows prompt in the prepared consciousness. The key to both Lady's expectation of resounding harmonies from heaven and the hope in "Il Penseroso" for ecstatic vision lies in the contribution of the soul's inner readiness and song's capacity to bring heaven itself within hearing.

As compared to Eden, however, the promptings of "Il Penseroso's" moments are not fully commissioned to bring forth a mounting succession comparable to Adam's evening songs, aubades, and orisons. The passage of the day from dawn to midnight slices mirth and pensiveness into subtly discriminated phases, into shades and plays of light. These reveal anew each topographical feature in a conversion of things into signs, until the storied windows bring us to a biblical accommodation and a quite different sign-referent relation that features the leap to religious ecstasy. In coming around to the rhyming of former moments, the second poem's revisiting carries it sufficiently above its forerunner to suggest "reproving" along with troping. Thus beside turning on points of difference from predecessors, Milton establishes his own small literary history within the controlled legend of the poet's growth from the first to the second outing. The anthems are finally the ear's reinforcement of surmised blessings that come when the right mood descends. The progression is more a spiral than a circle.

That mirth dwells in gestures and dimples, not in the epicurean excesses of a belly god, saves it from greater embarrassment later. The participatory liveliness of "L'Allegro" is fully justified in its way, which shows again in the restoring of a modified joy to pensiveness. The poet does not have any contamination to fend off as Lady does and is still enthralled with the actual sounds he hears at the end, in anthems even more acutely present than the songs of sad Philomela. What makes jest and youthful jollity attractive at the entry level—in an animation that prefigures Comus's trochaic chants and the playfulness of the writhed proboscis and pasturing fish of the creation—is their interplay of sounds and dancelike movement. Familiar items take on a capacity to lift the spirits, as do tales of intangible flails that thresh the corn as moving shadows. Mirth's pleasures can thus be both unreproved (for the moment) and undemanding. They do not bulge into grossness even in a stretched-out Lubber Fiend and do not demand argument or philosophical probing. They can also be Shakespearean in landscape intimacy up to the point at which Milton allows his neophyte poet to look beyond or within for more enthralling revelations. Melancholy has a greater potential almost from the outset because of the withheld joy of a far-off other world, glimpsed only through veils. It will not materialize in the landscape or its rustics, which are fully known.

"L'Allegro" and "Il Penseroso" together use rhetorical persuasion not to change the goddesses (the pensive goddess is asked to fix her wonted state in marble) but to bring them nearer as guides. We understand from the initial issuing of titles that the speaker is playing mainly with attitudes, and we see from his lack of exchanges with those he observes that nothing in the social and political structure is expected to contribute, any more than argument does. It is the frame of mind that sets up the succession of gifts. Sounds and sights, haunted forests, and towers both foster moods and are objects to be seen through them. The telling moment, however, is the collaboration of ear and eye at the end of "Il Penseroso." The meeting place of what is actually heard and what is imagined can only be the self or the assimilative mind. No sound will produce heaven by itself without preparatory learning; yet everything remains secondary to the music that produces it.

More Bent to Serve

Even Adam and Eve, assuming a purposeful function in everything they see, are momentarily puzzled at the apparent disconnection of remote phenomena from themselves. They edge toward a concept of purposelessness and, if not a universal blank, a blank of isolated localities that do not serve as prompts. Although their puzzlement is minor, it points to a parallel between their need to escape loneliness and narcissism respectively and a desire, very strong in both of them, for rational steps that will lead from what they see around them to what they must accept on faith. The enigma of superfluity and dispersal is never entirely explained. Milton's narratives all come to peaks and pitches and seek a principle of egress to a transported phase through some turn that cannot be fully anticipated from within but is usually known to the writer from without from predecessor texts taken as histories rather than fictions. Lacking that capacity to transcend their own stories, the speakers of "How Soon Hath Time" and "When I Consider" come to similar questions about providence and self-admonitions concerning the limits of knowledge. The ordeals of the sonnets are in that crucial respect unlike those of Milton's protagonists: they do not hold down a place in a completed fable. They fill the entire boundaries of the poem with their present-tense condition, which does not include a clear prophecy of the future. Where Samson's and Christ's trials are known and framed beforehand, the immobilized sonnet speaker cannot see even the next stage or define the service he would render. "L'Allegro" and "Il Penseroso" are also expectant poems without a definite future, but they use their present sequences to chart possible future gifts and are situated in a learning phase. The logic of growth and increasing powers saves them from speculations as to specific tasks to come. "Comus" is not locked into the present, thanks to Spirit's anticipatory narrative and expectant tiered myths and beckoning goals; *Samson Agonistes*'s dramatic present encloses its participants, but not those who know the whole story beforehand.

Progress toward some such completed narrative is precisely what the puzzled speaker of days flying with full career cannot manage. He writes about not writing, about wasted time and talent and the feel of contingency. A sonnet rhetoric applied to the lady and the suffering sonneteer is of little application to that futility. Although sonnets in sequence can string out the episodes of a real or imagined love, the end of the usual sonnet story is assumed to be love's fruition or frustration. More comprehensive is the metapoetic turn of Shakespearean sonnets that takes in the perpetuation of art and its memorializing of the subject. "Not marble nor the gilded monuments / Of princes shall outlive this powerful rime" and "So, till the Judgment that yourself arise, / You live in this, and dwell in lovers' eyes" are the familiar sounds of it. The edge of doom itself is love's terminal point in Shakespeare's 116th skirmish with time. It is a long way off, but it at least offers a project. That expansiveness catches Milton's interest, as "When I Consider Everything That Grows" catches his ear and sets up still another career-making contrast.[4] But from Milton's point of view, even the lasting power of monumental art looks into the future through too narrow an opening. In "Methought I Saw My Late Espoused Saint" the poet's dream foreshadows no less than the celestial state when the veil will be altogether lifted. Looking through the window the dream of the spouse provides, he contrasts that ultimate reunion to his benighted awakening before plunging back into the historical moment. What counts is not the cancellations of time but the discrepancy between the tantalizing dream and the unveiled presence he expects. The occasion produces an elegiac narrative of the moment in the context of a projected nuptial fulfillment.

In echoing Raleigh's careful weighing of Petrarch and Spenser in "Methought I Saw the Grave, Where Laura Lay," Milton keeps some specific sonnet conventions in sight as a measure of both the eventual return of the spouse and her current vanishing. Although the poet's waking dark is benighted by comparison to either Petrarch or Spenser, "once more I trust to have / Full sight of her" does establish, within the moment of denial itself, a hope that transcends the possession Raleigh describes. The return to dark is after all in the past tense. The current state holds both it and the future in balance, part narrative and dramatic because of the painful moment of the awakening.

Both "How Soon Hath Time" and "Methought I Saw" illustrate Milton's handling of the deprived present in the light of what desire projects. But "When I Consider," in its balancing of deflected ambition and anticipation, prepares more directly for the blind seer and for Samson and illustrates the limits of rational consolation. By naming patience directly, it gives prominence to the realization that the cancellation of ordinary achievements prepares for something unpredictable, likely to be complete but not at the moment coming any nearer. Milton is clearly resolved to stay within those limits of vision, however frustrating they may be, while simultaneously realizing the bustle of a magnificent scene in the battles of providential history that go on without him. As so often at the edge between ordeal and release, the key is the service, the vocational aspect of the greater design:

> When I consider how my light is spent,
>   Ere half my days, in this dark world and wide,
>   And that one Talent which is death to hide,
>   Lodg'd with me useless, though my Soul more bent

>   To serve therewith my Maker, and present
>   My true account, lest he returning chide;
>   "Doth God exact day-labor, light denied,"
>   I fondly ask; But patience to prevent
>   That murmer, soon replies, "God doth not need
>   Either man's work or his own gifts; who best
>   Bear his mild yoke, they serve him best; his State
>   Is Kingly. Thousands at his bidding speed
>   And post o'er Land and Ocean without rest:
>   They also serve who only stand and wait."

Most of the ways Milton stretches sonnets are evident here. Scored for two voices as a minidrama (working toward lyric but never quite getting there), the sonnet obviously does not pace itself through ordinary divisions. Its thinly disguised hope is for some authorized party to step in and redirect personal progress. Patience as a substitute for rational argument and for achievement speaks out of the aphoristic wisdom of self-denial. The writing of a sonnet itself is a substitute task related to greater missions as doing nothing is to kingly service. This suspension from work lies outside the shepherd-plowman-knight phases of the Virgilian career and on that account reveals something about the ultimate patron that no other career could. Those who are posted are much less likely to realize their uselessness. The formal indication of vexation is five straight lines that disregard end stops and a tone and syntax that keep their distance from song. "Who best / Bear his mild yoke, they serve him best" makes up a line in meter and a unit in grammar, but pounding at the *b*, it rises to its strained intensity as a kind of maverick. It sets up antithetical equivalents in "Man's work" and "his own gifts" that leave nothing of value for a would-be servant to do and no grounds for bargaining. These devices of spillover and thematic expansion overload a poem that obviously has no leisure to illustrate an initial theme in the Shakespearean manner.

Ordinarily Milton brings corrective views in by spirit or angel, the commissioned agents of eternity-time interactions or modal go-betweens who stitch drama to encompassing rationales. Patience offers a more tenuous principle, serving by not serving, although any advice is accommodating if it can link the greater chronicle to the life story at issue. Patience to be sure unfolds a panoramic vision that approaches epic without quite leaving earth for the regions of Attendant Spirit or Raphael; but that vision comes with no hint of a specific evangelical assignment of the kind the parable of the talents might lead one to expect. If the perspective opens enough to reveal the scale of the operation, it is only to expose the speaker's misreading of such parables. Was not the incarnate Word to have replaced other message-bearers with one who is collected and brings in his train those who serve in a different way? If so, how could a "talented" disciple so misapply the message? Certainly neither the speaker nor patience says anything about inner light or faith as a replacement for works and consolation for a wasted life, which acknowledges the secrecy of the design. A bustling activity that tells us how detailed God's interference can be merely compounds the futility of his commanding service at all. (Milton would presumably be thinking of the entire biblical record of such demands as well as recent English history.) Nor does the speaker entertain doubts about the line of command, since God's employed servants go "at his bidding." They are not mistaken, self-promoting entrepreneurs. What patience makes no attempt to explain—as if any move from general principle to specific prophecy were forbidden—is why some stand and some post. For the individual, no general plan is fully meaningful unless it gathers up the details of the chronicles he knows firsthand. Each has to live with the enigma of his own works or lack of them. The consolation is that, according to the doctrine of patience, serving by waiting has the same status as action: both are unnecessary to God.

Serving by waiting is not the only unexpected setback in Milton, nor is this sonnet its only instance. Raphael must realize that even angel ambassadors are less than instrumental when he is posted to prepare Adam and Eve against a fall that has already been announced and seems to be proceeding on schedule. The uncouth swain is not the one finally who wipes away Lycidas's tears, despite his announced purpose. With great inventiveness and daring exploits, angel warriors on both sides of the war in heaven prove ineffectual, and then they too serve by standing. The result here is the ending of the complaint through the realization of another kind of management. The sonneteer cannot elect his work, any more than the speakers of "Il Penseroso" and "How Soon Hath Time" can. To glimpse some grounds for lyricism in such a chastising lecture while denying personal achievement, patience works a triumph of compression and constraint. Altogether Milton squeezes into the fourteen lines a meditative phase in the speaker's voicing of the frustration of his biblical research, an account of the dramatic progress of discontent coming to a reversal, and a panoramic narrative coming to focus in an epigram. Standing apart from any particular episode, the final line is both a historical observation and a philosophical precept. "They" are all those who have ever been denied a specific calling but stand prepared anyway. Their talents are not hidden, although neither are they advancing a cause. The colon stops the bustle so that a calmer voice, speaking a regular iambic line, can reach its rhyme in "wait," in the march of wise regulation to completed form. The cautionary statement is heartening compared to what precedes, if discouraging compared to what one wants. Restoring hope, it restores a semblance of lyric, hovering between virtue as dramatically tense inaction and wisdom as relaxed transcendence.

It is perhaps worth noting in passing that sonneteers such as Spenser and Sidney suffer different disappointments and rewards. They may ultimately say the equivalent of "leave me O love" or go into some other line of work; the speaker here has nowhere to turn. But the relief that comes with the doctrine of patience is nonetheless greater. Sidney cannot fall back on the confidence that a fuller plan will someday be clear and may yet post him over land and sea. He writes sonnets, romances, and defenses of poetry as an alternative. Milton does not separate doubt-plagued history from eventual certainty; they are one and the same. God works on simultaneously large and minute scales, toward an end that makes waiting an image of eternity as well as an ordeal. We remember that Christ merely stands on the pinnacle while Satan, having worked industriously, "smitten with amazement," repeats his original and forever fall, ironically serving against his will a cause he cannot understand. The sonnet's unspoken alternative to standing patiently on the verge of lyric, but stuck in the anxiety of drama, is just such a headlong pitch. What the speaker does while waiting is to fill the vacuum with the brief narration itself and end it with a simple proposition. Perhaps the final irony is that so uncopious a statement, seemingly so assured and definitive, should be capable of projecting such enormous implications and so indefinite a duration. Stretched across that interim, drama is reduced to a struggle for interior discipline; lyric is restricted to a complaint that Milton measures against a merely conceivable transport, located for the time being solely in others.

Down Reason Then

I want to conclude with *Samson Agonistes* not because it is probably Milton's own final mixture of contentiousness and lyric but because it offers an opportunity to gauge his way with a subject that suppresses the visionary dimension. Samson is active on behalf of a community that has not heeded him but for its own good must learn to do so. He is not otherworldly in the manner of the later Judaic prophets, but under the conditions of witnessing that he, his people, and the Book of Judges recognize he has been marked by a special providence. His renegade tendencies are similar to those of the prophets and a source of the difficulties his countrymen have in accepting him as God's witness. Lawbreaking draws him away from them, and yet the group we see onstage is closer to him than those who have made peace with his conquerors, who prefer business as usual even in servitude. They cannot rise to modes of acclamation that in this play must pass through tragedy on the way to choral lyric.

To accept such a hero as their own, Samson's closer countrymen must put aside not only their temporizing but moral propriety and reason. If God is not bound to "his own prescript," it seems to follow that a Nazarite, "a person separate to God" as Samson describes himself, can be granted a similar exemption. But that makes it all the harder for his people to follow the twists and turns of God's "contrarious" ways toward his champion, especially when the situation requires the breaking of Nazarite vows and marriage customs. Samson has driven his countrymen away not merely by his first marriage with a "fallacious Bride, / Unclean, unchaste" and the betrayal of his secret to Dalila but by the slaughter of his enemies when most of them would prefer a peaceful coexistence. Such a figure cannot be reintegrated into the civil body as an ordinary citizen. He is not adept at living among the confusions of motive and mixtures of unheroic minor virtues that move Philistines to their holiday and move his father to tinkering with the status quo. He is better suited to be a self-sacrificial champion. His people are not called upon to follow that model, merely to understand what it portends for the future management of the dignity he restores to them.

It is Harapha who puts the case most forcefully and extracts one of Samson's three explicit self-defenses of his public function. To the charge that following his first marriage he became a peace-breaker, robber, and murderer, Samson calls upon his privileges and obligations as a Nazarite:

> I a private person, whom my Country
> As a league-breaker gave up bound, presum'd
> Single Rebellion and did Hostile Acts.
> I was no private but a person rais'd
> With strength sufficient and command from Heav'n
> To free my Country; if their servile minds
> Me their Deliverer sent would not receive,
> But to thir Masters gave me up for nought,
> Th' unworthier they; whence to this day they serve.
> I was to do my part from Heav'n assign'd,
> And had perform'd it if my known offence
> Had not disabl'd me.
>
> (1209–19)

The "did Hostile Acts" is a euphemism for the story Judges tells of the aftermath of that marriage: "And the Spirit of the Lord came upon him, and he went down to Ashkelon, and slew thirty men of them, and took their spoil, and gave change of garments unto them which expounded the riddle"

(Judges 14:19). Both the charges and the reply are revealing for their parallels to the Dalila case. Samson married both women to vex his enemies. As it turned out, he vexed his countrymen almost as sorely. His shift from the champion of his people to heaven's champion marks a turn from legality to illegality and from open to covert warfare. It is tempting to side with Empson and Joseph Wittreich in finding him a deluded fanatic and muscular terrorist in that renegade phase.[5] But we have the word of the Chorus and Manoa that both his original calling and his marriages were either vouched for by the angel visitations or given credence by subsequent marvellous exploits. The Chorus reinstates recollection of that evidence at the very point at which Milton adds still another divine prompting (this one not in Judges), and thereby nails down the parallels between them and the glorious witnessing of the victory over Dagon. The catastrophe thus finishes a long-term pattern of callings and establishes Samson as the moral backbone of a wavering people. Hence much as we may resist that reading of a "breeding order'd and prescrib'd / As of a person separate to God, / Design'd for great exploits" (30–32), neither Milton nor Judges offers us much choice except to break completely with the writers of the texts. An offstage force is all the while engineering a harvest of ironies too exact and well timed to be accidental. The upshot is that the uses of rational argument are primarily to show its limits and prepare for a leap into faith as the superior way into the providential plan. That way is abrupt, and the preparation leads to the point at which heaven stoops to a virtue enfeebled by betrayal but reinvigorated by a combination of repentant self-scrutiny and divine intervention.

That pattern of vengeance also fits everything we know of Old Testament righteousness. Given the prophets' inclination to foresee the ruin of their enemies and Milton's defenses of contemporary warrior saints in reform by violence, it is not likely that Samson's God wants the Israelites to find a peaceful settlement with the Philistines. The mission of heroes and the hectoring of prophets run against the inclinations of a murmuring, temporizing people. Yet it is "to prevent / The harass of thir Land" (256–57) that the men of Judah deliver Samson bound to Gath (241–76). Samson's final deed is like the earlier ones the Chorus finds perplexing and beyond the law. They return to that defeat of reason in realizing that the sayings of the wise "in ancient and in modern books" offer no consolation to such as Samson. Sayings of the Ecclesiastes and Proverbs type also go beyond rational consolation, reaching deep into the tragic experience of the people:

> with th'afflicted in his pangs thir sound
> Little prevails, or rather seems a tune,
> Harsh, and of dissonant mood from his complaint,
> Unless he feel within

> Some source of consolation from above;
> Secret refreshings, that repair his strength,
> And fainting spirits uphold.
>
> (660–66)

Hence from the public point of view, the dilemma of Nazarite privacy and the secret refreshings from within: the stigma of lawlessness and public disapproval goes with the specially prescribed breeding of those chosen by God; the way of humiliation is ironically the way to trap the Philistines and unseat the policy of appeasement.

The Chorus has more to go on than the glorious witnessing of faith that Samson provides them. It has only to examine a well-preserved record to discover similar gaps and tests of faith. The typical "I have said, and it shall be," with its linking of past to future, presupposes both an uncontestable authority and a period of doubt that falls between the prophecy and the event. That division between anticipation and end again shows that argument and dialogue are not adequate for "a dramatic poem of the kind called tragedy." What Samson says during his inactive (but talkative) period does not go much beyond reaffirming the justice of his suffering. He then acts with only a few taunting words. At issue in that disconnection of language from act is anyone's capacity to direct a course and emerge from its consequences in satisfying closure—not an isolated matter in Milton, as we have seen. Lady claims that unleashing words will devastate Comus but remains stuck and after she is freed falls silent. The uncouth swain's reversal comes without argument. The redemption of humankind in *Paradise Lost* circumvents argument in several ways. God establishes it on the grounds that Satan falls self-willed, humankind deceived; but Adam knows what he is doing (Milton gives him a soliloquy to make that clear), and Eve, although deceived about the serpent, knows well enough what tree she stands before. They can be reclaimed only by preemptive grace, not by a less damaging fall that makes them in any way justified on their own. Christ refutes Satan in *Paradise Regained* with learning and logic, but his resolve is generated by a purpose he does not articulate (beyond reiterating that he serves the glory of God), and he does not think it within his prerogative to influence the timing. When we put these limitations on argument and act together with nonetheless timely rescues and demonstrations of glory, it becomes apparent that providence pulls episodes loose from morality and causal logic and that the disconnection between the two journeys of "Comus" is not an isolated matter. We are led to question whether logic can survive and whether the transition from personal ordeal to act is not *necessarily* a reversal, based simultaneously on blind preparedness in the hero and God's unexpected bidding.

It certainly seems to be so in Samson's case. Over halfway toward his suicidal act, he is not appreciably closer than he was at the outset to knowing what he can do. That makes it difficult to concede the bit-by-bit advance that rationalized readings of the play urge. The complaints and debates do not change significantly through the middle, although his defiance of the Philistines grows in the interviews with Dalila and Harapha. As it picks a way through special signs and contributing errors, the personal narrative carries back and forth between confessional lament and anguished didacticism, without Lancelot Andrewes's accomplished method of turning enigmas into merely paradoxes:

> My griefs not only pain me
> As a ling'ring disease,
> But finding no redress, ferment and rage,
> Nor less than wounds immedicable
> Rankle, and fester, and gangrene,
> To black mortification.
> Thoughts my Tormentors arm'd with deadly stings
> Mangle my apprehensive tenderest parts,
> Exasperate, exulcerate, and raise
> Dire inflammation which no cooling herb
> Or med'cinal liquor can assuage,
> Nor breath of Vernal Air from snowy *Alp*.
>   (617–28)

No one who talks in this vein is spiritually helpless or backward, but neither is he likely to squirm loose from conscience and say with Donne that "mine enemy is not an imaginary enemy, fortune, nor a transitory enemy, malice in great persons, but a reall, and an irresistible, and an inexorable, and an everlasting enemy, The Lord of Hosts himselfe," and precisely because of this, an enemy who will outweigh this exceeding affliction with an exceeding glory.[6] The exchanges between Samson and the Chorus go well past this midpoint in Samson's ordeal without coming to any conclusions that we could call firm. Manoa's quarrels with him never approach the alternative the play elects except as an ironic misprediction of ransom. How to break the impasse is thus never clear until it is clear. Without seeing at all into his specific mission, Samson turns down alternatives that would disqualify him while renewing his hostility against the treacherous wife and his giantship. After remembering that he was God's "nursling once and choice delight," Samson is still saying very far along that "Hopeless are all my evils, all remediless" (648) and "my deadliest foe will prove / My speediest friend, by death to rid me hence" (1262–63).

Certainly while listing his errors in a mode halfway between monody and public argument, Samson does not earn his mission by any recognition of his contribution to the prophesied end. Since only tangentially does he seem to exercise free choice even in going to the arena, one has to agree with A. S. P. Woodhouse and G. A. Wilkes that divine guidance remains the main issue in his doing so.[7] The interplay of his and God's wills must be inferred from the act, coming as it does after a refusal to go that is guided by respect for Israelite law and custom. One indication of the suddenness of the change is that not until line 1381 is the reversal marked by the second answer. Even then, as Wilkes suggests, inspired *knowledge* is nowhere demonstrated in it, although a moved *will* is. Samson's end does not require us to disregard his previous self-examinations altogether, however. His escape comes through what appears to be backsliding, since it involves submission to further humiliation; but where revengers ordinarily stifle personal potential to do what they must, he gives full vent to a long-established combative nature, turning against what he hates most, ungodliness and idolatry. His reemergence as a public hero thus depends upon a resumed character, which has been given every opportunity to deteriorate. The personal appeal of the service is clear in his announcement to his tormentors, now his victims, "I mean to show you of my strength"—mean to give an exhibition—"as with amaze will strike all who behold" (1644–45).

This rehabilitation of the witty Samson who smites enemies is built upon the strength he regains in the Dalila and Harapha interviews. But by parodying religious solemnity and Sabbath celebration, the Philistine worship of sea idols actually comes nearer predicting his mission. In retrospect, morality and discipline are at best a holding action. The interviews get nowhere themselves, but they occupy time while the stadium fills, and the timing of the reversal is as important as its agency or its efficient cause. It reveals not only the power that lies behind it but foresight witnessed by the prophecies and the marriages. The arguments that the body of the play pursues prevent both the hero and his people from sinking below redeemability. The end comes when the Philistines are ripe for it and providence has its agent standing by.

Samson himself says almost nothing about his rousing except to reassure his countrymen that he will not violate taboos, which maintains some continuity between the notion he now begins to entertain and tribal laws. He realizes that the course he must follow requires before anything else a circus performance with "Gymnic Artists, Wrestlers, Riders, Runners, / Jugglers and Dancers, Antics, Mummers, Mimics." That added debasement, turned to stratagem, makes the best sense of his earlier contributions to folly, since what is continuous from beginning to end is blindness. Each stumbles toward his fate intending something entirely different. (The logic of events turned providential must be ironic and unexpected or else we could not see providence in it.) That part of Samson's ordeal gets more than enough attention:

> All otherwise to me my thoughts portend,
> That these dark orbs no more shall treat with light,
> Nor th' other light of life continue long,
> But yield to double darkness nigh at hand:
> So much I feel my genial spirits droop,
> My hopes all flat, nature within me seems
> In all her functions weary of herself;
> My race of glory run, and race of shame,
> And I shall shortly be with them that rest.
> (590–98)

Premonition hints at both the stoic fatalism of revenge tragedy and strong retribution. The plangency of the concluding commonplace has the cadence if not the metaphoric fireworks of Macbeth's sere and yellow leaf and perhaps some of the epic narrator's "Thus with the Year / Seasons return, but not to me returns / Day." That the race of glory is also the race of shame and both are soon to grow even more pronounced makes for a peculiar wordplay. Glory and shame become interchangeable; his shame is God's glory augmented, and his own too, seen from another angle. "Nature" includes muscular exertion. Weakness becomes strength armed with pillars, a paradox that a good many Philistines will tumble to a moment too late.

Although Samson's final state of mind is reported only from a distance, piety returns to his interpreters, who make him instrumental to their reconstruction of the divine purpose. God presumably does not require Samson's fall and his history of errors—not if he is the same as the one who "doth not need / Either man's work or his own gifts"—but he improvises once his servants have gone astray. He converts weaknesses into strengths by policy, doing so ahead of time. Similar ironies strike Manoa when the messenger reports the costly kind of redemption that is so unlike the kind he has been pushing through the bureaucracy. The chorus's theological corollary is that God hides his face to be seen, and his "faithful champion" buries himself in rubble to bear witness.

A parallel in terms of catharsis develops out of our relief over Samson's getting what he wishes, a sign that God has not abondoned him, and secondarily out of our realization that ungodliness does not prosper. The relation of hero to people is thereby relieved of some of its former troubles in the concept of the sacrificial rescuer. Since such signs always look the opposite of what they turn out to be, disclosure and reversal must come together.[8]

With the destruction of an impious people, but more doubtfully, comes God's willingness to proceed at whatever expense to his agents, this particular one needing the expiation as well as the deed. The celebrational aspect of tragedy makes it seem that Samson is not badly off if he can be so well remembered and perform so remarkable a rescue of his people. Milton is Aristotelian enough in his opening apology to ask tragedy for some such coincidence of recognition and reversal. Not every reader can follow him in that sanctifying of a hero who must be more terrorist than liberator, but we have no luck with the play as tragedy and find no way to the catharsis Milton describes unless we agree that the Philistines get what they deserve, as Samson does as well in agreeing to accept his greatest enemy as his speediest friend. If Aristotelian recognition is humanly dynastic, recognition here concerns servant and god first, followed by the next step down in tragic realization, namely, Manoa's of his son's glory.

Taking a Shakespearean route to this point conditions us to see that the hero's arousal is a variant not only of Greek drama but of other figures whose ordeals occasion poetic flights. It is partly a deflection into private second worlds that deprives Lear and Cleopatra and tragic protagonists such as Macbeth and Othello of a community. Milton's point may be in part that such figures are missing the only legitimate center of a people, their godliness. What they can accomplish is defined solely by the social structure; they do not collaborate in constructing a consensus transcendence. In denying Cleopatra's Antony, Dolabella voices an extensive breach between heroic dream and reality. If Cleopatra's own attendants are to join her, they too must do so suicidally and leave whatever lesser life that survival would have given them under Octavius. Lear leaves stricken sufferers behind in the aftermath, the props of the state having been kicked away. All motions toward greatness go with him. In contrast, what new trials may follow for Milton's Old Testament people is not part of the play's calculations; in the aftermath of Samson's bearing of witness, the future will be devoted to copious legend and rehearsals of his triumph. Although the liberty the hero wins has a political side, the better part of communal life hereafter will be artistic rather than governmental, "sweet lyric" being the people's choral response to the hero's beyondness. Poets have a large share in supplementing such a chronicle, which reaches into the mysteries of divine role assignment. A recounting of the sacrificial act is the best means to experience the "misnaming" of the dramatic ordeal, which continues to construe its signs wrongly until the last moment.

Although more self-concerned than Shakespeare in many respects, Milton's preference is to get beyond both himself and his protagonists to a company he begins imagining in the nativity ode and renders as the gathering of saints in *The Reason of Church Government,* "Il Penseroso," "Lycidas," and the epics. Most of Shakespeare's plays end with the restoration of a former chivalry or with a state crippled by departures from an ideal, both of these the outcome of an interplay between individual and social motives that has received explicit voicing and dramatic exploration. Failing to find a suitable kingdom manageable, Milton transfers it elsewhere both before and after the prose-writing interim, in the traditional manner of Christian eschatology swerving from millennialism. Some hint of that is present in the superior realization of role-playing that inactivity brings to one who knows the futility of lesser tasks. The shrinking of the attendant company in *Paradise Regained* does not prevent the chief bridger of realms from being "Brought on his way with joy" to his mother's house for more recordable deeds, in their midst, for their sake. But he undertakes these as the catalyst of a greater gathering, not as the champion, for instance, of better Rome-Israel relations. The concluding anthem and the end of the chronicle in that poem are not one and the same, but they render, respectively, an intimation of ultimate closure and a taking up of evangelical dissemination.

Samson Agonistes is less broadly applied to any project for a whole people, but the pattern is similar. The link between the dramatic climax and divine intent is by definition impossible to establish by accommodation or analogy, but enough intimations of it are available to suggest that what restores a Samson bodes well for others, provided that they too sit tight and wait. We know from the greater fable that those who are not elected have some version of Pandaemonium's rhetoric to occupy them and a quite different leader to look up to, the one Milton shows being commemorated, but not in "copious Legend, or sweet Lyric song." As epilogue to *that* play, in "Their universal shout and high applause," the chorus of fallen angels returns to misery just when it thinks to break into joyous shout—a "drie mock" or metonymic reduction of the transported style that Satan parodies elsewhere. The Prebend preacher in Donne puts it succinctly (and not incidentally points toward a similar concept of dramatic ordeal and lyric anthem) when he remarks that "Howling is the noyse of hell, singing the voyce of heaven; Sadnesse the damp of Hell, Rejoycing the serenity of Heaven" (p. 110). One is meaningless and always fixed in its frustration; the other is always in progress but also always final. They require each other to set their differences. On earth they meet as dialectic scaled down to the struggles of saints against Philistines, which does not allow many shades of gray or many areas of indifference.

What both the Shakespearean and Miltonic collaborations of drama and poetry suggest is that poetry is put in a squeeze by rhetoric and dialogue, which assume speakers who are eager to claim and develop their places in some collective venture. If we know anything about selves it is that such roles do not often totally absorb them, not even in the most single-minded and obsessed. The different escapes from limitations in Shakespeare and Milton are ways of mythologizing the intangible dimension left over from our political selves, or what we often credit to the imagination. We glimpse the advancements and retreats of such fugitive selves in the poetry more than in actual relationships, and they tend to subvert the commitment to act unless, as in Samson's case, a voice comes within to announce that now is the time and self-destruction the way. Among these fugitives, the author appears not so much within characters as in the language that gets uttered despite them, that escapes from them.

Eloquence is an inadequate title for that excess because it concedes too much to the intentional effects of rhetoric and suggests the posturing of a dynamic self engaged in ruling others. Much of what Shakespeare's cadences and diction bring almost into view does not move to action. We could resort to more purely aesthetic terms for these extra dimensions, but they too would very likely fall short. They are not "beauty" but something closer to personal force, applied to perception at the margins. When that quality of the peripheral comes with the poetry, it resembles the displaced meanings of dreams, riding on manifest images but not equivalent to them. Were it not for the images, we would not know them. But if it were not for the drama, poetry would also not have its occasions and its lines of articulated thought to nestle between. No poetry, then, without the rhetoric and dialogue; but then no verse drama of Shakespearean or Miltonic dimension without a countervoicing that keeps it from flattening out.

Notes

Introduction

1. See John Crowe Ransom, *The World's Body* (Baton Rouge: Louisiana State University Press, 1968), pp. 133, 271, 300, from the essays "Poetry: A Note in Ontology" and "Shakespeare at Sonnets." See also "Humanism at Chicago" and "The Literary Criticism of Aristotle," reprinted in *Selected Essays,* ed. Thomas Daniel Young and John Hindle (Baton Rouge: Louisiana State University Press, 1984), pp. 273 and 247. Although Ransom is not to blame for my bringing Milton into the rivalry of act and word, he has even more to say about departures of texture from structure in Milton than in the others in whom he locates that dichotomy.

Critics in the past decade or so have grown increasingly curious about Milton's relation to Shakespeare. See Paul Stevens, *Imagination and the Presence of Shakespeare in Paradise Lost* (Madison: University of Wisconsin Press, 1985), partly in answer to John Guillory, *Poetic Authority: Spenser, Milton, and Literary History* (New York: Columbia University Press, 1983); and Rachel Trickett, "Shakespeare and Milton," *Essays and Studies* 31 (1978): 23–35.

2. Joel Altman finds debate developing from training in rhetoric and in the Ciceronian spirit of open-ended questioning. See *The Tudor Play of Mind: Rhetorical Inquiry and the Development of Elizabethan Drama* (Berkeley: University of California Press, 1978), p. 2. On the occupation of the same space by dialogue, fiction, and rhetoric, see also the very useful chapter on "Propaedeutic for Drama," pp. 64–106. Although later plays use figures less frequently, Shakespeare's development did not leave rhetoric or set speeches entirely behind, as Robert Y. Turner makes evident in *Shakespeare's Apprenticeship* (Chicago: University of Chicago Press, 1974), p. 34.

3. Altman, *The Tudor Play of Mind;* William J. Kennedy, *Rhetorical Norms in Renaissance Literature* (New Haven: Yale University Press, 1978). Some of what is at issue between neutral rhetoric and rhetoric as "invisible bullets" can be seen in Michael McCanles's review of Kennedy in "The Authentic Discourse of the Renaissance," *Diacritics* 10 (1980): 77–87. Representative new-historicist readings are collected in *The Power of Forms in the English Renais-*

sance, ed. Stephen Greenblatt (Norman, Oklahoma: Pilgrim Books, 1982); also in *Genre* 15 (1982). It is from that collection that I have paraphrased Franco Moretti's "'A Huge Eclipse': Tragic Form and Deconsecration of Sovereignity," pp. 7–40, on soliloquy and Shakespearean "poetry," pp. 32–33. See also Thomas Cartelli, "Ideology and Subversion in the Shakespearean Set Speech," *ELH* 53 (1986): 1–26; Ann Rosalind Jones and Peter Stallybrass, "The Politics of *Astrophil and Stella*," *SEL* 24 (1984): 53–68, for distinctions between courtship and courtiership; Peter Erickson, *Patriarchal Structures in Shakespeare's Drama* (Berkeley: University of California Press, 1985); and John Alvis's introduction to *Shakespeare as a Political Thinker*, ed. John Alvis and Thomas G. West (Durham, N.C.: Carolina Academic Press, 1981), pp. 3–26.

4. Jane Donawerth, *Shakespeare and the Sixteenth-Century Study of Language* (Chicago and Urbana: University of Illinois Press, 1984), p. 115.

5. As Sigurd Burckhardt points out, words are corporeal, especially Shakespearean ones and especially in allowing rhyme connections and alliterative hookups quite apart from lexical and syntactical assignments. *Shakespearean Meanings* (Princeton: Princeton University Press, 1968), especially the essay on the poet as fool and priest originally published in *ELH* 23 (1956): 279–98.

6. Phyliss Racklin puts a similar case with admirable clarity in "Shakespeare's Boy Cleopatra, the Decorum of Nature and the Golden World of Poetry, " *PMLA* 87 (1972): 201–12.

7. Mark W. Booth goes in the right direction in making Feste's concluding song in *Twelfth Night* a showpiece for a view of song itself in *The Experience of Songs* (New Haven: Yale University Press, 1981), pp. 1–5, 27–28. Coburn Freer points out that character cannot be made into mere pretexts "for poetry clamoring to be written" but that play characters are nonetheless artificial creations: *The Poetics of Jacobean Drama* (Baltimore: Johns Hopkins University Press, 1981), pp. 16–17. The best reasons for retaining a concept of artfully imaged *life* are those that Jonas Barish brings to bear against Yvor Winters's extreme antimimeticism: our vicarious engagement of represented actions is after all mainly what attracts us to the theater. In "Yvor Winters and the Antimimetic Bias," in *The Anti-theatrical Prejudice* (Berkeley: University of California Press, 1981), pp. 418–49.

8. Stephen Booth, *King Lear, Macbeth, and Tragedy* (New Haven: Yale University Press, 1983), p. 129.

9. Bert O. States, *Great Reckonings in Little Rooms: On the Phenomenology of Theater* (Berkeley: University of California Press, 1985), pp. 120–21. Also aware of the effects of theatrical phenomena on our responses to plays are J.L. Styan, "Changeable Taffeta: Shakespeare's Characters in Performance," in *Shakespeare, The Theatrical Dimension*, ed. Philip C. McGuire and David A. Samuelson (New York: AMS Press, 1979), pp. 133–48; Ralph Berry, *Shakespeare and the Awareness of the Audience* (London: Macmillan, 1985); and Nicholas Brooke, "Language Most Shows a Man . . . ? Language and Speaker in *Macbeth*," in *Shakespeare's Styles: Essays in Honour of Kenneth Muir*, ed. Philip Edwards, Inga-Stina Ewbank, and G.K. Hunter (Cambridge: Cambridge University Press, 1980), pp. 70–71. Peter Szondi takes an opposing view in *Theory of the Modern Drama*, ed. and trans. Michael Hays (Minneapolis: University of Minnesota Press, 1987). Although his distinction between the epic "I" who addresses an audience and the absent dramatist is justified, it doesn't necessarily follow that the dramatist has no relationship to an addressed spectator (p. 8).

Chapter 1

1. Prolusion III, "Against Scholastic Philosophy," in *Complete Poems and Major Prose*, ed. Merritt Y. Hughes (New York: Odyssey Press, 1957). Milton quotations are from this edition. When classical commentaries on rhetoric from Aristotle to Quintilian take up the distinction

between rhetoric and poetry, ornamentation is usually the key difference. It is never a very firm distinction, however, where fictionality is not acknowledged and teaching is foremost. See Aristotle, *Rhetoric,* III.1, for instance. The common view is illustrated by Cicero's granting poets freer access to archaisms, metaphors, and rare words (*De Oratore,* Book III).

2. G. R. Hibbard, *The Making of Shakespeare's Dramatic Poetry* (Toronto: University of Toronto Press, 1981), p. 20, for example, and "'The Forced Gait of a Shuffling Nag,'" in *Shakespeare 1971,* ed. Clifford Leech and J. M. R. Margeson (Toronto: University of Toronto Press, 1972), pp. 76–88.

3. Harriett Hawkins, *Likenesses of Truth in Elizabethan and Restoration Drama* (Clarendon: Oxford University Press, 1972), p. 32. Both in this book and in *Poetic Freedom and Poetic Truth* (Clarendon: Oxford University Press, 1976), Hawkins discusses playhouse self-consciousness, as do Robert Egan, *Drama within Drama: Shakespeare's Sense of His Art* (New York: Columbia University Press, 1975); Bertrand Evans, *Shakespeare's Comedies* (Clarendon: Oxford University Press, 1960) and *Shakespeare's Tragic Practice* (Clarendon: Oxford University Press, 1979); Richard Fly, *Shakespeare's Mediated World* (Amherst: University of Massachusetts Press, 1976); Sidney Homan, *When the Theater Turns to Itself* (Lewisburg, Pa.: Bucknell University Press, 1981); James L. Calderwood, *Shakespearean Metadrama* (Minneapolis: University of Minnesota Press, 1971), *Metadrama in Shakespeare's Henriad* (Berkeley: University of California Press, 1979), and *To Be and Not To Be: Negation and Metadrama in Hamlet* (New York: Columbia University Press, 1983); Anne Righter, *Shakespeare and the Idea of the Play* (London: Chatto & Windus, 1962); Thomas F. Van Laan, *Role-Playing in Shakespeare* (Toronto: University of Toronto Press, 1978); and Sigurd Burckhardt, *Shakespearean Meanings* (Princeton: Princeton University Press, 1968).

4. That researching of history for models is another of the things the young Milton shares with his predecessors: "History, when it is handsomely related, can allay and compose the anxious troubles of the mind or anoint it with joy or, again, evoke tears, but gentle and calm tears, tears that bring a strange pleasure with their flow" (Prolusion III, p. 605).

5. F. W. Brownlow, *Two Shakespearean Sequences: Henry VI to Richard II and Pericles to Timon of Athens* (Pittsburgh: University of Pittsburgh Press, 1977); Terence Hawkes, *Shakespeare's Talking Animals: Language and Drama in Society* (London: Edward Arnold, 1973); Albert Cook, *Shakespeare's Enactment: The Dynamics of Renaissance Theatre* (Chicago: Swallow Press, 1976), pp. 139–56, for example; and Michael Black, *Poetic Drama as Mirror of the Will* (London: Vision Press, 1977). Among others who make a special point of keeping poetry in its dramatic harness are Ronald Watkins and Jeremy Lemmon, *The Poet's Method* (London: David & Charles, 1974), especially "The Actor's Task" and "The Poet-Playwright," pp. 120–93; and William C. Carroll, *The Great Feast of Language in Love's Labour's Lost* (Princeton: Princeton University Press, 1976).

6. Jonas Barish, *The Antitheatrical Prejudice* (Berkeley: University of California Press, 1981), pp. 187–88. The Kenneth Burke citation is from *A Rhetoric of Motives* (Berkeley: University of California Press, 1969), p. 270.

7. Wallace Stevens, *The Collected Poems* (New York: Alfred Knopf, 1978), p. 523. Transported language plays against both street language and the forum use of devices. Concerning the latter, the orator whom Cicero and Quintilian imagine—whom the Renaissance linked with the poet as educator—is not masked and does not rehearse fables complete in themselves, at least not for their own sake.

8. Dialogue in Milton moves toward symposium uses at times. Its in-between stature as imagined discourse in support of presumed events, partly dramatic and partly expository, is typical of dialogue from the beginning, whether the speakers are teachers and colleagues of Socrates or historical figures in Greek history. One reason Aristotle fails to develop a concept of it in either the *Rhetoric* or the *Poetics* may be that ambiguous status. The aim of philosophic

dialogues is to define general truths or locate universals in particulars. In mimetic narrative and drama, dialogue forwards plots, but it can also be lifted from dramatic interplay and staged for the sake of ideas, as in Raphael's long talk with Adam, which moves toward the kind of exposition that More's *Utopia* and Castiglione's *Book of the Courtier* exemplify. See K. J. Wilson, *Incomplete Fictions: The Formation of English Renaissance Dialogue* (Washington, D.C.: Catholic University of America Press, 1985), especially p. 14.

9. Francis Berry, *The Shakespeare Inset: Word and Picture* (New York: Theatre Arts Books, 1965), p. 99.

Chapter 2

1. Wilbur Samuel Howell, *Poetics, Rhetoric, and Logic: Studies in the Basic Disciplines of Criticism* (Ithaca: Cornell University Press, 1975), pp. 32–57. See also Howell's *Logic and Rhetoric in England, 1500–1700* (Princeton: Princeton University Press, 1956). The likenesses of poetry and rhetoric usually receive much more attention than their differences. See, for instance, Arthur F. Kinney, "Rhetoric as Poetic: Humanist Fiction in the Renaissance," *ELH* 43 (1976): 413–43; Baxter Hathaway, *Marvels and Commonplaces: Renaissance Literary Criticism* (New York: Random House, 1968), p. 23; and William G. Crane, *Wit and Rhetoric in the Renaissance* (Gloucester, Mass.: Peter Smith, 1964). On the common ground between fiction and rhetoric in the use of topoi, see Thomas Blount, *The Academy of Eloquence* (London: Humphrey Moseley, 1654), facsimile reprint by The Scolar Press, 1971, pp. 49–118. Blount's *formulae majores* emphasize the common passions—friendship, love, hate, anger—and the phrases and gestures by which these can be conjured whether on the podium or the stage. But common ground in the use of types and figures does not argue of course for a common purpose.

2. See Longinus, "On the Sublime," trans. A. O. Prickard (Clarendon: Oxford University Press, 1906), reprinted in *Criticism: The Major Statements*, ed. Charles Kaplan (New York: St. Martin's Press, 1975), pp. 56–57; Cicero, *De Oratore*, trans. H. Rackham (Cambridge: Harvard University Press, 1960), vol. 2, p. 121; compare vol. 1, p. 51: "The truth is that the poet is a very near kinsman of the orator, rather more heavily fettered as regards rhythm, but with ampler freedom in his choice of words, while in the use of many sorts of ornament he is his ally and almost his counterpart" (Book I.xv.70). Concerning Aristotle's distinction between rhetoric and poetics, see the *Poetics*, section IV, and *Rhetoric*, Book I. See also Richard McKeon, "Literary Criticism and the Concept of Imitation in Antiquity," in *Critics and Criticism*, ed. R. S. Crane (Chicago: University of Chicago Press, 1952), pp. 141–42 in the abridged edition (1957).

3. *Ben Jonson*, ed. C. H. Herford and Percy and Evelyn Simpson (Clarendon: Oxford University Press, 1947), vol. 8, *The Poems, The Prose Works*, p. 593.

4. Castelvetro, *On the Art of Poetry, An Abridged Translation of Poetica d'Aristotele Vulgarizzata et Sposta*, trans. Andrew Bongiorno (Binghamton, New York: Medieval and Renaissance Texts & Studies, 1984). Whenever the chief object of oratory is perceived to be the influencing of judgment, Cicero's three aims of rhetoric (*docere, delictare,* and *movere,* roughly equivalent to plain, moderate, and high styles) are likely to become an evaluative hierarchy. See Mazzoni, *Defense of the Comedy of Dante,* trans. Robert L. Montgomery (Tallahassee: University Presses of Florida, 1983), pp. 5–9, 72–79; Robert L. Montgomery, "Verisimilar Things: Tasso's *Discourses on the Heroic Poem* (1594), in *The Reader's Eye* (Berkeley: University of California Press, 1979), pp. 141–68; and John M. Steadman, *The Hill and the Labyrinth: Discourse and Certitude in Milton and His Near-Contemporaries* (Berkeley: University of California Press, 1984), p. 88.

5. Sidney, *An Apology for Poetry,* ed. Geoffrey Shepherd (London: Thomas Nelson, 1965),

pp. 52–55. Sidney finds objectionable any lover's style that catches up swelling phrases like those of the man who tells us that the wind is "at north-west and by south, because he would be sure to name winds enough," p. 137.

6. Sidney, p. 138.

7. Heinrich F. Plett, "The Place and Function of Style in Renaissance Poetics," in *Renaissance Eloquence: Studies in the Theory and Practice of Renaissance Rhetoric,* ed. James J. Murphey (Berkeley: University of California Press, 1983), pp. 364–75.

8. George Puttenham, *The Arte of English Poesie* (Menston: Scolar Press, 1968), p. 6 (first published in 1589).

9. Longinus, in *Criticism,* ed. Kaplan, p. 56.

10. See Teresa Coletti, "Music and *The Tempest,*" in *Shakespeare's Late Plays,* ed. Richard C. Tobias and Paul G. Zolbrod (Athens: Ohio University Press, 1974), pp. 185–99. On songs in general, see William R. Bowden, *The English Dramatic Lyric, 1603–1642* (New Haven: Yale University Press, 1951); Mark W. Booth, *The Experience of Songs;* James Anderson Winn, "The Rhetorical Renaissance," in *Unsuspected Eloquence: A History of the Relations between Poetry and Music* (New Haven: Yale University Press, 1981), pp. 122–93; and Mary Chan, "Shakespeare: *The Winter's Tale* and *The Tempest,*" in *Music in the Theatre of Ben Jonson* (Clarendon: Oxford University Press, 1980), pp. 301–31.

11. See Philip Brockbank, "'The Tempest': Conventions of Art and Empire," in *Later Shakespeare,* ed. John Russell Brown and Bernard Harris, *Stratford-Upon-Avon Studies* 8 (1967): 183; and Harry Berger, Jr., "Miraculous Harp: A Reading of Shakespeare's *Tempest,*" *Shakespeare Studies* 5 (1969): 277.

12. Joan Hartwig, *Shakespeare's Tragicomic Vision* (Baton Rouge: Louisiana State University Press, 1972), pp. 137–74.

13. E. E. Stoll, *Art and Artifice in Shakespeare* (London: Methuen, 1933), pp. 77–79. See also Arnold Stein, "Macbeth and Word Magic," *Sewanee Review* 59 (1951): 271–84; Albert Cook, *Shakespeare's Enactment,* pp. 139–42. Nicholas Brooke anticipates some of my conclusions about *Macbeth* in "Language Most Shows a Man . . . ? Language and Speaker in *Macbeth.*"

14. Simon O. Lesser, "*Macbeth:* Drama and Dream," in *Literary Criticism and Psychology,* ed. Joseph P. Strelka (University Park: Pennsylvania State University Press, 1976), pp. 150–73; Alexander Leggatt, "*Macbeth* and the Last Plays," in *Mirror up to Shakespeare: Essays in Honor of G. R. Hibbard,* ed. J. C. Gray (Toronto: Toronto University Press, 1984), pp. 201–6.

15. Harry Berger, Jr., "Text Against Performance in Shakespeare: The Example of *Macbeth,*" in *The Power of Forms in the English Renaissance,* ed. Stephen Greenblatt (Norman, Oklahoma: Pilgrim Books, 1982), p. 67.

16. Franco Moretti, "'A Huge Eclipse': Tragic Form and the Deconsecration of Sovereignty," in *The Power of Forms,* p. 33.

Chapter 3

1. Thomas Hardy, *Collected Poems* (London: Macmillan, 1952), p. 332.

2. J. Hillis Miller, *The Linguistic Moment: From Wordsworth to Stevens* (Princeton: Princeton University Press, 1985), p. 291. See also Peter M. Sacks, *The English Elegy: Studies in the Genre from Spenser to Yeats* (Baltimore: Johns Hopkins University Press, 1985), pp. 227–59. Both critics read the poems as the persistent vestiges of both Hardy and Emma, "as print or sign" in Sacks's words (p. 236).

3. Robert Ornstein, in "The Ethics of Imagination: Love and Art in *Antony and Cleopatra,*" in *Later Shakespeare, Stratford-upon-Avon Studies* 8 (1967): 31–48, notes a distaste in both

the play and "The Canonization" for stiff monumentalizing (p. 45). See also Antony B. Dawson, *Indirections: Shakespeare and the Art of Illusion* (Toronto: University of Toronto Press, 1978), p. 146; H. A. Mason, *Shakespeare's Tragedies of Love* (London: Chatto & Windus, 1970), pp. 299–76; and Peter Erickson, *Patriarchal Structures in Shakespeare's Drama* (Berkeley: University of California Press, 1985), pp. 127–29. In Ronald R. Macdonald's account of the submission of fact to recollective performance, the play encourages us to think less about the motives of stable characters than about the impromptu histrionics that prepare the image: "We are left not with a made or definitely made-up world," in his words, "but with characters making a world, dreaming, imagining, performing, and acting" in a "back-and-forth" chase of "possibilities that never crystalize into hard truths." To Michael Goldman too, "greatness" is mostly imaginative presence. The quarrel between moralists who concentrate on the deserved ruin and sentimentalists who dwell on greatness can be attributed in part to differences, between the mere self and the elegiac performance. Macdonald, "Playing Till Doomsday: Interpreting *Antony and Cleopatra*," *ELR* 15 (1985): 80, 89; and Goldman, *Acting and Action in Shakespearean Tragedy* (Princeton: Princeton University Press, 1985), p. 113.

4. Kenneth Burke, "Shakespearean Persuasion: *Antony and Cleopatra*," in *Language as Symbolic Action*, p. 112.

5. Julian Markels, *The Pillar of the World: Antony and Cleopatra in Shakespeare's Development* (Columbus: Ohio State University Press, 1968), p. 33. J. Leeds Barroll offers an extended and subtle portrait of Antony in *Shakespearean Tragedy: Genre, Tradition, and Change in Antony and Cleopatra* (Washington, D.C.: Folger Shakespeare Library, 1984), pp. 83–129.

6. Though M. R. Ridley suggests hoops of gold in that language of hooping and binding (from 2.2.110), a world given to breaking apart also lends itself to barrel hooping. Octavius hopes to make Antony one of several tightly bound staves. See the Arden edition of the play (London: Methuen, 1954).

7. Arnold Stein, "The Image of Antony: Lyric and Tragic Imagination," reprinted in *Essays in Shakespearean Criticism*, ed. James L. Calderwood and Harold E. Toliver (Englewood Cliffs, N.J.: Prentice-Hall, 1970), pp. 560–75.

8. As John Porter Houston suggests, extravagance is the chief device of the play's love talk, which moves from a hyperbole contested by meiosis (or belittlement) to a high style that Houston contrasts to Lear's rant, "a disorder of high forceful style," and to Othello's "violent low style." See *The Rhetoric of Poetry in the Renaissance and Seventeenth Century* (Baton Rouge: Louisiana State University Press, 1983), pp. 146, 150, 151–56. Unlike Lear, Cleopatra does not call upon the gods; she assigns Antony their postures and claims like powers for him. The effect is to seize for the self the energies that in Lear's world turn against everyone who tries to command them.

9. Matthew N. Proser, *The Heroic Image in Five Shakespearean Tragedies* (Princeton: Princeton University Press, 1965), pp. 233–35. Michael Goldman in *Acting and Action* has a similar view of Cleopatra's manipulating of Dolabella with verbal magic, pp. 19, 132.

10. Samuel Daniel, "Cleopatra," in *The Complete Works*, ed. Alexander B. Grosart (New York: Russell & Russell, 1963), vol. 3, l. 1662.

Chapter 4

1. Robert Ornstein, "The Ethic of the Imagination: Love and Art in *Antony and Cleopatra*," in *Later Shakespeare*, ed. John Russell Brown and Bernard Harris, *Stratford-Upon-Avon Studies* 8 (New York: St. Martin, 1967): 41; reprinted in *Antony and Cleopatra: A Collection of Critical Essays*, ed. Mark Rose (Englewood Cliffs, N.J.: Prentice-Hall, 1977), pp. 82–98.

Kenneth Burke explores a different version of the relation between character and playwright in several readings of Shakespearean tragedy, chastizing Bradley, for instance, for considering "Iago's conduct as though it were the outgrowth of his character" rather than looking at character as a function of the play, "so formed by the playwright that it would be a perfect fit for the kind of conduct the play required of him." Were he "one bit less rotten and unsleeping in his proddings," the play could not keep going "at such a pitch" (p. 157). See *"Othello:* An Essay to Illustrate a Method," *Hudson Review* 4 (1951): 165–203, reprinted in *Perspectives by Incongruity and Terms for Order,* ed. Stanley Edgar Hyman (Bloomington: Indiana University Press, 1964), p. 180.

2. Verdi's musical drama underscores the play's already prominent operatic qualities. What lingers and is developed in verse as such is often musical in structure and feeling. In both *Othello* and *Otello,* chivalric idealism gives that romanticized feeling many of its cues. See Graham Bradshaw, "A Shakespearean Perspective: Verdi and Boito as Translators," epilogue to James A. Hepokoski, *Giuseppe Verdi: Falstaff* (Cambridge: Cambridge University Press, 1983), pp. 152–71.

3. Thomas Rymer, *A Short View of Tragedy* (Yorkshire: Scolar Press, 1970), pp. 110–11, reprint of the London 1693 edition. Rymer is one of the first Shakespeare critics to use what Geoffrey H. Hartman calls "tea talk," which in critics like Addison and Arnold is well suited to extract the built-in judgments the common idiom makes of romantic excess. But in *Othello* it can blind us to excursions into literary adventurism. See Geoffrey H. Hartman, "Tea and Totality: The Demand of Theory on Critical Style," in *After Strange Texts: The Role of Theory in the Study of Literature,* ed. Gregory S. Jay and David L. Miller (University: University of Alabama Press, 1985), pp. 29–45. On Othello's romanticism, see James C. Bulman, *The Heroic Idiom of Shakespearean Tragedy* (Newark: University of Delaware Press, 1985), pp. 107–25; Richard S. Ide, *Possessed with Greatness* (Chapel Hill: University of North Carolina Press, 1980), pp. 50–74; and Mark Rose, "Othello's Occupation: Shakespeare and the Romance of Chivalry," *ELR* 15 (1985): 293–311.

4. Concerning style, see Helen Gardner, G. R. Hibbard, and others in *Shakespeare Survey* 21 (1968); Derick R. C. Marsh, *Passion Lends Them Power: A Study of Shakespeare's Love Tragedies* (New York: Barnes & Noble, 1976), pp. 89–140; H. A. Mason, *Shakespeare's Tragedies of Love* (London: Chatto & Windus, 1970), pp. 59–164; Michael Long, *The Unnatural Scene: A Study in Shakespearean Tragedy* (London: Methuen, 1976), pp. 37–58; and Robert B. Heilman, "Othello: Action and Language," in *Magic in the Web* (Lexington: University of Kentucky Press, 1956), pp. 137–68. Philip C. McGuire, in *"Othello* as an 'Assay of Reason,'" *Shakespeare Quarterly* 24 (1973): 198–209, holds that much of the play concerns the debasement of rhetoric and the erosion of judicial reason, and in that opinion he is joined by a number of critics.

5. *Othello* is not a demonstration of logic's relations to rhetoric, but the play does devote attention to Othello's shortcuts through the fields of probability. Rhetorical manuals usually make logic and rhetoric mutually supportive, but the relation can be uneasy. In *The Arte or Crafte of Rhetoryke,* ed. Frederic Ives Carpenter (Chicago: University of Chicago Press, 1899), Leonard Cox gives them the close association that Aristotle proposes. He assigns logic the task of disputing and observance of rules, rhetoric the statement of arguments "gay and delectable to the aere" (p. 48). See also Richard Rainolde, *The Foundacion of Rhetorike* (London, 1563), and Thomas Blundeville, *The Art of Logike* (London: John Windet, 1599).

6. See, for instance, Stephen Reid, "Desdemona's Guilt," *American Imago* 27 (1970): 245–62. On the play's view of women generally, see Gayle Greene, "'This That You Call Love': Sexual and Social Tragedy in *Othello,*" *Journal of Women's Studies in Literature* 1 (1979): 16–32; Madelon Gohlke, "'All That is Spoke is Marred': Language and Consciousness in *Othello,*" *Women's Studies* 9 (1981): 157–76; Eamon Grennan, "The Women's Voices in *Othello:* Speech, Song, Silence," *Shakespeare Quarterly* 38 (1987): 275–92; and S. N. Garner, "Shakespeare's Desdemona," *Shakespeare Studies* 9 (1976): 233–52.

7. Bernard Mc Elroy, *Shakespeare's Mature Tragedies* (Princeton: Princeton University Press, 1973), p. 92. In Mc Elroy's reading, the play is concerned less with Othello's gullibility than with his "ever-deepening isolation" after he has wagered everything on love and thinks he has lost.

8. See Rosalie L. Colie, *Shakespeare's Living Art* (Princeton: Princeton University Press, 1974), pp. 137ff.; Albert Cook, *Shakespeare's Enactment*, pp. 40–41.

9. Michael Goldman finds Othello's "bright swords" maintaining the exotic pitch of the role in a playful image ("look at your pretty swords"). See *Acting and Action in Shakespearean Tragedy* (Princeton: Princeton University Press, 1985), pp. 60–61.

10. Heilman, p. 106; and Robert Hapgood, "The Trials of Othello," in *Pacific Coast Studies in Shakespeare*, ed. Waldo F. McNeir and Thelma N. Greenfield (Eugene: University of Oregon Press, 1966), pp. 134–47.

11. Norman Maclean, "Episode, Scene, Speech, and Word: The Madness of Lear," in *Critics and Criticism*, ed. R. S. Crane (Chicago: University of Chicago Press, 1952), p. 112 in the abridged edition.

12. Jared R. Curtis, "The 'Speculative and Offic'd Instruments': Reason and Love in *Othello*," *Shakespeare Quarterly* 24 (1973): 188–97; compare Winifred M. T. Nowottny, "Justice and Love in *Othello*," *University of Toronto Quarterly* 21 (1952): 330–44.

Chapter 5

1. William Frost offers an interesting account of the first scene in "Shakespeare's Rituals and the Opening of *King Lear*," in *Shakespeare: The Tragedies*, ed. Clifford Leech (Chicago: University of Chicago Press, 1965), pp. 192–93. In his view, the "tramp-tramp" dramaturgy of commencements and rituals dampens individual character. This it does, however, in order to probe the relation of egoistic drives to the family and the state. See also Harry V. Jaffa's defense of Lear's strategy in "The Limits of Politics," Allan Bloom with Harry V. Jaffa, *Shakespeare's Politics* (New York: Basic Books, 1964), pp. 113–45.

2. On the disruption of our expectations, see Stephen Booth, *King Lear, Macbeth, Indefinition, and Tragedy* (New Haven: Yale University Press, 1983), pp. 1–58; and William Matchett, "Some Dramatic Techniques in *King Lear*," in *Shakespeare: The Theatrical Dimension*, ed. Philip C. McGuire and David A. Samuelson (New York: AMS Press, 1979), pp. 185–208. Also Derek Peat, "'And that's true too': *King Lear* and the Tension of Uncertainty," *Shakespeare Survey* 33 (1980): 43–54. I have not set out to answer these essays explicitly, but I have attempted to respond to them.

3. See Granville-Barker's comments on the final scene in *King Lear: Critical Essays*, ed. Kenneth Muir (New York: Garland, 1984), p. 74; David A. Samuelson, "Performing the Poem," in *Shakespeare: The Theatrical Dimension*, pp. 18–20; and Judah Stampfer, "The Catharsis of *King Lear*," *Shakespeare Survey* 13 (1960): 1–10, reprinted in *Aspects of King Lear: Articles Reprinted from Shakespeare Survey*, ed. Kenneth Muir and Stanley Wells (Cambridge: Cambridge University Press, 1982), pp. 77–86.

4. Lawrence Danson is surely right to speak of necessity with regard to the ending of Lear, although it has that appearance only after the play has looked at a variety of competing forms and options and rejected them as part of its housecleaning. See *Tragic Alphabet: Shakespeare's Drama of Language* (New Haven: Yale University Press, 1974), p. 188.

5. A. C. Bradley offers an extensive list of improbabilities in the play, for some of which Kenneth Muir proposes answers. See *Shakespearean Tragedy* (New York: Fawcett, 1968), pp. 200–274, and *King Lear*, ed. Kenneth Muir (London: Methuen, 1963), pp. xliii–l (the edition I have used). See also Emrys Jones, *Scenic Form in Shakespeare* (Clarendon: Oxford University

Press, 1971), p. 156; Maynard Mack on the combination of parable and acute realism, *King Lear in Our Time* (Berkeley: University of California Press, 1965), p. 56.

6. George Orwell, "Lear, Tolstoy, and the Fool," in *Selected Essays* (London: Penguin, 1959), pp. 119–36, reprinted in Muir, *King Lear: Critical Essays*. Michael Goldman puts the range of styles with its rages, vaunting, farce, bluster, and evasions in terms of virtuosity in *"King Lear: Acting and Feeling,"* in *On King Lear,* ed. Lawrence Danson (Princeton: Princeton University Press, 1981), pp. 25–47. It is Burckhardt's view that the values Lear assigns to words misconceive the word-referent relation. Accustomed to unchallengeable authority, Lear refuses "to submit to the demeaning necessity ordinary men are under: the necessity of suspiciously grubbing for facts by which to judge words," *Shakespearean Meanings* (Princeton: Princeton University Press, 1968), pp. 239–40.

7. Puttenham's illustrations of *merismus* or "the distributer" include one that he attributes to Chaucer, from which Shakespeare borrows. For comment on that borrowing, see Gary Taylor, *"King Lear: The Date and Authorship of the Folio Version,"* in *The Division of the Kingdoms: Shakespeare's Two Versions of King Lear,* ed. Gary Taylor and Michael Warren (Clarendon: Oxford University Press, 1983), p. 383.

8. Fool's prophecy is full of topical references that for the first Shakespeare audiences must have imposed contemporaneity on legend with some of the implications for a critique of institutions that John Murphy and Stephen Greenblatt find in Edgar's echoes of Samuel Harsnett. See John L. Murphy, *Darkness and Devils: Exorcism and King Lear* (Athens: Ohio University Press, 1984), pp. 171–85; and Stephen Greenblatt, "Shakespeare and the Exorcists," in *After Strange Texts,* ed. Gregory S. Jay and David L. Miller (University: University of Alabama Press, 1985), pp. 101–23.

9. That Lear could return repentant to Cordelia at any time is not conclusive proof of his continued folly. As Arnold Isenberg demonstrates by way of a psychological defense of the delay, Lear represses his shame, leaving it mainly to Kent to voice. See "Cordelia Absent," in *Aesthetics and the Theory of Criticism,* ed. William Callaghan et al. (Chicago: University of Chicago Press, 1973), pp. 125–27. I have drawn also upon Edgar Schell's weighing of the relationship between Cordelia and Lear in *Strangers and Pilgrims: From the Castle of Perseverance to King Lear* (Chicago: University of Chicago Press, 1983), pp. 151–96.

10. John Baxter, *Shakespeare's Poetic Styles: Verse Into Drama* (London: Routledge & Kegan Paul, 1980), p. 99.

11. Robert Grundin notices these pairings and others in *Mighty Opposites, Shakespeare and Renaissance Contrariety* (Berkeley: University of California Press, 1979), pp. 137–53.

12. The matter of rights has to concede something to Goneril and Regan. See Kathleen McLuskie, "The Patriarchal Bard: Feminist Criticism and Shakespeare: *King Lear* and *Measure for Measure,"* in *Political Shakespeare: New Essays in Cultural Materialism,* ed. Jonathan Dollimore and Alan Sinfield (Ithaca: Cornell University Press, 1985), pp. 98–106. The disadvantage of conceding those rights without judgment of them is a skewing of the play, especially the Cordelia-Lear relation, and a suggestion that the power struggle as such is not interpreted by the play, merely seen from Lear's viewpoint.

13. Concerning justice and closure, Harold Skulsky finds the play saying, in effect, abolish "all mere insignia of justice, human dignity, and love; abolish the divine, the civil, and the psychological gendarmerie behind justice, the power and trappings of dignity, the mere self-interest in love," and see then whether any "intrinsic values" still persist. Presumably, unless we locate such values the play has no compensation for its final catastrophe. Even if it does in Skulsky's view, an appropriate response must combine "bewilderment and mourning" with compassion. See *Spirits Finely Touched: The Testing of Value and Integrity in Four Shakespeare Plays* (Athens: University of Georgia Press, 1976), p. 166. On the possibility of specifically Christian compensations, see Robert G. Hunter, *Shakespeare and the Mystery of God's*

268   Notes

Judgments (Athens: University of Georgia Press, 1976), pp. 187–94; and William R. Elton, *King Lear and the Gods* (San Marino: Huntington Library, 1966), especially pp. 335–37 on the *deus absconditus* and *prisca theologia* or virtuous heathen traditions.

14. See Martha Andresen on *sententiae* and commonplaces and Rosalie Colie on biblical echoes and sources in *Some Facets,* pp. 117–44. For assessments of contrasts in style, see Winifred M. T. Nowottny, "Some Aspects of the Style of *King Lear,*" *Shakespeare Survey* 13 (1960): 49–57; and Emily W. Leider, "Plainness of Style in *King Lear,*" *Shakespeare Quarterly* 21 (1970): 45–53.

15. Tragedy ordinarily restores if nothing else the "gored state" and sets off as a *communitas* those who have been victimized but are now commemorated by some coalition of survivors.

Chapter 6

1. Robert N. Watson finds each setting deficient in itself, in *Shakespeare and the Hazards of Ambition* (Cambridge: Harvard University Press, 1984), pp. 236–40. Stylistic contrasts have attracted a good deal of interest. See Patricia Southard Gourlay, "'O my most sacred lady': Female Metaphor in *The Winter's Tale,*" *ELR* 5 (1975): 375–95; Carol Thomas Neely, "*The Winter's Tale*: The Triumph of Speech," *SEL* 15 (1975): 321–38; Jay B. Ludwig, "Shakespearean Decorum: An Essay on *The Winter's Tale,*" *Style* 8 (1974): 365–404; Anne Barton, "Leontes and the Spider: Language and Speaker in Shakespeare's Last Plays," in *Shakespeare's Styles,* ed. Philip Edwards, Inga-Stina Ewbank, and G. K. Hunter (Cambridge: Cambridge University Press, 1980), pp. 131–50; and A. F. Bellette, "Truth and Utterance in *The Winter's Tale,*" *Shakespeare Survey* 31 (1978): 65–76.

2. See Robert Egan, *Drama within Drama* (New York: Columbia University Press, 1975), pp. 56–89; Bertrand Evans, *Shakespeare's Comedies* (Clarendon: Oxford University Press, 1960), pp. 289–315; and Thomas F. Van Laan, *Role-Playing in Shakespeare* (Toronto: University of Toronto Press, 1978), pp. 226–38. Concerning stand-ins and delegates, see also Richard Fly, *Shakespeare's Mediated World* (Amherst: University of Massachusetts Press, 1976); and James L. Calderwood, "Self-Erasing Messengers: Go-Betweens and Get-Betweens," in *To Be and Not to Be* (New York: Columbia University Press, 1983), pp. 123–27. Robert W. Uphaus, in "The 'Comic' Mode of *The Winter's Tale,*" *Genre* 3 (1970): 40–54, identifies the royal attorneying of the play's separation with a "familial feel" at the end, but the shepherds and Autolycus seem further out of the family than he suggests.

3. Thomas Middleton and William Rowley, *The Changeling,* ed. N. W. Bawcutt (London: Methuen, 1958).

4. N. W. Bawcutt, p. lxi. On the play's contrasts, see Lois E. Bueler, "The Rhetoric of Change in *The Changeling,*" *ELR* 14 (1984): 95–113.

5. William H. Matchett argues plausibly that an alert first-night listener is likely to think Leontes right about his wife for at least an ambiguous moment. See "Some Dramatic Techniques in 'The Winter's Tale,'" *Shakespeare Survey* 22 (1969): 95–98. Concerning the suddenness of the jealousy, see Nevill Coghill, "Six Points of Stage-Craft in *The Winter's Tale,*" *Shakespeare Survey* 11 (1958): 31–41; Larry S. Champion, "The Perspective of Comedy: Shakespeare's *The Winter's Tale,*" *College English* 32 (1971): 428–47; Roger J. Trienens, "The Inception of Leontes' Jealousy in *The Winter's Tale,*" *Shakespeare Quarterly* 4 (1953): 321–26; Murray M. Schwartz, "Leontes' Jealousy in *The Winter's Tale,*" *American Imago* 30 (1973): 250–73; Norman Nathan, "Leontes' Provocation," *Shakespeare Quarterly* 19 (1968): 19–24; Stephen Reid, "*The Winter's Tale,*" *American Imago* 27 (1970): 263–78; and Charles Loyd Holt, "Notes on the Dramaturgy of *The Winter's Tale,*" *Shakespeare Quarterly* 20 (1969): 47–51. What we can know (and how we know it) about Leontes and about Hermione's innocence Stanley Cavell

looks at skeptically in *Disowning Knowledge* (New York: Cambridge University Press, 1987), pp. 193–221. See also Howard Felperin, "'Tongue-tied our queen?': The Deconstruction of Presence in *The Winter's Tale*," in *Shakespeare and the Question of Theory*, ed. Patricia Parker and Geoffrey Hartman (New York: Methuen, 1985), pp. 3–18.

6. Wallace Stevens, "Auroras of Autumn," in *The Collected Poems* (New York: Random House, 1955), p. 417.

Chapter 7

1. The political side of the Reformation is the subject of Quentin Skinner's *The Foundations of Modern Political Thought* (London: Cambridge University Press, 1978), especially the second volume, *The Age of Reformation*. See also Perez Zagorin, *The Court and the Country* (New York: Atheneum, 1970), "Social Structure and the Court and the Country," pp. 19–39, which makes the point that the civil rebellion crossed lines frequently and was not class oriented. It is difficult to come from Whitehall masques to "Comus" and not feel that Milton has decreased the aristocratic splendor measurably despite the "glozing courtesy" of the references to Lawes and the Egertons. John Diekhoff, however, does count 139 lines, or 16 percent of the whole, devoted to the first-night audience (*A Maske at Ludlow*, pp. 1–16).

2. See *Of Reformation* and *Apology Against a Pamphlet*, in *Complete Prose Works*, vol. 1, ed. Don M. Wolfe (New Haven: Yale University Press, 1953), pp. 614, 952.

3. We do not get decisive help in bridging the two destinations from the surrounding poems of the 1645 edition. It has proved plausible to read that volume as either a strong Protestant revision of Stuart and Caroline poetics or as evidence of a lingering patronage system and its cavalier modes. See Louis L. Martz, "The Rising Poet, 1645," in *The Lyric and Dramatic Milton*, ed. Joseph H. Summers (New York: Columbia University Press, 1965), pp. 3–34; and Richard Helgerson, *Self-Crowned Laureates* (Berkeley: University of California Press, 1983), pp. 185–282. My interest in distinguishing the second from the first journey and from the Shakespearean cyclical journey overlaps John Guillory's in *Poetic Authority* (New York: Columbia University Press, 1983), and Maureen Quilligan's interest in influence, the latter in *Milton's Spenser: The Politics of Reading* (Ithaca: Cornell University Press, 1983). See also Ethel Seaton, "*Comus* and Shakespeare," *Essays and Studies* 31 (1945): 66–80; Rachel Trickett, "Shakespeare and Milton," *Essays and Studies* n.s. 31 (1978): 36–64; Paul Stevens, *Imagination and the Presence of Shakespeare in Paradise Lost*, pp. 11–45; John M. Major, "*Comus* and *The Tempest*," *Shakespeare Quarterly* 10 (1959): 177–83; and Alwin Thaler, *Shakespeare and Our World* (Knoxville: University of Tennessee Press, 1966), "Shakespearean Recollection in Milton: A Summing-Up," pp. 139–228.

4. Milton is usually assumed to have known William Browne's *The Inner Temple Masque* (in *The Whole Works*, ed. W. Carew Hazlett), Townshend's *Albions Triumph* and *Tempe Restored*, and Carew's *Coelum Britannicum* as well as Jonson's *Pleasure Reconciled with Virtue*. Also typical of the masques in political rhetoric are Sir William Davenant's *The Temple of Love* (1634), *The Triumphs of the Prince D'Amour* (1635), and *Britannia Triumphans* (1637), which honor Henrietta and Charles and exercise the poet's Orphic powers on their behalf. See Enid Welsford, *The Court Masque* (New York: Russell & Russell, 1962, first published 1927), especially "The Caroline Masque," pp. 217–44, also pp. 324–49 on the masque elements of *A Midsummer Night's Dream* and *The Tempest*.

5. See O. Mannoni, *Prospero and Caliban: The Psychology of Colonization*, trans. Pamela Powesland (New York: Frederick A. Praeger, 1956); Roberto Fernandez Retamar, "Caliban: Notes toward a Discussion of Culture in Our America," *Massachusetts Review* 15 (1974): 7–72; for a feminist version, Lorie Jerrell Leininger, "The Miranda Trap: Sexism and Racism in

Shakespeare's *Tempest*," in *The Woman's Part: Feminist Criticism of Shakespeare*, ed. Carolyn Ruth Swift Lenz, Gayle Green, and Carol Thomas Neely (Urbana: University of Illinois Press, 1980), pp. 285–94.

6. Assuming that E. M. W. Tillyard's view of Cupid and Psyche is valid, Milton might be said to transfer the weddings of *A Midsummer Night's Dream* and *The Tempest* to a realm beyond reproach. See "The Action of Comus," in *Studies in Milton*, reprinted in *A Maske at Ludlow*, ed. John S. Diekhoff, pp. 43–57. In the same collection, however, see the opposing opinions of A. S. P. Woodhouse in "The Argument of *Comus*," pp. 17–42, and "*Comus* Once More," pp. 72–77, and Rosemond Tuve, p. 164. William G. Madson situates Cupid and Psyche among several ways of implicating grace *in* nature, which is closer to the view I have taken, with the reverse twist that Milton is also implicating nature in grace, both in a postponed state. See *The Idea of Nature in Milton's Poetry* (New Haven: Yale University Press, 1958), pp. 217–18.

7. Stephen Orgel, "New Uses of Adversity: Tragic Experience in *The Tempest*," in *Essays in Shakespearean Criticism*, ed. James L. Calderwood and Harold E. Toliver (Englewood Cliffs, N.J.: Prentice-Hall, 1970), p. 328.

8. William R. Bowden, *The English Dramatic Lyric, 1603–42* (New Haven: Yale University Press, 1951).

9. David Lindley, "Music, Masque, and Meaning in *The Tempest*," in *The Court Masque* (Manchester: Manchester University Press, 1984), p. 48. See also Julian Patrick, "*The Tempest* as Supplement," in *Centre and Labyrinth: Essays in Honour of Northrop Frye*, ed. Eleanor Cook et al. (Toronto: University of Toronto Press, 1983), pp. 162–80, concerning Ariel as a "winged spirit of creation that comes in response to a moment of crisis or imagined failure," p. 170.

10. Howard Felperin, *Shakespearean Romance* (Princeton: Princeton University Press, 1972), p. 281.

11. John D. Cox, "Poetry and History in Milton's Country Masque," *ELH* 44 (1977): 622–40. See also James Andrew Clark, "Milton Naturans, Milton Naturatus: The Debate over Nature in *A Mask Presented at Ludlow*," *Milton Studies* 20 (1984): 3–28.

12. William Kerrigan, *The Sacred Complex: On the Psychogenesis of Paradise Lost* (Cambridge: Harvard University Press, 1983), p. 58.

Chapter 8

1. See John Hollander, *The Figure of Echo: A Mode of Allusion in Milton and Others* (Berkeley: University of California Press, 1981), especially pp. 60–70; Gordon Braden, *The Classics and English Renaissance Poetry* (New Haven: Yale University Press, 1978); Roger Sale, *Literary Inheritance* (Amherst: University of Massachusetts Press, 1984); Richard S. Peterson, *Imitation and Praise in the Poems of Ben Jonson* (New Haven: Yale University Press, 1981).

2. Ruth Nevo, *Comic Transformations in Shakespeare* (London: Methuen, 1980), p. 2.

3. *Areopagitica*, cited from *The Complete Prose Works*, vol. 2, ed. Ernest Sirluck (New Haven: Yale University Press, 1959), p. 555.

4. See Louis Martz, "The Rising Poet, 1645," in *The Lyric and Dramatic Milton*, ed. Joseph H. Summers (New York: Columbia University Press, 1965), pp. 3–33; and on Milton's arrival at an epic subject specifically, Gordon Teskey, "Milton's Choice of Subject in the Context of Renaissance Critical Theory," *ELH* 53 (1986): 53–72.

5. *Christian Doctrine*, in *Complete Poems and Major Prose*, ed. Merritt Y. Hughes (New York: Odyssey Press, 1957), p. 915.

6. William Kerrigan and Gordon Braden, "Milton's Coy Eve: *Paradise Lost* and Renaissance Love Poetry," *ELH* 53 (1986): 27–52.

7. *Christian Doctrine,* p. 901.

8. William Kerrigan, *The Prophetic Milton* (Charlottesville: University Press of Virginia, 1974), p. 161. John Guillory speculates that Milton "wins for himself the identity of the prophet in the renunciation of the not sacred rather than the intention to produce a sacred text," but Milton's renunciations surely do not include "figuration itself." See *Poetic Authority,* pp. 94–145, especially p. 106.

9. Michael Lieb, *Poetics of the Holy: A Reading of Paradise Lost* (Chapel Hill: University of North Carolina Press, 1981).

10. John Smith, *Select Discourses, 1660* (New York: Garland, 1978), pp. 171–72.

11. Lancelot Andrewes, *XCVI Sermons* (London: Richard Badger, 1641), p. 111, sermon on Luke 2:12, reprinted in *Sermons,* ed. G. M. Story (Clarendon: Oxford University Press, 1967). The other references are also to the 1641 text.

Chapter 9

1. *An Apology Against a Pamphlet,* in *Complete Prose Works of John Milton,* ed. Don M. Wolfe (New Haven: Yale University Press), I.949. On zeal and vehemence in the rhetoric of the masque, see Christopher Grose, *Milton's Epic Process* (New Haven: Yale University Press), pp. 85–93.

2. George William Smith, Jr., "Milton's Revisions of the Design of *Comus,*" *ELH* 46 (1979): 56–80. Robert Wilcher also focuses on debate and recalls Tillyard's identification of Milton's university disputations in the early poems. "Milton's Masque: Occasion, Form and Meaning," *Critical Quarterly* 20 (1978): 3–20. See also John M. Major, "Milton's View of Rhetoric," *Studies in Philology* 64 (1967): 685–711.

3. See William C. Carroll, *The Great Feast of Language in Love's Labour's Lost* (Princeton: Princeton University Press, 1976), pp. 205–41.

4. In Jonathan Goldberg's account of Milton's echo of Shakespeare's "When I Consider Everything That Grows," *Voice Terminal Echo: Postmodernism and English Renaissance Texts* (London: Methuen, 1986), pp. 124–58, the two poems fall into a neat antithesis, Shakespeare's all generation, Milton's tomblike. "Shakespeare engrafts; Milton engraves." That contrast seems too nifty. Although Milton is concerned with the expunging of light and the burial of a talent that cannot grow in the dark, the sonnet delays rather than denies gratification.

5. William Empson, *Milton's God* (London: Chatto & Windus, 1961), pp. 211–28; and Joseph Wittreich, *Interpreting Samson Agonistes* (Princeton: Princeton University Press, 1986).

6. *Donne's Prebend Sermons,* ed. Janel M. Mueller (Cambridge: Harvard University Press, 1971), p. 97.

7. A. S. P. Woodhouse, "Tragic Effect in *Samson Agonistes,*" *University of Toronto Quarterly* 28 (1958): 205–22; and G. A. Wilkes, "The Interpretation of *Samson Agonistes,*" *Huntington Library Quarterly* 26 (1963): 366–70. See also Edward W. Tayler, *Milton's Poetry: Its Development in Time* (Pittsburgh: Duquesne University Press, 1979), pp. 105–22; Albert C. Labriola, "Divine Urgency as a Motive for Conduct in *Samson Agonistes,*" *Philological Quarterly* 50 (1971): 99–107; and Arthur E. Barker, "Calm Regained through Passion Spent: The Conclusions of the Miltonic Effort," in *The Prison and the Pinnacle,* ed. Balachandra Rajan (Toronto: University of Toronto Press, 1973), pp. 3–48.

8. Catharsis depends on how we understand both the disclosure and the reversal. See Arnold Stein, *Heroic Knowledge* (Minneapolis: University of Minnesota Press, 1957), pp. 192–202; Paul R. Sellin, "Sources of Milton's Catharsis: A Reconsideration," *JEGP* 60 (1961): 712–30; and Martin F. Mueller, "*Pathos* and *Katharsis* in *Samson Agonistes,*" *ELH* 31 (1964): 156–74.

Index

Accommodation, 230–37, 243, 247, 257
Aeschylus, 30
Altman, Joel, 4, 259 nn. 2, 3
Alvis, John, 260
Amplitude, 10, 39–43, 58, 70, 100, 106–7, 205, 217, 225–26. *See also* Hyperbole, Sublime (the)
Andrewes, Lancelot, 234–36, 253, 271 n. 11
Aristotle, 4, 9, 11, 26, 37, 40, 45, 47, 256, 261 n. 1, 262 n. 8
Augustine, 233

Bacon, Francis, 10, 40
Barish, Jonas, 28, 261 n. 6
Barroll, J. Leeds, 39
Bawcutt, N. W., 158, 268 n. 4
Baxter, John, 134
Berger, Harry, 54, 57, 263 nn. 11, 15
Berry, Francis, 35, 262 n. 9
Bible, 11, 44, 195, 222, 225, 228, 230–36, 248, 249, 250–51
Black, Michael, 27, 28–30, 261 n. 5
Blount, Thomas, 262 n. 1
Blundeville, Thomas, 265 n. 5
Boito, 91
Bombast. *See* Decorum, Hyperbole, Sublime (the), Vehemence
Booth, Mark W., 260 n. 7

Booth, Stephen, 15, 260 n. 8, 266 n. 2
Bowden, William, 210, 270 n. 8
Braden, Gordon, 229, 270 n. 6
Brockbank, Philip, 54, 263 n. 11
Browne, Thomas, 42
Brownlow, F. W., 27, 28, 261 n. 5
Burckhardt, Sigurd, 260 n. 5
Burke, Kenneth, 28, 76–77, 81, 261 n. 6, 264–65 nn. 4, 1

Calderwood, James, 261 n. 3, 270 n. 7
Carew, Thomas, 186, 187, 201, 269 n. 4
Castelvetro, 40, 262 n. 4
Character, 2–4, 7, 9, 12, 21, 27–31, 56–61, 92–93, 118–22, 123. *See also* Decorum
Chivalry, 2, 4–6, 7, 13, 24, 39, 91, 95, 97, 104, 107, 109–11, 115, 119, 139, 149, 221, 227, 257
Cicero, 25, 32, 38, 42, 162, 262 n. 2
Colie, Rosalie, 102, 266 n. 8
Contention, 8–9, 32–33, 49–50, 53, 55, 76–77, 79, 81, 83, 85, 88–91, 101, 108–9, 133, 154, 172–73, 184, 186, 188, 193–94, 204, 207, 215, 223, 225, 231, 239–45, 249, 258, 261–62
Cook, Albert, 27, 28, 102, 261 n. 5, 266 n. 8
Copiousness. *See* Amplitude

Cox, John D., 213, 270n. 11
Cox, Leonard, 39, 265n. 5
Curtis, Jared, 118, 266n. 12

Daniel, Samuel, 4, 5, 42, 264n. 10
Debate. *See* Contention
Decorum, 25, 28, 37–43, 45, 47–49, 60, 92–93, 95, 104–5, 144, 154–55, 167, 169, 177, 178, 231. *See also* Character
Dialogue. *See* Contention
Donawerth, Jane, 10, 260n. 4
Donne, John, 65–67, 76, 85, 109, 228–29, 257, 271n. 6
Dryden, 6, 38, 82
Dynasty, 14, 31–32, 48, 51, 54, 124–25, 132–36, 139–44, 147, 149–52, 155, 159, 175, 178, 184, 187, 188, 190, 201, 220–21, 223, 226–27, 256

Egan, Robert, 155, 261n. 3, 268n. 2
Egerton, Alice, 210
Egerton, Thomas (Earl of Bridgewater), 184, 186
Elegy, 65–67, 69–70, 75, 76, 77, 81, 114, 136, 141, 207, 211, 216–17, 255
Eliot, T. S., 92
Emerson, Ralph Waldo, 81
Empson, William, 251, 271n. 5
Erickson, Peter, 260n. 3, 264n. 3
Escher, M. C., 12, 13
Evans, Bertrand, 155

Felperin, Howard, 213, 270n. 10

Genre, 23, 31–32, 37, 45–46, 123–26, 127, 130, 136, 164, 179, 219–20, 222–23, 230, 232, 233, 239–44
Green, Robert, 169, 176
Guillory, John, 259n. 1, 269n. 3, 271n. 8

Hall, Joseph, 38
Hardy, Thomas, 65–67, 76, 263n. 1
Hartwig, Joan, 54, 263n. 12
Hawkes, Terrence, 27, 261n. 5
Hawkins, Harriet, 20, 261n. 3
Heilman, Robert, 112, 266n. 10
Herbert, George, 230–31, 233, 234
Heywood, John, 8
Historicism, 2, 4–7, 30, 34, 39
Hibbard, G. R., 19, 27, 28, 261n. 2, 265n. 4

Hollander, John, 219, 270n. 1
Homer, 13, 37, 187, 194, 229
Houston, John Porter, 264n. 8
Howell, Wilbur Samuel, 262n. 1
Hyperbole, 91–93, 96, 99–100, 109–10, 119, 121, 195–96, 222. *See also* Amplitude, Sublime (the), Vehemence

Jones, Inigo, 184
Jonson, Ben, 37, 38, 39–40, 43, 140, 184, 196, 201–2, 204, 205, 206, 214, 220, 262n. 3

Kennedy, William, 4, 259n. 3
Kerrigan, William, 218, 229, 232, 270n. 6, 271n. 8

Lawes, Henry, 186, 210, 214, 240
Leavis, F. R., 92
Lesser, Simon O., 57
Lindley, David, 210, 270n. 9
Lipsius, 38
Lodge, Thomas, 169
Longinus, 39, 44, 57, 200, 262, 263

McCanles, Michael, 259n. 3
McElroy, Bernard, 100, 266n. 7
Maclean, Norman, 117, 266n. 11
Magnitude. *See* Amplitude, Sublime (the), Vehemence
Mannoni, O., 194, 269n. 5
Markels, Julian, 79, 264n. 5
Marlowe, 30, 32, 38, 40, 43
Marvell, 195–96, 225–26
Middleton and Rowley, 158, 170, 172
Miller, Hillis, 66, 263n. 2
Milton: *An Apology against a Pamphlet*, 185, 240; "L'Allegro" and "Il Penseroso," 214, 241–44; "Arcades," 207; *Areopagitica*, 219, 222–23, 231, 232, 236, 257; *Christian Doctrine*, 228, 231–32, 233; "Comus," 12, 32, 152, 180, 183–218, 222, 223, 226, 228, 229, 231, 237, 239, 240–41, 244, 247, 252; "How Soon Hath Time," 229, 245, 246, 248; "Lycidas," 34, 194, 196, 203, 209, 220, 226, 248, 257; "Methought I Saw," 246; the nativity ode, 234, 236; *Paradise Lost*, 32–33, 34, 43–44, 190, 196, 200, 208, 220, 223–28, 229–30, 243, 245, 247, 248, 252, 257; *Paradise Regained*,

10–12, 32, 185, 187, 190, 204, 222, 223, 226–27, 228, 236, 252, 257; Prolusion III, 19, 260n. 1; *The Reason of Church Government,* 232, 233, 257; *Of Reformation,* 204; *Samson Agonistes,* 32, 188, 245, 249–58; "When I Consider," 33–34, 229, 245, 246–49

Montaigne, 10

Moretti, Franco, 5, 58, 260n. 3, 263n. 16

Narrative, 34, 106–8, 156, 157, 162, 170, 171, 174–76, 178, 188, 203, 225, 226, 229, 231, 232, 245, 248, 249. *See also* Plot

Nevo, Ruth, 220, 270n. 2

North. *See* Plutarch

Orgel, Stephen, 208, 270n. 7

Ornament. *See* Decorum

Ornstein, Robert, 88, 263n. 3

Orwell, George, 127, 267n. 6

Ovid, 4, 13, 37, 52, 187, 201, 225

Patriarchy. *See* Chivalry, Dynasty

Patrizi, 20

Petrarch, 246

Plato, 33, 39–40

Plett, Heinrich, 41, 263n. 7

Plot, 9–12, 26, 45–47, 52, 82, 90, 134, 144–46, 190, 221, 255–56. *See also* Narrative

Plutarch, 4, 5, 79, 80, 82

Proser, Matthew, 82, 264n. 9

Puttenham, 25, 26, 39–43, 87, 129, 150, 263n. 8, 267n. 7

Quintilian, 25, 32, 39, 41–42

Racklin, Phyliss, 260n. 6

Raleigh, Walter, 246

Ransom, John Crowe, 1, 3, 4, 5, 259n. 1

Retamar, Roberto, 194, 269n. 5

Rymer, Thomas, 90, 92–93, 96, 265n. 3

Scaliger, 20

Seneca, 38, 161

Sentiment, 47–51, 102, 105, 114, 119, 126, 141, 144–47, 149–52, 153, 158, 159, 167–68, 173, 175, 176, 178, 221

Shakespeare: *Antony and Cleopatra,* 1–6, 8, 9, 12, 15, 16, 20–26, 28, 35, 45, 56, 65–86, 87–88, 94, 99, 103, 109, 120, 121, 179, 203, 221–22, 256; *As You Like It,* 12, 13, 39, 45–51, 56, 103, 166, 168, 174, 187, 214, 217, 220; *Coriolanus,* 118, 221; *Hamlet,* 14, 15, 34, 88, 94, 101, 114, 117, 125, 137; *1* and *2 Henry IV,* 8, 28, 38, 45, 110, 167, 179, 226–27; *Julius Caesar,* 221; *King Lear,* 4, 8, 9, 12, 13–14, 15, 16, 20, 43, 45, 50, 56, 94, 97, 114–15, 117, 118, 120, 121, 123–52, 172, 178, 203, 222, 256; *Love's Labour's Lost,* 4, 8, 12, 40, 241–42; *Macbeth,* 5, 8, 9, 10–11, 27–31, 39, 43, 56–61, 114, 125, 222, 255, 256; *A Midsummer's Night's Dream,* 12, 20, 166, 168, 174, 187, 189, 190–93, 197, 204, 212, 214, 215; *Othello,* 9, 23, 27, 31, 44–45, 59, 87–122, 125, 136, 137, 172, 173, 178, 256; *Richard II,* 12, 28, 38–39, 110, 118, 121; *Richard III,* 28; *Romeo and Juliet,* 12, 81, 158; sonnets, 245–46; *The Tempest,* 39, 45–48, 52–56, 58, 117, 166, 168, 173, 179–80, 183–218, 220, 222, 223, 229, 241; *Troilus and Cressida,* 23, 110, 119, 121, 221; *Twelfth Night,* 130, 166, 174; *The Winter's Tale,* 20, 46, 56, 103, 153–82, 184, 187, 211, 212

Shepherd, Geoffrey, 40

Sidney, Philip, 38, 39, 40–41, 42, 43, 44, 46, 49, 140, 233, 249, 262–63n. 5

Skulsky, Harold, 267n. 13

Smith, George William, 240, 271n. 2

Smith, John, 234, 271n. 10

Soliloquy, 5, 35, 37, 46–47, 117, 174

Song, 12–13, 35, 37, 38, 45–54, 56, 66, 76, 101–2, 103, 105, 130, 153, 165–67, 180, 184, 188, 190, 196, 198–99, 205, 206, 210–11, 212, 216, 236, 239–45, 257, 263

Sophocles, 37

Spenser, 49, 184, 201, 203, 209, 220, 225, 246, 249

States, Bert O., 15, 260n. 9

Stein, Arnold, 79, 263, 264, 271n. 8

Stevens, Paul, 259n. 1

Stevens, Wallace, 1, 30, 31, 76, 179, 205, 261n. 7, 269n. 6

Sublime (the), 25, 43–45, 57–61, 95, 115–17, 121, 131, 199–200, 242. *See also* Vehemence

Topoi, 3, 4, 8–9, 59, 77, 91, 98, 115, 125, 150, 168, 243, 251–52, 262
Townshend, Aurelian, 186, 187, 269n. 4
Transport. *See* Amplitude, Sublime (the), Vehemence
Trickett, Rachael, 259n. 1

Van Laan, Thomas, 155, 268n. 2
Vehemence, 19–20, 23–24, 26, 29, 31, 32 38, 42, 58, 61, 88–90, 99, 102, 103, 134, 135, 160–61, 172, 208, 230
Verdi, 91, 265n. 2
Virgil, 4, 13, 37, 78, 214, 225, 247

Webster, 30
Wilkes, G. A., 254, 271n. 7
Wilson, K. J., 262n. 8
Wilson, Thomas, 10, 39
Winters, Yvor, 57
Wittreich, Joseph, 251, 271n. 5
Woodhouse, A. S. P., 254, 270n. 6, 271n. 7

Zagorin, Perez, 269n. 1